FIELDS OF
GLORY

Jim Miles

FIELDS OF GLORY

A HISTORY AND TOUR GUIDE OF THE WAR IN THE WEST, THE ATLANTA CAMPAIGN, 1864

SECOND EDITION

Jim Miles

CUMBERLAND HOUSE

NASHVILLE, TENNESSEE

Copyright © 1989, 1995, 2002 by Jim Miles

Published by
CUMBERLAND HOUSE PUBLISHING, INC.
431 Harding Industrial Drive
Nashville, Tennessee 37211
www.cumberlandhouse.com

Unless otherwise noted, photographs are by the author. Pictures credited to *Mountain Campaigns in Georgia* courtesy of the Atlanta Historical Society or taken from Joseph M. Brown, *The Mountain Campaigns in Georgia: War Scenes on the W&A* (Buffalo, N.Y.: Matthews, Northrup & Co., 1887).

Cover design by Bateman Design, Nashville, Tennessee.

Library of Congress Cataloging-in-Publication Data

Miles, Jim.
  Fields of glory : a history and tour guide of the war in the West, the Atlanta Campaign, 1864 / Jim Miles.—2nd ed.
    p. cm. — (The Civil War explorer)
  Includes bibliographical references and index.
  ISBN 1-58182-256-1 (alk. paper)
  1. Atlanta Campaign, 1864. 2. Georgia—History—Civil War, 1861–1865—Battlefields—Guidebooks. 3. United States—History—Civil War, 1861–1865—Battlefields—Guidebooks. 4. Historic sites—Georgia—Guidebooks. 5. Georgia—Guidebooks. 6. Automobile travel—Georgia—Guidebooks. I. Title.
  E476.7.M636 2002
  973.7'371—dc21

                                                                            2002009542

Printed in the United States of America.

1 2 3 4 5 6 7 8 9 10—05 04 03 02

To my wife, Earline, my driver and research assistant,
and our children, Paul and Melanie

CONTENTS

INTRODUCTION

MADE IN ATLANTA.

William Tecumseh Sherman kicked at the shell casing in disgust. All around him lay the debris of war—cannon abandoned in haste by their gunners, wagons with broken axles, rifles dropped by panicked or wounded men, canteens, and dead Rebels who lay scattered across the ground. Stamped or stenciled on virtually every last item, even the buttons on uniforms of the casualties, was that hated notation, *Made in Atlanta.*

Sherman had seen that script on a dozen battlefields extending from Mississippi to Tennessee. Gazing south from Lookout Mountain, he imagined he could see the young, bustling city that had become the manufacturing center of the Confederacy. New factories turned out enormous quantities of cannon, rifles, pistols, shells and cartridges, wagons, uniforms, spurs, shoes, and swords. An Atlanta rolling mill even produced steel plate for the dangerous Rebel ironclad warships.

Across the heartland of the Confederacy—Mississippi, Alabama, and Georgia—farmers had abandoned their traditional cotton crops to raise vegetables, grains, and fruits of every kind; and herds and flocks grew fat. This food was funneled into Atlanta where, along with the war materiel, it was shipped on a nearly continuous stream of trains to supply not only his adversary, the Army of Tennessee, but allowed the resilient Army of Northern Virginia to keep fighting in the East. The four railroads that met in Atlanta were also the key to transportation in the Confederacy.

Within a few months Sherman took charge of all armies in the West. Ulysses S. Grant, appointed general in chief of all Federal armies, gave Sherman this order: "You I propose to move against Johnston's army, to break it up, and to get into the interior of the enemy's country as far as you can, inflicting all the damage you can against their war resources."

In Sherman's mind, before the war could be brought to a victorious conclusion, this meant that Atlanta had to be destroyed and the Confederacy denied its precious products. From that day, Atlanta was a doomed city.

INTRODUCTION TO THE SECOND EDITION

T HE CIVIL WAR EXPLORER series began in 1989 when heritage tourism was in its infancy. The concept has proved extremely popular, and states, cities, and counties across the eastern United States have begun preserving and promoting their Civil War sites and preparing driving and walking tours so visitors can enjoy this precious heritage. Many of them have been inspired by this series of books.

This updated second edition incorporates dozens of new tour guides and many new Civil War sites, most of them accessible to the public for the first time. The resources section has been updated completely. Much information is still mailed from visitors bureaus and historical societies, but an incredible amount of material is available on Web sites, an excellent resource for historical travel.

The population of the Southeast has exploded over the past twenty years, particularly in the cities, making it even more important to carefully plan your trips and to have a traveling companion so one can drive while the other directs.

Watch for the development of a state park at Resaca and significant additions to Cobb County's growing Civil War sites. Perhaps most exciting is the current development of a Civil War trails system. The trails will connect national, state, and local parks and related historic sites from Ringgold to Atlanta, much like the Civil War Explorer series. If successful, other Civil War tours of the state will be developed, including Sherman's March, Jefferson Davis's escape route, Wilson's Raid, and others.

TIPS FOR ENJOYING THE TOUR GUIDE

The driving tour to historic sites has been exhaustively researched. However, readers need to bear in mind that highways and streets occasionally are altered, and the names and designated numbers of roads are often changed. That is why we have included written directions, mileage, and maps. These should enable you to circumvent any changes that might be made to the tour route in coming years. (We will update with each new printing.) Also, remember that odometers can vary considerably. Our .8

might be your .9, so please take this into account. When in doubt about your location, don't hesitate to ask residents for directions. While preparing this guide, we were frequently "misplaced."

For safety's sake, it is obviously best to tour the Atlanta campaign with a companion. While one drives, the other can read and direct. It is also advisable to read the touring information before hitting the road. Familiarizing yourself with the tour will enable you to choose the sites you would like to visit beforehand.

Traffic in parts of metropolitan Atlanta can be fast and hazardous, so please exercise caution in stopping to view historic sites and in reentering the traffic flow.

By all means, be respectful of private property. Do not trespass on land or call on the residents of a private historic home. It is extremely difficult to live in or on a part of history, and there are too many vandals and arsonists around to expect owners to be tolerant toward uninvited visitors. Fortunately, many historic homes are open as part of community tours around Christmas and during the spring. Check calendars of events for specific dates.

The tour route is designed to follow historic events of the Atlanta campaign. In doing so, it traverses some neighborhoods where crime is common. Exercise caution in determining when and under what circumstances you should visit sites in these areas.

The route is seldom far from Interstate 75, a very busy north-south artery. Food of every variety, hotels, campgrounds, and service stations abound for the weary and hungry explorer.

FIELDS OF
GLORY

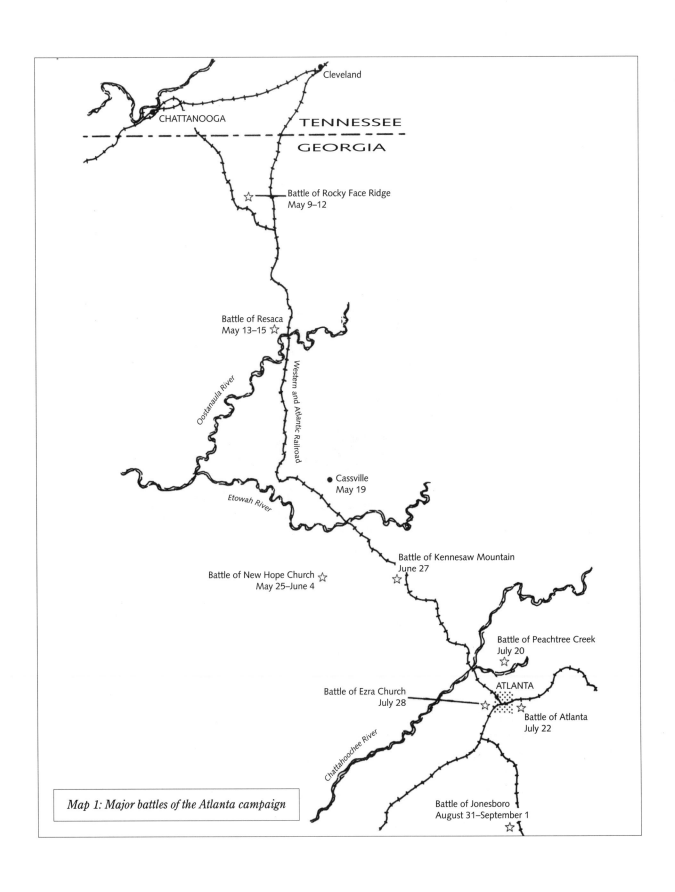

Cleveland

CHATTANOOGA

TENNESSEE

GEORGIA

Battle of Rocky Face Ridge
May 9–12

Battle of Resaca
May 13–15

Oostanaula River

Western and Atlantic Railroad

Cassville
May 19

Etowah River

Battle of Kennesaw Mountain
June 27

Battle of New Hope Church
May 25–June 4

Battle of Peachtree Creek
July 20

ATLANTA

Battle of Ezra Church
July 28

Battle of Atlanta
July 22

Chattahoochee River

Battle of Jonesboro
August 31–September 1

Map 1: Major battles of the Atlanta campaign

1

The Path of War Leads to Georgia

DURING THE FIRST DAYS of May 1864, the roads leading south from Tennessee into Georgia were choked by the traffic of one hundred thousand marching soldiers. An incredibly destructive force was advancing on Atlanta.

The fighting in the Civil War was entering its fourth catastrophic year. Four years of the most intense and deadly warfare experienced by any nation had brought the full fury of war to Georgia. Numerous bloody battles had been fought, and many more remained to be waged before the war would draw to a close in another year. What happened in Georgia during the next three months would contribute heavily to that final outcome.

The Civil War was fought on two fronts. According to traditional thought, the major theater was in the East, where enormous Federal armies under a succession of inept commanders attempted to destroy the Army of Northern Virginia and capture the capital of the Confederacy, Richmond. Every attempt to attain these goals was thwarted by the brilliant strategist Robert E. Lee, the Confederacy's beloved Gray Fox, whose tattered soldiers consistently delivered devastating defeats to far superior forces. However, Lee's two efforts to invade the North and end the war victoriously for the South had also failed. In the spring of 1864, the situation in the East was at stalemate.

Only in the western theater had Union forces prevailed. Early in the war, President Abraham Lincoln directed that the South be divided in half by the Federal seizure of the Mississippi River. A long and costly effort, it ultimately was successful.

In 1862 Ulysses S. Grant skillfully combined infantry and a fleet of gunboats to subdue the Confederate fortresses of Henry and Donelson, thereby securing Federal control of the Tennessee and Cumberland Rivers and

A Controversial Plan

Patrick R. Cleburne was one of the Confederacy's best generals. He had been born in Ireland and served in the British army before joining his family in immigrating to America, where they settled in Arkansas. His Confederate service had been exemplary, and for his valor at Ringgold Gap, Cleburne had been nicknamed "Stonewall of the West."

Joseph E. Johnston had been commander of the Army of Tennessee less than a week when Cleburne approached him with a stunning proposal. After three years of costly war, the Irishman announced, the South needed additional soldiers. Therefore, slaves should be allowed to fight for the Confederacy; their reward would be emancipation. This would solve the South's manpower shortage, encourage European recognition of the Confederacy, and remedy a terrible social problem.

Johnston found himself mediating between generals who had an open mind on the issue and generals like William T. Walker who called the proposal "treason." Cleburne's suggestion was quickly silenced in Richmond, and the general's outstanding career came to a sudden standstill.

Cleburne was killed in November 1864 at the battle of Franklin, and his visionary plan did not come to light until twenty-five years after the war ended.

establishing a stout reputation for himself. In April Grant beat back a furious Confederate assault at Shiloh to win the first great battle in the West.

Union control of Missouri and Arkansas was assured after a Federal victory at Pea Ridge, Arkansas. Following successful battles for New Madrid and Island Number 10, Federal forces had cleared the upper Mississippi River of Confederates; the southern end of the river was closed when Adm. David G. Farragut's fleet courageously captured New Orleans.

An attempt by Confederate Gen. Braxton Bragg, commander of the Army of Tennessee, the South's second largest army, to wrest control of Kentucky from the Federals failed when he was repulsed at Perryville by Don Carlos Buell. Bragg retreated to central Tennessee, where William S. Rosecrans, Buell's replacement, won a narrow but costly victory at Stones River.

Grant and William Tecumseh Sherman, Grant's chief lieutenant, had initiated operations against Vicksburg, the last remaining obstacle to Union control of the entire Mississippi River, late in 1862, but their first advances ended in dismal failure. Throughout 1863 Grant moved against Vicksburg, overcoming many obstacles and eventually surrounding the city. On July 4, 1863, the city was starved into submission, resulting in the closure of the Mississippi River to the Confederacy. The fledgling nation was split into two halves.

Rosecrans spent six months rebuilding his army, and in September 1863 he finally moved against Chattanooga. Bragg, outmaneuvered, abandoned the city, but at Chickamauga Creek, just across the Georgia border, he turned and assaulted Rosecrans with great ferocity. On the second day of battle, Confederate Gen. James Longstreet pierced the Federal line, and Rosecrans, with most of his army, literally ran for the safety of Chattanooga. At Chickamauga, one of the bloodiest battles in American history, thirty-six thousand men fell in two days of bitter fighting.

Bragg's victory had cost his own army so dearly that he was unable to follow it up vigorously, and he had to be content with besieging Chattanooga, surrounding the city in hopes of forcing its surrender. Unfortunately for this strategy, Grant, after his magnificent victory at Vicksburg, was promoted to lead all Western armies and arrived outside Chattanooga with sixty thousand additional troops from Mississippi.

After opening a supply line into Chattanooga in November, Grant launched several attacks against the Confederates entrenched atop Lookout Mountain and Missionary Ridge. The Southern defenders were routed, and the Army of Tennessee reeled into Georgia.

Grant was soon called to Washington and made lieutenant general, the first since George Washington. As commander of all Union armies, Grant assumed personal control of the Eastern troops in Virginia and immediately promoted Sherman to command the Western forces. Grant then formulated a plan to bring about a Federal victory in the war. For the first time there would be coordinated offensives in the East and in the West. When spring arrived, he would launch an attack against Lee and shatter the Army of Northern Virginia, while Sherman would advance south from Chattanooga, destroy the

ALFRED WAUD

Evidence of a revival in the spirits of the Army of Tennessee—a famous snowball battle fought in March 1864.

Army of Tennessee, and divide the Confederacy once again by capturing Atlanta and marching to either the Atlantic Ocean or the Gulf of Mexico.

Grant instructed George Gordon Meade, commander of the Army of the Potomac: "Lee's Army will be your objective point. Wherever Lee goes, there you will go also." For Sherman: "Joe Johnston's Army being the objective point and the heart of Georgia his ultimate aim."

After realizing that Atlanta provided food, clothing, munitions, and equipment of all kinds to the Confederate armies in the field, Grant was determined that the city must fall. If Lee were denied the enormous natural resources of Georgia, Grant was convinced Lee could not continue the fight.

Another factor that made Atlanta's destruction imperative was its railroads. Atlanta was one of the Confederacy's last remaining transportation centers. Four major railroads converged there from throughout the South. The Western and Atlantic extended north to Chattanooga and into Tennessee; the Georgia Railroad line to Augusta, Charleston, Wilmington, and Richmond was a direct funnel to Lee in Virginia; the Macon and Western served Macon and Savannah; and the Atlantic and West Point extended to one of the South's last major ports, Mobile. Atlanta was the economic, manufacturing, political, and transportation center of the remaining southernmost states in the Confederacy, and it had to be destroyed to bring the war to a successful conclusion.

Triumph in Georgia was also a political necessity. The capture of Atlanta was needed to guarantee the reelection of Lincoln, which seemed in doubt during much of 1864. The administration needed decisive victories to convince the people of the North to persevere and bring the war to a victorious military conclusion. Without the capture of Atlanta, an antiwar candidate might win the presidency and make a settlement with the South that would permanently split the United States. That must not be allowed to happen.

The conduct of the Atlanta campaign was determined by two factors: the disparity in numbers between the contending armies and the personalities of the commanders. Sherman had 110,000 troops at his disposal; his adversary, Joseph E. Johnston, began the campaign with only 40,000 men.

Sherman had been a dissatisfied peacetime soldier, but he proved himself an effective fighter during war. After graduating sixth in his class at West Point, he left the military after seventeen years, later writing, "I was not considered a good soldier." In civilian life he was a failure in law and banking then became superintendent of Louisiana State Seminary, which later became Louisiana State University. He reentered military service at the start of the war, and at the battle of First Manassas his brigade was one of those that panicked and ran from the field. Transferred west, his antics convinced Northern newsmen that he was dangerously insane, and he was nearly driven from the army. While commander of the Army of the Tennessee, however, Sherman won fame first while helping Grant at Shiloh and then in the capture of Vicksburg.

Sherman was held in high esteem by his men. They called him "Uncle Billy" and preferred his rumpled appearance and grumpy demeanor to the stiff formality of other officers.

At the beginning of the campaign, Sherman's forces were divided into three armies. Commanding the enormous sixty-thousand-man Army of the Cumberland was George H. "Pap" Thomas, one of the few Virginians who had remained with the Union. Thomas gained fame at Chickamauga when the rest of the army, including Rosecrans, fled the field in panic. Thomas occupied a defensive position and repulsed numerous Confederate assaults, saving the army from destruction by buying time for its escape to Chattanooga. When Grant arrived, he relieved Rosecrans and placed Thomas in command. Sherman's only complaint with the "Rock of Chickamauga" was a tendency to caution when Sherman expected immediate and vigorous action, prompting Sherman's personal nickname, "Old Slow Trot."

The second Union army, the Army of the Tennessee, was twenty-three thousand strong and formerly commanded by Grant and Sherman. Command was bestowed on James Birdseye McPherson, a young favorite of his superiors who had risen from captain to major general in one year. Before the Atlanta campaign began, he had asked Sherman for leave so he could marry his fiancée in Baltimore, but Sherman had refused, explaining that marriage would have to wait until the war was over.

Sherman's smallest corps, the seventeen-thousand-man Army of the Ohio, was led by John McAllister Schofield, an intellectual who would become secretary of war and commanding general of the army after the war.

The cavalry was led by Hugh Judson Kilpatrick, a youngster who started the war with the famous Fifth New York Zouaves and rose to command Meade's cavalry at Gettysburg.

Grant had great confidence in Sherman, as his orders indicated. Sherman was instructed to destroy the Army of Tennessee, capture Atlanta and render it useless to the prosecution of the war, and inflict as much damage on Georgia's productive breadbasket region as possible. How Sherman accomplished these broad goals was left to his discretion. From Atlanta, Sherman would be free to advance on Andersonville, Columbus, Mobile, Macon, Savannah, or wherever he thought he would have the greatest effect.

When he marched south from Chattanooga, Sherman had a rough plan for the campaign. Thomas would attack Johnston's front to keep the Confederates pinned down, McPherson would flank Johnston to the west, and Schofield, accompanied by Joseph Hooker's corps, would circle to the east. These maneuvers would force Johnston to continuously retreat toward the first objective: Atlanta. It also raised the possibility of Sherman cutting off the Confederates' supply line and severing their line of retreat, which would force Johnston to fight on Sherman's terms.

At some point Johnston would have to attack to stop the offensive, and Sherman's veteran armies would be ready to stop the assault. They would then counterattack and destroy the inferior Confederate command.

Johnston was born in Virginia fifteen days after Robert E. Lee and graduated with him from West Point in 1829. During his military career,

A Commanding General First and Last ■ Joseph E. Johnston

Joseph E. Johnston was a member of the West Point Class of 1829 and spent only one year out of uniform between then and the opening of the Civil War. When the country was thrown into civil war, he chose to fight for his home state of Virginia.

During the first major conflict of the Civil War, Johnston shared command of the Rebel forces in the field with P. G. T. Beauregard. As the Union army approached Manassas, Johnston rushed his men to the battle by rail, and their redeployment turned the tide of the fighting for the South. A year later, in 1862, Johnston demonstrated his skill in executing deft withdrawals (a cursed habit, his critics believed) up the Yorktown Peninsula in the face of Union Gen. George B. McClellan's massive force.

With the Union army within sight of Richmond, Johnston launched a furious counterattack at Fair Oaks to blunt the Federal advance. While reconnoitering the battle front in the early twilight, Johnston (exercising a profound propensity for attracting lead) was seriously wounded. Although few expected his replacement to succeed, Robert E. Lee proved masterful.

Johnston was transferred from Virginia and given nominal command of the western theater, but he was ineffective in stemming the Union tide that flowed through Tennessee and down the Mississippi River. In December 1863, after Braxton Bragg's retreat from Chattanooga, Johnston was grudgingly appointed to command the Army of Tennessee.

As William T. Sherman's armies advanced relentlessly into Georgia, Johnston managed to keep his army intact, but he retreated to Atlanta's outskirts without initiating a major battle. Distressed by Johnston's reticence to keep him informed, Davis dismissed Johnston at the same time that Sherman's force approached Atlanta.

Eight months later—the Army of Tennessee reduced to tatters by a disastrous campaign in Tennessee— Johnston was renamed the army's commander. Meanwhile, Sherman's armies had reformed, marched across Georgia, and advanced into the Carolinas. Johnston rushed his men to North Carolina and desperately threw his lean ranks against Sherman at Bentonville. Caught unaware, the

Federals fought hard to regain the advantage. Two weeks after Lee surrendered to U. S. Grant at Appomattox Court House, Johnston capitulated to Sherman.

Johnston was wounded ten times, leading Lee to remark that he seemed to attract lead. When Virginia seceded, Johnston resigned from the U.S. Army and offered his services to the Confederacy. He was soon embroiled in controversy with President Jefferson Davis, who ranked him fourth among Confederate generals. Johnston felt that his service and seniority earned him first ranking. This reignited a long-running feud that had begun at West Point when Johnston allegedly bested Davis in fisticuffs over the affections of a young lady. Johnston originally commanded the Confederate armies in Virginia, but he was wounded at Fair Oaks in 1862 and was replaced by Lee. After convalescing, he directed the Department of Mississippi during the Vicksburg campaign in 1863.

Following the Army of Tennessee's rout from Missionary Ridge in November 1863, Bragg asked Davis to relieve him. William Joseph Hardee, a corps commander, was offered the position, but he gallantly refused to keep it, insisting that Johnston deserved the command. On December 27, 1863, Johnston arrived at the railroad depot in Dalton, Georgia, to take command. Unfortunately, Davis recalled the disgraced Bragg to act as his principal military adviser. This dreadful mistake allowed the embittered Bragg to reinforce Davis's distrust of Johnston by continually criticizing his successor.

In fact, Johnston inherited a ruined army. During the rout from Chattanooga, the once proud Army of Tennessee had abandoned thousands of rifles, a number of cannon, and supplies of every sort. At Dalton, Johnston found a pitiful force of tattered, hungry men. They were six thousand rifles short, and "the number of bare feet was painful to see," the general noted.

The new army commander immediately ordered an amnesty, influencing thousands of men who had deserted since Chattanooga to rejoin the

The Man Who Made War Hell ■ William T. Sherman

Sherman, considered to be one of the greatest generals in American history, definitely had one of the country's most unusual military minds. He was named Tecumseh at birth for the famous Indian warrior. William was added by his adoptive parents, whose daughter, Ellen, he later married.

He was ranked sixth in the West Point Class of 1840, and his subsequent service covered much of the South and included the war with Mexico. Weary of trying to earn a living in the military, Sherman entered civilian life in 1853 and failed miserably in business. He seemed to have found his niche as commandant of a military school, which would become Louisiana State University, when the Civil War began. Sherman rejected a Confederate commission, one of the few offered a native Northerner, and rejoined the U.S. Army. He commanded a brigade at First Manassas.

Sherman's volatile temper and absolute contempt for newspaper correspondents embroiled him in conflicts that almost led to his dismissal. The general allegedly pondered suicide, but his star began to rise when he assisted Ulysses S. Grant at Shiloh and in the campaign to capture Vicksburg. After the pair relieved the Confederate siege of Chattanooga, Grant went east and left his trusted friend in charge of the Western armies.

Sherman's brilliant maneuvering won him Atlanta, and his virtually unopposed march to Savannah and through the Carolinas was a stroke of genius that pierced the hollow shell of an exhausted Confederacy. Paradoxically, when that campaign was over, Sherman was harshly censored by Congress for granting overly generous terms to surrendering Confederates.

After the war, Sherman refused to challenge Grant for the presidency, and he continued to resist the temptation of political office for the rest of his life. He remained in the army until 1883. To the North, Sherman was a conquering hero; to the South, he was evil incarnate. To all, he was a temperamental, unpredictable military phenomenon.

army and redeem themselves by fighting selflessly for their new leader. Johnston furloughed the entire army in shifts, allowing the men, some of whom had not seen home in two years, to visit their families. Johnston requisitioned better food and new uniforms and found footwear for the soldiers. A program of intense drilling and training instilled a sense of pride, confidence, and discipline. Morale was bolstered by battles fought throughout the winter with snowballs. When Johnston judged their progress as satisfactory, a formal review was conducted. Forty thousand men paraded past his reviewing stand with bands playing and regimental banners flying. The army also experienced a religious revival. By spring, Johnston believed the Army of Tennessee was ready once more to defend the heartland of the South.

But defense of the fledgling republic was not what Davis expected. During the winter he plagued Johnston with telegraphed orders to take the offensive, to recapture Chattanooga and invade Tennessee to claim it for the Confederacy. Sherman had massed 110,000 troops in Chattanooga; Johnston had 40,000. Sherman had 254 cannon; Johnston had 124. The odds prohibited offensive action; so Johnston informed Davis that when Sherman advanced, he planned to defeat the enemy then drive north. A trifle impertinent, Johnston added that if Davis would send him all the idle soldiers in the Deep South who were on useless garrison duty, he could recapture Tennessee. Davis did order the 15,000-man Army of the Mississippi, commanded by Leonidas Polk, to join Johnston in early May.

Johnston's army was divided into two corps. Hardee, a Savannah native and author of West Point's standard strategy textbook, led one corps. The second was commanded by John Bell Hood, a Kentuckian. Hood had been one of Lee's best divisional commanders in Virginia. A wound suffered at Gettysburg, however, had cost Hood the use of an arm, and he lost a leg at Chickamauga. The courageous general had to be helped into his saddle, where straps held him in place, and he could walk only with the aid of crutches. Although there was ample evidence that Hood's pain medication impaired his judgment, he was made a corps commander. Regarding Johnston, Hood considered the new commander cowardly for assuming a defensive posture and was highly critical of how he handled the army, attitudes he freely expressed in letters to Davis and Bragg.

Johnston, an intelligent, formal man, kept his own counsel, sharing his thoughts and strategy with no one. This trait made Davis, Bragg, and Hood suspect that he had no plan. Davis's distrust of Johnston increased as the campaign progressed, a feeling greatly fueled by false reports from Hood.

Polk, who had resisted Bragg's attempts to take the offensive at Chickamauga, was obstinate in his own way. Thus Johnston could not trust two of his three corps commanders to carry out his orders conscientiously. "If I were President," Johnston stated, "I would disperse the generals of the army over the Confederacy." Of his corps commanders, Johnston trusted only the loyal and reliable Hardee.

Johnston's cavalry was led by the impetuous Joseph Wheeler, who had gained a reputation in the Tennessee campaign as Jeb Stuart's equal. The colorful soldier announced his raids on Union lines by shouting, "The war child rides tonight!"

Like Sherman, the uncommunicative Johnston won the admiration of the soldiers who fought for him. He was concerned for his infantrymen and took care not to waste lives in foolhardy actions. His men loved, trusted, and admired Johnston, who wrote that the army "was my true friend"—he had few enough in Richmond.

Johnston formed his counterstrategy while awaiting Sherman's offensive. He would establish strong defensive positions and entice Sherman to attack in hopes of whittling down the enemy. Johnston planned to withdraw deeper into Georgia, stretching Sherman's supply lines while constricting his own. Sherman would be forced to leave troops behind to guard each depot, railroad bridge, and town he occupied. While Sherman would have to cope with the ever present danger of Confederate cavalry raids cutting the vital railroad, Johnston would gather strength as his garrisons joined the main army. After attrition had taken a toll on Sherman's armies, Johnston planned to attack him at a time and position favorable to the Confederates.

This grand chess game would be played for two months in the beautiful countryside of northern Georgia. Sherman attacked and flanked; Johnston established successive defensive positions. Compared to the awful carnage taking place between Grant and Lee at Virginia's Wilderness, Spotsylvania, and Cold Harbor, losses were light. Several times Sherman would become impatient with his own strategy and play Johnston's hand, with bloody results. When Sherman relied on his own strategy, he steadily gained ground. Johnston, busy much of the time executing deft retreats, attempted on several occasions to take the offensive to isolate and shatter parts of Sherman's giant army, but his efforts always failed.

Sherman had tremendous respect for his opponent, stating that Johnston was "in all the elements of generalship equal to Lee." Sherman praised Johnston's "lynx-eyed watchfulness" and his habit of remaining in an exposed position until the last second to inflict all possible casualties on an enemy, then slipping away unscathed. His "model of defensive warfare," Sherman declared, neutralized his own numerical superiority.

In turn, Johnston had a healthy respect for Sherman, for he had been ineffective in stopping Grant and Sherman from seizing Vicksburg while he was in charge of the Department of Mississippi. Johnston was well aware of Sherman's consummate military skill and of the large number of men and enormous quantity of supplies that the Union commander would have available. He fully realized that the impending campaign would determine the fate of the Confederacy.

On May 1, 1864, Grant telegraphed Sherman that he was moving against Lee. The struggle for Atlanta was about to begin.

2

Feints, Fights, and Flanks

THE QUIET VALLEYS OF northern Georgia came alive with activity as an irresistible wave of Federal skirmishers swept Confederate cavalry pickets from Ringgold and other outposts north of Tunnel Hill. Behind this screen advanced miles-long columns of blue-clad soldiers—110,000 of them—accompanied by hundreds of artillery pieces, brass bands, and a seemingly endless wagon train carrying supplies to sustain an enormous army on an extended campaign.

The soldiers marched slowly south from their winter quarters in Chattanooga and Cleveland, Tennessee. The ponderous force could not move quickly over the few country lanes leading south; so the armies spread out on a wide front, taking advantage of the narrow roads and natural gaps through the rugged ridges that dominate this part of Georgia. Johnston's army was waiting at Dalton behind a strong natural barrier: Rocky Face Ridge. Sherman intended to assault it frontally while sending a force around the ridge to outflank the Confederate position.

George H. Thomas's massive Army of the Cumberland occupied Ringgold on May 4 and advanced along the western slope of Taylor's Ridge in the Chickamauga Creek Valley. On the morning of May 5, he crossed Taylor's Ridge at Nickajack Gap, emerging into the Dogwood Valley near Mill Creek Gap. Kilpatrick's cavalry led the advance and screened the troop movements through this gap and others to the south so the Confederates could not determine the strength of the offensive or the primary direction of the thrust.

John M. Schofield's Army of the Ohio marched to the east of Ringgold from Cleveland, Tennessee, and Red Clay. Federal units that had camped at the antebellum watering hole of Catoosa Springs on May 6 advanced on Tunnel Hill and the Crow Creek Valley past Lee's Chapel on the following

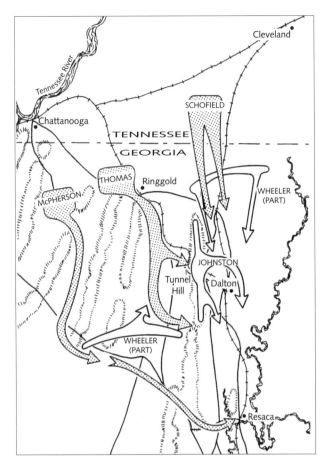

Map 2: The campaign begins

day. Sherman, Thomas, and Schofield watched the troops advance from a ridge near the church, which is considered the spot where the Atlanta campaign began.

The route of the Federal armies was lightly contested by Wheeler's cavalry. Confederate skirmishers established temporary firing positions in the woods and felled trees across the roads to delay the march, but they were forced to fall back under heavy pressure.

Schofield occupied Varnell after a sharp skirmish with Wheeler, then marched through Harris Gap, where Rocky Face Ridge breaks up into a series of small hills. He then approached Tunnel Hill, his first major objective. When the Federals arrived at 9 A.M. on May 7, they forced the Southern horsemen out of town but found Chetoogeta Ridge over the railroad tunnel bristling with a slight line of cavalry and a few small guns. The Federal skirmishers charged, and the Confederate cavalry fired a volley, then mounted up and galloped off for scouting duties west of Dug Gap. Federal Gen. Oliver O. Howard remarked simply, "The ball is opened."

The Confederates had neglected to close the railroad tunnel with explosives, an oversight that presented Sherman with an unexpected, but greatly appreciated gift. His supply trains would be able to keep pace with the offensive. Sherman would maintain his headquarters in Tunnel Hill throughout the Dalton operations.

From the top of Chetoogeta Ridge, Sherman and Howard had their first view of Rocky Face Ridge—a high, formidable wall of stone. Through his glasses, Sherman studied the impressive Rebel defenses. The first barrier on the road to Atlanta lay before him.

To the west, the third Federal force, James B. McPherson's Army of the Tennessee, was quietly sneaking around Rocky Face Ridge through Snake Creek Gap to attack Johnston's weak flank by surprise. The gap skirts the southern edge of Rocky Face fourteen miles south of Dalton, opens into Sugar Valley, and leads to the small town of Resaca, ten miles south of Dalton along the railroad. If the rails could be severed, Johnston would be trapped in Dalton between two Federal armies.

On May 7 McPherson marched through the old Chickamauga battlefield and turned southeast. He camped for the night at Chestnut Flat, dispatching a brigade to seize Ship's Gap (Maddox Gap on modern maps) over Taylor's Ridge. The next morning McPherson marched over winding Ship's

HARPER'S WEEKLY

Ringgold, Georgia, had seen a great deal of action by the time Union Gen. George H. Thomas's Army of the Cumberland arrived at the beginning of the Atlanta campaign. Not much remained of the railroad depot.

Gap into the beautiful West Armuchee Valley and seized Villanow, a small crossroads settlement, then continued east to seize Snake Creek Gap with no opposition.

North of Villanow was Gordon Springs Gap, where two corps of the Army of the Cumberland crossed into Dogwood Valley opposite Rocky Face Ridge to participate in the assault against Dug Gap and Mill Creek Gap. Kilpatrick's cavalry, having screened Federal infantry movements from Ringgold to Mill Creek, crossed Gordon Springs Gap in the opposite direction and led McPherson's advance out of Snake Creek Gap. The Federal armies were in position.

Dalton was a strategic city, thirty miles southeast of Chattanooga and eighty miles north of Atlanta on the Western and Atlantic Railroad. It was protected by the strongest natural obstacle in north Georgia: Rocky Face Ridge, a long, fifteen-hundred-foot-high ridge with a razor-sharp summit that extends north to south three miles west of the city.

After the Confederate army was routed from Missionary Ridge in November 1863, Bragg halted his troops at Dalton and fortified the ridge, expecting immediate pursuit by the Federals. When the Yankee advance was blunted by Patrick Cleburne's heroic rear-guard stand at Ringgold, the Army of Tennessee camped in Dalton for the remainder of the winter of 1863.

Shortly after Johnston replaced Bragg, he strengthened the works along the ridge, particularly at three accessible routes over and around the mountain barrier. The first was Mill Creek Gap, a natural passage just northwest of Dalton that was carved out of the mountain by Mill Creek. The railroad and main wagon road to

The Ringgold depot, damaged by artillery fire in November 1863, was repaired with lighter colored stones.

Horse Soldiers ■ The Cavalry

Both North and South produced a number of distinguished cavalry leaders such as Jeb Stuart, Philip H. Sheridan, Joseph Wheeler, and James H. Wilson. The role of the cavalry, however, was changed drastically by the war.

In earlier conflicts, cavalry tactics were designed to crash into the enemy, riding down infantry and slashing with sabers from their mounts. New weapons technologies, particularly longer-ranged rifles, made the cavaliers, and particularly their huge horses, an easy prey. After several thousand years, infantry finally triumphed over the horsemen.

During the Civil War, the mobility of the cavalry was utilized to strike deep behind enemy lines in lightning raids whose goals were to destroy supplies and lines of communications. Yet these raids were frequently more flashy than constructive. Cavalry also served as the eyes of the army, performing vital reconnaissance. The best horse soldiers, as typified by Confederate Gen. Nathan Bedford Forrest, were the equal of any infantry when fighting dismounted.

Catoosa Springs was an antebellum resort and was used as a campsite for Federal troops advancing into Georgia in May 1864.

Chattanooga passed through this bottleneck. Two miles to the south is narrow Dug Gap, an eight-hundred-foot-high passage over the mountain. A third point of concern was the Crow Creek Valley, which lies several miles north of Dalton and east of the protection afforded by Rocky Face. To repulse an expected attack from that direction, Johnston established a defensive line along a string of high hills that ring the exposed valley.

This was Sherman's second attempt to capture Dalton. In February 1864 he learned that Johnston had weakened his army by sending Hardee to reinforce Polk in Mississippi, and he responded to this opportunity by sending the Army of the Cumberland to test Dalton's strength. Thomas occupied Ringgold and Tunnel Hill, then assailed the fortifications at Mill Creek Gap, Dug Gap, and Crow Creek Valley simultaneously. When every attack was repulsed by the defenders, Sherman withdrew to Chattanooga to wait for spring, when he planned to launch a general offensive with additional troops promised by Grant.

Confederate scouts immediately alerted Johnston to Sherman's initial movements south from Ringgold. On the morning of May 8, he ordered his men to take their stations in the works along the ridge and in the passes.

Later in the day, the powerful Federal armies appeared north and west of Rocky Face, which Sherman called the "terrible door of death." Yet even without McPherson, his forces dwarfed Johnston's. The warriors in blue marched up in parade-ground formations, proudly flying Old Glory and the flags of their individual units. Bands passionately played "The Star-Spangled Banner," "America," "Hail, Columbia," and other martial airs. The music wafted upon the breeze to the Confederate troops, moving patriotic feelings for the United States in the most staunch of Rebel hearts.

From their vantage points on the heights, the Southerners had a grand view of Sherman's approach. The ragged, but proud, Rebel troops were impressed by the spectacle but not awed. Legend states that a Federal soldier stepped forward at Mill Creek Gap and boldly read Lincoln's Emancipation Proclamation. The Southerners listened politely, then, when the Yankee had finished, they punctured the document with a hail of rifle fire.

The defenders hoped the Federals would launch direct assaults on their lines. The common thought was that all the Union soldiers would be killed in short order, and they could go home. Cleburne said that he could hold this line indefinitely and destroy all attackers. But Sherman knew, and Johnston surely suspected, that this was a grand charade. Sherman would not cripple his army by dashing it against what was called Georgia's Rock of Gibraltar. The purpose of this demonstration was to distract Johnston's attention from his rear, so McPherson could push around the Rebel flank undetected.

Mill Creek Gap, known then as Buzzard Roost Gap, is a bold opening in Rocky Face Ridge. The heaviest fortifications around Dalton were here, giving the Confederates a great defensive advantage. Batteries of concealed artillery, which had been laboriously hauled up the vertical slope by hand, fired punishing salvos that the Federals could not return. Thousands of

The now abandoned railroad tunnel through Chetoogeta Ridge was Sherman's first objective.

The assault on Buzzard Roost Gap began, as usual, with artillery.

infantrymen crouched along the slopes, hidden from the enemy by thick foliage, but their view of the troops below was unimpaired. Confederate marksmanship devastated the Union ranks as they advanced in smartly dressed lines to meet death.

When the major Federal attack began, John Bell Hood's men lurked behind heavy entrenchments in the gap and in virtually impregnable stone breastworks on the slopes to either side. Combat engineers had dammed Mill Creek to create an artificial lake that barred entrance to the gap. On May 8 Thomas's troops made three valiant but futile efforts to destroy the dam so Federal troops could storm through the gap, then they attempted to bridge the lake to no avail. A concerted attack up the southern slope of the ridge was bloodily repulsed by a hail of fire from all along the heights.

Sherman watched this grim but expected slaughter from the peak of Blue Mountain. He could only hope that McPherson was having greater success at Resaca.

Dug Gap is a narrow pass in Rocky Face Ridge. Early pioneers cut a road to it from the sheer cliff to connect Dalton and LaFayette, and just east of the gap lay Johnston's vital railroad supply line. A Confederate officer said the terrain surrounding the gap was such a strong natural defense that a handful of resolute men could hold it without adding fortifications.

A Bright Star Lost ■ James B. McPherson

"If he lives, he'll outdistance Grant and myself."

That was William T. Sherman's assessment of his protégé, thirty-five-year-old James Birdseye McPherson. That opinion was shared by all who knew the Ohioan. McPherson had graduated from West Point first in his class and was a fine engineer before returning to the academy to teach.

He had fought valiantly in all the Army of the Tennessee's encounters, and Ulysses S. Grant and Sherman groomed him for further advancement. Their perception of his potential was shared by soldiers of all ranks who respected his intelligent, energetic leadership.

The handsome six-footer attracted many female admirers, but he had made his decision concerning matrimony. When the war allowed, he would marry Emily Hoffman, the proud exception to a Baltimore Secessionist family.

The Atlanta campaign, however, did not add to McPherson's sterling reputation. Timidity at Resaca wasted a golden opportunity to destroy Johnston, and his assault at Kennesaw Mountain had been easily repulsed. At the moment when his career should have crested, when Hood launched a crushing attack against his army, McPherson was slain when he refused to surrender as he surveyed the situation.

"You have killed the best man in our army," his orderly called out to the Confederates who shot McPherson. Thousands of soldiers, including Sherman, echoed that sentiment in their hearts.

HARPER'S WEEKLY

The infantry assault on Dug Gap was undertaken by John Geary's division.

Keeping the Confederates at Dug Gap from scouting to the west was important to Sherman's plans. Across Dogwood Valley to the west were two passes leading over Taylor's Ridge. Beyond it was McPherson, stealthily marching toward Snake Creek Gap, only twelve miles southeast of Dug Gap.

To screen McPherson's movements, Joseph Hooker's Twentieth Corps had crossed Taylor's Ridge via Nickajack Gap on the afternoon of May 7 and had camped in Dogwood Valley near Liberty Church, midway between Dug Gap and Mill Creek Gap. On the morning of May 8, John Geary's division marched over Taylor's Ridge via Gordon Springs Gap to attack Dug Gap.

At the foot of western Rocky Face was a small community centered around Joel Babb's plantation. Confederate cavalry under Col. W. C. P. Breckinridge had withdrawn from Tunnel Hill and Mill Creek to camp here below Dug Gap and patrol the valley. At 1:30 P.M. on May 8, they discovered Federal troops swarming through Dogwood Valley. Two hours later Geary arrived at Babb's, deployed a brigade to either side of the gap, and began his assault. A battery of guns was unlimbered to cover the attacking men, and shells began falling among Confederate positions on the mountain.

Southern boys were thickly sown across the lower slopes, crouching behind logs, trees, and rocks to snipe at the approaching enemy. Geary called their fire "galling and destructive." They took a toll on the attackers then scrambled to defensive positions farther up the ridge.

Union soldiers struggled up Rocky Face Ridge to attack Confederate positions at Dug Gap.

Geary's men fought well, springing between the cover of rocks and trees. The Confederates—Arkansas troops and Breckinridge's dismounted Kentucky cavalry—took up their main works: a stout stone wall erected along the summit of the knife-edged ridge. To keep the advancing enemy off balance, the defenders rolled huge stones down the slope onto them. In post-war accounts, outraged Federals expressed the belief that this was a breach of fair play.

A Northern newspaper correspondent wrote that there was a "fierce fire behind every cliff or rock. Huge rocks were even rolled from the top of the ridge, which came plunging down from crag to crag, crushing and tearing among the trees and sweeping through the advancing line."

The following Southern account of that famous episode was written by Breckinridge.

> At first, in a mere spirit of exuberant fun, some of the men rolled stones down the mountain-side; but when the effect was noticed they were directed to use these means as part of our defense; great stones were rolled down on the supporting lines on the mountain-sides or at its foot; and as these boulders would go leaping, crashing, breaking off limbs, crashing down saplings, we fancied we could see the effect of the unexpected missiles. It also proved a valuable resource for us, for without them our ammunition would have given out, indeed it was about exhausted when the attacks ceased.

A second assault was also parried successfully, and the thin line of defenders held the Federals at bay until two Confederate brigades arrived to reinforce Dug Gap, but they were not needed. A few Union soldiers had gallantly struggled to the summit of Dug Gap, but the pass was so narrow that only five men could enter at one time. The Confederates, crouched behind the stone wall to either side of the gap, quickly cut them down and cleared the crest of Yankee troops. The fighting subsided as a smoky dusk fell over the battlefield.

Geary lost 49 men killed, 257 wounded, and 51 missing to 50 Confederate casualties. Concluding that he had accomplished his objective of diverting Confederate attention away from Snake Creek Gap, Geary wisely elected not to renew the uneven contest on the following morning. He camped at the foot of the mountain and threw an occasional and ineffective shell up at the defiant Rebels.

The cries of Federal wounded, scattered across the slope, haunted the mountain that night. At dawn Confederates rescued the enemy casualties and carried them into Dalton for care. Cleburne said that the assaults were "repulsed with great slaughter" and contended that the Union fallen equaled the number of defenders present at Dug Gap when the fight began.

A third battle took place in Crow Valley, where the Confederate defenses began atop Rocky Face just north of Mill Creek Gap. It extended across several wooded ridges to Potato Hill, where artillery was emplaced to anchor the line.

Confederate infantry crouched behind this stone wall and repulsed a Federal assault at Dug Gap.

A Rifleman's War

The Civil War was the first conflict to be dominated by firearms. Muskets employed in earlier wars were one-shot smoothbores that were inaccurate and extremely limited in range. Reloading was a difficult, time-consuming job. Furthermore, primitive flintlocks would not function when wet—and only 80 percent of the time under ideal conditions.

Percussion caps soon replaced the unreliable flintlocks, and experiments with rifled muskets were progressing. A revolution in infantry warfare was sparked by a Frenchman, Claude E. Miniè, who in 1849 designed a bullet (not a "ball," as most Civil War participants referred to it) that was smaller than the diameter of the gun barrel and could easily be inserted. When fired, the base of the projectile expanded to fit the rifling, giving the bullet a stabilizing spin for greater accuracy and range.

Prior to Miniè's design, muskets had a range of two hundred yards against a column of men and only one hundred yards against an individual. The rifled miniè bullet was effective against targets six hundred yards distant. Its high-velocity impact inflicted terrible internal damage on its victims, which was responsible for the awful piles of amputated limbs that resulted from every Civil War engagement.

Riflemen on the defensive ruled the Civil War. Few assaults survived the hail of fire that began at long range and increased in horrible intensity as the troops advanced. Battles were still fought as stand-up fights between infantry, in the old European style, but rifled long arms quickly drove soldiers into earthworks that presaged World War I trench warfare.

The Federal occupation of Buzzard Roost Gap was sketched by artist J. E. Taylor for Leslie's Illustrated Newspaper.

On May 9 two of Schofield's divisions deployed in battle lines before Crow Creek. Rebel skirmishers delayed the Federal drive then fell back until the enemy was deep in the valley. Shells from masked Confederate batteries on Potato Hill and volleys of musketry from invisible infantry on top of eastern Rocky Face stopped the charge cold.

Federal forces remained in front of the Confederate positions at Dalton for several days, maintaining a constant pressure to keep the Confederates occupied. Sherman did not order them to renew the suicidal assaults. He was waiting for McPherson's bold strike on Resaca.

A Tour from Ringgold to Dalton

This tour of the Atlanta campaign begins in Ringgold, twenty miles south of Chattanooga and ten miles north of Dalton in Catoosa County. Rugged Taylor's Ridge, which runs north to south immediately south of the town, is visible for miles. Piercing the mountain is narrow, steep-sided Ringgold Gap. The old wagon road and railroad hugged the southern slope of the gap, and U.S. 41-GA 3 and the railroad still follow the same path; Interstate 75 was laid out below the western slope. When passing through on I-75, note the stone terraces carved out to prevent rock slides.

Turn off Interstate 75 at Ringgold (exit onto GA 151) and proceed east to U.S. 41-GA 3 (Nashville Street). Turn right. At the southern end of Ringgold, just before the railroad underpass, the old stone depot is on the left. Turn in.

The depot is listed on the National Register of Historic Places. Both slopes of Ringgold Gap are visible beyond the railroad underpass from the parking area in front of the depot. Erected in 1849 with locally quarried sandstone blocks, the walls of the depot are fourteen inches thick. It was in continuous use on the Western and Atlantic Railroad until recent decades, although the structure was badly damaged by artillery fire during the battle of Ringgold Gap in November 1863 (see appendix A) and later burned. It was repaired with lighter colored blocks. The extensive damage suffered at the southern end and along the roof line and around the windows is easy to distinguish. Legend has Grant and Hooker arguing here over the latter's failure to pursue Bragg aggressively.

By comparing the large size of the depot and its strong, skillful construction to other depots found along the Western and Atlantic in northern Georgia, one can grasp the importance that Ringgold once enjoyed in the region's economic life. Considerable wheat was shipped from here.

A three-hundred-thousand-dollar restoration has recently begun on the depot, which hosts weekend bluegrass concerts. When completed, there will be historic exhibits inside and signage to mark the beginning of the Georgia Civil War Trail.

By the spring of 1864, Ringgold had seen more Civil War activity than any other community in Georgia and had been largely destroyed. Only a few homes and churches survived the war. In April 1862 the famous Great Locomotive Chase ended just north of town when Federal saboteur James Andrews, who had stolen the engine *General* in Big Shanty, eighty

Map 3: The Ringgold area

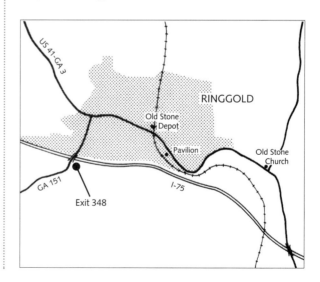

miles south of Ringgold, abandoned his daring mission because of William A. Fuller's heroic pursuit on the *Texas.*

A stone monument marking the place where the chase ended is on GA 151 beside the railroad, two miles north of Ringgold on Ooltewah Road. The raiders scattered into the woods but were captured.

In 1862–63 Ringgold was host to many military hospitals, particularly after Stones River. More than twenty thousand Confederate soldiers convalesced in churches, homes, the courthouse, hotels, and warehouses, cared for by many gracious ladies. The hospitals evacuated to the south in September 1863 to avoid capture by advancing Federal forces during the Chickamauga campaign.

The present courthouse (1939) is the third on this site. Union soldiers spared the original courthouse (1854) because it also housed a Masonic hall. The Baptist and Presbyterian churches, still on their original sites, served as hospitals. The Methodist church, no longer on its original site, was financed by Northern congregations.

After the battle of Stones River, Fannie Beers, a nurse whose husband was a Confederate surgeon, asked for the use of the courthouse and churches. Pews were thrown into the snow, straw was placed on the floors, and every room was crowded with wounded. By the spring of 1864 only the courthouse, depot, and churches remained.

In September 1863 William S. Rosecrans's Union Army of the Cumberland and the Confederate Army of Tennessee under Braxton Bragg collided just a few miles to the west in the second bloodiest battle of the war, Chickamauga. Touring the battlefield, museum, and monuments of the Chickamauga and Chattanooga National Battlefield Park would be a day well spent (see *Piercing the Heartland,* another of the Civil War Explorer books). Following the battle of Ringgold Gap that November, Ringgold became a no man's land between the Federals in Chattanooga and Confederates in Dalton.

At 309 Tennessee Street, two blocks from U.S. 41, is the Whitman-Anderson House (1850), listed on the National Register, which was used by Ulysses S. Grant as headquarters after Ringgold Gap. Legend claims that the general offered the woman of the house fifty U.S. dollars for her trouble, but she refused, demanding Confederate currency instead.

"She certainly is not whipped yet," Grant quipped, and Federal soldiers cheered her spirit. Her family had watched the fighting in Ringgold from the second floor. Local food stocks were exhausted, and the Federals distributed rations to prevent starvation. At Nashville and Guyler Streets is the Evans home, where Confederate nurses were boarded.

Just to the north of Ringgold, in Graysville, is the Gray home, which was spared by Sherman because the owner was a Mason. Federal troops were stationed on the grounds, and Grant used the structure as a headquarters.

Turn left from the depot onto U.S. 41-GA 3 and pass beneath the railroad. Note the twin stone pillars that welcome visitors to Ringgold; immediately on the right at .5 is the first of five unique interpretive pavilions. Note the sign designating this as the Ringgold Gap Historic Area.

Each of the pavilions describing the Atlanta campaign was erected during the 1930s by the Works Progress Administration and have enhanced historical interest along U.S. 41, which was the main traffic artery for the region at that time. These enchanting fieldstone constructions are equipped with picnic tables, a metal plaque describing the actions that occurred nearby, and a large stone table in the center with a giant relief map of the area that accurately depicts the battles and movements of both armies during the campaign. The markers, designed by John Steinichen, were cast at the Georgia Tech foundry. Construction was delayed by World War II and completed in 1946. The total budget was $27,500. There are occasional efforts to clean and restore the pavilions and replace missing markers and maps. At the rear of this one is a short path to a large granite monument with a bronze plaque near the railroad that marks the spot of furious fighting at Ringgold Gap in November 1863. It honors Col. John Ireland's New York Brigade. The pavilions provide ideal places to get oriented to the details of the campaign, allow the children to romp a bit, eat lunch, or lounge on the stone benches within the enclosures while enjoying the shade on a hot day.

The Atlanta campaign is considered to have begun on a ridge several miles east of here near Lee's Chapel on GA 2, where Sherman, George H. Thomas, and John M. Schofield watched their armies advance on Dalton. Thomas marched west of this spot along the route of GA 151, on the opposite side of Taylor's Ridge, to approach Mill Creek Gap. He camped for the night of May 6 at Pleasant Grove Church, Peavine Church, and Leet's Tanyard, where Bragg maintained his headquarters during part of the battle of Chickamauga. Schofield advanced to the east to seize Tunnel Hill and enter the Crow Valley.

With good maps, visitors can explore rugged Peavine Ridge around Beaumont and cross Taylor's Ridge over narrow, beautiful Nickajack Gap on SR 192-326, off GA 151 at Wood's Station, as H. Judson Kilpatrick and an infantry division did on May 7, 1864. This route approaches Dalton through Trickum, which was Thomas's route. Gordon Springs Gap to the south, through which John Geary and two divisions moved on May 7 to attack Dug Gap, is in southwest Whitfield County off GA 201 (Lookout Mountain Scenic Highway), but the road no longer crosses the ridge. West of GA 201 on Dunnagan Road near Liberty Church in the Dogwood Valley is the Anderson house, which was Joseph Hooker's headquarters during the Dalton operations.

Catoosa Station on the Western and Atlantic was not far from here. Bragg maintained a headquarters in the station's freight room during a portion of the battle of Chickamauga, and James Longstreet's corps was forced to disembark there the next day, September 18, to join the battle because the bridges farther north had been burned.

Continue south on U.S. 41-GA 3 through Ringgold Gap.

This portion of north Georgia is particularly beautiful as the highway hugs the sheer stone face of White Oak Mountain to the left and twists beside Chickamauga Creek to the right. As the narrow gap broadens into a valley, lovely farm country is framed against towering Taylor's Ridge in the background.

After 1.8 miles, at the intersection of U.S. 41-GA 3 with GA 2 at Tiger Creek, turn immediately left into the landmark Old Stone Church.

This church was organized in 1837 by Scotch-Irish Presbyterians, who first used a log cabin and in 1845 constructed Dogwood Campground. The church was constructed in 1850–52 with sixteen-inch-thick sandstone walls quarried from White Oak Mountain, which stands to the north. The use of stone for a church was rare in Georgia, and the 150-year-old structure is one of the oldest in the region. The attic timbers and pews, dating to the campground, are all hand-hewn, and the church retains its original foot-pedal organ. Note the thick, hand-cut windowsills. The hymn "Leaning on the Everlasting Arms," written by Dalton residents A. J. Showalter and E. A. Huffman and pastor Mark Matthews was first sung here.

After the battles of Missionary Ridge and Ringgold, the pews were removed and makeshift beds installed to transform the church into a hospital as evidenced by bloodstains that are still visible on the

The Old Stone Church (two views below) is just south of Ringgold. During the war, it was used extensively as a hospital. Today the building is a museum, and its floors are still stained with blood.

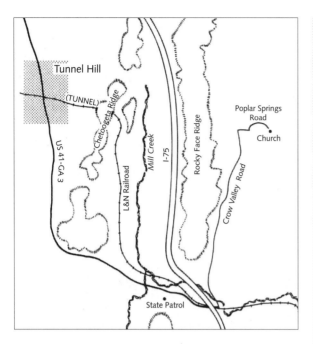

Map 4: Tunnel Hill and Mill Creek areas

floor. Federals used the structure for a hospital and livery. The pews, placed facing each other and used as horse feeding troughs, still have visible tooth marks from the animals. The sanctuary, which retains the original altar and pews and has bullets embedded in the stone walls, has since been used by many different denominations, but only sporadically since 1920. In the 1930s the church was nearly demolished for a tourist camp. The building, listed on the National Register, was donated in 1995 to the Catoosa County Historical Society for use as a museum. Additional land has been purchased for a separate museum in the future. Civil War artifacts are currently displayed inside the church.

Prior to the war, Catoosa County was famous for its hundreds of mineral springs. Believed to be healthful, these spas were frequented each summer by wealthy travelers to "take the cure," drinking and bathing in the mineral-enriched water. On GA 388 to the east, in beautiful Cherokee Valley was Cherokee Springs, used as a Confederate hospital from 1862 to 1863. Thousands of soldiers were treated for battle wounds or disease there, including Bragg and his wife. The hospitals were moved farther south in May 1863.

East on GA 2 and northeast on a county road is Catoosa Springs, perhaps the finest spa in pre–Civil War Georgia; it also was used as a Confederate hospital. Skirmishes were fought between Confederate and Federal cavalry on the grounds, and the Federals later used the facilities for camps while awaiting the push to Atlanta. The hospitals at Cherokee Springs and Catoosa Springs both accommodated five hundred. Some twenty thousand men were treated here before the hospitals moved in May 1863. The fine homes, hotels, and other facilities have vanished, but the current owner maintains the grounds and ponds created by the springs. Although several bathhouses remain, Catoosa Springs is not open to the public.

Also in the area was a saltpeter cave, an important Confederate facility that produced material for the manufacture of gunpowder.

Research preceding a housing development on Old Mill Road turned up the old Vincent Cemetery. The largest headstone is that of James Watkins, a Federal cavalryman who married a Vincent daughter, Setitia, and made his home here until his death in 1899. These graves may be moved, as was that of a soldier found during construction on White Oak Mountain.

Rejoin U.S. 41-GA 3 as it turns south opposite Old Stone Church to Tunnel Hill. The six miles between Ringgold and Tunnel Hill was a no man's land between November 1863 and May 1864. At 5 miles cross the railroad bridge on U.S. 41-GA 3 and immediately turn left onto Oak Street. Round the curve; up the railroad tracks at .2 to your right are the tunnels through Chetoogeta Ridge.

Prior to its restoration, Tunnel Hill appeared to be little more than a hole in the wall.

The larger, modern tunnel is to the left, the original to the right. The town of Tunnel Hill sprang up after the railroad was completed in 1850. The tunnel, the first in the Deep South and still the longest, was hewn through the ridge by two separate parties that started from opposite ends and met in the center of the mountain. Until it was completed train cargoes were unloaded at either end of the tunnel, transferred to oxcarts, and carried over the ridge. Jefferson Davis made a rousing speech at the depot early in the war. Confederates maintained a camp here through the winter and spring of 1864; a famous Confederate snowball battle involving thousands of troops was staged in this area. When the Federals arrived in May, the Southerners made a brief stand on the ridge over the tunnel, then retreated. It was here that Oliver O. Howard said to Sherman, "The ball is opened." They rode to the top of the ridge to observe Confederate positions on Rocky Face. The tunnel was initially a boon to the Confederacy, enabling supplies and troops to be rapidly shifted from the east to Atlanta then up to Tennessee. When Sherman arrived, however, a dispute erupted over whether the shaft should be destroyed to hamper the Federal war effort. Johnston wanted to collapse the tunnel, but Gov. Joseph E. Brown and Jefferson Davis opposed the plan. Apparently destroying the tunnel would be an admission that north Georgia and Tennessee had been irretrievably lost.

In 1863 Governor Brown called for eight hundred men to protect vital places along the railroad. The force, primarily composed of those exempt from Confederate service and men too old or too young to serve in the regular army, was designated the Georgia State Guards, First Regiment. The contingent raised locally was known as the Tunnel Hill Guards. Led by Capt. Hamilton Young, the unit served for six months before returning home.

Turn right on the road alongside the railroad tracks (Clisby Austin Road).

On the approach to a small, modern covered bridge spanning a trickling stream, across the tracks to the left is the Tunnel Hill depot, now part of an agricultural company. It was constructed of stone dug from the tunnel. To the right is the Clisby Austin house, also known as Meadowland, which was built as a resort hotel to take advantage of the scenery and two springs. After John Bell Hood's leg was amputated in the Armuchee Valley following Chickamauga, he recuperated here. On a grim note, because Hood was expected to die from infection, as large numbers of amputees did during the war, the leg was brought with him so his body could be buried whole. Hood survived, and his leg was interred in the family cemetery. Austin, a Unionist who welcomed Sherman and encouraged him to use Meadowland as headquarters during the fighting around Dalton, wisely slipped away when the Federals withdrew. Sherman's headquarters were established on the grounds for six days, May 5–9, 1864, and reportedly the general stayed in the same room that had sheltered Hood. Here he refined his campaign against Atlanta, heard of James B. McPherson's initial success at Snake

The restored tunnel offers visitors an intriguing peek at the railroad past as well as the Civil War.

Creek Gap, and first formulated his plan for marching to the sea.

While the home was being renovated in the 1980s, a horror movie was filmed here. The story line of *The Offspring* was that Southern war orphans who occupied a ruined mansion watched as Yankees captured and executed a squad of Confederates. The orphans kidnapped the Union leader and burned him at the stake. The three-story structure has been fully restored. A reenactment called the Battle of Tunnel Hill is held annually on the weekend after Labor Day.

Just before the road starts to climb Chetoogeta Ridge at .3, turn left into the parking area for the tunnel.

Most of the interior of the tunnel is lined with six feet of locally fired clay brick laid without mortar. The lower walls were finished with limestone blocks three inches thick. Inside are four alcoves, where pedestrians took shelter when trains caught them as they hiked to and from Dalton. At each end the portals are constructed of blocks of stone. The tunnel was christened with holy water from the River Jordan and bottles of wine and brandy before the first train passed through on May 9, 1850. This was the first railroad to cross the Appalachian Mountains, opening trade as far as the Rocky Mountains, and helping to establish the city of Atlanta. When the line was completed, the Western and Atlantic Railroad was 137 miles long and had a five-foot gauge. The tunnel remained in use until 1920, when the larger

tunnel was constructed adjacent to it. Reportedly, larger train cars had occasionally became stuck in the narrower excavation.

Not long ago the fourteen-hundred-foot-long tunnel, eight feet high and twelve and a half feet wide, was owned by the railroad and too dangerous to enter. Water seeped from the walls and gathered in deep pools on the floor of the tunnel, and large chunks of masonry often fell from the arched ceiling and sides, leaving piles of debris. The tunnel was in danger of collapsing. The remaining smoke-stained bricks were covered with moss. In 1996 the state of Georgia turned over the deed to the city of Tunnel Hill. It has since been repaired with nearly a million dollars of federal, state, and local funding. The ceiling was sealed with concrete, the bricks and limestone slabs repaired, and debris cleared. Plans call for information kiosks and eventually a visitors center to be constructed.

Research at the Foster Cemetery on GA 201 has revealed one Civil War tombstone belonging to a member of the Thirty-third Alabama and dated 1864. It is displayed in an old country store in Tunnel Hill, and the graves of dozens of other Confederates, who died in hospitals here, are believed to be at the back of the graveyard.

This quiet village, originally called Tunnelsville, was a busy railroad town 140 years ago when James Andrews and his raiders emerged from the tunnel and raced through Tunnel Hill, closely followed by the *Texas,* which must have presented a curious sight rushing up the tracks backward. Tunnel Hill is filled

Rugged Rocky Face Ridge (two views below) marked the Confederate line around Dalton and blocked Sherman's advance.

today with beautiful antebellum, Queen Anne, Victorian, Gothic Revival, and Colonial Revival homes.

Return to U.S. 41-GA 3 and turn left toward Dalton.

East on GA 201 at the intersection with GA 2 is the Varnell house (1847), which was used as a Confederate and Federal hospital and served as headquarters for several Union generals. A number of skirmishes were fought around the house, including one on May 12, 1864, when Joseph Wheeler swung around Sherman's left flank and drove the Federals briefly from the town, inflicting 150 casualties and capturing 100 prisoners, including 9 officers. The Varnell house still bears bullet scars.

Dalton and Calhoun, on U.S. 41, were once known as the capital of the hand-tufted and chenille bedspread industry. Numerous billboards attest to their continued leadership in carpet manufacturing.

On the outskirts of Dalton, at 4 miles, turn right into the Georgia State Patrol Post.

The patrol post is perched on the southern slope of Rocky Face Ridge. In front of a parking area below the station and overlooking the highway is the well-maintained second Atlanta campaign National Park Service pavilion. The relief map describes Sherman's unsuccessful attacks on Mill Creek Gap, Crow Valley, and Dug Gap, McPherson's successful flanking movement to the southwest, and Johnston's evacuation of Dalton (events of May 7–13, 1864). Hood held

A relief map interprets the action at Mill Creek Gap.

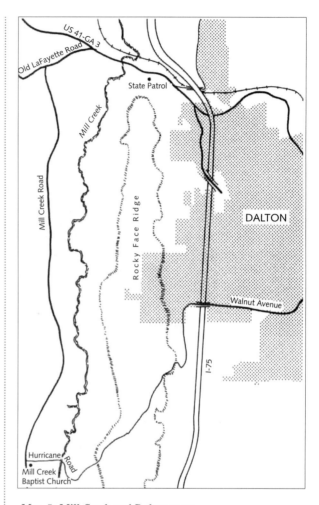

Map 5: Mill Creek and Dalton areas

the Crow Creek Valley, William J. Hardee Rocky Face Ridge; Leonidas Polk's corps were just reaching Resaca from Mississippi.

This is Mill Creek Gap, a large, level entrance to Dalton. The ridge rises abruptly in front and behind. Here Thomas's troops fruitlessly assaulted the Confederate works in the gap and on the ridge. The Southerners also held the northern slope, directly across the highway. North of Mill Creek Gap is Blue Mountain, where Sherman observed Union operations from its summit.

Local, state, and federal money has been recently combined to save Civil War fortifications on Rocky Face Ridge north of Mill Creek Gap from development. The land has extensive infantry trenches and artillery emplacements, and trails are planned to these and natural sites. Facing northwest on the ridge are breastworks of stacked stone, and below are four separate lines of parallel berms. Whitfield County will control the land as part of the Georgia Greenspace program. Many of the works were endangered, and several decades back construction of a giant water slide obliterated sections. Federals probed the works in February and May 1864.

Atop the ridge is the grave of Orphan Brigade member Pvt. George Disney, a thirty-eight-year-old tailor from Owensboro, Kentucky, and part of a "living telegraph line" that watched Federal moves. During a Union bombardment on February 25, 1864, comrades saw Disney sit up, yawn, then apparently lay back down to sleep. Later they discovered that he had been killed by a bullet that entered his mouth and penetrated his brain. He was buried on the spot, the grave marked by a pine board. The grave was forgotten until Boy Scouts stumbled across it in 1911. A year later they had a marble headstone placed at the site, and in 1953 a Georgia historical marker honoring Disney was erected at the base of Rocky Face.

Continue south on U.S. 41-GA 3 toward Dalton, but turn sharply left onto Willowdale Road at .3 and cross the bridge that spans Mill Creek. Cross the railroad, pass under I-75, and turn left onto Crow Valley Road at .2.

Traveling north on Crow Valley Road, the eastern slope of Rocky Face Ridge rises abruptly to the left. Note the beautiful bands of exposed stone.

At 2 miles, a historical marker (currently missing) indicates the point where the Confederate defensive line in Crow Valley began.

The eastern defenses of Dalton began high on top of the mountain, where a signal station was maintained, extended to the valley floor, and continued several miles to the hills on the east, then bent back south along Hamilton Mountain. Schofield's forces were stopped cold before these works.

Continue .8 to the stop sign, turn right onto Poplar Springs Road, and drive around the sharp curve to turn right at .4 into the Poplar Springs Baptist Church parking lot.

The large hill to the northeast is Potato Top, the Confederate artillery position instrumental in turning back the Federal attack. As part of Johnston's efforts to improve discipline in the ranks when he first assumed command of the army, a number of deserters were shot in the valley.

With very good regional maps, adventuresome visitors can trace Schofield's scenic path from Red Clay to Cohutta and Varnell through Harris Gap, just north of here at GA 201 and New Hope Road, to the Crow Valley. Red Clay, just yards across the Tennessee line, was an important Cherokee council site (their last eastern capital) and a vital Federal supply depot. It has been preserved as a Tennessee state park and features a visitors center–museum, a reconstructed Cherokee farm and cabins, a sacred council spring called the Blue Hole, and several other interesting attractions.

The three-story Prater's mill, on the National Register, is two miles east of GA 71 on GA 2. Built in 1859, the mill has three underwater turbines that turn huge milling stones, sifters, and grinders. On February 23, 1864, when Thomas probed Dalton's defenses, six hundred Union soldiers under Col. Eli Young camped on the grounds. On April 13, as the Atlanta campaign was being prepared, twenty-five hundred Confederates spent the night. Twice a year—on Mother's Day weekend and the second weekend in October—one of Georgia's finest fairs is held here, offering Civil War encampments, great country food, entertainment, arts and crafts, and canoeing. The setting is idyllic. Contact information is found in appendix E.

Return to U.S. 41-GA 3. Driving back down Poplar Springs Road to Crow Creek Valley Road offers one of the finest views available of dramatic Rocky Face.

Turn right onto U.S. 41-GA 3 and note the mileage, retracing the route past the State Patrol Post. At .9 is Mill Creek.

To the left a trail leads beside the creek to a point where a strong Federal attack up the southern slope was repulsed. In this area was the large artificial lake created for defense when the Confederates dammed the stream.

Continue. At .4 turn left from U.S. 41-GA 3 onto the Old LaFayette Road.

To the right before the turn is Blue Mountain, where Sherman observed the assaults on Mill Creek Gap.

At .6 turn left onto Mill Creek Road to enter beautiful Mill Creek Valley. Rocky Face Ridge rises boldly to the left beyond forests, homes, and farms. Other ridges appear equally grand to the right.

At 5 miles, turn left beside Mill Creek Baptist Church onto Hurricane Road at what was Babb's Settlement. Here Geary deployed his men and set up artillery to fire on Confederate defenders on the ridge.

Take the next left at .8 onto Dug Gap Battle Road and wind to the razor-sharp summit of Rocky Face Ridge. Dug Gap Battlefield Park is at 1.4 on the left.

The scenery on both sides of the ridge is spectacular, and the best views are available at this site. A small parking area affords a wonderful view of Dalton and ridges to the east, and a path leads to a 1,237-foot-long segment of the defensive stone wall from which a few brave Confederate soldiers from Arkansas and Kentucky repulsed Geary's men, who outnumbered them ten to one. It is easy to imagine how they could stop the Federals laboring up the sheer sides. Enormous boulders like the ones Confederates levered down on their approaching enemy are near the parking area on the west side of the ridge. The Dalton Civil War

Map 6: Dalton

Roundtable established the two-and-a-half-acre park. To arrange tours, call the Murray-Whitfield County Historical Society (see appendix E).

Continue east down the mountain on Dug Gap Road toward Dalton. At 1.3 turn right into the Northwest Georgia Trade and Convention Center.

A wide selection of information about Dalton is available here as well as information about many attractions in northwest Georgia.

Continue east as Dug Gap Road becomes GA 52-Walnut Avenue, then turn left at 2 miles onto Greenwood to the stop sign at Emory at .3. The rolling, terraced hills of Westhill Cemetery will be in front. Take the entrance nearly straight ahead and the second right within the cemetery to Soldier's Rest Confederate Cemetery, which is to the left in front of the maintenance buildings.

The iron-fenced enclosure, shaded by several large oaks, contains the graves of 421 unknown and 4 known Confederate soldiers, and 4 unknown Federal soldiers. These men died of wounds suffered at Stones River, Perryville, Chickamauga, Lookout Mountain, Missionary Ridge, and raids on Dalton and of disease in camp. Four hospitals in town nursed thousands of men, but they were evacuated south in May 1864. A small granite monument to the unknown soldiers who died in these hospitals was dedicated on May 10, 1892. The first memorial services were held in 1866. At the opposite end of the fence is a monument of Italian marble topped by a simple statue of a Confederate soldier, dedicated by the United Daughters of the Confederacy (UDC) on April 26, 1898, to honor the men who died at Chickamauga, Rocky Face, Dug Gap, and Resaca. It originally stood in Memorial Park on Thorton Avenue. The Memorial Wall, sponsored by the Civil War Roundtable and UDC, was added in April 1999. Marvin Sowder spent twenty years researching the names of the 400 unknown Confederate dead here. One side of the memorial lists the names, and the other side lists local historical sites.

Return to Emory, turn left, travel east .3 to U.S. 41-GA 3 (Thorton Avenue), and turn left.

The statue of a Confederate soldier guards the graves of Southern warriors in Dalton.

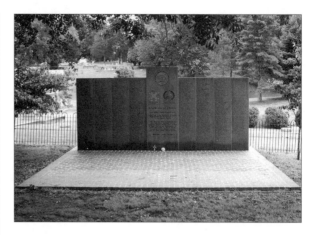

One side of a memorial wall in the cemetery lists the names of the Confederate dead; the other side lists noteworthy sites.

The fourth house on the left at 506 Thorton is the Blunt house (1848), constructed by Ainsworth E. Blunt, a minister who had arrived in the 1820s. He helped establish several churches and was Dalton's first mayor and postmaster. When war broke out, Unionist sympathies led him to flee with his family to Illinois, and the house was used as a Confederate hospital in the fall of 1863. During the winter and spring of 1864 the structure was headquarters for Confederate officers. Occupying Federals used the house and grounds for a hospital, covering the yard with temporary shelters called brush arbors and consuming the fences and trees. Blunt returned after the war and was horrified by the damage to his property. He filed a claim, and the U.S. government paid the family $1,815 for damages. In 1978 Blunt's descendants donated the house to the Murray-Whitfield Historical Society, stipulating only that it be placed on the National Register. Considerable original family furnishings—beds, chairs, drapes, dishes, etc.—are preserved here. Tours can be arranged by calling the historical society.

Turn right at .4 onto Crawford and drive through the next two intersections (Selvidge and Pentz); at .2 to the left is a statue of Joseph E. Johnston.

The bronze statue, which cost six thousand dollars, is the work of Belle Kinney of Nashville. The Bryan M. Thomas Chapter of the United Daughters of the Confederacy raised it in 1912. Johnston, a controversial Confederate leader, led the Southern armies in Virginia before Lee and was twice commander of the Army of Tennessee. Hated by Confederate politicians, he was loved by his men and respected by Federal opponents. While Virginia has erected numerous statutes of Robert E. Lee, Stonewall Jackson, Jefferson Davis, and lesser Confederate notables, it has snubbed this son. Only Dalton has honored Johnston's service.

Turn left onto Hamilton.

To the right and down the next street is the Dalton Western and Atlantic Railroad depot. Construction for the depot began in 1846 on land sold to the state by Mark Thorton for this specific purpose, and the first train arrived in 1847. The depot, in service until 1978, is one of only a few surviving original Western and Atlantic depots and saw a great deal of war activity. James Andrews sped the *General* through Dalton in 1862, pursued closely by the *Texas,* which dropped off a young man, seventeen-year-old Edward Henderson, to telegraph Chattanooga for assistance. Later that year the facility was used as an ordnance depot. In 1863 cheering citizens showered food on Longstreet's corps, en route to Chickamauga. Days later the railcars returned with thousands of wounded. The women of Dalton stripped their beds of sheets to make bandages when the building became a hospital receiving station. The depot was slightly damaged as Union troops occupied Dalton. After a million-dollar

Joseph E. Johnston, commander of the Army of Tennessee, is honored with this statue in Dalton.

renovation in the early 1990s, the depot now serves as a restaurant, preserving the original freight scales and other railroad paraphernalia.

Much of Dalton was ruined during the long Federal occupation.

Dalton had a machine shop that produced thousands of canteens and eight thousand straps for artillery rounds, buckles, and harness rings sent to Atlanta and Richmond. During the winter the shops turned out stoves and pots and pans for cooking, coffee pots, plates, water buckets, and lanterns for use by military personal and hospitals in town. As war approached, the facility was moved to Macon, where it functioned until March 1865. Nearly fifty men were organized into a local militia unit, the Dalton Machine Guards under Maj. James H. Bard.

A number of slaves ran away from their owners and entered Union lines in Georgia and Tennessee. During the war 3,500 black Georgians served in the Federal army or navy. One regiment, the Forty-fourth U.S. Colored Troops (U.S.C.T.), composed of 600 former slaves with a smattering of free blacks and led by 26 white officers, garrisoned Dalton to protect the railroad after Sherman passed farther south. On the morning of October 13, 1864, part of Hood's army, attempting to ruin Sherman's supply line, surrounded the garrison's fortifications. Ten cannon, placed in the city graveyard, bore on the works, and twenty guns were massed on a hill only five hundred yards away. A skirmish forced the Federals into the fort, resulting in 29 Confederate casualties. The 751 Union soldiers were heavily outnumbered, and Hood's ultimatum stated that no prisoners would be taken if they were forced to assault the works. Union Col. Lewis Johnson felt required to surrender. White officers were paroled, but black soldiers were to be returned to their owners. Confederates took clothing and shoes from their captives then marched them toward Tunnel Hill, where they were ordered to tear up two miles of railroad tracks. One man who refused to work was executed. Some of the prisoners were given to owners, including free blacks "claimed" to be escaped slaves, and 350 were marched to Selma, Alabama, and Corinth, Mississippi, where they worked on the railroads.

The primary fortification of the garrison, a blockhouse, was several streets to the east at Fort Hill.

The Cook-Huff house (316 Selvidge, 1850s) was Johnston's headquarters. It was constructed of handmade brick and hand-hewn logs. Here on March 4, 1864, Patrick Cleburne's controversial plan for emancipating slaves who fought for the Confederacy was proposed and hotly debated.

At .2 turn left onto Hawthorne for 20 feet and immediately turn right onto Chattanooga. At .3 proceed straight through the intersection with Tyler.

On the left are the beautiful Hamilton house (1840) and a stone springhouse. During the winter of 1863–64 the commander of the Orphan Brigade, Joseph M. Lewis, maintained his headquarters in a tent near the spring. Both armies used the residence for a hospital from 1863 until the end of the war. John Hamilton, a civil engineer who owned one thousand acres of land, constructed his house with solid brick walls. His four sons all served in the Confederate army. The house has been purchased by the Whitfield-Murray Historical Society as a museum and now houses a Civil War Room containing the flag of the Thirty-ninth Georgia, a large collection of local battlefield artifacts, and other historical displays. Call for hours.

At .2 turn left into Crown Gardens and Archives.

Until recently this was headquarters of the Dalton-Whitfield Historical Society. There were exhibits of Civil War artifacts, some excavated by the Dalton

Civil War Roundtable from the grounds of the Orphan Brigade camp. The society has a collection of books, Confederate records, and historical, genealogical, cemetery, and Daughters of the American Revolution files. There is also a picnic area and large scenic spring at what was once an extensive cotton mill.

Several years ago airport employees working at the end of a runway discovered a Confederate fort used as a lookout post. The small position had six-foot-high earthen walls.

Antebellum culture died slowly here. The 1873 Whitfield County Fair, a four-day affair, featured young Confederate veterans attired as knights from a Sir Walter Scott novel. They mounted horses and charged with leveled lances, not at other men, but suspended rings, and they took up swords to behead wooden warriors. Among the speakers were former President Andrew Johnson and Georgia's wartime governor, Joseph E. Brown.

South of Dalton, on Five Springs Road, is Walnut Grove (1852), which saw service as a Union headquarters and a stable. Initials remain written on interior walls, but it was spared destruction because the Sutherland family painted a large U.S. flag on the roof. The structure has eighteen-inch-thick brick walls and some original glass. The Starke house (1859) was ransacked and pillaged in May 1864. A Federal captain noticed Masonic materials in the house and spared it from burning.

In 1864 residents of Murray County, just to the east, found the corpse of a sixteen-year-old Federal soldier in a barn, apparently lost or deserted from his company. He was buried in an unmarked grave at the Spring Place Cemetery, and in 1976 the local American Legion post placed a headstone that read, "Little Unknown Soldier." Also interred there is a Confederate officer killed during a Federal expedition to clear the mountains of guerrillas in April 1865.

Return to Tyler and turn right for .1 then turn left onto U.S. 41-GA 3 (Thornton). To tour Tilton, at 9.1 turn left onto Tilton Road.

Tilton Road loops to Tilton near the pretty Conasauga River and intercepts U.S. 41-GA 3 farther south as Nance Springs Road. The countryside is beautiful, the town attractively sleepy. Sherman's advance was sharply checked at Tilton by a Confederate rear-guard action on May 13. After the fighting moved south, the Federals built a wooden blockhouse on the northern edge of the town and garrisoned it with three hundred soldiers. When Hood's army attacked on October 13, 1864, the Federals retreated into the blockhouse, but Hood brought up his artillery and after several hours the fort was battered into submission.

If you forego the Tilton side trip, continue south. At 2.8 the Tilton loop emerges on East Nance Springs Road.

3

A Clash of Armies

J AMES B. MCPHERSON'S TROOPS threaded through the narrow, five-mile-long passage between Mill Creek Mountain and Horn Mountain, emerging unopposed into Sugar Valley on May 9. McPherson's message announcing his arrival at the strategic position prompted Sherman to shout triumphantly, "I've got Joe Johnston dead!" His optimism was somewhat premature.

McPherson immediately deployed his troops to advance across Sugar Valley and occupy Resaca, certain that he would trap Johnston between his army and the bulk of Sherman's forces. The enemy would be destroyed before the campaign was fairly begun.

If Johnston had bothered to fortify the narrow gap with a few guns and men, he could have bottled up McPherson indefinitely, but for some reason he had failed to do so. The situation was made more critical by the failure of Joseph Wheeler's cavalry to discover McPherson's maneuver until the Federal army was pouring out of the pass and into Sugar Valley. One of Johnston's subordinates blamed this serious oversight on disobeyed orders. That was a common infantryman's complaint, that the horse soldiers preferred exotic, flashy deeds of derring-do over routine but vital reconnaissance. Regardless of who was at fault, McPherson slipped unopposed into the Confederate rear, where his orders from Sherman were to break the railroad at Resaca then return to Snake Creek Gap to dig in and await reinforcements. He would hit the Confederate flank when Johnston hurriedly withdrew from Dalton.

As McPherson advanced, dismounted Confederate cavalry bravely threw themselves at the advancing Federals. The skirmishers, including boys from the Georgia Military Institute in Marietta, drove back the first line of advancing Yankees. They fought desperately among abandoned

BATTLES AND LEADERS

Federal troops launch a spirited attack against Confederate defenders at Resaca in May 1864.

cotton fields and farm buildings then fell back to prepared works erected on a ring of hills west of Resaca, stubbornly resisting all the way. They had accomplished their purpose—to give the surprised Rebel defenders precious hours to ready their positions.

When the Union troops marched within range, Resaca's garrison met them with a withering fire. McPherson, stunned by the fierce resistance, was further confounded to find the eastern ridges of Camp Creek honeycombed with freshly dug earthworks and bristling with Confederate cannon and muskets.

The ever crafty Johnston had sent a small force of infantry and cavalry to Resaca to guard the railroad bridge over the Oostanaula River at his rear. These men had prepared the extensive works that caused McPherson's consternation, and providence had provided soldiers to man the line. The first five-thousand-man division of Leonidas Polk's Army of the Mississippi conveniently arrived from Rome to put up the skillful resistance, but their commander, James Cantey, had considerable cause to worry. He had five thousand men to counter McPherson's twenty-three thousand.

When word of McPherson's threat reached Johnston, he dispatched John Bell Hood and William J. Hardee to inspect Resaca's defenses. The corps commanders arrived as Cantey calmly awaited the seemingly inevitable and doubtless disastrous Federal strike. "We must hold until dark," Hood said simply, but the expected attack never materialized.

McPherson had been surprised to find the town, so far behind Johnston's main line, defended. In reaction, he supposed there were more Confederates than there actually were. The young general, noting his supplies were running low and fearing Johnston would isolate him from the main Federal army and destroy his force, moved cautiously. The Yankees slowly inched forward, pushing in the Rebel skirmishers and sharpshooters. Late in the day, McPherson decided he could not capture Resaca and ruin the railroad before nightfall, so he fell back to the gap and entrenched. McPherson penned a second message to Sherman, informing him that Resaca was too strongly fortified to be captured by assault.

Sherman, directing feints at Dalton's tough defenses from his Tunnel Hill headquarters, was exasperated. He grudgingly admitted that McPherson's actions were justified by his orders, which Sherman granted that he had worded poorly. Later the Union commander wrote that McPherson's fumbled opportunity to destroy an entire enemy army "does not occur twice in a single life."

McPherson had advanced to within a mile of the strategic railroad. With his overwhelming numerical advantage, he could easily have broken through the thin gray line, but he lacked the boldness to accomplish the mission. Instead he sat idly in his works at the mouth of Snake Creek Gap for three days waiting for the rest of Sherman's army to join him. The first opportunity to win a quick victory had been lost.

Sherman had never intended to waste his men by dashing them against Dalton's deadly ridges. He detailed a small force under Gen. Oliver O. Howard to hold the Confederates in place and to occupy Dalton when Johnston withdrew. Then he sent George H. Thomas on May 11, and John M. Schofield on the next day, south over Taylor's Ridge at Gordon Springs Gap to follow McPherson through Snake Creek Gap and around Rocky Face Ridge. He would unite his entire force in Sugar Valley for a full assault on Resaca and destroy whatever Confederate force held it.

The bulky Federal army moved slowly over the primitive mountain roads, choking the narrow passages with masses of men, horses,

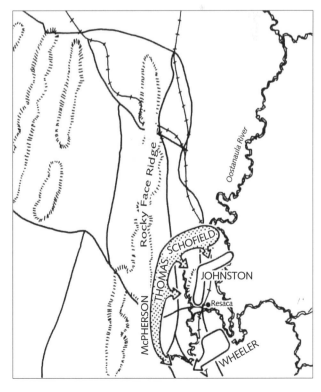

Map 7: The battle of Resaca

47

wagons, and cannon. Rain turned the dirt tracks into quagmires that forced soldiers to wrestle their heavy equipment through knee-deep mud.

Johnston was in no hurry to leave his comfortable Dalton camp, refusing to evacuate the army until the night of May 12. With his usual foresight, the Confederate commander had previously sent his wagons and draft animals south of Resaca so his withdrawal would not be hindered. He had improved the country roads leading to Resaca and knew that his troops using these roads and rail transportation could easily reach Resaca before Sherman. Besides, he had a much shorter distance to travel and had faith that his men could hold off McPherson, if he attacked, until relief arrived.

Wheeler's cavalry reported as each Federal unit was withdrawn, but Johnston continued to rest his men in Dalton. He knew where the Yankees were going and how long it would take them to get there. His own officers were terrified that the army would be trapped, and Oliver O. Howard feared the unpredictable Rebel leader would assail and eliminate him before the Confederates withdrew.

At midnight on May 12, the remaining Federals reported fierce fighting still occurring with the Confederates. Four hours later, there was silence. Johnston's army had vanished as cleanly as if it had never existed. One of Sherman's officers reported that he was "profoundly impressed by the skill of the withdrawal." Johnston had decamped south with forty thousand soldiers in a matter of hours without leaving a single biscuit behind. At 10 A.M.

Under cover of darkness, Federal soldiers dismantle a Confederate earthwork at Resaca and seize several cannon.

MOUNTAIN CAMPAIGNS IN GEORGIA

the Southerners slipped into the works before Resaca as easily as they had left Dalton, dumbfounding the enemy and originating a legend about Johnston's mysterious ability to anticipate an opponent.

Howard occupied Dalton and marched directly to Resaca from the north. He drove against a stubborn Confederate rear guard and was temporarily checked by a sharp skirmish at Tilton. Howard termed the pursuit "slow and spasmotic."

The Confederates had just settled into their prepared works when McPherson's troops deployed opposite them on the ridge west of Camp Creek. On the march McPherson had fought a fierce action with Confederate cavalry that left Kilpatrick, the Union cavalry commander, wounded. The Southerners, dressed in butternut, watched quietly as the rest of Sherman's bluecoats emerged over the hills and took up positions alongside McPherson.

At Resaca, Johnston was delighted to find Polk, who had fortuitously arrived from Mississippi with ten thousand men. Polk was a West Point graduate, but he had resigned his commission almost as soon as he received it. He left the military in 1827 for the ministry and had been the Episcopal bishop of Louisiana for several decades. In 1861 he offered his services to the Confederacy.

The Confederates occupied a double row of trenches that extended for three miles along the low, wooded hills west and north of Resaca, forming a rough semicircle overlooking Camp Creek Valley. Their left lay south on the Oostanaula River and continued north, parallel to Camp Creek, protecting Resaca and the railroad, which were several hundred yards east of the line, then turned sharply east and ended at the railroad and Conasauga River. The Federal position paralleled the Confederates. John Bell Hood held the right side opposite Thomas, William J. Hardee occupied the center opposite Schofield, and Polk invested the left against McPherson. A Federal officer stated that this horseshoe-shaped defensive alignment was similar in strength to the Confederate position at Fredericksburg, Virginia, site of a bloody Union defeat in 1862.

The two armies spent the remainder of the first day skirmishing to obtain better positions. When the action started, Polk occupied a bald hill west of Camp Creek, but McPherson's batteries commenced a furious shelling that inflicted heavy Confederate casualties and weakened Polk's works. McPherson's men charged forward, initiating a furious three-hour battle that forced Polk to the east side of Camp Creek. Polk dug in along the ridge overlooking Resaca, which was occupied by the rest of the Confederate army, but on the afternoon of May 14, the Federals stormed across Camp Creek and drove the Rebels from this second line. Polk's vigorous attempts to retake the ridge proved fruitless, so he withdrew to establish a new position in front of the railroad on the outskirts of Resaca. Discovering that his captured ridge overlooked the Resaca river crossings, McPherson brought up his guns and began to shell Johnston's only line of retreat.

Attack and Die ■ Civil War Tactics

Civil War generals were schooled principally in the tactics developed by Napoleon, who fought his final battle in 1815. Napoleon advocated assaults on a narrow front by massed columns of infantry. His human battering rams smashed into the opposing ranks, then French soldiers dispatched the enemy with bayonets.

Such tactics were successful at the turn of the nineteenth century only because muskets were notoriously inaccurate, difficult to reload, and had a limited range. Attackers were subjected to only one or two volleys before they overran the defenders.

By the time of the Civil War, musket range and reloading time had increased by as much as 300 percent. Confederate Gen. William J. Hardee had modified American military thinking to adjust for this development in his textbook, *Rifle and Light Infantry Tactics*. Troops advanced in an extended line shoulder-to-shoulder and two ranks deep. A company of one hundred men covered twenty-five yards; a regiment three thousand yards; a brigade ninety-five hundred yards. In addition, skirmishers who preceded the main attack skillfully scrambled from one point of concealment to another, firing sporadically to force defenders to keep their heads down.

Unfortunately for the infantry in both armies, field commanders still expected soldiers to march across hundreds of yards of open ground in the face of devastating rifle and artillery fire then dispatch the opposition with the "cold steel" of bayonets. Few Civil War assaults reached the enemy's works; they were usually shattered far from their objective.

LIBRARY OF CONGRESS

The Resaca battlefield: trenches in the foreground, town and bridges over the Oostanaula River in the background.

This was the only advantage the Federals would gain at Resaca, because the valley of Camp Creek was not favorable to offensive action. Attackers were forced to leave the security of their works on a heavily wooded ridge, march down a steep slope to the floor of a broad valley, crawl through thickets of brush and trees, flounder through pools of deep water, struggle through bogs, cross ravines, and charge up a steep ridge in the teeth of massed infantry and artillery fire.

On May 14 Schofield's troops surged across the valley to strike the center of the Confederate line. They climbed halfway up the opposite slope before being hurled back with heavy losses. The survivors took shelter below the creek bank until dark then crept back to their own lines. One of them termed the Confederate fire "terribly deadly."

Sherman launched a second assault that day on the angle of the Confederate line where it turned east toward the railroad. The men charged forward in a line five deep, bands playing stirring airs and regimental banners snapping in the breeze. The Confederate gunners were so eager to cut down this parade-ground spectacle that their officers could hardly restrain them until the Federals were within effective range, about two hundred yards. They opened a murderous fire that cost the Yankees six hundred soldiers; the rest took refuge along Camp Creek. Three successive waves of attackers were handily repulsed by the spirited Confederates, who enjoyed the gunnery practice. The approaching enemy made such an inviting target that artillery crews were "double shotting," firing two deadly charges at once. A few Federal soldiers reached the Rebel line but were rapidly driven out. The Union general responsible for these poorly coordinated attacks was subsequently relieved for incompetence.

A Northern correspondent recorded one of the mad charges: "Over the hill they swept, down the valley in double quick time, across it, raked by withering fire from the Rebel artillery; up the opposite hill toward the crest, where they met a regular shower of shell and bullets. Yet on they swept, plunged through the woods, striving desperately to gain its ascent." Few did, and those were cut down.

The Confederates did not escape unscathed. Volleys of well-aimed Federal artillery fire, faithfully signaled by a bugle call, had nearly leveled the Confederate earthworks at the angle by day's end.

Acting on intelligence from Wheeler's scouts that the northeastern flank of the Union line was lightly held, Johnston ordered Hood to lash out with an attack at 3:30 P.M. Hood's men rushed over the Yankee parapets, carried the enemy entrenchments, and surged around the left end of the position. Regiments started to break for the rear, but Sherman threw in reinforcements at this critical moment and restored the line. The Confederate advance stalled, and Hood was forced back to his original line, denied a critical victory. Sherman, the master flanker, had come perilously close to seeing his own flank turned and rolled up.

Throughout the day Johnston, who had been wounded in the Mexican War and earlier in the Civil War, rode his horse to the scenes of conflict. Bullets from Union snipers whipped past him, but he disdainfully refused to take cover. The ground trembled from the cheers of his men as he rode among them with encouraging words. They were outnumbered and outgunned, but their spirits were excellent.

The War Child ■ Joseph Wheeler

The short history of the Confederacy produced many able and flamboyant cavalry leaders. Joseph Wheeler deserves to be ranked with Jeb Stuart and Nathan Bedford Forrest. Wheeler, a self-professed "War Child," fought in an incredible 127 battles and skirmishes. He suffered three wounds, and sixteen horses bearing him in combat were killed. The attrition rate among his staff officers was legendary.

The diminutive warrior—he was only five feet five inches tall and weighed 120 pounds—commanded the Army of Tennessee's cavalry in all its major campaigns, which made him the country's acknowledged expert in covering retreats. His most important role was harassing Sherman's March to the Sea, which he accomplished with such vigor that Confederate President Jefferson Davis praised him for constricting the area of destruction.

After the war, Wheeler served in Congress and entered private business. When the Spanish-American War broke out, he reenlisted in the U.S. Army and led a division of cavalry against the Spanish in Cuba. Rumor persists that, flushed once again with the heat of battle as he led his men into combat, he yelled, "Come on, boys! Let's whip those damn Yankees!" He later averred that he had not used profanity on that occasion.

Wheeler retired as a brigadier general in the U.S. Army and was buried with full military honors in Arlington Cemetery.

When darkness fell, artillery batteries shelled the opposing ridges as both armies extended their lines in efforts to outflank each other. The Federals made one attempt to surprise the Southern defenders in the dark, but their advance was detected by Confederate pickets, and the alarm was sounded. The Confederates fired a large barn to illuminate the field, then twelve cannon opened a punishing fire against the attackers in blue. One participant, torn from sleep, wrote, "Volcanic fire leaps forth from the cannon's mouth . . . the air trembles violently with the din of battle." This Union foray was quickly repulsed, and the soldiers went back to sleep.

A far different activity was taking place just behind the Confederates' lines that night. After Hood and Polk were reunited at Resaca, the two generals were inspecting their lines when Hood remarked to the bishop that he had never received the communion of his church and asked that Polk perform the rite. Polk agreed, and Hood soon stood before him on crutches (Hood's numerous wounds prevented his kneeling) in a candlelit tent. Polk appeared resplendent in his ministerial robes, which were worn over his Confederate uniform. He baptized Hood from a tin basin with Hood's staff present as witnesses. A participant later wrote that Hood's face was "like that of an old crusader" as Polk administered the religious act.

Several days later Johnston approached Polk with the same request. In a similar ceremony in a tent at Cassville, Polk baptized this old campaigner.

Meanwhile, the first day of battle had ended inconclusively. Sherman's test of the Confederate defenses had proved them impregnable to frontal assault, and the Confederates had come close to winning a significant victory. Sherman noted that the exchanges "rose all day to the dignity of a battle" that turned the area into a forest of shattered stumps. Resaca was shaping up as the first major conflict in the Atlanta campaign.

At noon on May 15, Schofield and Thomas concentrated for a strike against Hood's sector, but the Rebel works could not be pierced. The attack was marked by general confusion—Federal brigades fired volleys at each other, then the units milled together, making an organized assault impossible. The Yankees did manage to overrun an exposed four-gun battery, unwisely placed eighty yards in front of the gray line, but other Confederate positions opened a withering fire on the attackers, forcing a hasty retreat. The Federals crept back after dark, quietly dismantled the front of the log-and-earth lunette, and dragged the four guns back to their lines by hand as trophies of war.

When Sherman deployed along Camp Creek two days earlier, he had dispatched his cavalry to search the north bank of the Oostanaula River for an undefended crossing. If one were found, he could threaten Johnston's flank as he had at Snake Creek Gap by driving troops into the Confederate rear, exposing their railroad supply line to attack, and possibly trap them between two Federal forces.

On May 14 the cavalry crossed the river at Lay's Ferry, near the mouth of Snake Creek, on two pontoon-boat bridges. They drove off a fierce attack

HARPER'S WEEKLY

After several days of hard fighting, Federal forces occupy Resaca.

by Confederate cavalry guarding the opposite bank of the river, but the game of lost advantage continued. The Union horsemen withdrew because of a rumor that the Rebel army was crossing the river above them. Fearing they would be cut off, the Federal cavalry retreated to the northern shore and dug in for the night.

Johnston responded to the threat at Lay's Ferry by sending a division to throw the Federals back across the river. Finding the crossing deserted, the men marched back to Calhoun to await developments. On May 15 the Federals recrossed the river and were reinforced by McPherson's troops, who were shifted south from Resaca. This development, coupled with the Union shelling of his bridges, presented a serious danger to Johnston.

Hood had prepared a second attack against the Union left flank late in the afternoon, but his troops were recalled when Johnston learned that Federal troops were crossing in force at Lay's Ferry. It was time for another strategic withdrawal.

Once more Johnston's army disappeared like the night mist at dawn. When the sun rose on May 15, Sherman found the field deserted except for hundreds of bodies that littered the battlefield. The dead lay scattered across no man's land, cut down by bullets and shells long before they reached the enemy. A few attackers who breached the opposing trenches lay dead in the works, skulls crushed by rifle butts or bellies laid open by bayonets.

The corpses of Rebel and Yankee soldiers were intermingled in death. There are no accurate casualty figures for this small battle, but the best

MOUNTAIN CAMPAIGNS IN GEORGIA

Confederate troops vainly try to recapture Lay's Ferry and save Johnston's position at Resaca.

estimates are that Sherman lost thirty-five hundred men killed and wounded at Resaca, Johnston twenty-six hundred.

Veteran officers on both sides of the field must have wondered about a curious coincidence. Many had fought in the Mexican War at the battle of Resaca de la Palma, and here they fought each other at a small Georgia village named for that American victory.

Resaca set the tone for the remainder of the campaign. It was immediately obvious that determined defenders positioned behind stout works could confidently hold off a much larger attacking force. Direct assaults would always fail, with great loss of life to the attackers. Sherman would react to this discovery by using his numerical advantage to outflank his adversary, while Johnston would try to maneuver Sherman into positions where either he would be goaded into attacking the Confederate defenses or Johnston would have an opportunity to successfully strike Sherman.

A Tour of Tilton and Resaca

This driving tour begins between Dalton and Resaca at the intersection of U.S. 41-GA 3 and Nance's Springs Road.

After the Confederate evacuation of Resaca, some of John M. Schofield's troops crossed the Conasauga near here at Hogan's Ford and at several ferry points, including Fife's, to advance on Adairsville from the east. They camped at Old Holly Post Office in Murray County.

James B. McPherson emerged from Snake Creek Gap on May 9. Finding Resaca fortified and mistakenly fearing he was outnumbered, he withdrew to await Sherman. By May 13 Johnston's entire army was firmly entrenched north and west of Resaca as Federals began clearing skirmishers off the hills west of Camp Creek. On the following day three Union assaults against Johnston's angle were easily repulsed with heavy Federal losses. After Joseph Wheeler notified Johnston that Sherman's left was poorly defended, John Bell Hood was ordered to strike. He drove the Federals past Nance's Springs Road but was stopped by Union reinforcements and the Fifth Indiana Battery and returned to his works. Late in the day McPherson attacked and drove Leonidas Polk to the edge of Resaca.

On May 15 Sherman again struck the Confederate right, overrunning Capt. Max Van Den Corput's Confederate battery, unwisely emplaced in advance of the infantry. The Federals were driven back but the Confederate assault was punished. That night Federals demolished the front of the abandoned work and pulled the guns into their lines. Learning that Union forces were threatening his rear by crossing the Oostanaula River downstream, Johnston withdrew, burning the railroad bridge and taking up his pontoons. Of 160,000 troops engaged, making it one of the largest battles fought in Georgia, there were 6,000 casualties—3,560 Federal, 2,600 Confederate.

Hood held the east-west segment of the Confederate line, ending at a large bend in the Oostanaula River. William J. Hardee formed the Confederate center, from the angle toward the south, and Leonidas Polk held the southern end of the line at Resaca and the river at the railroad bridge. Oliver O. Howard and Schofield attacked the northern angle, augmented by Joseph Hooker, who was shifted from his position farther south.

This tour basically follows the Resaca Battlefield Driving Tour prepared by Friends of Resaca Battlefield, Inc. (write or e-mail them for a copy) but in a different order. Eventually the state will develop its own driving tour, but that is several years away.

From U.S. 41-GA 3 southbound turn left onto East Nance's Springs Road.

The troops of Hooker and Howard gathered here, driven from a position farther east by Hood's attack the previous day, for their May 15 attempt against Hood. Farther west was the site of the Indiana battery that fought to turn back Hood's furious assault of May 14.

Note a small monument designating Nance's Spring, where an old church cemetery still exists. At the railroad near Nance's Spring was John H. Green's wood station, a fueling stop on the Western and Atlantic in the 1860s where James Andrews stopped for wood on April 12, 1862. On May 9, 1864, at the start of Sherman's offensive, Federal raiders burned the station and cut the telegraph wires between

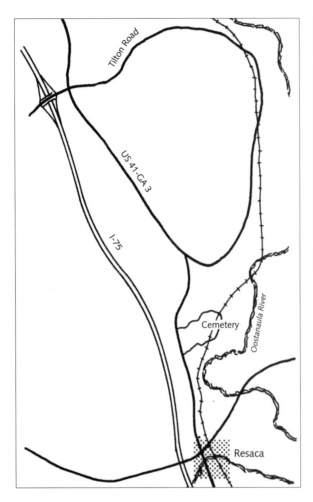

Map 8: The Resaca area

The Federal line at Resaca occupied the crest of this ridge. Union troops advancing to attack Hood's position marched in formation along this route.

At .4 turn left onto a small country road, Chitwood, at two historical markers, and drive to the dead end. This leads to a hilly area where much of the Resaca fighting occurred.

Hood's corps, which occupied the ridge to the left, repulsed repeated Federal assaults on May 15. In the area at the dead end Hood staged his troops for failed assaults against the Federal left flank on May 14 and 15.

Each year during the third weekend in May, an important reenactment of the battle is staged at the Thurmond Chitwood farm, where the hills form a natural amphitheater for the simulated fighting. The reenactment includes infantry combat, cavalry clashes, and artillery duels. The city of Resaca, the Gordon County Chamber of Commerce, and the Gordon County Historical Society sponsor the event. Check the Web sites in the Resources section for specific information.

Return to U.S. 41 and turn left. After .4 turn right on to Rooker Road, another dead end.

To the right is a continuation of the ridge occupied by Hood, where his troops prepared to attack the Union lines. Several Federal assaults were turned back in heavy fighting as Thomas attacked from the west and north across Camp Creek Valley.

Return to U.S. 41 and turn right then almost immediately left to the third Atlanta campaign pavilion.

Here a marker and relief map describe the battle of Resaca and the Federal flanking movement at Lay's Ferry, which forced Johnston to evacuate Resaca and retire farther south. This station is well maintained, and on the corner is a small monument that commemorates the establishment of the Resaca Confederate Cemetery.

Take County Road 297 (Confederate Cemetery Road) beside the pavilion .4 to the Confederate cemetery where the road ends.

Dalton and Atlanta. Two local women, Miss Carrie Sims and her sister, a Mrs. Bachman, became heroines by splicing the telegraph wires together to maintain Confederate communications.

After .4 turn right on Nance's Spring, an unmarked cul-de-sac.

Respect the private property and just look from your car. Hood's May 14 attack drove Federals across the ridge visible here and on to U.S. 41, where it was stopped by superior Union forces.

Return to U.S. 41 and turn left. Just before the Gordon County line at .4, a historical marker draws attention to a ridge through which the highway cuts.

56

In this area the Confederate line ran west to east from the Camp Creek Valley to the railroad and Conasauga River just north of the road. Also north of here Hood almost broke Sherman's left flank with a determined assault, and Hood's four-gun battery changed hands several times on May 15 as his gunners were forced to abandon the pieces. Then the Federals were driven away. The guns sat in no man's land until that night when future president Benjamin Harrison led the Seventieth Indiana to breach the front of the earthworks. In the midst of a furious firefight the Federals used ropes to drag the trophies off. The earthworks still exist in woods on private property not far from U.S. 41.

When the armies had continued south, a local resident, Mary J. Green, with her sister Pyatt and father, Col. John Green, buried two Confederates in their flower garden. Mary later organized the women of Resaca to give all the dead decent burials. They gathered more than four hundred bodies of Confederate soldiers and buried them here, where many had fallen on Hood's battlefield. A sturdy stone wall with a high entrance arch now surrounds the cemetery; on it is a bronze marker erected by the Atlanta chapter of the United Daughters of the Confederacy. This marker honors Green's service in establishing the first Confederate cemetery in Georgia and one of the two oldest in the country.

The graves of 421 unidentified Confederate soldiers killed at Resaca are laid out in circles around a central stone monument topped by a granite cross that honors the "Unknown Dead." There are nine different sections, representing seven Confederate states, unknowns, and the CSA. Some of the graves were later marked by family members who traveled from across the South to find the resting places of sons, brothers, fathers, and husbands. Carefully cultivated flowers surround the monument, and a stand of giant oak trees shades the cemetery and imbues it with a serenity that stands in marked contrast to the manner in which these men died. On Confederate Memorial Day, small Confederate flags are placed on each grave. Memorial services are held then and during the reenactment. Also buried here is Mrs. E. J. Simmons, who helped establish the cemetery. Just outside the cemetery is an information board. Inside is a stone monument; lift the metal lid for information about the cemetery.

This is a good spot to discuss the second battle of Resaca, this one fought for preservation of the battlefield in the late 1990s. It was sponsored by Friends of the Resaca Battlefield, formed in 1994 for this purpose, with help from the Georgia Civil War Commission. In 1999, with strong support from the governor, state legislature, Atlanta Historical Society, and news agencies, it looked as though the state was about to purchase twelve hundred acres, or 65 percent of the original battlefield. Unfortunately, the ever fragile negotiations failed when the property was sold to a private party that didn't embrace the idea of a state park. The state then exercised its power of eminent domain.

In March 2000 the state acquired 505 acres as well as a protective easement on 60 additional acres. The wooded hills, valley, and fields contain miles of

As time has passed, the Atlanta campaign pavilions have become subtle markers. Below is the Resaca pavilion.

All of the pavilions have a relief map of the significant action that occurred on their respective sites in mid-1864.

undisturbed infantry trenches and artillery emplacements, including all surviving Confederate works and 90 percent of the Federal works. The land, in an excellent state of preservation despite highway construction damage, was the last large Civil War battlefield with open land still available for park use. This was considered the most pristine unprotected Civil War battlefield in the country.

The property now belongs to the Georgia Department of Natural Resources, which is developing a general interpretive plan. The Global Positioning System has been used to map trenches, batteries, and other prominent physical features. Parking, hiking trails and interpretive markers will be developed first, with a visitors center to be constructed later, on the model of the Pickett's Mill battlefield farther south, which is highly regarded by preservationists.

Particularly prized is the hilltop line of Hardee's corps that faces a ridge held by two divisions of Schofield's 23d Corps, and of course the valley over which the Federals attacked. Currently the only monument on the field is a tombstone-sized memorial to the 103d Ohio. Unfortunately, one of the major sites on the Resaca battlefield that was not included in the purchase is the battery on the Chitwood farm near the annual reenactment site.

Resaca is split by I-75, the most heavily traveled highway in the country, and the future park is well positioned to become a popular historic site. It is hoped that the park will became the anchor for a Civil War driving tour, like the highly successful Virginia Civil War Trails, a gateway for an exploration of Sherman's 1864 Atlanta campaign and part of a chain of state and federal parks and historic sites stretching between Ringgold and Jonesboro, south of Atlanta.

The federal government may be convinced to construct a pulloff in the southbound lane of I-75 at a high spot at the northern head of Camp Creek Valley, which has an excellent view of the battlefield.

Return to U.S. 41-GA 3 and turn left to pass through the village of Resaca, which has roughly the same population today as it had in 1864.

No longer a stop on the Western and Atlantic, Resaca consists of a post office, a gas station, an arts and crafts exchange, and several stores. It was incorporated a decade ago with a population of 350. The town

The Confederate cemetery at Resaca honors the Southerners who died in the fighting here.

was a tiny but vital transportation hub. On the main road from Atlanta to Chattanooga, and with roads leading east and west, Resaca marks the confluence of the Conasauga and Coosawattee, where the Oostanaula is formed, and here the Western and Atlantic crossed the Oostanaula on an important bridge.

In the 1850s railroad workers named Resaca for a Mexican War battle, Resaca de la Palma. The rough, hilly countryside supported isolated farms, but most of the area remained woods choked with underbrush. Several local companies of Confederate soldiers were trained here, and it was a staging area for troops traveling to the fighting in Tennessee. When Sherman started south in May 1864, Johnston requested reinforcements. Two divisions came with Polk from Mississippi. They were held here and set to work fortifying the strategic position. McPherson saw their activity, overestimated their numbers, and retreated to Snake Creek Gap. That October, as Hood invaded Tennessee, he marched through this valley.

At 1.8 turn right onto GA 136 toward LaFayette.

On the outskirts of Resaca, Polk occupied works after McPherson threw him back from an advanced position.

Cross I-75 and at .6 park on the right side of the road by Camp Creek.

Walk to the bridge and face north to examine the valley, cleared for the construction of the interstate.

This view of Camp Creek Valley is from the Confederate line opposite the Union position. Sherman's attacks were repulsed.

Extensive photographs taken by George Barnard shortly after the battle proves the topography has changed little.

Left, or northwest of here, is McPherson's route through Snake Creek Gap (see appendix C), followed by most of Sherman's forces. They marched to Resaca along this route over the gap on the western horizon to establish a position on the western ridge. The Confederate line was to the east, right, somewhat altered by the construction of U.S. 41-GA 3 and I-75. The line extended north nearly three miles parallel to Camp Creek then turned sharply east to Hood's position near the cemetery and the Conasauga River. Hardee's battle line to the northeast is well preserved. These ridges were heavily wooded, and the meandering stream was choked with trees, underbrush, and bogs. At no other site of the Atlanta campaign is it possible to view so much of a battlefield. Near this spot McPherson swept Polk back from the ridge on May 14, brought up artillery, and started unsuccessfully shelling the railroad and wagon bridges. Polk attempted to recapture several hills here (destroyed by highway construction) but failed. Farther north Sherman launched a series of unsuccessful assaults.

The road McPherson used ran through the field ahead. He occupied the position on May 13, and his attack on May 14 drove Polk back to Resaca. Behind and to the south, Confederate skirmishers were driven back by Federal cavalry.

Farther north in the valley Federal troops deployed their battle lines, worked their way down the western ridge under deadly accurate artillery fire from the Confederate defenders, and plunged through the creek. They charged up the eastern slope in the face of galling fire from screaming Rebel infantry then retired in disarray to lie in the creek until darkness hid the land. It is easy to visualize the carnage left in the valley by the clear fields of fire enjoyed by the Confederates, and it seems incongruous to watch cattle grazing on the western slopes of the peaceful farms and the traffic and intrusive signs along the interstate.

In this area on May 14 the Ninth Illinois Mounted Infantry was advancing toward Resaca when 150 young soldiers in fancy uniforms emerged from the woods and carrying short rifles. They were the cadets, aged fifteen to eighteen, of the Georgia Military Institute in Marietta. The Union soldiers ridiculed them until the youngsters formed a line behind a rail fence and fired, killing and wounding a number of Federals. The Union troopers charged, and according to which side one favors, the cadets were routed or withdrew in good order, firing as they went.

Continue west on GA 136 for 1.2 and turn left onto Hall Memorial Road for .1 then left on Hall Road.

From this area on May 13 McPherson's infantry and Kilpatrick's cavalry concentrated. Kilpatrick cleared Confederate skirmishers and then protected McPherson's right as the infantry attacked the hills to the east.

Follow Hall Road for .5 back to GA 136. Drive straight across the highway onto Pine Road for .4, an area of extensive skirmishing on May 13.

At Fain Brown Road, where McPherson drove back a Confederate brigade on May 13 there is a great view of Camp Creek Valley.

Turn right onto Fain Brown Road to GA 136 at .2 and turn left, back to Resaca. After 1.1 turn right toward Calhoun.

To the southeast is Lay's Ferry, where McPherson flanked Johnston out of Resaca. The site is no longer accessible, but by proceeding north off Grogan and Leg Roads from GA 156 west of Calhoun, one can approach the site, which occupies a scenic setting.

The Oostanaula River is crossed at 1 mile.

The railroad bridge to the left was constructed on the original foundations of the bridge that Confederates torched as they retreated. In 1862 Andrews's raiders crossed through a covered bridge that had been their primary target. Closely pursued, Andrews was forced to abandon the attempt. He backed up to "throw" two cars, hoping they would slam into his pursuers, but the Southern railroad men successfully coupled the cars to their backward-racing locomotive and continued the chase. On a ridge east of the railroad bridge are the ruins of a Union fort constructed to protect Sherman's supply route along the railroad. It was so formidable that Hood chose not to attack it in October 1864.

4

Race to the Etowah

OHNSTON'S MEN EVACUATED THEIR lines soon after dark on May 15 and withdrew from Resaca across two pontoon bridges and the railroad trestle that spanned the Oostanaula River. The Confederates destroyed the railroad bridge at 3:30 A.M. on May 16 and removed the pontoon boats to delay pursuit then retreated toward Calhoun in search of a new defensive position. Hardee remained behind to slow the Federal advance and to prevent an attack on the cumbersome Southern wagon train.

To facilitate rapid movement on a broad front over the rough country roads, Sherman split his massive force into three groups, hoping to trap Johnston's army while it was scattered in withdrawal. James B. McPherson crossed the river over two pontoon bridges six miles south of Resaca at Lay's Ferry and moved to the west toward Rome, sending Jefferson C. Davis's division to capture that important industrial center. George H. Thomas quickly built two bridges over the Oostanaula at Resaca and followed Johnston directly to Calhoun, while John M. Schofield, accompanied by Joseph Hooker's corps, spanned the Coosawattee River at Field's Ferry and marched east of Calhoun through Cash and Sonoraville in an attempt to slip around the Confederate right at Adairsville.

Johnston found the terrain south of Resaca lacking in strong defensive features. Below Dalton there were no rugged mountains, only low, gently rolling hills that were easy to flank and valleys too wide for his limited number of troops to hold. In this terrain Johnston would find himself constantly frustrated in his attempts to hold a defensive position, always outflanked by Sherman's superior numbers. The open country placed Johnston at a disadvantage, but it was perfect territory for Sherman to maneuver his large armies.

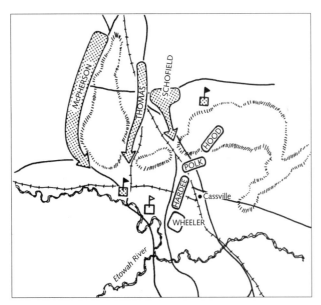

Map 9: Confrontation at Cassville

Johnston had hoped to fight at Calhoun, but the open plain before the town was split by the swollen Oothcalooga Creek. Johnston could not risk separating his army to defend both banks, but he did stop to allow his exhausted men a few hours of precious sleep.

When the Confederates withdrew south of Calhoun, William J. Hardee still commanded the rear guard and had orders to fight a delaying action. On May 16 at the battle of Rome Cross-roads, he engaged two divisions of McPherson's army and stopped them for twenty-four hours, ensuring the escape of the long wagon train below Adairsville. When McPherson exerted strong pressure against the Rebel position, Hardee withdrew to Adairsville and rejoined the main Confederate column.

Johnston had reason to be optimistic as he approached Adairsville on May 17. Maps showed a narrow, defensible gap between two ridges north of the town, but a personal survey of the area shattered his plans. The valley was wider than indicated, and Johnston worried that he lacked the men to hold it. The Confederate commander warily ordered his soldiers to establish a line and seriously considered bringing Sherman to battle here, but intelligence gathered by cavalry scouts indicated that Federal troops were flanking his position to the east and west of town. As Thomas deployed on the valley below, Johnston decided to abandon Adairsville.

Johnston disliked surrendering more territory, but according to his military philosophy this was preferable to wasting men in an unwise battle. Furthermore, during the days of retreat he had developed an offensive strategy. Feeling that the situation south of Adairsville was perfect for its execution, Johnston ordered the plan put into effect. Sherman would be lured into a trap.

When Johnston began his withdrawal south, Benjamin F. Cheatham's division of Hardee's corps was left to fight another delaying action in the trenches before Adairsville to buy time for the wagons to reach Kingston safely. The skirmish raged for several hours with heavy exchanges of artillery and rifle fire, but Cheatham held the Federals until several divisions deployed in line of battle for a full attack on his works. Then he skillfully withdrew during the night and marched to Kingston on the morning of May 18.

When Sherman arrived at Adairsville, he took his staff forward to reconnoiter the enemy position. There an alert Confederate battery opened fire on them, killing several horses. Sherman wryly remarked that it was probably a mistake to expose the army's general staff to such danger, and they retired to a safer observation post.

Sherman noted that the Confederate action at Adairsville approached the intensity of a full battle. During the afternoon of May 17, two hundred Union soldiers were killed, but the dawn of May 18 revealed that Johnston had pulled his vanishing act once again. Except for the stout fieldworks, there was no evidence that an army had ever occupied the ground. After the Confederate evacuation, Sherman briefly rested his armies at Adairsville while preparing to march on Kingston, where he assumed the Confederates would finally make a stand. Before following Johnston south, Sherman cared for his wounded, replenished his supplies, and destroyed a Confederate arsenal at Adairsville and nearby factories.

Behind Sherman's advance, Union engineers performed a miraculous job of repairing the railroad. While men fought at Resaca, Federal supply trains entered Dalton. When Union troops seized Calhoun, the rails reached Resaca, and engines chugged into Adairsville while Sherman briefly tarried there. The repair of telegraph lines kept pace with the railroad, keeping Sherman in constant communication with his supply bases in Tennessee.

The Union commander split his forces for the pursuit from Adairsville, intending to outflank Johnston and cause the Confederates to retreat closer to the ultimate objective: Atlanta. Thomas followed directly to Kingston, McPherson passed to the west, and Schofield and Hooker pursued to the east, all in a repetition of their earlier pattern. Johnston was counting on that.

As the Confederates continued to retreat, refugees became a growing problem. Some people chose to remain in Union-controlled territory to care for their farms and businesses, but thousands flocked before the Southern army, clogging the roads, straining local resources, and often panicking other citizens with frightening stories of destruction. As each mile of territory was relinquished, there were more civilians urging Johnston to turn and destroy the hated Yankee invaders. He intended to do just that.

Johnston had retreated thirty miles from Dalton, but he was determined to stop Sherman before the Union general forced him across the Etowah, the last river barrier remaining before the Chattahoochee. Johnston had studied his adversary's accomplished flanking maneuvers at Snake Creek Gap, Resaca, Calhoun, and Adairsville. Now he planned to turn Sherman's tactics against him.

The Confederate commander anticipated that Sherman would send the bulk of his army to Kingston, following the railroad and major wagon roads. Johnston believed his adversary would split his forces as he had done before, sending the smallest command—Schofield's Army of the Ohio, accompanied by Hooker's corps—to the west toward Cassville, the next stop after Kingston on the railroad, to flank the Southerners out of Kingston. Johnston decided he would mass his army at Cassville to destroy Schofield and Hooker before the other armies could arrive to assist their beleaguered colleagues.

Johnston sent William J. Hardee and Joseph Wheeler's cavalry, with all the wagons, to Kingston, ten miles south of Adairsville. That would make

Drill, Drill, Drill ■ The Soldier's Guide to Survival

Successfully loading a Civil War musket was an exercise in exasperation. The process was complicated, and performing it amid the din and slaughter of battle—with an enemy shooting back—required iron discipline and constant training in camp.

In the 1850s, to teach the proper firing procedure to new troops, William J. Hardee (who later resigned from the army to accept a general's commission in the Confederate army) broke down the process into nine steps in his *Rifle and Light Infantry Tactics:*

1. Hold the rifle barrel up, stock firmly on the ground.
2. Take a cartridge from belt and tear it open with teeth.
3. Pour the gunpowder down the barrel, followed by the paper cartridge as wadding and place bullet in barrel, pointed end up.
4. Take rammer from beneath barrel.
5. Ram bullet down the barrel.
6. Cock hammer halfway back and extract old percussion cap.
7. Take new cap from pouch and place on nipple under hammer.
8. Cock hammer back fully, bring rifle to shoulder, and sight.
9. Fire.

A well-trained soldier could fire three shots a minute.

Curious things happened in combat. Often a gun failed to fire, and with the sounds of battle surrounding him, a rifleman might not notice. He would reload, and the gun might fire the two loads or it might explode. A number of men were impaled by rammers that excited soldiers had neglected to extract from the barrel before firing.

the road look obviously traveled to Sherman's scouts. The bulk of the Confederate army, the corps of Hood and Polk, marched to Cassville, five miles south of Adairsville and east of Kingston, on a minor road that led directly from Adairsville. The wagon train continued immediately from Kingston to Cassville, but Hardee was to execute a fighting withdrawal, tearing up the railroad tracks and obstructing the roads behind him in order to delay McPherson and Thomas from coming to relieve Schofield and Hooker.

Johnston was delighted by the terrain he found at Cassville. North of the town was a ridge where he would entrench Polk's army. In front of Polk was a wide, open plain over which Schofield would advance: a perfect killing field. Behind the town was another ridge where the Confederates emplaced their artillery, and a rear guard stationed there could protect their flank.

Hood was positioned northeast of Polk. His assignment was to assault Schofield's left flank, then Polk would pour out of his works to hit the badly outnumbered and thoroughly surprised Federals from the front. Hardee, advancing from Kingston, would strike the Federals from the west and roll up their right flank. Schofield and Hooker would be destroyed before reinforcements could intervene, and Sherman might be forced to retreat to Chattanooga to regroup.

Johnston began to evacuate the women and children of Cassville, a thriving commercial and cultural center of northern Georgia. He also hurriedly converted a women's college into a hospital to receive the inevitable flood of casualties. The attack was scheduled for dawn on May 15.

The Southern commander announced the impending combat in an order that was read to all his troops. Johnston congratulated the men for having "repulsed every assault." He praised their courage and skill in facing the enemy. Then he delivered the message for which they had long waited: "You will now turn and march to meet his advancing columns. I lead you in battle!"

A Confederate officer noted, "The men were burning to fight," particularly those Southerners whose homes had been occupied in Kentucky, Tennessee, and northern Georgia and those whose families lay in the path of hostilities to Atlanta. Great cheers echoed among the hills as each regiment heard the order, but the ragged Rebels were due another disappointment.

As Schofield marched unwittingly into the trap, Johnston waited anxiously for the sounds of battle. They never came. The plan failed when Hood claimed he had been outflanked by powerful Federal forces, which turned out to be a small contingent of lost Yankee cavalry. Hood promptly fell back to establish a defensive position on the ridge beside Polk. Johnston, bitterly disappointed by the loss of a perfect opportunity to turn the tide of this campaign, was outraged that Hood had not bothered to ask for instructions. Instead, the crippled general had withdrawn then informed Johnston of his action hours later. Johnston called Hood's conduct "extraordinary disobedience."

The bulk of Sherman's armies followed Hardee to Kingston, camping at Conesena Creek on May 18 and arriving in Kingston at 8 A.M. on May 19.

Sherman was extremely puzzled and more than a little troubled when he reached the town. His troops met only light resistance on the march, and Kingston had been relinquished without a fight. Since Johnston had not defended Calhoun, Adairsville, or Kingston, Sherman believed the wily Confederate had retreated across the numerous bridges and shallow fords along the serpentine Etowah River just south of Kingston. A hasty cavalry reconnaissance reported no Rebels across the river and no evidence that an army had recently used the roads.

At midday on May 19, Schofield, not realizing his narrow escape from disaster, stumbled upon Johnston's army entrenched at Cassville. Riders quickly informed Sherman, who saw Schofield's danger and immediately shifted Thomas and McPherson from Kingston as rapidly as he could push through Hardee's interference. Sherman's hard ride over primitive roads brought him to Cassville an hour before dark. Thomas's huge corps and the bulky wagon train advanced over the main roads and deployed in front of Cassville then waited for McPherson, who marched cross-country and over poor back lanes to arrive several hours later.

For the assault against Schofield, Johnston's position on the ridge north of Cassville was perfect, but it was not a good line of defense. From his position, Johnston was unable to attack the entire Federal army advantageously, which was once again united in front of him. At 4 P.M. Johnston ordered his men to establish a new line on the ridge south of town. He and Polk reconnoitered the terrain and marked positions they wanted occupied.

As the withdrawal progressed in the late afternoon, an aggressive Federal strike drove the Confederates back from the women's college in Cassville. The Southern trenches were rapidly seized by an Ohio artillery battery that opened a deadly fire on the retreating Confederates. Under a

The Unsung Rock ■ George H. Thomas

A number of notably incompetent generals rose to command, but one of the Union's greatest leaders has long been one of the most unheralded. George H. Thomas was born in Virginia in 1816, but he lost his family in 1861 when he declined a general's commission in the Confederate army and chose to fight for the North. His sisters turned his picture to the wall and never spoke his name again.

Thomas accepted an early role in the Army of the Cumberland, fighting at Shiloh, Perryville, and Stones River. At Chickamauga he possibly saved the Union. There the Federal army was put to flight, but Thomas and his command occupied a precarious position and repulsed furious attacks until nightfall, preventing the Rebels from completely destroying the army of William S. Rosecrans. For this heroic action, Thomas was nicknamed the "Rock of Chickamauga."

After steady service in the Atlanta campaign, Sherman dispatched Thomas to contain Hood in Tennessee. Hood laid a pathetic siege to Nashville while Grant harried Thomas to attack. Just as Grant was preparing to board a train to relieve him, Thomas launched a shattering assault that inflicted the worst defeat suffered by a Confederate army in the entire war. For that action, Thomas was nicknamed the "Hammer of Nashville."

Thomas was one of the North's best tacticians, but after many of his plans were successfully implemented, more colorful generals reaped the rewards. Thomas refused to seek the presidency in 1868 and died two years later at his post. As a recognition of his contributions to the outcome of the Civil War and a public demonstration of the regard in which he was held, more than ten thousand people attended his funeral.

On May 23 Federal armies crossed the Etowah River, which Sherman called the "Rubicon of Georgia" in his dispatches to the War Department. Rough terrain, however, stalled his advance, allowing Johnston to fall back before his supply line could be severed.

heavy bombardment in the oppressive evening heat, the Rebels tumbled into their new line. A Confederate officer made this note in his diary: "Late in afternoon, considerable skirmishing and artillery [fire], enemy's skirmishers occupy town."

Amid much noise, dust, and confusion, the Confederate wagon train, artillery, cavalry, and infantry fell back to the southern ridge under constant fire from Federal batteries. Experienced officers coolly waded into the melee and restored order, directing the wagons to wait while the fighting men and cannon took up positions from which they returned the galling Union fire.

The terrified residents of Cassville found themselves exposed in a free-fire zone. A Confederate diarist recorded: "Many flee, leaving all, some take away few effects, some remain between hostile fire."

The new Confederate position extended four miles, from a point east of Cassville to west of the railroad at Cass Station. Arriving from Kingston, Hardee anchored the western end of the line, Polk occupied the center, and

Hood was to the east. Ironically, the line skirted the home of Gen. W. T. Wofford, who at that moment was fighting desperately in Virginia's Wilderness with Robert E. Lee, unaware that war was ravaging his home.

When Sherman arrived at Cassville, Howard informed him that the Confederates had withdrawn in perfect order to the opposite ridge. Surveying the heights through his field glasses, Sherman found it covered with freshly dug works. *At last,* he must have thought, *Johnston has found a favorable place to fight.*

Federal troops quickly occupied the evacuated Confederate works, and throughout the night of May 19 a furious artillery duel took place between Rebel and Yankee batteries. Shells shrieked across the beautiful valley as skirmishers fiercely fought in the streets of Cassville. Fine homes and buildings were riddled with shot and shell, and some structures were torched by troops for illumination. Civilian casualties among those who did not flee the fighting are unknown.

The Confederate rear guard barely escaped capture in the town by swarming Union soldiers. One of the last Confederates who fell in Cassville was Legare Hill, son of Joshua Hill, a congressman from Madison who knew Sherman's brother John, a U.S. senator from Ohio. Federal troops watching from nearby hills held their fire as two friends carried Hill's body into a house, pinned his name to his clothes, and left. The Federals who occupied the town buried the young man and marked the grave by carving his name on a piece of wood, thus sparing him the ignominy that many soldiers on both sides of the war feared—an unknown grave.

After surveying his new lines, Johnston believed he had a good defensive position. The ridge towered 140 feet above the valley floor and commanded the ground over which Sherman had to advance. The eager Confederates had an unobstructed field of fire. Johnston called the position "the best that I saw occupied during the war." Having been denied victory here once, Johnston decided it would still be the site of the first decisive battle in the Atlanta campaign.

After riding along the line to encourage his men, the Confederate commander entered his tent to rest. There he found an invitation to supper with Hood and Polk. When he arrived at Polk's headquarters, Hood immediately argued that his position was vulnerable to artillery fire from the side as well as from the front, a dangerous situation known as being enfiladed. He claimed the Union guns were in a position to slaughter his troops. Johnston responded that the problem had been noted, and engineers were digging traverses to protect Hood's works. Hood, however, insisted that his line could not be held. Polk concurred, leading many to believe that the generals had conspired to induce Johnston to change his plans. Hood and Polk advised their commanding general to withdraw behind the Etowah and fight on a better field.

Johnston was dumbfounded. These two officers, particularly Hood, had frequently criticized him for not meeting Sherman in aggressive battle.

Furthermore, Hood grossly violated the proper chain of command by writing letters to President Davis in which he condemned Johnston's strategy. And Hood was the one who just that day had thrown away a golden opportunity to destroy Schofield's army. Johnston surely remembered that Polk had given Braxton Bragg grief in 1863 when he proposed to take the offensive. Bragg had relieved Polk of command for failing to attack at Chickamauga, but his decision was countermanded by the Confederate president. Now these two wanted to withdraw when Johnston had decided to confront the enemy.

Johnston's reflections were interrupted by the arrival of Hardee at the conference. The respected tactician was outraged that Hood and Polk had confronted Johnston with such a suggestion. His own position was the least desirable, but Hardee foresaw a great Confederate victory on this ground.

The final decision was Johnston's. Considering the possibility of victory in a battle where two of three corps commanders questioned his judgment and felt that defeat was probable, he angrily determined to retreat.

During the night the bewildered Southern soldiers received orders to withdraw. By dawn not a trace of the Army of Tennessee remained at Cassville. After the sun rose to reveal that the enemy had disappeared, Sherman wandered among the empty Confederate trenches. His astonishment was matched by that of the Confederate soldiers who were tramping across the Etowah River and burning the bridges behind them.

Johnston was severely criticized by Southern newspapers from Atlanta to Richmond for retreating behind the Etowah without bringing Sherman to battle, but they did not realize that the decision had been forced on him by two sullen subordinates. The "Cassville Controversy," Hood's failure to attack followed by his confrontation with Polk against Johnston, would be fought on paper for decades after the war ended.

A Tour from Adairsville to Cassville

This driving tour begins at the Oostanaula River bridge south of Resaca. The route is the same as that followed by Joseph E. Johnston and George H. Thomas after Resaca, while John M. Schofield crossed the Conasauga River to the east and James B. McPherson advanced to the west.

At the intersection of U.S. 41-GA 3 and GA 225 at 3.2, pull over to inspect the two interesting monuments in the traffic island.

At the entrance to the little park is an arch with figures of a Confederate soldier on the left and a World War I doughboy on the right. One suspects that when this monument was erected no one could imagine the country would be involved in larger or more destructive wars than those represented here. Through the arch is a bronze statue of Sequoya, the Native American who developed a syllabary for his language and established a Cherokee newspaper at New Echota, a fascinating state historical development to the east on GA 225.

New Echota was capital of the Cherokee Nation before their forced removal on the Trail of Tears. Historical buildings have been moved there and restored or recreated. There are houses, a tavern, a supreme court building, a print shop, and an interesting museum.

Continue south on U.S. 41-GA 3 through downtown Calhoun. At two miles to the right is Court Street. You may turn right here for .1 and the original, pre–Civil War railroad station is to the left. During the Great Locomotive Chase, James Andrews nearly collided with a southbound passenger train here.

At Oothcaloga Creek, west of Calhoun on GA 53 Spur, Hardee's three divisions put up a strong rear

An unusual memorial in Calhoun incorporates a Confederate soldier (far left below) and a World War I soldier (far right below) and in the background (as seen through the arch) a statue of Sequoya.

New Echota, near Calhoun, was the capital of the Cherokee nation. The building below housed a Cherokee-language newspaper, the Phoenix.

guard fight, delaying McPherson for twenty-four hours at the battle of Rome Crossroads

If you visited the railroad station, return to U.S. 41-GA 3 on Court and turn right. On the right in Calhoun at .2 is Oakleigh.

Sherman is said to have established a temporary headquarters here. It is now home to the Gordon County Historical Society and houses a doll collection.

Continue south on U.S. 41-GA 3.

The highway from Calhoun to Adairsville passes through beautiful, pastoral country in a broad valley. It is easy to see why Johnston had to retreat through Calhoun and south to Adairsville; the ridges east and west—actually low, rolling hills—were too widely separated to establish a defensive line across the valley. Johnston and Thomas traveled this route; Schofield passed east through Cash and Sonoraville; and McPherson went west, sending a detail to occupy Rome and destroy its industrial facilities.

If you have plenty of time, ample county maps, and a great deal of patience, you may want to explore the river crossings east of here and the lovely countryside that Schofield traversed on his route to Adairsville and Cassville. Bridges span the Coosawattee River just before it joins the Conasauga to form the Oostanaula at the sites of Field's Ferry, McClure's Ferry, and Harlan's Crossroads. County roads run

from Redbud to Cash, where Schofield camped beside Dew's Pond, which has a beautiful mill and falls, and to Sonoraville. Schofield advanced into Bartow County via Mosteller's Mills (a plantation-manufacturing center of the 1860s where little remains today), and crossed Cedar Creek to proceed through Pleasant Valley toward Cassville. Drive back to Calhoun to avoid long periods of being lost while exploring this route.

You can trace the route of Federal cavalry and infantry to Rome west of here. On May 15 Kenner Garrard's cavalry left Villanow and camped at Floyd Springs on GA 156. The next day he continued four miles to Farmers Bridge on Armuchee Creek, skirmished briefly with Confederate cavalry, crossed the creek at the U.S. 27 bridge, and rode eight miles to DeSoto Hill on the east bank of the Oostanaula River near the railroad underpass on U.S. 27. That day, Confederate Gen. Samuel G. French arrived from Alabama to prepare a defense, but he soon received orders to withdraw and assist in the planned attack at Cassville.

Garrard was scouting for Union Gen. Jefferson C. Davis's infantry, which reached DeSoto Hill on May 17; on the following day Davis forced a crossing under fire to capture the city. He remained until May 24 then followed McPherson to Dallas through Aragon on GA 101. Rome was garrisoned until November and was reinforced during Hood's erratic campaign into Alabama and Tennessee. Sherman rested there on October 17 and returned on October 28. When the March to the Sea began, all military

Oakleigh served as Sherman's headquarters and now is the headquarters of the Gordon County Historical Society.

equipment and factories were destroyed. The city was abandoned on November 10.

When Garrard left the Rome area, he protected McPherson's right flank on the move to Kingston via Barnsley's Gardens, breaking the Rome Railroad south of the city and passing near Shannon on May 17 and 18. On May 17 McPherson left Calhoun for Barnsley's and camped at McGuire's, where GA 53 and GA 140 intersect. Shannon is two miles southwest on GA 53.

Evidence of U.S. 41-GA 3's importance before the nearby interstate was built is provided by the old red tile service stations and restaurants that line this route. Note the scenic old concrete bridges over streams beside the main highway and barns. During the Great Locomotive Chase, James Andrews covered the nine-mile distance between Calhoun and Adairsville in seven and a half minutes, an unheard-of time. Conductor William A. Fuller followed at a leisurely, but still suicidal, mile a minute.

At 8.8 miles turn right onto GA 140, left at .1 onto Main Street, and right at .6 onto Public Square Road for .1 to the public square in downtown Adairsville.

The region surrounding Adairsville, the Oothcaloga Valley, was an important breadbasket to the Confederacy. The town was also of vital railroad interest as it had been designated a terminus of the Western and Atlantic and machine shops and a roundhouse had been constructed, in addition to a gun and gunpowder factory. Much of the town was burned during the war.

This view of the Oostanaula River is just east of Calhoun. It was the site of Schofield's crossing after the battle of Resaca.

At the Old Courthouse (1884) on the public square is a stone monument commemorating the Great Locomotive Chase. Each October the community celebrates the event at a Great Locomotive Chase Festival. (Contact information is found in the Resources section.) The yellow-frame antebellum depot, listed on the National Register, witnessed the chase and was partially destroyed by Union troops. It has been recently restored to its wartime appearance as a Cartersville–Bartow County Convention and Visitors Bureau welcome center and The Age of Steam Museum. Here conductor Fuller had the *Texas* shunt cars onto a siding and set out to pursue the *General* backward.

Adairsville is a perfectly preserved example of a small Georgia town. There is a gazebo and a row of old-fashioned stores, most of them still open. Inside are traditional wooden floors and broad counters. Clustered in the downtown area are pretty churches and old homes, and nearby are recreational facilities. Adairsville is alive.

The entire town is on the National Register. The Thedfort house on North Main Street has bullet holes from the war, and at the Bowdoin-Price house off South Main Street is a tree where Federal soldiers rested and plotted their depredations, according to locals. The Watts house on South Main is reputed to have a secret tunnel used to hide slaves on the Underground Railroad. In Eastview Cemetery, on U.S. 41 east of town, are the graves of two Confederate soldiers, killed and buried as unknowns along the railroad for more than a century. In a

Scenic Mill provided a campground for the Federals marching toward Adairsville and Cassville.

71

The Western and Atlantic Railroad depot in Adairsville witnessed the Great Locomotive Chase as well as the passage of Johnston's and Sherman's armies.

strange story, a local woman determined their identify during a table-tapping séance and confirmed it with historical research. The U.S. government provided one with a gravestone.

Johnston temporarily established a defensive line just north of town and skirmished with Sherman before setting his trap. Here he split the Army of Tennessee. Most of the army retired directly to Cassville along the modern route of U.S. 41-GA 3. Hardee, with Thomas and McPherson following, went to Kingston along the railroad. So will we.

Turn right at .1 and drive west beside the old warehouse on Park Street for .4 to Hall Station Road and turn left. At 1.7 turn right onto Rock Fence Road.

Scenic Snow Valley coincides with the route followed by McPherson to Barnsley's Gardens, a plantation where he camped the night of May 18 before moving to Kingston. Thomas marched straight to Kingston along Hall Station Road, but this route is infinitely more attractive. Schofield followed the eastern route of U.S. 41 toward Cassville, inadvertently approaching Johnston's trap. Eight cavalry clashes occurred in this area between June and September 1864.

Travel this winding road slowly to appreciate the beauty of this secluded valley. Wooded ridges rise all around, and creeks babble beside the road. Cows graze in the lush fields and in summer submerge all but their heads in the streams and ponds, separated from the road by old wire strung on decaying fence

posts. Behind tree-lined fence rows are fields littered with wonderfully weathered farm buildings, outhouses, wells, and old homes with tin roofs and double chimneys.

Bear left at the next three branches to a stop sign at 4.6. Turn right onto 106 and left at .4 onto Barnsley Church Road. Barnsley Church is on the left at .7.

Barnsley Church is on what once was an extensive plantation. The quaint little church has twin outhouses and a wonderful covered picnic area for dinner on the grounds.

From the church, return to 106 and turn right, passing Rock Fence Road. At 1 mile, to the right, is the entrance to Barnsley's Gardens.

Godfrey Barnsley arrived in Savannah from Great Britain and made his fortune in cotton and shipping goods between the United States and Europe in his fleet of ships. In 1840 he purchased thirty-six hundred acres in Cass County halfway between Rome and Marietta, hoping the mountain air would help his wife's tuberculosis. His father-in-law was William Scarborough, a partner in the construction of the *Savannah,* the first steamship to cross the Atlantic Ocean. Barnsley began building a grand three-story, twenty-eight-room brick Italianate manor, named Woodlands, which remained under construction for several decades. A mahogany dining room table could seat 40, and a special stove could cook enough food for 150 guests. A three-hundred-gallon tank provided hot and cold running water to the house and flush toilets. Marble was imported from Italy, doors and paneling from England, and rare trees and plants from around the world. The grounds were as magnificent as the mansion, featuring acres of gardens, goldfish ponds, and exotic trees from several continents. There were English boxwood gardens, a bog garden with five thousand aquatic plants, rose gardens, rock gardens, an Oriental garden, and statuary. The operation required the labor of one hundred servants and sixteen slaves. Unfortunately, Barnsley's wife, Julia, died in 1844.

In late May 1864 the Army of the Tennessee passed Barnsley's. As the Federals approached, Confederate Col. Richard G. Earle, a friend of Barnsley's, raced to warn the Englishman of the threat. While riding away, Earle was killed by Union soldiers and fell on a gravel walk in the gardens, shot five times while surrounded by a hundred varieties of roses, wrote witness Charles W. Willis of Illinois. He is buried on the grounds, his grave a prominent landmark. Earle's troopers, angered, charged and captured one hundred Federals before being driven off by Union reinforcements.

An alternate story, and probably closer to the truth, is that Earle's Second Alabama Cavalry drove a regiment of Union cavalry from the outskirts of Kingston to the main Federal cavalry line at Barnsley's, where Earle was killed near the house by Union

Map 10: From Adairsville to Kingston

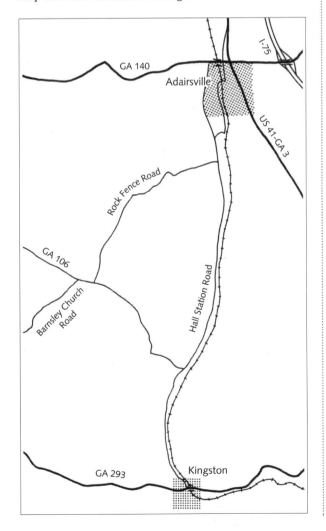

Pvt. Thomas H. Boner. He was buried by the women of the family on a terrace near the home.

Barnsley flew the British flag and claimed neutrality, despite the fact that most of his assets were invested in Confederate war bonds and his two sons, George and Lucien, fought in the armies of the South. Reportedly he sold all the metal on the plantation to the Noble Foundry in Rome to be melted down for arms. McPherson, who called the plantation "a little piece of heaven," issued orders that Woodlands should not be harmed. After camping on the grounds on May 18, the main Federal body continued south, but stragglers broke into the cellar and supposedly consumed two thousand bottles of wine. The drunken men then started a bonfire, fueling it with exquisite furnishings while they smashed objects of marble and porcelain. Whatever survived was looted. One story claims that a Union soldier asked Barnsley the time then snatched the gold pocket watch and fled. A housekeeper named Mary gave chase and jumped the man, but was knocked senseless by a rifle butt. Mary took the offense to McPherson, who allowed the woman to identify the man and the watch was returned. McPherson was considered a gentleman surrounded by ruffians.

Barnsley filed a claim for $155,000 in damages against the Federal government through the British consulate in Washington. He collected nothing.

Moreover, Barnsley lost his fortune in the war. His bonds were rendered worthless, and of the twelve ships he offered to the Confederacy, two were sunk attempting to run the blockade. His sons refused to take the oath of allegiance to the United States and emigrated to the famed Confederate colony in Brazil. Two children died, and when Barnsley died in New Orleans in 1873, his body was returned here in a copper coffin. A surviving daughter buried him at Woodlands and managed the plantation. The daughter, Julia, was married to Capt. James P. Baltzelle, who served under Robert E. Lee. Heirs were forced to sell off parcels of land, and a tornado in 1906 ripped off the roof and forced the family to live in the right wing, now a museum, until 1942.

The plantation house and grounds fell into decay, with kudzu covering outbuildings and trees taking root in the manor. In 1988 German investors purchased sixteen hundred acres here and spent several million dollars clearing the land, stabilizing the striking three-story ruin, restoring the extensive gardens with tens of thousands of plants, and opening a café, a gift shop, a golf course, and a theater. The museum in the right wing displays Civil War artifacts excavated on the grounds, which were a campground and skirmish site, and weapons, uniforms, and currency. Regular programs are sponsored, including a Confederate ball and Civil War days. In 1997 an elderly man visited Barnsley's and remembered that his great-grandfather told him of stealing a fiddle from a mansion in north Georgia in 1864. This was the site, and 135 years later the instrument was returned.

The eight-room Rice house (1854) was cut in two and hauled thirty-two miles by truck from Rome to Barnsley's for use as a restaurant. It has floor-to-ceiling windows and French doors inside. Family legend maintains that the owner, Fleming Rice, a business associate of Barnsley, used whiskey to convince Union soldiers not to harm the house. Rice Springs farm, which produced wheat on thirteen hundred acres along the Alabama Road, was overrun on October 13, 1864, by thousands of Union soldiers heading for Rome. The Federal force surprised eight hundred Texans, routing many, capturing two cannon, and inflicting seventy casualties to their own fourteen. The front of the Rice house has four bullet holes, and many artifacts, including cannonballs, were found on the Floyd County property.

After McPherson had camped overnight, he continued on to Wooley's plantation, just west of Kingston and south of GA 293 on a county road loop. A few buildings remain there, but they are not accessible to the public. Most of the Army of the Tennessee crossed the Etowah River there on a covered bridge, while the remainder crossed the river at Gillem's Bridge and a pontoon bridge at Milam's Bridge.

Continue east to Hall Station Road at 2.5 and turn right. To the left are the low Cassville Mountains, which separated Thomas's and McPherson's columns from Schofield's.

On May 18, 1864, Confederate and Federal armies marched past Spring Bank plantation, between Adairsville and Kingston, and Oliver O. Howard briefly occupied the house. The owner, the Reverend Charles H. Howard, ran an academy and raised the Sixty-third Georgia Infantry Regiment. Daughter

Wartime Kingston was destroyed in late 1864, when Sherman began the March to the Sea. This is the oldest surviving building, the DeSoto Hotel, famous to generations of traveling salesmen.

Frances T. Howard spied for the Confederates and wrote about local Civil War events in the book *In and Out of the Lines.* At war's end Gens. William T. Wofford and Henry M. Judah may have met in the parlor to arrange surrender terms. The home burned in the 1970s, but the family cemetery contains the grave of Everett B. D. Julio, a French artist who painted *The Last Meeting of Lee and Jackson,* a famous painting prominently displayed at the Museum of the Confederacy in Richmond. The presence of the New Orleans painter is a mystery—it is claimed he taught at the school or was simply passing through when he fell ill with tuberculosis. He died in 1879 and is buried in a rock-lined grave surrounded by a wrought-iron fence.

At 4.7 stop at the sign and turn left onto GA 293 into Kingston. At .5 turn right beside the store and gas station onto Shaw Street for .1 to the stop sign.

To either side are rows of old stores on Railroad Street, which faces the tracks and park. Many of the buildings, closed for decades, are opening again.

The original business district, constructed in the 1830s, stood across the tracks, but Sherman burned it when he left for the coast. Rebuilt on the north side after the war, all the buildings except the brick, two-story, fourteen-room DeSoto Hotel (1890) on your right, now on the National Register, were destroyed in a second devastating fire in 1911. By 1915 forty stores, banks, and hotels flourished here. The DeSoto was a favored stop for salesmen, and its food was renowned throughout the region. Kingston was once an important commercial center.

To your front is a large, well-kept park that has witnessed a great deal of Southern history. Hardee's corps passed through on May 18 on their way to Cassville, with most of Sherman's army following.

On May 12, 1865, Confederate Gen. William T. Wofford surrendered the last Confederate troops in the state, and the last east of the Mississippi River (most of the four thousand men were Georgians) to Federal Gen. Henry M. Judah in this park. The terms were signed at the McCracey-Johnston house on Main Street, although Spring Bank makes the same claim. Judah generously issued the hungry Rebels rations and released them to return home and work their farms.

Kingston is one of many sites claimed to be the spot where Sherman planned or began his infamous March to the Sea, and this community has a better claim to that honor than most. Sherman established his headquarters here on May 19, after Johnston's Cassville trap malfunctioned, to plan his advance on Dallas. He remained until May 23 and returned in October after chasing Hood into Alabama, requesting permission from Grant to campaign against Savannah. Sherman was quartered in the Thomas Van Buren Hargin house, which burned in 1947.

Several street names in Kingston are confusing, so ignore the signs and follow these directions. From the stop sign at Shaw and Railroad Streets, turn right onto Railroad then left on Johnston Street to cross the railroad tracks. Continue straight at the four-way stop at Johnson and Main, but note down the street to the left a monument recognizing Kingston as the site of eight Confederate hospitals that treated ten thousand men from 1862 until the spring of 1864.

Dr. William W. Tippin converted a store for the first hospital, and other businesses and homes were used. Surgeon B. W. Avent was also instrumental in the operation. Two of the hospital structures still stand, the Reynolds house, center of a large plantation west of town, and the Goulding house (.6 mile east of Kingston on GA 293), owned by Dr. Francis R. Goulding, who claimed to have invented the first sewing machine. In 1864 the wounded and sick were evacuated to Atlanta out of the path of the contending armies. The monument also honors local women who cared for the men. Once Kingston was occupied, the hospital facilities were used by Union troops until Sherman left for Savannah.

During the Great Locomotive Chase, conductor William A. Fuller was able to close the distance on the raiders while the *General* was delayed here sixty-five minutes by several passing trains and James Andrews argued with the stationmaster. Southbound trains blocked Fuller, so he abandoned the *Yonah* and commandeered the engine *William R. Smith,* which had steam up and was ready to go. Faint remains of the stone depot foundation are found in the park in front of the DeSoto Hotel and traces of the spur line to Rome can be found near the railroad tracks to the west. Eight skirmishes occurred around Kingston between May and September 1864, including several Confederate cavalry raids.

Continue for .4, then turn left into the city cemetery and proceed to the prominent Confederate portion.

Here lie 249 unknown Confederate dead, 1 known, and 2 unknown Federal soldiers who died in the hospitals. The only identified warrior here is Sterling F. Chandler, a twenty-nine-year-old infantry private from Georgia. The sight of these blank headstones is a chilling reminder of the true cost of war.

Inside the enclosure is a small monument to the unknown soldiers and an obelisk erected to honor the Confederate dead. For almost 140 years women from the United Daughters of the Confederacy have laid wreaths at the obelisk and small Confederate flags at each grave. Descendants of original Kingston families keep the tradition alive. Confederate Memorial Day (or Decoration Day, which is held to remember Southern men who died in the Civil War) was held in Kingston in April 1864, the first observance in the United States and a continuous one. When ladies first requested permission from Gen. Henry M. Judah to decorate Confederate graves, he agreed if they would also grace Federal graves with flowers. They did.

Across the small parking area is a monument to Kingston's Confederate veterans, all of whom lived full lives following the Civil War. From this hillside cemetery is an impressive view of hills to the north.

Return to the four-way stop at Johnson and Main and turn right to the Methodist church at .1. The extensive park is on your left. The Kingston Woman's History Museum–Confederate Memorial Museum (13 East Main Street, Kingston, GA 30145; 770-387-1357) is in the small building in the park to the left. It contains a collection of Civil War artifacts—weapons, munitions, money, photos, and scrapbooks—of Kingston's extensive Civil War role, and memorabilia of 140 years of Memorial Day celebrations. It is open on a limited basis.

Built in 1854, the Methodist church is the only original house of worship left from the time that Sherman occupied the town. For several years it hosted all denominations, served as the local school, was the scene of the first Confederate Memorial Day services and later the site of temperance rallies. A pastor of the church was Confederate general and noted Civil War historian Clement A. Evans, who edited the multivolume *Confederate Military History,* and the famed evangelist Samuel P. Jones preached from its pulpit. A superbly crafted bell hanging in the tower was a gift from John Pendleton King, president of the Western and Atlantic Railroad and a U.S. senator, for

Bespeaking of Cassville's former status is the imposing Confederate monument.

The restored Atlanta campaign pavilion at Cassville illustrates Johnston's failed attempt to trap Schofield.

whom the town was named. The bell, audible for four miles, saw use as the town fire alarm and was rung to announce peace following four wars.

Continue to the notable Baptist church at .1 and turn left onto Church. Turn right at .3 for the short drive to Cassville on GA 293.

Sherman's affection for the Etowah Valley can be understood by the beauty seen along this stretch. In 1975 the U.S. Department of Agriculture designated the Etowah Valley as Georgia's largest historic district, forty thousand acres. The highway winds gently beside creeks, rolling hills, beautiful green fields, and farms. George H. Thomas and James B. McPherson raced across this land when they realized the threat to John M. Schofield, who had found Johnston entrenched before Cassville.

On the trip across Gravelly Plateau to the east, Schofield's soldiers camped at Mosteller Springs, an early industrial center long used locally for baptisms, picnics, and reunions. Most of the buildings have long disappeared, but the springs remain on private property along GA 140, five miles east of U.S. 41. On GA 140 one mile east of the junction with U.S. 41 is the Trimble house. A son of the owner fought on the property under Joseph Wheeler, and two Confederate troopers from the First Georgia Cavalry killed nearby are buried here. The wounded were treated in the house.

At 5.7 turn left onto Spur 293-C to the stop sign, and turn left for .4 to the intersection with U.S. 41-GA 3. Cross the four-lane highway to Cassville-White Road. Immediately on your left is the fourth Atlanta campaign interpretive pavilion.

This station is the largest of the five. It was once in terrible condition, with crumbling walls, a missing relief map, and poor maintenance, but it has been restored to its original glory, the map replaced by the local Sons of Confederate Veterans. The marker describes the action that took place at Cassville, or almost occurred, just east of this spot, when Schofield's small Army of the Ohio and Hooker's corps barely escaped destruction. Relax at one of the picnic tables and reflect on a civilian tragedy that occurred around you.

Cassville, established in 1833, was the seat of Cass County and one of the most prosperous cities in northern Georgia before the Civil War. The courthouse was surrounded by a number of dry goods stores, four hotels, three carriage shops, a bookstore, a blacksmith shop and a shoemaker, four churches, separate colleges for men and women, and many fine homes. Four doctors and a number of

This WPA monument on the old courthouse square commemorates the once thriving village of Cassville.

prominent lawyers practiced their profession. The first decision of the Georgia Supreme Court had been rendered here in 1846. The local newspaper, the *Cassville Standard,* was widely read. In 1861, at Gov. Joseph E. Brown's suggestion, the Georgia legislature changed the county name to Bartow to honor Georgia Gen. Francis S. Bartow, who died at First Manassas (Bull Run for those of the Northern persuasion), and the town was renamed Manassas. After the war the U.S. Postal Service refused to recognize the new name.

The Cassville Female College stood on a hill northwest of town, and on May 20, 1864, hundreds of Union soldiers were spotted sitting at desks in the

The Western and Atlantic Railroad depot in Adairsville witnessed the Great Locomotive Chase as well as the passage of Johnston's and Sherman's armies.

A road pierces the ridge occupied by the Confederates. Nearby is the house in which Johnston was dissuaded from attacking, thus spawning the Cassville Controversy.

The old Presbyterian church in Cassville survived Sherman's destruction of the town.

library quietly reading. On May 24 Wheeler's cavalry made a daring dash around the Federal left to Cassville, where they intercepted a Federal supply train. After driving off the Union cavalry guard, they burned 180 wagons and brought 70, loaded with supplies, and 250 teams of mules, 200 prisoners, and many head of cattle back to their lines below the Etowah River, where they were gratefully received.

Two months after Atlanta fell, Union soldiers marched into town on November 5, 1864, with orders to raze it. The two thousand people of Cassville were given little time, merely twenty minutes, to evacuate homes and businesses. They saved a minimum of belongings. "We cried to hearts of stone," resident Lizzie Gaines remembered. The town was soon blazing fiercely, and by sundown only smoking timbers and charred chimneys were left to mark the site of the formerly thriving city. The people were left to care for themselves in a cold rain with no shelter. Some died of exposure and malnutrition during the hard winter. Only three churches and three homes, used to house the sick, were spared destruction. Cassville was never rebuilt, and the county seat, most of the people, and all the busi-

nesses were relocated to Cartersville, just north on the Western and Atlantic after voters approved the decision in a referendum.

The reason for Cassville's destruction remained a mystery for over a hundred years. Legend held that it was because of the name change, or because earlier in the war a dozen women waved black aprons, symbolically wishing them death, at Union POWs passing on a train, but a diary entry by a Federal officer explained Sherman's action. The area surrounding Cassville was a center of guerrilla activity, and in early November 1864 the men of a Union patrol were found dead. The grisly scene suggested that they had surrendered to guerrillas and had then been executed. To retaliate, Sherman, in an apparently unrecorded order, directed every structure within five miles of the murders to be burned. Cassville lay within that range.

Proceed east on Cassville-White Road.

The Baptist church to your left at .8 is on the original location of a former sanctuary that was spared the conflagration of November 1864. The Federals used it as a stable, turning the pews into troughs.

At .1 on the right is the old Presbyterian church, the same that survived the fire and was used as a Union hospital. Just down the road at .2 is a sign indicating the historic Methodist church to the right on Church Street. Turn right and follow that narrow road .1 to the

Historic Cassville Methodist Church survived the community's postwar decline.

beautiful church, which has been slightly altered but is the original building.

Continue on Church Street around the curve, down a straight stretch, through an intersection, and around another curve. At .4 the old Cassville Cemetery is directly in front of you. Turn right then enter the second drive on the left and circle the cemetery to the Confederate section on the eastern slope of the hill.

Eight Confederate hospitals were established in Cassville from late 1861 until May 1864, treating ten thousand soldiers before being evacuated south. Of the five hundred Confederates who died in those hospitals, three hundred were buried here, but only one, W. M. Barrow, a twenty-year-old from Louisiana, is identified. In May 1899 the Cassville chapter of the United Daughters of the Confederacy honored the unknown men by placing headstones over each grave. Towering above the Confederate graves is an obelisk, dedicated on April 26, 1878, by the Ladies Memorial Association in recognition of the bravery and sacrifice of these men. The obelisk carries several inscriptions such as, "Is it death to fall for freedom's cause?" "It is better to have fought and died than not to have fought at all," "You loved liberty more than life," and "Rest in peace, our own Southern heroes." Above the fallen flies a Confederate flag, and ancient cedar trees shade their resting place.

Gen. William T. Wofford, a Cassville native, is also buried here. He was a cavalry captain in the Mexican War and rose to the rank of major general in the Con-federate army. Wofford fought at Manassas, South Mountain, Antietam, Fredericksburg, Chancellorsville, and the Wilderness. After Thomas R. R. Cobb was killed at Fredericksburg, Wofford assumed command of his Georgia troops until January 21, 1865, when the War Department in Richmond reassigned him to north Georgia. Gov. Joseph E. Brown directed Wofford to raise seven hundred soldiers and patrol for marauding bushwhackers who terrorized the region after the collapse of organized government that inevitably followed Sherman's destructive visit. In May 1865 it was his duty to surrender the remaining Confederate soldiers in the region at Kingston.

The second Confederate line at Cassville skirted the cemetery to the south. The Federal line occupied the northern ridge, extending through the female college and just north of the male college. The city lay in the valley between the lines.

From the cemetery drive back the way you came, round the curve, and at .2 turn right at the intersection onto Cassville-White Road. After .2 turn left. To the immediate left is a large park area that marks the old courthouse square.

In 1936 the Works Progress Administration (WPA) created a monument here in memory of vanished Cassville. All that remains of the town today are the churches, the cemetery, one store, a post office, and a new fire station across the street from the empty courthouse grounds.

Most of the Confederates interred at Cassville died in the many military hospitals of the area.

Johnston's soldiers occupied the ridge on which the cemetery is situated. Sherman's Federals invested the opposite ridge.

Drive west on Cassville-White Road .5 and turn left onto Mack Johnson Road. At .3 you pass through the ridge that was Johnston's second line.

Leonidas Polk's headquarters—the residence of William L. McKelvey, where he and John Bell Hood dissuaded Johnston from attacking and thereby ignited the Cassville Controversy—stood just south of the ridge.

Continue 1.5 through this lovely tree-lined valley with a stream flowing beside the road. At U.S. 41-GA 3 you may want to drive straight across the highway then turn right onto GA 293 and left on Burnt Hickory Road to the railroad.

This is Cass Station. To the right, the shell of the original depot stands behind an abandoned building. During the Great Locomotive Chase, Andrews and Fuller thundered past surprised and disappointed travelers. Cass Station was a major shipping point for agricultural produce and manufactured goods and marked the end of the Confederate line in May 1864.

At U.S. 41-GA 3 turn left onto the highway to drive south on the four-lane highway into Cartersville and beyond. Below the city, enjoy the lovely green peaks that are scattered about. If you are continuing with the next portion of the tour, at 7 miles turn right off the highway where the signs call attention to Cooper's Furnace, and then left on River Road (306).

5

Desperate Fighting in a Georgia Wilderness

AFTER PURSUING JOHNSTON'S FORCES to ensure they retreated south of the Etowah River, Sherman decided his men deserved a break from three weeks of continuous fighting and marching. He returned north to the pleasant town of Kingston on May 20 and remained there until May 24. During that time he planned the next phase of his campaign. Sherman was satisfied with the progress his army had made, but the Confederate force remained intact, and Atlanta was still distant, separated from him by considerable rough country and many determined men. One of Sherman's officers confided in a letter home, "We will have some bloody work before that place."

Sherman allowed his troops three days' rest in Kingston, Cassville, and around Cartersville on the north bank of the Etowah. When the railroad was repaired into town, the officers' luggage arrived on the first train, along with tons of mail for all ranks and supplies that refreshed the men. The wounded were tended, and time was taken to gather the dead from a half-dozen battlefields and give them decent burials.

The Northern soldiers were enchanted by the beauty of the Etowah Valley. Oliver O. Howard described it as "a country picturesque with its natural features, with farms and woodlands as quiet and peaceful as if there had been no war." Sherman was fond of this region and took time to revisit the "remarkable Indian mounds" (the Etowah Mounds) to which he had taken a fancy on an earlier tour of the area.

The Confederates dug earthworks and rested south of the river, watching for Sherman's next move. Pickets glared at their counterparts across the river, but exchanges of fire were rare, and many friendly insults and commodities were traded when officers were absent.

The railroad bridge over the Etowah River was supported by these stone piers. After Johnston burned the span, Sherman rebuilt it then dismantled it and stored the timbers at the beginning of the March to the Sea.

Sherman realized that if he chased Johnston's army along the railroad, he would be forced to fight through a rugged country known as the Allatoona Range. As a young lieutenant in 1844, Sherman had been stationed briefly at Marietta. Horseback rides across the region had given him an intimate knowledge of the terrain, and he knew the natural strength of Allatoona Pass and assumed that Johnston had fortified it heavily. It would be suicidal to attack the gap, so Sherman abandoned that possibility. If somehow the strongpoint could be avoided, he mused, then Johnston would be forced to abandon the fortress.

The steep Allatoona Mountains protrude one thousand feet above the surrounding countryside several miles south of the Etowah River. The railroad passed through a narrow defile in the mountains, a forbidding sixty-five-foot-deep gap with high rock ledges to either side that were studded with cannon and riflemen. The position was far stronger than Dalton, and Johnston hoped Sherman would attempt to storm Allatoona to follow the railroad to Acworth, Big Shanty, Marietta, and Atlanta. Since an attack would result in a slaughter of the Federal horde, Johnston sensed that Sherman would not follow that potentially disastrous course. As a precaution, he stationed cavalry along the Etowah River to detect the Union direction of advance.

Sherman finally decided to execute a long flanking movement by swinging twenty miles southeast of Kingston and following a network of rough country roads that converged at Dallas, southwest of Johnston's Allatoona citadel. From Dallas his armies would advance over other primitive roads to the Chattahoochee River and Atlanta, hopefully before Johnston could oppose the movement. If the advance achieved surprise, Sherman could trap Johnston north of him, destroy the Confederate army, and march unopposed into the city. At worst, Sherman felt Johnston might recover to meet him in battle close to Atlanta.

The Union commander severed his railroad supply line and ordered the men to carry all the provisions and munitions they would need for several days. On May 23 Sherman's army began crossing the Etowah River by fords, covered bridges left unburned by Rebel cavalry, and pontoon spans.

"The Etowah is the Rubicon of Georgia," Sherman recorded in his diary. "We are now all in motion like a vast hive of bees and expect to swarm along the Chattahoochee in a few days." After crossing the Etowah, his troops converged on Euharlee and Stilesboro then split into the three separate armies.

James B. McPherson composed Sherman's right wing on the advance to Dallas. He veered far to the west from Stilesboro to Taylorsville, Aragon, and Van Wert. Returning from Rome, Jefferson C. Davis followed McPherson's route a day later. On May 24 McPherson turned east toward Dallas, marching over Dugdown Mountain at York, and camped for the night at Pumpkinvine Church, two miles southeast of Dallas. On May 25 he broke camp before dawn, drove the Confederate cavalry out of Dallas, and occupied the town by 2 P.M. His progress was abruptly halted just east of town when he unexpectedly ran into the resolute defense of William J. Hardee. McPherson was stunned that the Confederates had reacted so swiftly. He would have been further surprised had he known his men would be locked in desperate combat here for the next two weeks.

From Stilesboro, George H. Thomas and John M. Schofield—Sherman's left wing—continued directly south over several poor rural lanes. They marched just east of the Allatoona Range, staying close enough to support each other in case Johnston lashed out from his mountain redoubt. Sherman had learned a valuable lesson from his near disaster at Cassville and was being more cautious. The Federals skirmished with Southern cavalry at Raccoon Creek then stopped to rest for twenty-four hours at the tiny community of Burnt Hickory to give McPherson, who was wheeling far to the west, time to reach Dallas. On the afternoon of May 25, they continued the march and approached New Hope Church, a crossroads settlement five miles northeast of Dallas.

The entire Union army, from Sherman to the lowliest infantryman, soon regretted this foray into what they felt was the worst region in Georgia. Their admiration for the Etowah Valley turned to disgust at the terrible conditions around Dallas, fourteen miles south of the Etowah River. They found the countryside desolate, a Georgia wilderness broken by a few scattered farm clearings. No accurate maps of the area, one of the wildest in northern Georgia, existed. Rolling hills were choked by thick forests and underbrush

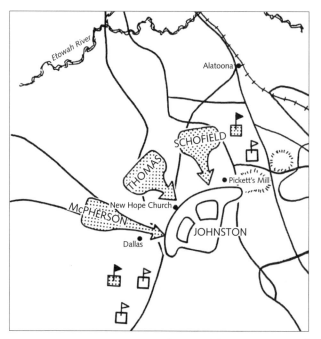

Map 11: The battles of New Hope Church and Pickett's Mill

that pickets found impossible to penetrate. Tangled hogbacks fell into deep ravines then ran into steep ridges. The soil was loose and sandy, the lowlands were swampy, and quicksand was common. Sherman tersely noted, "The country was almost in a state of nature."

Furthermore, the heat was intolerable, and the torrential rain that began to fall continued for a month. Roads were turned into quagmires, adding to the misery of the men engaged in this deadly game. The season was the wettest spring on record, resulting in epidemic levels of colds, flu, and pneumonia among the soldiers. Sickness felled more men than bullets. Road conditions impeded resupply efforts, and the men went hungry.

Adding to the problems caused by nature were the Confederates. Sherman was shocked to discover he had to contend with the complete Army of Tennessee. He had hoped to pass through Dallas in a few days; but the terrain, weather, and Johnston's skillful maneuvers would force the Federal commander to waste his strength in weeks of furious fighting under wretched conditions.

Sherman had barely broken camp on May 23 when Joseph Wheeler's cavalry detected the direction of his movement and sent word to Johnston, who promptly shifted his forces west to counter the advance. Hardee was immediately dispatched from Allatoona to Dallas, where he stopped McPherson's march and anchored Johnston's left. John Bell Hood remained a day longer at Allatoona in case one of the three Yankee armies abruptly moved back to the railroad, then he followed Hardee in time to intercept the Federals at New Hope Church. There Hood became the center of the Confederate line. Leonidas Polk was ordered to Lost Mountain, a point halfway between Dallas and Allatoona, so he could provide support to either position that Sherman might threaten. When it became obvious that all of Sherman's forces were moving through Dallas, Polk was directed to form Johnston's right near Pickett's Mill Creek. All the Confederate forces would find plenty of action in this phase of the campaign.

Hood rushed to New Hope Church and erected log-and-earth breastworks along a ridge. Some of his men found shelter behind gravestones in a Methodist church cemetery, and sharpshooters were sent forward to act as skirmishers. To support his five thousand infantrymen, Hood unlimbered sixteen cannon. Just hours after he arrived, Joseph Hooker's command emerged from the woods directly in front of the Confederate works.

Federal scouts informed Hooker that a large force of entrenched Rebels was entrenched at New Hope Church. He sent John Geary's division to drive in the Confederate skirmishers then energetically attack what he assumed was a weakly held fine. Surprised to find a well-manned defense, Geary fell back, threw up works of his own, and sent word to Sherman of the situation. Sherman, drawn to the scene by the sound of artillery fire, refused to believe that Johnston was blocking his path and regarded the resistance as little more than pesky Confederate cavalry. He admonished Hooker's hesitancy, asserting that there were no more than twenty Rebels in the area. Rejecting the advice of Hooker and Geary, the Federal commander ordered a quick assault to brush aside this nuisance.

At 4 P.M. Geary, reinforced by Hooker's other two divisions, marched out of the forest on a narrow lane in a line only six men wide. The foolish attack on Hood's barricades was handily repulsed with heavy Federal losses. The Union ranks were decimated as hundreds of soldiers were felled within minutes by what one Federal officer called an "effective and murderous fire."

Hooker's men courageously regrouped and repeatedly battered the Confederate works, slogging to within fifty yards of their line. They received fire from three sides, and the dead piled up in heaps, forcing the attackers to struggle over the corpses of comrades. A heavy storm drenched the troops, and great peals of thunder added voice to the Rebel cannon that belched deadly shot point-blank into the assaulting men. Volleys of rifle fire disintegrated whole ranks while canister blew gaping holes in the Federal formation. Three times the Union soldiers charged, and three times they were shattered and thrown back with frightful casualties.

Hood offered his divisional commander additional troops to stem the Federal attacks, but the offer was rejected. There were plenty of men for the target practice at hand. Confederate cannon unleashed fifteen hundred deadly rounds into the surging Union ranks over three hours, but the artillerymen did not escape unscathed. In the batteries, fifty-four horses were hit and forty-seven gunners were felled.

Fighting raged into the night. Then the disheartened Federals withdrew and fortified an opposing position. Hooker lost eighteen hundred men in the savage fighting and failed to dent the Confederate line. One of his officers reported that the men had met "murderous fire from all sides"; another noted, "We have struck a hornet nest at the business end." Surviving soldiers appropriately called New Hope Church the "Hell Hole."

In the darkness a house behind Federal lines was hastily transformed into a hospital. "Torchlights and candles lighted up dimly the incoming stretchers and the surgeon's tables and instruments," a Union soldier wrote. "The very woods seemed to moan and groan with the voices of sufferers not yet brought in."

During the night Schofield's horse stumbled and threw him, disabling the Army of the Ohio's commander for several days. Scattered skirmishing occurred throughout the next day between the entrenched armies, although the soldiers could seldom see a target.

Sherman, who slept behind a log near New Hope Church that night, rose the following morning to find earthworks everywhere. He was mystified to find himself stymied at Dallas and New Hope Church. Determined not to be stalled, he ordered his line extended to the east in another attempt to flank Johnston. On May 27, thinking he had reached the end of the Confederate defenses, Sherman attacked at Pickett's Mill, several miles northeast of New Hope Church, with hopes of enveloping Johnston's right end and imposing himself between the Confederates and Atlanta.

Johnston had correctly anticipated Sherman again. In extending his right, Johnston occupied a hill near Pickett's Mill and stationed one thousand unmounted cavalrymen to secure his flank across Pickett's Creek. When skirmishers discovered the advancing Federals, the Southerners were ready. Sherman massed three brigades for an attack in the center, with smaller diversionary efforts to strike either side. These were designed to hold the Confederates in place and isolate the beleaguered center.

At 5 P.M. Schofield's infantry advanced slowly over the wild terrain, driving back the cavalry screen, picking their way across a ravine, and pushing through thick woods that covered the slope. The fifteen thousand troops were as startled as Hooker's men had been at New Hope Church two days earlier to find five thousand Rebels—Patrick Cleburne's full division—confidently deployed and waiting for action. These troops, considered among the best in the Confederate army, lay on the open ridge with a tremendous field of fire stretching before them. Two cannon the Confederates had wrestled over the muddy roads and fields were poised for support.

Showing little regard for the perilous situation, the Federal soldiers bravely broke into a run toward the Confederate line screaming, "Damn you, we have caught you without your logs now!" It was soon obvious to the attackers that the Rebels did not need their accustomed log-and-earth works. Cleburne reported that his men "slaughtered them with deliberate aim." A regimental standard was planted fifteen feet from the rapid-firing Southerners to encourage the failing Federals, but five bearers were shot down before the flag was recovered and borne to the rear. The men were blinded by a solid wall of muzzle flashes that felled five hundred charging soldiers in minutes, some at the foot of the Confederate line.

The first brigade was broken, its survivors fleeing in disarray through the second brigade, which pressed a determined charge only to run into a withering crossfire between the two cannon firing grapeshot and dismounted cavalry firing rapidly from the flank. The Federal ranks were shattered as seven hundred additional blue-clad bodies fell heavily to the earth. The third brigade staged a demonstration so the wounded could be extracted. The supporting attacks to each side had been poorly coordinated in the dense forest, allowing the Rebels to concentrate their fire on the main assault in the center. A Union soldier remarked, "The Rebel fire swept the ground like a hailstorm."

Two brigades had been destroyed.

MOUNTAIN CAMPAIGNS IN GEORGIA

The May 25 fighting at New Hope Church was part of a week of fighting that led the soldiers to refer to the site as the "Hell Hole."

During the heat of battle, Confederate soldiers, referring to reports in Northern newspapers that Johnston's army had lost its will to fight because of recent retreats, yelled at the Yankee force, "Come ON! We are demoralized!" as they loaded and fired like men possessed.

Hundreds of Federals found retreat as deadly as the attack had been. The crashing din of rifle volleys and the insidious whine of bullets snapping away tree branches chased them to earth. The men hugged every crease in the ground for shelter or crawled into the ravine to wait for dark before filtering back to their own lines. The fighting had petered out by 7 P.M., but at 11 P.M. the Confederates, invigorated by the easy victory and irritated by the sound of the enemy slithering away, fixed bayonets and swarmed out of their freshly dug works to charge across the darkened field "like a whirlwind, screaming like demons," said one terrified Yankee survivor.

The maniacal charge struck fear into the remaining Federals, who fled the field accompanied by a swarm of rabbits flushed by the crazed Johnnies. The exultant Southerners captured 250 prisoners, including many wounded who had been abandoned by the routed Union troops. One Confederate described the charge as a "desperate and reckless thing" that would have been cut to ribbons if the Federals had resisted, but having exhausted their ammunition, the bluecoats were helpless.

Cleburne lost 35 men killed in the attack, 500 total casualties counting wounded and missing; Union losses were 1,500. The attack cost one unit 203 of 400 men; another lost one-third of its men in an advance measured in yards. In forty-five minutes 500 Federals fell, 300 in another half-hour. A Union soldier involved in the assault commented, "This is not war; it is butchery." One Yankee officer at the scene, writer Ambrose Bierce, later penned an article titled "The Crime at Pickett's Mill." The battle, he wrote, was "fordoomed to oblivion." It was one of the bloodiest battles in the Atlanta campaign.

Schofield's battered men fell back several hundred yards and established a defensive line parallel to the Confederates and centered on a hill where a four-gun battery was placed to stabilize the position. That night the hillside was littered with wounded, and flickering campfires illuminated men "with broken limbs or disfigured faces." Howard was among the wounded.

Dawn's faint light revealed a ravaged woodland strewn with hundreds of corpses. Confederates noted that some of the youthful faces expressed peace; others were fearfully contorted from agonized deaths. Gazing at the grisly sight from the safety of their rifle pits, the men in gray were sickened by the terrible slaughter they had accomplished. The Federal dead were left

By the Book ■ William J. Hardee

William J. Hardee was a native Georgian who spent all of 1864 desperately defending his homeland—in vain. Born in Camden County, he attended West Point and fought the Indians and Mexicans before the Civil War erupted.

In 1856 he wrote a manual of arms published as *Rifle and Light Infantry Tactics* and popularly known as *Hardee's Tactics,* which was adopted for use by the army and the classrooms of West Point. With the outbreak of the war, many officers in blue and gray used the manual to train hundreds of thousands of civilian soldiers.

Hardee earned the sobriquet "Old Reliable" for his steady leadership in every battle fought by the Army of Tennessee: Shiloh, Perryville, Stones River, Chickamauga, and Chattanooga. After Braxton Bragg was reassigned, Hardee declined command of the army, preferring to serve under Joseph E. Johnston.

Following Johnston's removal from command, the new army commander, John Bell Hood, blamed Hardee for the series of disastrous defeats suffered by the Confederates. Hardee had no confidence in Hood's leadership and reacted by demanding a transfer. When Hood marched away to Tennessee, Hardee was assigned to head the Department of South Carolina, Georgia, and Florida. His foremost responsibility at this time was to protect Georgia from Sherman's legions.

While Sherman steadily moved across Georgia, Hardee assembled a scratch force of ten thousand men in Savannah. When sixty thousand hardened Union veterans invested the city at Christmas 1864, Hardee managed to slip his command across the Savannah River in an audacious move that caught Sherman by surprise.

During the last months of the war, Hardee once again served under Johnston, just as he had begun the Atlanta campaign the previous year. Johnston returned to command the pitiful remains of the Army of Tennessee, and he rushed to oppose Sherman in North Carolina.

Tragedy struck Hardee in one of the final battles. Succumbing to the pleas of his fourteen-year-old son, Hardee allowed the boy to join the cavalry at Bentonville. Hours after kissing his son good-bye, Willie Hardee was killed in his first combat.

on the field for several days, creating a stench the burrowing combatants could not escape and would never forget. Burial details later counted seven hundred Union corpses, many in drifts three and four deep. They were gathered for burial in two mass graves that could not be found after the war.

Pickett's Mill marked the low point of Sherman's otherwise brilliant strategy. Although he chose not to mention the disaster in his memoirs after the war, he did term this a "wretched week" that was a "wearisome waste of time and strength."

In the two battles of New Hope Church and Pickett's Mill, the Federals lost three thousand men, the Confederates eight hundred. Following these twin defeats, Sherman decided to move far to the east of the Dallas–New Hope–Pickett's Mill line. On May 28 he sent George Stoneman's and Kenner Garrard's cavalries to occupy the abandoned Confederate positions at Allatoona and to seize Acworth, a railroad station to the south.

Sherman planned to shift McPherson from the extreme western end of the Dallas line, behind Thomas and Schofield, to the east toward Acworth, Big Shanty, and Marietta. He urgently needed to regain the railroad to resupply his hungry army, and the move would place him in better position for an attack on Atlanta. The Federal commander had quickly realized that this type of warfare was not to his benefit. Like Grant in Virginia, Sherman knew there would be no decisive battle fought in this wilderness.

Johnston anticipated Sherman's move and ordered Hardee to attack McPherson during the vulnerable withdrawal, hoping to destroy the Army of the Tennessee and turn the Union right flank. The comedy of errors, however, continued—this time at Confederate expense. Johnston's reasoning was faultless, but the timing was catastrophic. McPherson was not withdrawing, and his troops were strongly entrenched. At 3:45 P.M. on May 28, according to a Union report, "a heavy column of Rebels rose from the brush with a yell the devil ought to copyright" and attacked.

The Confederates surged recklessly forward and carried the first line of Federal works and a three-gun battery by ferocity alone. Punishing salvos from the primary Union trenches, however, decimated their ranks. The Southerners determinedly fought off McPherson's fierce counterattacks. They were subsequently overwhelmed when Union Gen. John A. Logan leaped his horse over the earthworks and led a charge to recapture his guns and works.

Because they found themselves in a hopeless situation, the attacking Confederates did not order waiting units to join the assault. Unfortunately, on the far end of Hardee's line, the commander of a Kentucky brigade feared he had missed the signal to attack. The Kentuckians attacked alone. They occupied some works, capturing several guns and some prisoners, but intense Federal artillery and rifle fire from the main position halted the advance. When the original attacking force retreated, the Kentuckians missed the withdrawal signal and were left to stubbornly fight on alone. After suffering frightful losses in a struggle to within twenty yards of the

Federal line, the Kentucky commander seized his brigade's flag and started for the rear, forcing his men to abandon the hopeless mission. They had lost half their number. Ironically, these men were already known as the Orphan Brigade because Kentucky had not seceded; this battle would make their name synonymous with heroism and tragedy in the short history of the Confederacy. At the conclusion of the futile battle of Dallas, the Rebels lost 610 men, the Yankees 380.

In his memoirs, Sherman wrote of this battle, "Fortunately, our men erected good breastworks and gave the enemy a terrible and bloody repulse." Johnston, however, referred to it as a minor affair.

On the night of May 27 Hood was dispatched to execute a long march designed to strike McPherson's left flank by surprise. Hardee and Polk were to join the assault to destroy the entire Federal army. When the battle was scheduled to begin, Hood reported to Johnston that the Federals were too strongly emplaced to attack. The bold plan was canceled. For a second time Johnston angrily charged Hood with disobedience of orders, stating that he lacked the will to attack and noting that after a ten-hour march Hood had only advanced the distance of a rifle shot. This was yet another round in an increasingly contentious relationship.

Johnston continued to extend his works to parallel the Union line and prevent Sherman from outflanking him. Constant deadly skirmishes erupted as the two armies faced off in this Georgia wilderness. Their lines eventually extended ten miles: from the edge of Dallas three miles northeast, across the high ridges of Ray's Mountain and Ellsberry Mountain to New Hope Church, and northeast to beyond Pickett's Mill. The heavily wooded ridges, choked with briars and heavy brush, were soon crisscrossed with miles of extensive earthworks.

By May 29 Johnston was certain that Sherman would shift his troops east to sidestep to the railroad and flank him out of this strong position. To counter this, he ordered a series of night attacks on McPherson to keep the Federals from withdrawing and sliding down the line. Some Union troops reported being attacked seven times in a single night by screaming Rebel phantoms who stormed abruptly out of the darkness. One Federal officer recorded in his diary, "Oh God, what a night!" The attacks continued until June 1, frustrating McPherson's efforts to execute an orderly withdrawal.

McPherson finally inched out of his position by devising a new tactic for this unique situation. Part of his force would dig a defensive line behind the main works, then the men would fall back into the new trenches. This exhausting process of creeping backward was repeated many times. Johnston's men, meanwhile, scurried to occupy the abandoned trenches and keep up a relentless pressure.

The fighting in the thickets around Dallas introduced a new form of warfare to the campaign: isolated combat between small groups of soldiers. The combatants were often within voice range, and the fighting was constant and vicious. Both sides turned hills, ravines, and stands of trees into natural fortresses. A Federal soldier compared the operations around Dallas to "Hell and its awful fires." Another officer paid homage to the courage of the fierce Confederates who were defending their homes: "Braver men never shouldered a musket than those Rebels as they came up to drive us out of our works" charging blindly from the dark, hats pulled down over their eyes, "like men who care only to throw away their lives."

When troops advanced or retreated, they needed no orders to dig in. Making "the dirt fly," as they said, was a simple matter of survival. Skirmishers fanned out in front of the new line to slow the enemy advance and protect the main force of soldiers who stacked their guns and broke out shovels to dig trenches. Others grabbed axes and felled trees for logs used to reinforce the parapets; they also cleared deadly fields of fire in front of the breastworks. From such stout fortifications, experienced soldiers could hold off the most determined assaults.

Given an hour, a regiment would systematically protect itself against infantry attack and artillery bombardment by digging connecting trenches and placing huge logs on top of the parapet, which were then covered with dirt. The earthworks had a wall of logs for a backing, and a log was placed over the ditch to protect the soldiers' heads. The men fired from gaps beneath the head logs. The head logs rested in grooves cut into two other logs that extended to level ground behind the trench. If an artillery shell hit the head log, it would skitter harmlessly over the soldiers instead of falling into the pit and crushing the defenders. Such works were safe but uncomfortable. As the spring rains continued to fall, the works turned into miserable quagmires.

The Hard Luck Army ■ The Army of Tennessee

In November 1862 the Confederate armies that had been brought together under Albert Sidney Johnston several months earlier to blunt U. S. Grant's advance into Tennessee were formally recognized as the Army of Tennessee, the South's second great military force—second to the Army of Northern Virginia. Made up of fighting men from Tennessee, Kentucky, Georgia, Arkansas, Alabama, Louisiana, Mississippi, and Missouri, this army was responsible for the defense of a huge region of the South, which was three hundred miles wide and six hundred miles long.

This valiant army never matched the exploits of the Army of Northern Virginia largely because of its poor leadership. Its first commander, Braxton Bragg, was a brilliant planner, but he seemed to lose confidence at crucial times. Bragg's health was also poor, and he was prone to fits of despondency. Furthermore he alienated virtually everyone he knew. During the Mexican War, one of his soldiers allegedly tried to kill him, and during the late 1863 siege of Chattanooga several witnessed Nathan Bedford Forrest threaten to kill him.

In the fall of 1862, Bragg launched a short-lived invasion of Kentucky. After an inconclusive battle at Perryville, he retreated to Chattanooga. Advancing to Murfreesboro in central Tennessee, Bragg attacked the Federal army on New Year's Eve 1863, winning an incomplete victory. The contest was later renewed with inconclusive results, and Bragg decided to withdraw. At Chickamauga in October 1863, Bragg routed a Union army but failed to pursue and destroy it. After Grant relieved the siege of Chattanooga, the Army of Tennessee retreated in disarray to Dalton, and Bragg resigned.

Joseph E. Johnston restored the army's morale then led it on a hundred-mile retreat to Atlanta in 1864. There John Bell Hood commanded the army in four disastrous defeats around Atlanta, then he finished its destruction with a winter campaign into Tennessee. Hood recklessly sacrificed his men at Franklin and Nashville. Johnston returned to lead the army in a final battle, attempting to blunt Sherman's drive through North Carolina.

In fighting spirit and ability, the Army of Tennessee equaled its famous Virginia counterpart, but in terms of sacrifice and endurance, the men of this army exceeded their comrades under Robert E. Lee. Although the Army of Tennessee never won a complete victory, the men persevered to the bitter end.

These entrenchments around New Hope Church reflect the redefinition of military tactics during the war, when many found it prudent to huddle close to logs and earth rather than hurl themselves toward the enemy. Riflemen were kept busy here until Johnston abandoned this line on June 4.

Another mode of defense used extensively since the fighting at Resaca was the incorporation of gabions, containers of wattle filled with earth—sometimes fifteen feet thick—that could stop artillery fire. On the Dallas and Kennesaw lines, and particularly in the forts around Atlanta, Confederate defenders energetically produced chevaux-de-frise, a primitive but wicked form of barbed wire made by piercing large logs with long, sharpened stakes. These devices slowed down attackers considerably. After clearing fields of fire, soldiers would leave many trees lying where they fell, creating a natural obstacle of tangled branches.

An intricate trench system like that which would cover France fifty years later in World War I quickly developed. A Federal observer said an area ten miles by twenty miles looked like an enormous furrowed field. He estimated that four hundred to five hundred miles of earthworks were constructed in six weeks.

West Point graduates in blue and gray worried that this style of defensive fighting meant the men had lost their nerve for conventional infantry action. Instead of charging across open no man's land, they sneaked into enemy trenches at night. Hood, who was particularly disturbed by this new brand of trench warfare, feared his men were losing their offensive edge. Schofield took the side of the soldiers, believing this new form of war to be an all-American endeavor. A soldier was like a civilian in business, Schofield

The Confederate line held up to Federal assaults, but the constant pressure eventually allowed Sherman's men to force the Southerners to fall back—albeit to another line that proved stronger than the improvised earthworks of Dallas, New Hope, and Pickett's Mill.

said: "He wanted to see a fair prospect that it is going to pay." In this enterprise, payment meant survival.

During the last week on the Dallas line, the soldiers fought no pitched battles but constantly sniped, skirmished, and volleyed. The Army of the Cumberland expended two hundred thousand rounds of barely replenishable rifle ammunition daily in this disorganized conflict. Moreover, trench warfare exacted a heavy toll on the exhausted men. For weeks they endured the strain of constant alarms, living among the screams of the wounded and the stench of the unburied dead. Men were isolated for days with no rations or water, but they fought with a ferocity seldom matched in the Civil War. Unrecorded heroism was common.

Sherman had committed a grievous error by advancing into an area that a defensive genius like Johnston could put to deadly advantage. The Confederates had become invisible. In two weeks the Federal commander saw only a half-dozen Rebels dodging between trees and rocks to snipe at his troops. Severe casualties mounted daily in what Sherman called a "big Indian war."

It was inevitable that Sherman's superior numbers would gain control of the situation on the Dallas front. To the east, at the extreme left of the Federal line, Schofield's troops closed in on the Dallas-Acworth road. Hardee, transferred from Dallas to form the Confederate right, stretched his troops to meet the threat, but on June 4 Confederate cavalry protecting the vital road were driven off. Johnston was forced to abandon Dallas. Sherman had finally broken the deadly stalemate in the wilderness.

Federal cavalry captured Allatoona on June 1, and on June 6 they occupied the railroad town of Acworth. When the rails were repaired and a bridge over the Etowah River rebuilt, Sherman reestablished his supply line north to Chattanooga. Sliding down the rails, they drove Joseph Wheeler's cavalry out of Big Shanty, situated between Acworth and Marietta, on June 9, ending ten days of continuous fighting. Sherman bitterly realized that he was no closer to Atlanta then he had been at Dallas. The destruction of the previous two weeks had been a complete waste.

Within a few days most of the Federal army reached Big Shanty, and Sherman halted there for several days to rest the men, await reinforcements, and resupply his command. He was itching to continue the offensive, but he was unable to get around Johnston. His adversary had been flanked out of the formidable Dallas position, but the Confederate army was again blocking the path to Atlanta.

A Tour from Cartersville to Pickett's Mill

This portion of the driving tour begins south of Cartersville, on the north bank of the Etowah River off U.S. 41-GA 3, driving east on River Road (360).

Drive slowly 2.4 miles down the winding road that follows the Etowah River to the right. Beyond the I-75 overpass, trees overhang the road and create a dark green canopy. The road leads to Cooper's Furnace Historic Day Use Area, and the furnace is on the left.

Cooper's Furnace, listed on the National Register, is equipped with grills, picnic pavilions, and facilities for children's play. There are two historical trails: one (.7 mile in length) follows the route of the Civil War–era railroad spur used to ferry manufactured products from the Etowah River to the Western and Atlantic main line to the west. Near Allatoona Dam at the end of the road is an enormous outcropping of stone that should not be missed, but the centerpiece of the park is the imposing furnace.

After Jacob Stroup built an iron foundry here along Allatoona Creek in the 1840s, this became one of the most prosperous areas in northern Georgia. In 1858 the foundry was bought by Mark Anthony Cooper, a businessman and politician who named the facilities the Etowah Iron Works. He established a rolling mill, a flour mill that produced three hundred barrels a day, and factories for the production of guns, the South's first railroad iron, tools, nails, spikes, and utensils of all descriptions. England's Queen Victoria once wrote Cooper to praise his fine flour, produced in a four-and-a-half-story mill. The town of Etowah had a school, church, boarding house, bank, brewery, store, post office, log houses, and a bordello. It supported up to four thousand residents, five hundred to six hundred of them workers. Gold and copper mines operated in the area.

The railroad engine *Yonah,* which was involved in the Great Locomotive Chase, was Cooper's yard engine, used to carry his products over the small spur line to the main Western and Atlantic tracks several miles west. During the chase it was commandeered by William A. Fuller. Cooper's company prospered, particularly when the Civil War broke out and the Confederacy suddenly needed quantities of iron no longer available from the North. Cooper sold the works in 1862 for $450,000 to William A. Robinson and William T. Quim, of Memphis, who were arms manufacturers. After paying off his debts, Cooper had $200,000 left, which he invested in the Confederacy and of course lost everything. The state of Georgia took control of the facilities in 1863. When Johnston abandoned Cassville, he retreated along the route of U.S. 41-GA 3, followed by Schofield. After a skirmish on May 21, Schofield's men destroyed the ironworks then rejoined Sherman at Kingston. Some of the facilities were rebuilt after the war, but they could not compete with cheaper Northern production.

At its height, Cooper had several cold-blast iron furnaces operating on Allatoona and Story Creeks. Iron ore and limestone were mined nearby, and charcoal was created from local timber. Ore, limestone, and charcoal were carried on trestles to the furnaces and dumped in layers. The charcoal was ignited and heat increased by blasts of cold air forced into the furnaces by pumps driven by overshot waterwheels. The water was carried to the site by flumes from nearby creeks. As the iron ore and limestone melted, the limestone absorbed impurities in the ore and rose to the top to be skimmed off as slag. The molten iron was released from the furnaces through plugs and drained into casting trenches that resembled pigs eating at a trough, thus the name "pig iron." Twenty tons were produced each week.

This large stone structure is all that remains of Cooper's enterprises, which once stretched for several miles along the Etowah River and included twelve thousand acres in four counties. The town that housed the employees was a mile from the works, but it and other ruins are now beneath Lake Allatoona.

Retrace your route. Just before you reach U.S. 41-GA 3, turn into the graveled area on your left and park near the stone piers in the Etowah River.

These five piers supported the original 620-foot-long bridge when the Western and Atlantic Railroad was constructed in the 1840s. Johnston burned the bridge after he crossed; Sherman repaired the span then destroyed it as he headed for Savannah in the fall. The railroad rebuilt the bridge a mile downstream. During the Great Locomotive Chase, James Andrews unwisely elected not to destroy the bridge, though one doubts he could have done it much harm, but he should have damaged the little engine he saw on the siding. Fuller soon arrived on a handcar to appropriate the *Yonah* and motorize his determined pursuit.

Before leaving the parking area, look at the high hill immediately across the road to the north. A historical marker indicates that after Sherman passed south, he built a fort on top of this hill and garrisoned it to guard the rebuilt railroad bridge from Rebel cavalry raids. Since there were no raids, the men were bored. They swam in the river, hiked the hills, picked blackberries, and played a newly developed pastime, the first baseball games seen in the region. A few soldiers were captured by Confederates when they left the fort to hunt wild game.

Several hundred yards west was a line of Confederate earthworks built to protect the north bank of the Etowah River. They were destroyed by construction of the new railroad and U.S. 41-GA 3.

Return to U.S. 41-GA 3, heading south. If you are in no hurry, at .9 you will want to turn left onto Powerhouse Road (294) at the sign for Allatoona Dam. The road leads to the base of the huge dam.

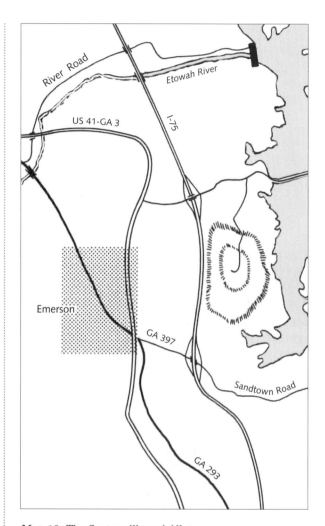

Map 12: The Cartersville and Allatoona areas

A scenic drive along the banks of the Etowah River affords marvelous views of surrounding peaks and the beautiful Etowah Valley. At the dam the Etowah is wide and weed-choked, but it becomes narrower and deeper and flows faster farther downstream. Features include camping, picnicking, and fishing areas just before the road dead-ends at the enormous dam. A long flight of stairs invites a strenuous climb to the top of the dam, but the view is worth the exertion. Inside the dam is a visitors center where employees are eager to explain how the mammoth facility works.

The Lake Allatoona Visitors Center is at the top of the dam, on Spur GA 20. It has wonderful views of the Etowah River, the valley, the dam, the site of the town of Etowah below, and Lake Allatoona, which covers twelve thousand acres and has a shoreline of 270 miles. Hiking trails lead to the valley below. The museum in the visitors center, operated by the Army Corps of Engineers, has interpretive displays that explain Bartow County's geology, Native Americans, Mark Cooper and the ironworks, and the lake. The Civil War along the Etowah is also explored, with an artillery tube and other artifacts, a painting of the nearby battle of Allatoona that occurred October 5, 1864, photographs, and descriptions.

Continue south on U.S. 41-GA 3 and at 1.1 is a sign for Red Top Mountain to the left, on S1665. The park offers all the recreational facilities of a state park.

Continue on U.S. 41-GA 3 south through the outskirts of Emerson.

Emerson was named in 1889 for Georgia Civil War Gov. Joseph E. Brown's middle name. The town was known as Steagall's Station when Johnston camped here on May 20, 1864. The Steagall house (GA 293-Main Street, 1845), home of railroad agent John P. Steagall was thought to have been the first stop for Andrews's raiders after they stole the *General*. It has recently been preserved and after restoration by a private company will be given to the city of Emerson.

At 1.5 exit right off U.S. 41-GA 3 and turn right at the stop sign. A sign in front indicates GA 293, which will shortly turn right, but continue straight on 397. Cross under Interstate 75 and wind through a gap in the one-thousand-foot-high Allatoona Mountains, past fields of kudzu. The road turns sharply right and winds down to the tiny village of Allatoona.

Drive slowly beside the massive thirty-foot-high retaining wall of earth and stone that blots out the view of everything opposite little Allatoona, seemingly unchanged by time. At 2.3 turn left into the parking lot.

After Johnston was denied the chance to fight a decisive battle at Cassville, he retired across the Etowah River and established an impregnable position in the Allatoona Mountains. There he waited for Sherman to follow. Sherman chose not to, and later established a strong garrison here. Although the armies did not fight here in May, a desperate battle was waged in the pass above Allatoona in October 1864 after Sherman had occupied Atlanta and Hood tried to draw him into Tennessee. For a detailed account of this battle, see appendix B. The fighting inspired the noted hymn, "Hold the Fort, for I Am Coming."

Look across the road to the only surviving structure from Allatoona. The Clayton house (1830s), a two-story clapboard structure, was built by John C. Clayton, a prosperous miner who died a month after the battle. His home had been used as a headquarters by the Federals and as a Confederate hospital during the battle and a Union hospital following it. The walls retain bullet holes, blood stains the floors, and twenty-one unknown Confederates are buried in the backyard. A communal marker stands in the front yard, and individual stones have been placed to mark the graves. Beyond the Clayton house, the depot was on the left, or western side, of the tracks, and the ration

Scenic views of the beautiful, historic Etowah Valley at Allatoona Dam (left) and along the Etowah River, which provided Confederates with a strong defensive position.

The Clayton house, below Allatoona Pass, was used as a hospital after the October 1864 battle.

warehouses and a siding were on the right. The brick building (1892) on the western side of the highway was a general store. During the war Allatoona was a small community with fewer than ten structures.

The tracks formerly ran to the east of this building, along this parking area. The deep railroad cut through the pass is a dramatic sight here; the steep walls are sixty-five feet high. To the left of the cut (and right of 397 at the curve) are the major fortifications erected by the Southerners and strengthened by the Federals, including the star fort. To the right of the cut are lesser works. The Confederates advanced north of 397 and west of Allatoona to attack.

In 1862 the locomotive *General* raced past the community and through the cut, followed by William A. Fuller and Anthony Murphy on their pole car, soon to appropriate the *Yonah.*

The Etowah Valley Historical Society (EVHS) has been aggressively preserving Bartow County's extensive historical heritage for decades and sponsors tours of Allatoona Pass, historic homes, cemeteries, and other places.

In 1995 EVHS received a twenty-thousand-dollar grant to prepare a preservation plan for Allatoona Pass, and that organization and the U.S. Army Corps of Engineers agreed to create a trail system with signs. Volunteers cleared brush and trees. The work concluded in 1996 when the corps created the parking lot. The corps owns three hundred acres, including all of the eastern redoubt. The EVHS and the state of Georgia have identified a number of acres of privately owned land to add, particularly at the star

fort. In 2001 Bartow County received state funds to purchase six acres there. That same year EVHS, the state of Georgia, and the Civil War Preservation Trust declared Allatoona Pass one of the ten most threatened Civil War sites in the country. They are attempting to purchase additional land.

The 160-year-old pass is 360 feet long, 60 feet wide, and 65 feet deep, the deepest cut on the Western and Atlantic between Atlanta and Chattanooga, forming a natural choke point. As a young lieutenant, Sherman had ridden through the pass in 1844. Impressed at the engineering marvel, he remembered the natural strength of the position when he returned with his armies in 1864. He refused to attack the position and opted to flank Johnston to the west.

After outflanking the Allatoona position, Sherman's troops occupied it, repairing the railroad and establishing a garrison on June 7. The area was quiet until the fall. The little known (even in Georgia) October 5, 1864, battle was one of the fiercest engagements of the Civil War. In four hours 1,603 men, including 70 officers, of the 3,276 Confederates (commanded by Maj. Gen. Samuel G. French) and 2,025 Federals (led by Maj. Gen. John Corse) became casualties—30 percent, one of the highest casualty rates of the war.

As soon as Allatoona Pass was secured in late spring 1864, Capt. Orlando Poe, Sherman's chief of engineers, designed fortifications to defend this vital railroad line and primary supply depot. The steep heights overlooking the railroad cut were covered by the star fort to the west and the eastern redoubt on

The deep railroad cut at Allatoona Pass was the scene of Hood's desperate attack in October 1864.

the opposite side, protecting the Tennessee road. A footbridge spanned the sixty-foot-wide cut and allowed troops and ammunition to move from one bastion to the other. A huge pine tree was used as an observation post on the eastern side, where an artillery stable was kept. Blocking the Alabama road on the western side, north of the present Emerson-Allatoona Road, was Rowett's Redoubt. Headquarters of the Fourth Minnesota was to the east, and the Ninety-third Illinois was to the west.

The fortifications were twelve feet thick, six feet high on the inside (with exterior ditches six feet deep on the outside) and buttressed with extensive trenches and rifle pits to the front. When the Confederates attacked, nine thousand head of cattle were penned north of the pass, and warehouses held three million rations of hardtack.

Jefferson Davis, after meeting with Hood, revealed the general's plans to the Confederate press, which promptly published it. Hood would strike north, destroying the Union supply line and forcing the Federals to follow him. Sherman read the newspapers and knew he must reinforce Allatoona Pass, thirty-five miles north of Atlanta and housing his primary supply base. The position was held by 976 men under Lt. Col. John E. Tourtelotte. Maj. Gen. John Corse, whose men were garrisoning Rome, was immediately ordered to Allatoona. He arrived early on the morning of October 5, 1864, with 1,050 reinforcements, only two hours before the battle began.

Confederate Maj. Gen. Samuel G. French was given an impossible mission. He had thirty hours to

Earthworks remain intact from the star fort, the primary Federal position that won the battle of Allatoona Pass.

march his division, numbering 3,250 men, twenty-five miles, capture Allatoona Pass, destroy Union supplies, fill the pass with debris, and return to the Army of Tennessee.

At 6:30 A.M. French opened with an artillery bombardment and pressed four determined assaults from the north and west to within one hundred yards of the primary fortifications. The outer works were captured and considerable casualties inflicted, but the Confederates could not take the position and were forced to withdraw, their valor wasted. The Southerners did not discover the warehouses until after the battle and were unable to burn them.

Allatoona Pass is a wonderful, compact site that preserves more original earthworks and other physical landmarks than most other Civil War battlefields. The defenses are among the best preserved and pristine in the Southeast, particularly the star fort.

At the parking lot are interpretive markers, provided by EVHS. Face north, toward the railroad cut. The lake embankment is on the right, and the road and Clayton house are to the left. This is the original roadbed of the Western and Atlantic. The primary road from Atlanta began at Montgomery's Ferry on the Chattahoochee River and was known as the Old Sandtown Road to this point. The Alabama road passed in front of the Clayton house and turned west, north of the existing road by which you arrived, and was protected by Rowett's Redoubt. The Tennessee wagon road branched to the right (north) and was protected by the eastern redoubt.

Walk into the railroad cut. Signs point out a trail to the right, the Tennessee road, traces of which are still visible. That trail intersects another trail. To the right is the eastern redoubt and sites of the stable, observation post, headquarters of the Fourth Minnesota, and the lake. To the left are earthworks and the eastern edge of the railroad cut.

If you can only take one hike here, save it for the railroad cut, which grows deeper and deeper and resembles a cave as the rock walls rise on both sides. The sight is impressive. Pause to read all the historical markers. At the deepest part of the cut, where the sixty-foot-wide footbridge spanned the sixty-five-foot-deep cut, climb the stairs to the left and follow the path into the star fort. The walls and embrasures are clearly visible. To the west is Rowett's Redoubt. Confederates attacked from the west and north, overrunning the redoubt and pressing close to the star fort, scene of the heaviest fighting in the battle.

The footbridge may eventually be reconstructed. The original earthen abutments remain. During the battle, runners carried ammunition over it to the star fort. One brave man made four harrowing trips. A reconstructed observation post would contribute to a better understanding of the battle. The site contains an estimated three hundred Confederate dead, who were probably thrown into the earthworks and covered with dirt. After the war Gov. Joseph E. Brown visited Allatoona and found the observation tree dying. He ordered it cut down and the wood made into gavels and cigar boxes that were presented to the Confederate officers who fought the battle.

Allatoona Pass has only one monument. It honors Gen. Francis M. Cockrell's First Missouri Brigade (C.S.). During the war these Missourians marched two thousand miles and fought in thirteen major battles, including Allatoona Pass, in seven states. Considered by many (and Jefferson Davis) to have been the best fighting unit on either side of the war, the Missouri Brigade lost 91 killed or mortally wounded here and 270 total casualties. Weeks later it suffered 68 percent casualties at the battle of Franklin, Tennessee. The seven-foot-high slab of Georgia granite, carved in the shape of the state of Missouri and resting on a base of red Missouri granite, was dedicated in 2001.

Return down the stairs to the parking lot. The trail continues north for a view of the Tennessee wagon road to the right; to the left is the original grave of an unknown Confederate. The path offers good views of Lake Allatoona.

Architect and historian Bill Scaife estimates that 1.8 million cubic feet of material would have been required to fill the massive cut. Even had the Confederates won this battle, it is doubtful they would have been able to do much damage to the railroad.

Turn left from the parking lot. After .4, just beyond the railroad tracks where the road branches, look to the right for a small fenced plot and a sign that reads "An Unknown Hero."

Allatoona is famous for this grave of an unknown Confederate soldier, but confusion reigns over its origin. The local folk tale claims that a decaying body arrived in a sealed box labeled simply Allatoona, Georgia. In

The grave of an unknown Confederate at Allatoona was tended by railroad crews.

an attempt to discover the identity, six courageous women opened the box but found only the remains of an unidentified Confederate soldier. They buried the man and marked the grave with a crude marker. Because the grave would be covered by construction of the lake, in 1940 it was relocated a short distance so railroad workers could tend the site. In 1980 surveyors placed a gravestone. The grave had been east of the railroad, its original location later lost. An alternate story asserts that a train crew found the body beside the tracks after the battle and buried it there

In reality, there were two graves of unidentified Confederates killed in the battle at Allatoona, and they were buried on opposite sides of the railroad. One, lesser known, was buried in the pass on the east side of the railroad with no marker. The second soldier was buried where he died at the northern edge of the railroad cut west of the tracks. He was identified as Pvt. Andrew J. Houston of the 135th Mississippi. To prevent its being covered by the lake, in 1950 the railroad relocated the grave here, a half mile south of the original burial site, and it was maintained by rail workers.

The hill where Confederate artillery was emplaced to fire on Federal positions at Allatoona is just south of this spot. The site of a blockhouse manned by eighty-four soldiers captured by the Confederates at the time of the battle is now covered by Lake Allatoona. To the east on the lake is a boat ramp, beach, and tent and trailer camping.

From Allatoona we pick up Sherman's trail from Kingston, where he retired to rest and plan the remainder of his campaign. He chose to advance on Dallas rather than Allatoona, and Johnston shifted west to Dallas from Allatoona.

Retrace your steps on 397 past I-75 and return north on U.S. 41-GA 3 into Cartersville. Turn left onto GA 113-GA 61 and start your mileage. At .3 to the right is Friendship Plaza, Cartersville town square.

The Cartersville railroad depot is the original, dating to 1854, four years after the railroad reached the city. On May 19, 1864, the Confederate rear guard barricaded the depot, knocking out bricks for firing slits. During the engagement, Union artillery inflicted damage to the structure. The Confederates withdrew on May 20, and by the time Sherman left, the wooden roof and floor had been burned. It was repaired in 1865, and in 1902 additions to each end made the depot a block long. The building was almost completely razed in the 1970s, leaving only a small portion of the original depot. That remnant is 40 feet wide and 124 feet long with a granite-topped entrance, grand arches, and huge bay windows. The depot is being restored to its original appearance for use as a visitors center. Sixty trains a day still rumble through the heart of the city.

Sherman made his final plans for the March to the Sea a few miles from here in Kingston, but it was at this depot that he ordered the telegraph severed, cutting off communications with the North. His last message to George H. Thomas in Tennessee was,

"All is well." Sherman aide George W. Nichols wrote, "We have cut adrift from our base of operations."

Entrepreneur Mark Cooper, finding himself one hundred thousand dollars in debt during the panic of 1857, offered to sell his industries to satisfy the debt. Thirty-five friends signed notes for the sum, and by 1860 Cooper had repaid them. In appreciation he erected a fourteen-foot-high monument of Georgia marble with the names of his friends inscribed on it. Originally sited near Cooper's office on the Etowah town square, the memorial was moved before the inundation of the site by Allatoona Lake to downtown Cartersville. In the 1960s there was a need for additional parking downtown, so the monument was moved again, this time by the Corps of Engineers to a scenic overlook at the dam above Cooper's Furnace. In 2001 the monument, the only known tribute to creditors, was returned to this site in Cartersville.

Friendship Plaza features the Fence of Fame, where plaques honor outstanding local residents, including governors, judges, U.S. cabinet members, writers, women's advocates, congressmen, preachers, missionaries, and baseball players. From the Civil War are Confederate generals P. M. B. Young, the youngest major general on either side of the conflict, and Gen. William T. Wofford. Note also the large granite map of Bartow County.

Currently on the square but soon to move to the restored 1870 courthouse is the excellent Bartow History Museum, which preserves the exciting natural and historical heritage of this area. In the Civil War

Cartersville's railroad station was a Rebel stronghold in 1864, and the building was severely damaged in the fighting. It is being renovated into a visitors center.

Mark Cooper's monument to the generosity of his creditors once overlooked the Allatoona Dam. It has since been moved to downtown Cartersville.

room are displays on the Great Locomotive Chase (including a section of rail from the Western and Atlantic), the battle of Allatoona Pass, operations of a local saltpeter cave (which was part of the gunpowder manufacturing process), wall maps, period illustrations, photographs of the extensive Civil War activity in the county, the history and personal possessions of local Confederates, and weapons—rifles and pistols, swords and knives, and projectiles.

The 1870 Italianate courthouse, the first built here after the county seat was shifted from Cassville, is at the corner of Church and Railroad Streets. A Confederate monument stands on the grounds.

Roselawn, the grand Victorian home of famed nineteenth-century evangelist Samuel P. Jones, is at 224 West Cherokee Avenue. The United Daughters of the Confederacy has a collection of Civil War artifacts on display.

At the eastern corner of Main and Bartow is the First Presbyterian Church (1853), with wonderful stained-glass windows and hand-carved details. It was damaged during use as a Union stable. The 1856 First Baptist Church (227 West Cherokee Street) was so abused by the Federals that the government paid five thousand dollars in damages. That church was demolished and replaced by a two-story brick structure, which is now a private home. This was the home church of renowned missionary Lottie Moon. The new church is just down the street.

Union Pvt. A. O. Granger, Sherman's military secretary and confidant in Georgia, grew attached to Bartow County. In 1889 he moved to Cartersville, made his fortune in mining, and purchased the Young-Granger-Evans home (1841) at the end of West Main Street atop Granger Hill. He greatly expanded the modest house to a three-story structure with twenty-six rooms and an observatory that housed the South's second largest telescope at that time. Granger called his house Overlook.

Currently under construction is the Booth Western Art Museum, slated to open in late 2002. The four-acre downtown grounds will contain an eighty-thousand-square-foot facility with six galleries. Among several permanent collections will be a Civil War gallery featuring eleven Don Troiani originals, including a special painting commissioned by the museum, *The Battle of Allatoona Pass,* and works by Mort Künstler. There will also be a large theater, a multimedia room, and a café. For updates: contact cheryl@boothmuseum.org.

There are many interesting things to see in and around Cartersville, including the magnificent Etowah Indian Mounds, which made a deep impression on Sherman during his 1844 tour of the region when he was a guest at Glencoe.

Gen. Pierce M. B. Young (1836–96), who would have graduated in the West Point class of May 1861, is buried in Oak Hill Cemetery. He had corresponded with every prominent Georgian asking whether he should resign his appointment or remain and earn his commission, and all had advised his departure. He served in Virginia with Jeb Stuart's cavalry while Federals occupied his Cartersville home, Walnut Grove.

Cartersville resident Bill Arp, a Confederate soldier who became one of Georgia's great humorists, is also buried here. Of his Civil War service he wrote, "I killed as many of the Yankees as they killed of me." Arp, whose real name was Charles H. Smith, died in 1903, aged seventy-seven.

Curiously, after the war, Sherman's son Tom marched to Cartersville in a demonstration for peace.

Drive past GA 31 to Dallas. At 6.7 you will pass scenic Raccoon Creek Church and cross meandering Raccoon Creek. Confederate and Federal cavalry clashed here during Sherman's advance to Dallas.

On this stretch of highway notice the mountains to the right, several with large sections cut away. Bartow

In 1844 Sherman visited the ancient Etowah Mounds, which includes one of the largest mounds in North America.

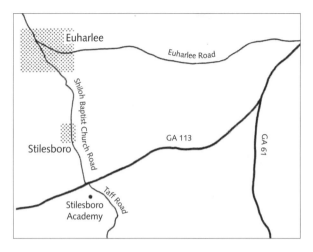

Map 13: Euharlee and Stilesboro

County is one of the richest mineral regions in Georgia, and a great deal of mining has occurred here for 130 years. As you approach Stilesboro, Georgia Power's enormous Plant Bowen grows larger in the distance. Just before reaching the town you will pass under three lines of giant pylons that appear to march across the countryside as they carry electricity to much of the Peach State.

At 1.7 in Stilesboro turn left onto Taff Road for .1 and park on the grounds of the magnificent old wooden building to your right, Stilesboro Academy.

Sitting majestically on a hill, the massive academy is a national treasure. Built in 1859 at a cost of five thousand dollars, it consists of two wings, each containing a single huge classroom. Between the classrooms is a chapel-auditorium. Broad wooden steps lead to enormous sixteen-foot-high double doors. The walls of the structure are twenty feet high, and long shuttered windows extend across the rear. The academy possesses a commanding view of the Etowah Valley, as befits such a sentinel of learning, but today that view is dominated by Plant Bowen. Enormous oaks shade the grounds and a sheltered picnic area. The academy closed in 1861 when many students went to war or took their fathers' places in the fields, but it was reopened after the war and was used for many additional decades.

Sherman's troops moved south from Kingston and Cartersville and crossed the Etowah River at numerous bridges and fords, then they converged on Euharlee and Stilesboro. McPherson marched in front of the academy to swing on Dallas from the west; Thomas and Schofield moved to the east, camping here for one night. Thomas passed through Stilesboro on May 23 and 24.

Return to the highway, turn left onto GA 113 for .1 and immediately turn right onto Stilesboro Road and down a straight stretch that leads toward Plant Bowen. Note the abandoned businesses of old Stilesboro. When stopped at the first sign at .5 turn left over the railroad tracks and pass the beautiful old Stilesboro Methodist Church and grounds. At .5 turn left then right at .1 at the stop sign onto Covered Bridge Road.

On the left is the settling pond where mountains of burned coal-ash are dissolved, parts of it looking like black tidal pools. To the right are the enormous coal-fired generating plants, four huge cooling towers, and an earthen retaining wall that conceals enormous stores of coal.

Out of sight to the right is the Etowah River site of Milam's Bridge, a covered structure burned by retreating Confederate cavalry. On their march to Dallas, Federal troops crossed on a pontoon bridge here, at Gillem's Bridge (now Harden Bridge) on the Kingston-Euharlee road (now Harden Bridge Road), and at Island Ford to the west, which is no longer accessible. McPherson passed Macedonia Church west of here on the way to Van Wert.

Imposing Stilesboro Academy witnessed the passage of Sherman's armies in May 1864.

After 1.9 in Euharlee turn left to the Lowery Covered Bridge, which is nestled off the road in a wooded cove with a picnic area.

The bridge, which spans Euharlee Creek, is a 116-foot-long single span, town-lattice structure built in 1886 to replace a bridge that was swept downstream by floodwater. Each piece of wood was numbered before construction, leading historians to believe that it was built in a nearby field to ensure proper assembly then disassembled and reconstructed over the creek, a common practice at the time. The numbers are still visible. Records indicate that grain mills were established along this creek in 1844. Soon after that, a ferry was replaced by another covered bridge, which Federal forces crossed in 1864 on their way to Dallas.

The western entrance to the bridge is long and curved, with two raised wooden tracks in the center like a wide railroad. Inside you can see crossed wooden beams on the sides and the creek below between floor planks. Note the wooden pegs used instead of nails to hold the span together. The bridge is supported twenty feet above the water by concrete piers. Considering its age and the fact that it carried vehicular traffic until two decades ago, the weathered structure is in excellent shape. There are remains of a stone mill in the creek and on the west bank between the covered bridge and the concrete bridge.

This small community was chartered in 1976 so as to obtain the grants necessary to preserve the town's pre–Civil War buildings. Euharlee purchased sixty-five acres in the center of town, including the bridge, millers house, blacksmith shop, commissary, militia district courthouse, and calaboose. Guided by experts in historical architecture and preservation, they restored the 1900-era Militia District Courthouse, where a justice of the peace presided until the 1950s, and the calaboose, which was a local jail used to hold minor offenders or public drunks. Behind the courthouse and calaboose are a fifteen-acre park and picnic grounds used for civic gatherings. The community hosts the annual Covered Bridge Festival.

Another landmark is the F&M Grocery, Euharlee's only store, and the post office, a 130-year-old building with a foundation of hand-hewn logs. Near the bridge are a quaint, covered public well, protected from the elements by a wood-shingled peaked roof, and several attractive wooden warehouses. A

The current Euharlee covered bridge occupies the same site as an earlier span that was used by Civil War armies.

little farther down the road are two beautiful old churches, Baptist (1853) and Episcopal (1852) and their graveyards. Sherman was too hurried to devastate Stilesboro and Euharlee the way he did later to Cassville and other communities in his path.

Between Kingston and Euharlee, north of Gillem's Bridge on the Etowah River, was the Bartow Saltpeter Works. Saltpeter, potassium nitrate, found in limestone caves and used as fertilizer and in food preservation and medicines, was a valuable war resource. The material was mixed with sulfur and charcoal to produce gunpowder at Augusta. Mining started in 1804 and intensified during the War of 1812. In 1862 the cave was purchased by two Atlanta druggists. Josiah Gorgas, head of the Confederate Ordnance Department, created the Nitre Bureau under Isaac M. St. John. The government tested caves across the Confederacy and found this to be one of the best. On May 31, 1862, the works here were impressed and the owners paid $28,500.

This soon became the largest Confederate niter works, producing one thousand pounds of salt crystals a day. A thirty-man work crew, many of them slaves, worked two windlasses and twelve buckets to lift dirt to the surface. Water was run through the dirt in settling troughs; boiling left the crystals exposed. The facility consisted of one house, six shanties, a kitchen, an office, and three work sheds. Other caves were mined in Cherokee and Chattooga Counties. Federals destroyed the works on May 18, 1864. The cave, operated commercially for a time, was a picnic site early in the twentieth century for

Ruins of the old stone mill beside the Euharlee covered bridge mark the center of a local historical park.

many locals and tourists, and a dance hall was briefly popular. The cave is marked by a descriptive sign but was closed to the public and fenced in 1983 because of vandalism. Organized cave exploration groups mount occasional tours. The walls are marked with hundreds of carved names of visitors, including Col. William T. Wofford of the Eighteenth Georgia, and vertical slashes that recorded production. There are manmade tunnels, and waste rock litters the floor. Fossilized bones dating back ten thousand years have been found.

Several fine antebellum plantation homes with Civil War histories can be found along Robert Stiles Road off Euharlee Road northeast of and overlooking the scenic Etowah River on heights near Euharlee. Valley View was the headquarters of the Union occupation commander, Gen. George W. Schofield, who remained for three months. Area lore has the iron balcony railing sent to Cooper's Iron Foundry for use in making bullets (unlikely), and the piano was used as a trough.

On May 23, 1864, while camped near Etowah Cliffs at the William H. Stiles house, Union Gen. Milo S. Hascall wrote to Sherman describing the "wanton destruction of private property and works of art" committed by Federal soldiers. It was a common practice, as he had seen half a dozen grand homes burning at one time in the neighborhood.

Popular myth claims that while Sherman was attending West Point, he courted and was rejected by Cecelia Stovall, mistress of Shelman Heights (which burned in 1911) when the Union army passed

through the area. She was not at home, but when Sherman discovered that this was her property, he ordered that the home not be burned. Stories of these mansions, present and vanished, can be read in Medora F. Perkerson's *White Columns in Georgia.* Enjoy the tales, but beware the romantic legends.

Return to GA 113 on Covered Bridge Road past Stilesboro and turn left onto 113 at 3.4, toward Cartersville. At 5 miles take GA 61 south (right) to Dallas.

Schofield and Thomas advanced on parallel roads to Dallas; Schofield via Sligh's Mill (where he camped one night) to Burnt Hickory, and Thomas in the center to Burnt Hickory on a more westerly route. Following McPherson's wide sweep to the west toward Dallas can be an interesting side trip. Follow county roads west of Euharlee to Taylorsville and Aragon, GA 101 to Rockmart and Van Wert, U.S. 278-GA 6 to Yorkville atop Dugdown Mountain, and east on 278-6 into Dallas.

Notice the rough nature of the countryside, rolling hills interspersed with farms. In 1864 the roads were narrow tracks, and Sherman's men suffered miserably trudging through the sparsely settled wilderness.

At 5 miles is the site of Sligh's Tanyard, where Schofield camped for a night, and at 3.3 Burnt Hickory (the present community of Huntsville), named for a tree accidentally set afire that blazed for days, amazing the locals and becoming a landmark. Gold was mined in three area creeks. Federal troops demolished Mount Moriah Baptist Church for materials to bridge Pumpkinvine Creek.

Here Federal armies turned southeast to New Hope Church. That route no longer exists, so continue into Dallas. At 7.5 miles in Dallas turn left onto GA 6. The courthouse is ahead on the right, a Confederate monument on the left.

Gen. John A. Logan held the extreme Union right at Dallas; William J. Hardee comprised the extreme Confederate left around Ray Mountain. On May 28, 1864, expecting Sherman to shift troops from his right to his left to outflank the Confederates, Johnston ordered an attack against the Federal lines at Dallas by Brig. Gen. Joseph M. Lewis's Orphan Brigade, hoping to catch them as they withdrew. The Union troops, however, were still strongly entrenched, and

105

in three futile attacks the Orphan Brigade suffered 600 casualties to 380 Federals lost.

The Dallas battlefield, along Old U.S. 278 just southeast of Dallas, survived intact until the summer of 1995 when much of it was bulldozed and the soil trucked away as filler for a shopping center. The property had earthworks and was thought to contain the graves of more than three hundred Confederates who had made the futile assault. The site will be developed for commercial purposes or apartments; however, twenty acres, which contain trenches that the Orphan Brigade occupied at the eastern edge of Dallas days before the fatal attack, have recently been saved from development. Plans for historical interpretation are being formulated.

Just south of Dallas, on the eastern side of Academy Drive off Hardee Street, is the grave of an unknown Confederate soldier. He was probably killed during the futile attempt to turn the Federal flank and was buried in the Morris family cemetery. Sherman's headquarters during operations around Dallas was the Henderson house on East Memorial Drive.

The Paulding County Museum (295 North Johnston Street, 770-505-3488) has been established in a building designated by the state as the town's first

Map 14: New Hope Church and Pickett's Mill

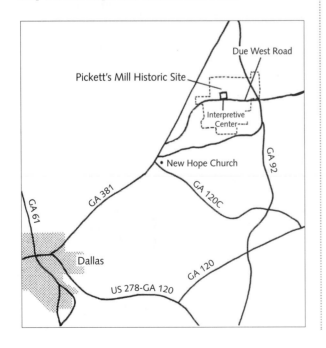

This structure marks the site of the original New Hope Church.

school in 1860. It saw use as a hospital during the Union occupation.

At .3 take a sharp left on GA 381 to New Hope; the main highway (GA 6) curves right.

To the right on the outskirts of town are the peaks of Ray's Mountain and Ellsberry Mountain, part of the long Confederate line at Dallas that was never attacked. Johnston maintained observation stations on the peaks. The Confederate works crossed the highway just west of New Hope Church and again farther east.

At 3.3 turn right to New Hope Church, the wooden one on the west side of the road.

This is the site of one of the bloodiest battles of the Atlanta campaign. The defenders were A. P. Stewart's division of Hood's corps, primarily Georgians from Brig. Gen. Marcellus A. Stovall's brigade; the attackers were from Joseph Hooker's corps. The original New Hope Church, a log structure, stood across the highway at the site of the stone store. The church burned during the war, was rebuilt, and burned again. The battle occurred just north of the church, with some of Hood's men firing from behind gravestones in the cemetery. A number of Confederates are buried there in several mass graves, including seventeen unknown soldiers beneath a tall marker. Some of the older stones bear scars from the battle. In 1999 the Sons of Confederate Veterans erected a monument for 2d Lt. Benjamin W. Pickett of the First Georgia Cavalry, killed at Chickamauga in September 1863, less than a year before the war enveloped his family's farm and mill several miles from here. Comrades sent his saddle, boots, gold pocket watch, pistols, shotgun, and coat to his widow.

Behind this modern church, shaded by oaks and pine trees, is the grave of Lt. Col. John Herrod of Mississippi, who died here. Behind that are two original trenches used as part of the Rebel defenses. Picture the scene of ten thousand Federals charging during a fierce thunderstorm. Five thousand Confederate rifles and several cannon turned the ground into a field of slaughter. Until recently a small historic park, established by the Gen. William Hardee Camp, Sons of Confederate Veterans, was behind the church. It consisted of a small marble Georgia Historical Commission commemorative monument to the battle, a short sidewalk, and a pole for a Confederate flag, all enclosed by a wooden rail fence. However, after twenty years the church ordered the park removed. Bobo Road separates the two churches here, and .7 miles south on it is the site of the William Wigley house, Johnston's headquarters from May 26 to June 1; the house no longer stands.

Directly across Bobo Road, behind the Baptist church, is the last Atlanta campaign station, a small, raised monument. This memorial has only a marker and relief map explaining Johnston's interception of Sherman on the Dallas line, the two-week stalemate here, and Sherman's ultimate success in flanking Johnston out of Dallas and regaining the railroad before Johnston's new Brushy Mountain Line and later Kennesaw Mountain Line. Beside the highway

in front of the Baptist church is a WPA marker erected in 1936 to honor all the soldiers, Northern and Southern, who served at New Hope Church.

The Georgia Battlefield Association has purchased five acres of the New Hope Church battlefield around a wooden ravine called the Hell Hole, and the Atlanta History Center owns fourteen acres in this rapidly developing area. Hopefully, these acres will be developed as a state preserve with parking and interpretive signs, which would be a welcome accompaniment to Pickett's Mill State Park. Portions of the battlefield have already been destroyed.

Four miles to the north on GA 381, at the community of Roxana, was the intersection of the Dallas-Acworth and Burnt Hickory roads. Hood and Hardee marched past there on May 24 to meet Sherman at New Hope and Dallas, and on June 5 McPherson moved from Dallas to outflank the right side of the Confederate line and break the stalemate.

Turn right onto GA 381–Dallas-Acworth Highway. After .3 turn right onto Due West Road. After 1.4 turn left onto Mount Tabor Church Road at the sign for Pickett's Mill State Park. Turn right into Pickett's Mill. The parking area for the visitors center is reached after .9.

Stymied at New Hope Church on May 27, Sherman ordered an attack against the Confederate right, and George H. Thomas selected Oliver O. Howard's Fourth Corps for the assault. The march, however, was delayed, and it was midday before Howard believed he had reached Johnston's right. The Federals were slowed by dismounted Confederate cavalry

Part of the Confederate trenches around New Hope Church (left), and a WPA monument (right) honors the men who fought here.

and Johnston detected the Union move. Patrick Cleburne, of Hardee's corps, prepared ten thousand men to meet the threat. They occupied a ridge overlooking a steep ravine, with two 12-pounders positioned to enfilade the ravine, near Pickett's Creek.

Pickett's Mill was constructed by Malachi Pickett on Little Pumpkinvine Creek (known now as Pickett's Mill Creek) in 1832 to grind corn and wheat. His son, Benjamin Pickett, was killed at Chickamauga. His widow and four children lived near the mill but fled as war approached. Federals torched the mill after the battle.

The Pickett's Mill battlefield, which is on the National Register, is a unique Georgia historical preserve. Before the recent purchase at Resaca, it was the only Atlanta campaign battlefield owned by the state and is considered to be the best-preserved Civil War battlefield in the country, the site little disturbed since 1864. The state bought the land in parcels from 1973 until 1981 and opened the park in 1990 on 765 acres. The new visitors center features exhibits and an audiovisual program with a seventeen-minute video that explains the battle of Pickett's Mill.

The park has developed a living history program, and tours of the site are organized with the assistance of volunteer demonstrators. Authentically garbed men and women demonstrate the daily life of both Union and Confederate troops during the war, featuring surgeons, mess camps and cooking techniques, a sutler's store, firing of artillery, and infantry drills.

The terrain at Pickett's Mill is little changed and has not been developed since the war. The roads used by the troops are still in use, with the addition of a few logging roads, and many well-preserved earthworks are evident, illustrating the use of skirmish lines, reentrant lines, and primary defensive positions. Park staff, with the invaluable help of volunteers and Boy Scout troops, have improved trails, built footbridges, and cleared fields to resemble the landscape of 1864. Visitors are advised to travel light and wear good walking shoes as the tours require several hours of hiking, and the ground is moderate to steep.

Three hiking trails have been established through the park, highlighting much of the battlefield, including the Confederate battle line, the Federal attack routes, the mill site along the creek, the steep-sided ravine, miles of Confederate and Federal infantry

A Confederate banner still flies over the graves of casualties from the fighting at New Hope Church.

trenches, and earthworks that protected a four-gun battery. The trails, 1.1 to 1.7 miles in length, require one to two hours to hike and are well marked by numbered and color-coded wooden posts that indicate what direction to face.

If you must choose only one of the three trails, follow the Red Loop, at 1.7 miles the most comprehensive. It traces most of the Confederate line before descending to the creek and mill site, ascends a steep slope to the start of the Federal assault, follows the Union advance where hundreds fell, then descends into the ravine before emerging at the visitors center.

The route starts at the ravine overlook. A stream in the steep ravine literally ran red with Union blood. To the front, unprotected along the wartime road, was Brig. Gen. Hiram S. Granbury's Confederate brigade, which repulsed three Federal assaults.

Station 1 (Red Loop) was the end of Granbury's line, where he saw William B. Hazen's troops attempting to flank his exposed right. He asked Brig. Gen. Daniel C. Govan, on his left, for help, and two regiments, the Eighth and Nineteenth Arkansas, commanded by Col. G. F. Baucam stopped the threat.

Federals in the ravine below charged through thick woods (the same terrain as today) and fell upon Granbury's men. Hand-to-hand combat erupted before the Northerners were repulsed.

The clearing at Station 1 (Red Loop) was a cornfield when Hazen's Union brigade emerged from the far side to attack the Confederate rear here. Baucum stopped Hazen, and the arrival of Brig. Gen. Mark P.

Lowrey's Confederate brigade drove the Federals across the field, where they rallied and stopped the Confederate counterattack. Nevertheless, Hazen's threat had been neutralized.

The trail follows a line of works constructed by Lowrey's men after the battle at the edge of the field, which was more extensive in 1864. This is Station 2.

Station 3 is along the ravine, where Lowrey's men advanced, reaching the Union rear and threatening to encircle the Twenty-third Kentucky (U.S.), which escaped capture only by a rapid retreat.

As Hazen's men withdrew, they rallied at Station 4, a fence along the cornfield and brought the Confederate assault to a halt. At dusk two Federal brigades made a juncture here.

The Red Tour joins the Blue Tour at Station 4, site of the miller's residence, which was burned during the battle. A hand-dug well was lined with stone.

The remains of Pickett's Mill, where locals ground corn and wheat, are found at Stop 5, consisting today of a few stacks of stone. At 5 P.M. on May 27, Federal Col. B. F. Scribner advanced but was checked here in heavy fighting with Brig. Gen. John H. Kelly's dismounted Confederate cavalry firing from a hill to the rear. Some of the cavalry then crossed the creek to seize the hill in front, which allowed them to enfilade Scribner's line at the edge of a wheat field. Scribner launched a two-pronged attack against Kelly, one against the Confederate-held hill while three regiments crossed the creek. Kelly was forced to withdraw, but he had delayed the Federal attack. When Scribner reached the cornfield at 7 P.M., he was too late to assist Hazen.

The visitors center at Pickett's Mill State Park.

Station 7 features infantry trenches constructed by the Federal units that were held in reserve during the battle. After the fighting ceased, Scribner retreated to this position.

The trail ascends a hill, following a trench line to the right, to Station 8, where a second line of works was constructed at a right angle to the first. This second line served two functions—to protect the men dislodged from the primary line by a Confederate attack and to defend against enfilading fire from across the creek.

The trail to the next portion of the tour is lined with Federal earthworks to the left. At 4:30 P.M. Hazen assembled his first attack at Station 9, and two solid lines of infantry stepped off through the woods. The attack was meant to be made by the entire division, but only Hazen initially advanced. After Hazen's repulse, the brigades of Cols. William H. Gibson and Frederick Knefler followed, one at a time. The piecemeal attack was defeated in detail.

Station 10 illustrates Hazen's trenches, which stretched continuously for three-quarters of a mile.

At Station 11 Hazen's second line, after losing sight of the first line in the wilderness, veered left, crossing the ravine and climbing a hill before engaging the Confederates in the cornfield.

Station 12 marks the opposite end of Granbury's ridgetop line. The Federals were situated across the ravine, which has steep slopes on each side. Hazen's men topped the hill and plunged down the slope, reformed in the relative safety at the bottom, then charged uphill into a devastating fire at short range, briefly engaging in hand-to-hand combat. Hazen was thrown back, and the action was played twice again as Gibson then Knefler, at dusk, threw their brigades against the Confederate line. The wounded and other survivors crowded at the bottom of the ravine.

At Station 13 is the position held in succession by Hazen, Gibson, and Knefler. Granbury, reinforced by Edward C. Walthall's brigade, held the ridge ahead. To the right front were two Confederate cannon, under Capt. Thomas Key, which poured canister into the Federals. Many of the Union dead carpeted this area—one tree displayed two hundred scars from bullets. At 10 P.M., hearing Federals still in the ravine, Granbury attacked in the dark, capturing 250 prisoners and forcing Knefler to retreat.

Return to the visitors center.

A Civil War–era road snakes through Pickett's Mill State Park.

The Blue Loop (1.5 miles) explores the center of the Confederate line, the creek and mill ruins, the initial Union position and advance route, and the ravine. The only significant site not included on the Red Tour is Station 3, the hilltop on which Kelly's dismounted Confederate cavalry fought. Rifle pits utilized by his men are still visible.

The White Loop (1.1 miles) examines the left side of the Confederate line, the initial Union position, and the attack into the ravine and up the opposite slope. Unique here is Station 1, a road junction that was the site of the two Confederate 12-pounder howitzers that raked the ravine, protected by Brig. Gen. Daniel C. Govan's brigade positioned in the wheat field. Station 2 explains the Confederate trenches, started as rifle pits before the attack then deepened and connected to form a continuous line that started at New Hope Church and extended five miles to the east. This is the original Civil War road, part of it sunken due to long use.

Station 3 marks the scene of a scouting expedition personally led by Howard. Observing Rebels digging rifle pits, he decided this was the Confederate flank and ordered the attack. Howard remained ignorant of the ravine, which impeded his assault. The three Union attacks extended into the wheat field here, but they were battered by ten Confederate guns.

One reason for the Federal failure was the lack of artillery support. After the assault, guns were brought forward. That night four horseshoe-shaped pits were constructed to protect a Union battery, which fired at Confederate artillery the following day. Those earthworks are at Station 5.

In the two-hour contest, 4:30 to 6:30 P.M., the Federals suffered seventeen hundred casualties of fourteen thousand engaged. The Confederates lost five hundred of ninety-six hundred men.

From the entrance to Pickett's Mill Historic Site, turn left onto Mount Tabor Church Road. At Due West Road turn left and start your mileage. At the stop sign after 1.8 turn left onto Dallas-Acworth Highway for .1 then right back onto the Due West Road, which was a wartime road.

After crossing Mars Hill Road, Lost Mountain is visible through gaps in the trees to the right, or south. A dirt road runs through the woods along its western base and well-preserved earthworks remain, but the summit is inaccessible. Polk passed the mountain on his way to Dallas-New Hope Church on May 23–24, then held the left, western anchor of the Brushy Mountain Line here in early June, although little fighting occurred. There are plans for placing interpretive markers here and perhaps preserving the fine view of Kennesaw Mountain and the surrounding historic countryside.

The famed Lost Mountain Store (1881), at the crossroads of the Marietta-Dallas Highway and Mars Hill Road, had been threatened with destruction by the massive development occurring in Cobb County, but the solid brick structure was moved a short distance, restored, and incorporated into a shopping center that swallowed its original location as a bank branch. The venerable landmark was constructed in 1881 by local landlord A. Lafayette Bartlett. When he was thirteen, Union troops burned his home and he became a Confederate spy, slipping in and out of Union lines. Local legend claims that he was captured, sentenced to death, and rescued by Confederate scouts. The building was once a stagecoach stop.

At the traffic light after 4.9 continue straight onto Kennesaw–Due West Road. Turn left into the small parking lot at a section of restored earthworks near the former site of Gilgal Church.

6

Stalemate and Slaughter

BIG SHANTY WOULD BE the Federal supply base for June. Sherman established his headquarters in the top of a cotton gin on the edge of town. From there he could see Kennesaw Mountain, the central peak of a low range of hills that barred his advance to Marietta.

"Kennesaw, the bold and striking twin mountain, lay before me," he wrote. "To our right, Pine Mountain, and behind it in the distance, Lost Mountain. On each of these peaks the enemy had his signal stations. The summits were crowned with batteries, and the spurs were alive with men busy in felling trees, digging pits, and preparing for the grand struggle impending. The scene was enchanting, too beautiful to be disturbed by the harsh clamor of war, but the Chattahoochee lay beyond, and I had to reach it."

Despite heavy fighting in the month-old campaign, troop strength remained stable. Sherman had suffered 10 percent losses since leaving Chattanooga, but on June 8 he received 9,000 men, two infantry divisions and a cavalry brigade under Gen. Francis F. Blair from Alabama. These men were added to James B. McPherson's command, and the Union army now mustered 113,000. Johnston had lost 6 percent of his manpower but welcomed 6,000 additional men. Soldiers in both armies were much encouraged by the arrival of reinforcements.

Sherman believed Kennesaw Mountain would be the center of a heavily fortified line, and he knew there would be some serious fighting before he reached it. The country before Kennesaw consisted of thickly wooded hills and ridges broken by steep ravines and creeks swollen by three weeks of heavy rain. The few existing roads were impassable muddy tracks, and Johnston's crafty band of veterans had turned the countryside into a

111

fortress. Sherman would probe, feint, and fight his way to Kennesaw Mountain in a series of battles that would last a week.

On June 10 the Federal commander dispatched his cavalry south to identify the first Confederate line, and his entire army followed close behind. By the next day he had uncovered the Brushy Mountain Line, an interconnected maze of infantry trenches and artillery batteries that Johnston prepared after withdrawing from Dallas. The Rebels were again patiently waiting for the Yankees to come to them.

Johnston's right, defended by John Bell Hood, and the flank beyond, which was protected by Joseph Wheeler's cavalry, lay across the railroad to the east at Brushy Mountain. It extended west for ten miles across Pine Mountain, which William J. Hardee held in the center, and ended at Lost Mountain on the western end, Leonidas Polk's responsibility. Polk's flank was held by William Jackson's cavalry. McPherson slid down the railroad to oppose Hood; George H. Thomas pressed against the Confederate center at Pine Mountain; and John M. Schofield closed on Polk around Lost Mountain. This line, anchored by the three hills, was not intended to fend off Sherman's massive advance permanently. Johnston admitted that it was "much too long for our strength"; Sherman humorously commented, "I suppose the enemy, with his smaller forces, intends to surround us."

The Confederates benefited from the torrential rains that continued to fall, forcing Sherman to alter his strategy. The ground was too boggy for maneuvering his superior numbers around Johnston, so Sherman determined to press forward and find weak spots where he could break through Johnston's thinly held front. He hoped Johnston would submit to a fair fight on this ground, but his opponent was too wise to allow that. Johnston contracted and strengthened his line in response to Sherman's pressure.

Johnston, the master of defense, had chosen his field perfectly. The heights offered such a sweeping view of the area that he was immediately aware of Sherman's movements and could effectively counter them. The Federals were forced to move slowly and exercise extreme caution, inching forward under successive lines of trenches while engaged in sharp, continuous combat. "Not a day, not an hour, not a minute was there a cessation of fire," Sherman wrote. Conditions required him to convert his cavalry into dismounted infantry for use in what he termed "desultory fighting."

In 1844 Sherman had ridden across this countryside and up to the crest of Kennesaw Mountain several times. Remembering the potential defensive strength of the terrain, he swore, "I will not run head on against his fortifications." Yet the situation continued to aggravate his always volatile emotions. As each day passed with inconclusive skirmishing, Sherman grew impatient and so evil-tempered that subordinates avoided him to escape his frequently severe rebukes. The Federal commander restlessly paced his lines and smoked one cigar after another in nervous agitation. His troops were equally edgy and depressed by the nerve-wracking forest fighting. Every forward movement became a furious firefight with Confederate sharpshooters sniping from behind rocks and trees. Scurvy plagued the troops, and the dismal weather turned minor wounds gangrenous. A common belief developed that the heavy cannonades had rent the heavens and caused the constant downpours.

The Confederates constructed log-reinforced earthworks as fast as the Federals could root them out of their previous trenches. The bulwarks were so obscured by brush that "we cannot see them until we receive a sudden and deadly fire," Sherman reported. The Yankees were forced to protect themselves in like manner, which further slowed their progress. "As he [Johnston] did, so did we," a Federal general claimed. "No regiment was long in front of Johnston's Army without having virtually as good a breast-work as an engineer could plan."

Pine Mountain, a large, conical knoll with a heavy growth of timber on its steep slopes, was the highest point on the Confederate forward line when Thomas advanced from Mars Hill Church on June 10. His initial probes revealed that Pine Mountain was a salient, a formidable redoubt located a mile north of the main Rebel line. The base was ringed with a double row of infantry trenches that protected artillery batteries posted on the summit. The mountain was held by William B. Bates's division of Hardee's corps and supported by the famed Washington Artillery of New Orleans.

The Confederates cleared fields of fire by chopping down countless trees on Pine Mountain, and the logs strengthened their trenches and supplied chevaux-de-frise for defense against assault. As the Federals approached, they felled more trees to use in their protection against the deadly, accurate fire from the mountain. At Dallas and Kennesaw the sound of axes was more common than gunfire.

The Fighting Bishop ■ Leonidas Polk

Leonidas Polk was born into a prosperous North Carolina family in 1806. He had intended to follow a military career, but only six months after graduating from West Point in 1827, he resigned his commission to enter the ministry. He soon became an Episcopal priest and served throughout the South and Southwest, becoming the bishop of Louisiana in 1841 and helping to found the University of the South (Sewanee) in 1861. Jefferson Davis was a year behind Polk at the U.S. Military Academy, and Davis was somewhat starstruck with Polk and several other upperclassmen, which included Albert Sidney Johnston.

When the war began, Davis offered Polk a major general's commission and a post in the West, which the bishop accepted. Polk participated in all the momentous battles of the Army of Tennessee. While his courage was never questioned, his military aptitude was frequently disparaged. After Polk failed to attack at Chickamauga, Braxton Bragg threatened to dismiss him from command and court-martial him. Davis's patronage saved his career and, ironically, sealed the general's doom.

In June 1864, in the company of Joseph E. Johnston and William J. Hardee, Polk observed the movement of Sherman's army from Pine Mountain. Sherman, however, took exception to the reconnaissance of the generals and ordered a battery to fire on the distant figures. The portly, dignified Polk refused to hurry to safety, and a shell struck and killed him instantly.

Polk had been a stubborn and sometimes inept general, but he had been greatly loved by his troops. He had imparted a sense of decency and morality to the soldiers, and even the leaders of the army had been favorably affected by his presence. While Polk's loss was less than "irreparable" to the cause, as Davis lamented, his inglorious death was a symbol of the South's overall declining fortunes.

Rain hampered the Federal advance, and it was not until the morning of June 14 that Union pincers were threatening to isolate Pine Mountain from the Confederate line. Three Federal corps advanced north, south, and west of the salient while artillery softened its works. That day dawned clear. The ground began to dry somewhat as Johnston, Hardee, Polk, and Bates rode to the summit of Pine Mountain to observe the Yankee movements and weigh whether the position should be abandoned. Standing above the forward parapets, Hardee pointed out the danger of his post's being surrounded, which would cause the loss of valuable infantry and cannon. Johnston, seeing the enemy only half a mile away, was convinced the post should be evacuated after dark.

Ironically, Sherman was at the front prodding his generals when he noticed a cluster of men, obviously officers, watching his operations before "Pine Top." Irked that his maneuvers were being so casually observed— "How saucy they are," he commented—Sherman ordered a nearby battery to lob a few shells at the crest to force the men to take cover. Oliver O. Howard, the divisional commander, demurred, explaining that Thomas had issued directions to conserve ammunition. "Fire anyway," the irate Sherman snapped.

As the first shot screamed overhead and burrowed into the parapet, Johnston, Hardee, and Bates scurried for cover. The dignified, corpulent Polk walked casually toward the trenches, calmly watching the cannon firing at him from below. The second shell hit him squarely in the chest, tearing out his lungs and killing him instantly. Johnston and the others raced to the bishop's side. Weeping, Johnston muttered, "I would rather anything than this." In Polk's pockets he found three books of spiritual guidance that were inscribed as gifts for Johnston, Hood, and Hardee.

Down on the plains, Sherman wondered who he had just killed, a question that was quickly answered. His signal officers had broken the Confederate cipher and could decode messages flashed between Rebel stations. The Federal commander was soon informed that an intercepted signal from Pine Mountain to Kennesaw Mountain read, "Send an ambulance for Polk's body."

As a religious figure, Polk had aroused controversy in the North for taking up arms; many felt he had received his due. Sherman's laconic report on the following day read, "We killed General Polk yesterday, and have made good progress today."

During the night, the Confederates withdrew to their main line a mile south. When Federals occupied Pine Mountain at daybreak, a Northern newspaper reporter found a crudely lettered sign attached to a broken ramrod: "You Yankee sons of bitches have killed our old General Polk."

To the grieving army Johnston delivered a eulogy for their fallen leader. "You are called upon to mourn your first Captain, your oldest comrade-in-arms. In this distinguished leader we have lost the most courteous of gentlemen, the most gallant of soldiers. This Christian patriot has neither

LESLIE'S ILLUSTRATED

Joseph Hooker's men assault and occupy Lost Mountain on June 16, 1864.

lived nor died in vain. His example is before you; his mantle rests with you." The Confederate commander added that "in every battle he had distinguished himself," a genteel misstatement uttered for the troops' benefit.

Polk's body was carried to the Marietta depot for transportation by rail to Atlanta, where on the following day the largest funeral Atlanta witnessed during the war was held at St. Luke's Episcopal Church. The reality and nearness of battle were revealed to the thousands of Atlantans who wept over the coffin.

Polk's death was not a significant military loss to Johnston. The bishop had been awarded great devotion and respect by his men, who were saddened by his death, but Polk's officers regarded him as a harmless and ineffectual commander. He had given both Braxton Bragg and Johnston considerable grief, and his greatest contribution had been in influencing many Louisiana men to serve the Confederacy when he joined the Southern cause in 1861.

Johnston appointed William W. Loring temporary commander of the Army of the Mississippi, and the grinding combat continued unabated. The Federals occupied Pine Mountain, but behind it Kennesaw rose like a fist in defiant challenge.

With Pine Mountain lost, Johnston began to shorten his line west and north of Kennesaw during the following week. The primary weakness of the position was the proximity of the Chattahoochee River to his rear. Mindful that he might be forced to abandon Kennesaw, Johnston ordered his

Pickets atop Lost Mountain face a seemingly peaceful dawn.

chief military engineer, Francis A. Shoup, to prepare two lines of field forti-fications between Kennesaw and the river, one at Smyrna, another on the north bank of the river itself. Shoup hired one thousand slaves from local planters to build the works. If he had to retreat, Johnston would not allow Sherman to trap and destroy him against the Chattahoochee.

The people of Atlanta grew increasingly concerned over the approach-ing conflict, which seemed to creep closer each day. The mayor declared a day of prayer and fasting, and a newspaper headline proclaimed, OUR CITY IS IN A STATE OF SIEGE.

With the capture of Pine Mountain, the center of the Confederate fine was revealed before Thomas, and Schofield began probing the Rebel left, anchored on Lost Mountain. It was a natural bastion that allowed the defend-ers to observe approaching troops and greet them with damaging fire.

On May 24 Polk had marched past Lost Mountain on his way to Dallas from Allatoona, and on June 4 he had withdrawn from the Dallas line and established a position here, while William Jackson's cavalry covered the extreme southern left, southwest of the mountain. On the night of June 9, Johnston transferred Polk to the peaks of Big and Little Kennesaw, and Jackson assumed the defense of Lost Mountain.

On June 15 and 16 George Stoneman's cavalry drove off the Confeder-ate cavalry screen in front of the mountain and penetrated between Lost Mountain and the primary Confederate line behind it at Gilgal Church. This action threatened to separate Lost Mountain from the rest of the army; so Jackson was forced to abandon it. He fought a spirited rear-guard clash as Johnston's line was again contracted, this time to a position behind Mud

Creek. In the skirmishes for this strongpoint, the Federals suffered 300 casualties, the Rebels 150.

While possession of Lost Mountain was being challenged, elements of Schofield's army assailed the main Confederate works at Gilgal. On June 15 Hardee's men were driven from a line of rifle pits and scampered over several thinly wooded ridges in a running skirmish, then they dropped into prepared trenches and log barricades at Gilgal. A determined assault late in the afternoon was decimated by the protected Southern infantry and artillery, leading Schofield to stop and entrench a line parallel to Hardee. Howard reported gallant fighting all along the line that day, which cost the Federals 500 casualties to Hardee's 150.

On June 16 Schofield positioned his artillery on high ground to sweep the Rebel defenses and roads leading to the rear, so Johnston withdrew his men from Gilgal and Lost Mountain that night. The left portion of the Confederate line swung back like a hinged door to a readied position behind Mud Creek, forming an angle to the north at the Latimer place, where it joined the existing Confederate trenches behind Pine Mountain.

Schofield was at his best, alertly observing the Confederate withdrawal and following swiftly. At the new Rebel line, one division of Union soldiers maintained a rapid fire that forced the defenders to keep their heads down while other Federals quickly dug in only four hundred yards from the Confederate works. One Union brigade made a reckless charge that carried a Southern skirmish line and captured many prisoners. A second brigade occupied a Confederate position, lost it to a savage counterattack, then retook it in the wake of a hot barrage from rifles and cannon.

Schofield quickly brought up his heavy guns and placed them on a ridge overlooking the Confederate position across Mud Creek. In the close-range artillery duel that followed, the Federal guns were brilliantly served.

The Long Arm ■ Artillery

Field artillery changed little since the early 1800s. Most cannon were bronze Napoleons, muzzle-loading smoothbores of 1840s vintage, but there were several types of heavy guns. The average range was around seventeen hundred yards. Each weapon weighed around two thousand pounds and was mounted on stout, horse-drawn carriages. Ammunition was carried in an accompanying limber.

An artillery battery commonly consisted of six guns with a crew of as many as 150 men. Confederate batteries might have no more than four guns and smaller crews, with several men performing multiple jobs. The guns were extremely mobile and could be moved quickly by teams of six horses per gun.

Smoothbores were inaccurate at long range, but the guns could throw six- to twelve-pound solid iron balls into advancing infantry with deadly effect. Over the course of the war, rifled tubes were introduced, and accuracy and range improved proportionally.

The gunners had an assortment of ammunition. As the enemy approached within eight hundred yards, batteries fired case shot—hollow balls filled with a small powder charge that exploded and spewed deadly lead pellets into the charging troops.

At three hundred yards the gunners switched to canister—thin-walled tin containers packed with iron balls that spread out like a shotgun blast and cleared lanes through advancing enemy soldiers.

When a battery was close to being overrun, bundles of large, solid shot were thrust into the muzzles. Upon firing, the balls immediately sprayed out to destroy anyone in front of the battery. In times of extreme danger, crews would fire two loads of canister, or grape, at once.

Rates of fire varied. In general the guns fired one round every two minutes; in practice and under combat conditions, the gunners usually managed two shots a minute, or more if using canister.

Confederates manhandle their artillery up Kennesaw Mountain.

Two Confederate cannon were blown over, two disabled, and the crews of the rest scattered. John W. Geary proudly wrote that his men "opened a rapid and accurate fire [that] produced great havoc among the enemy's works and guns."

Cleburne's men endured a terrible pounding from the massed batteries, and his own cannon were unable to return fire. One shell seriously injured Gen. Lucius E. Polk, nephew of the bishop. The wound, his fourth, forced Polk to retire from military service.

On June 18 rain stalled all offensive operations, and Geary's infantry spent a miserable day in the swollen creek bed. That night Cleburne was instructed to fall back, an order he was relieved to obey after holding an untenable position for forty-eight hours.

Geary recorded that Confederate snipers had hidden in trees across Mud Creek, and his sharpshooters knocked several out of their "elevated hiding place." Other Confederates cut bushes and placed them in their belts, effective camouflage, Geary said, which on a "dark, misty day, rendered them almost indistinguishable." The Confederates had become expert at this style of fighting.

Just north of Mud Creek was the center of Johnston's original line at the Latimer place, also know as Hardee's Salient. It was held by Samuel G. French's division against twice as many Federals under Howard's command. The Yankees made a quick thrust on the night of June 17 that forced Confederate pickets to sprint for safety to avoid capture, and Howard occupied the Confederate outer works. The Federals brought up their artillery to the north and west of the line and dropped shells down the length of the Rebel trenches. There was no defense against this brutal enfilading fire that pinned down the Confederate troops. Realizing that a major Union assault would rupture the entire line, Johnston evacuated it and withdrew to another prepared position two miles south: the famous Kennesaw Mountain Line.

After successfully crossing Mud Creek, Sherman decided to concentrate on forcing the western end of Johnston's position. Since there had been little action between McPherson and Hood to the east around the railroad and Brushy Mountain, he shifted McPherson west to face Loring opposite Kennesaw Mountain. Thomas moved farther south but remained in the center, opposing Hardee, and Schofield and Hooker slid southwest beyond the Confederate line in an attempt to flank Johnston out of Kennesaw Mountain and precipitate a hazardous retreat to the Chattahoochee barrier.

Schofield advanced on the Sandtown Road in a long and muddy march from Lost Mountain against Jackson's stubborn cavalry. The Federals reached flooded Nose's Creek at dark on June 19, forded it the following day, and drove off Rebel skirmishers guarding the opposite bank. On June 21 Schofield rebuilt the bridges and resumed his slow, methodical advance to Olley's Creek.

Seeing this threatening development, Johnston ordered Hood's three divisions to march through the night from Brushy Mountain and establish a line that would stem the dangerous Union sidestep. Arriving from his swing behind Loring and Hardee, Hood initially faced his men in the wrong direction. After discovering the error and correcting his deployment, Hood decided to attack and turn the Federal right flank, unaware that he was facing the center of a strongly held line.

On the morning of June 22, Hooker occupied a ridge near Valentine Kolb's farm, with Schofield guarding his right flank. He had fourteen thousand infantrymen distributed on a one-and-a-half-mile-long line. For support forty pieces of artillery were emplaced on high ground with excellent fields of fire. Hooker then ordered two regiments to skirmish as far south as possible and warn him of approaching enemy forces. For several hours they chased their Confederate counterparts across creeks, hills, and fields, springing between cover and firing sporadically. The Confederates finally dropped into a line of rifle pits, and the Union advance ground to a halt.

Late in the morning Federal skirmishers captured thirty Rebels and hustled them to the rear for interrogation. Hooker was surprised by Hood's sudden appearance and disturbed to learn the aggressive field commander was preparing an immediate assault. Familiar with Hood's fearsome reputation from the Virginia battlefields, Hooker ordered his men to dig in. Federal soldiers abandoned their berry-picking in the pleasant summer sunshine and hurriedly dismantled fences for barricades and scooped out shallow holes from which to fight. Artillery crews cleared their guns for action.

In front of Hooker the Federal skirmishers watched apprehensively as eleven thousand Confederates formed three long lines for battle. When the Rebels advanced, the Northerners ran like foxes for the security of their own lines. Hooker's forces held their fire until the men sped past, then at a range of five hundred yards his batteries opened a brutal fire on the steadily approaching Confederate ranks.

At the battle of Kolb's farm, the artillery work became legendary. Forty crews served their guns as if they were part of the weapons themselves. Like enormous shotguns, canister spewed deadly iron balls into the air, shredding men instantly and cutting lanes into their formation; case shot timed to explode in the air above the Confederate ranks sent hails of iron shrapnel raining down onto vulnerable men; solid shot bounced wildly across the uneven ground, smashing bodies, breaking limbs, and severing heads with sickening thuds. The crews fell into a well-trained rhythm— load, fire, load, fire—alternating canister, case, and solid shot, volley after volley, often discharging double loads. When the Confederates drew close to the Federal line, they were exposed to a maelstrom of ninety artillery rounds a minute blazing from front and flank.

Federal infantry opened fire at two hundred yards, and the plucky Southerners reeled from the hurricane of destruction. Hundreds fell, but the remainder staggered forward through the gale of hissing shot, firing at their antagonists but unable to pause and reload in such a dangerously exposed position. The decimated Confederates courageously charged to within thirty-five yards of the Union line then broke under the debilitating fire and ran for the safety of a ravine where they regrouped and gallantly mounted other attacks, each time with fewer men.

The slaughter was so appalling that many Confederates surrendered on the field to escape certain death. Federal officers quickly snapped orders not to fire on the Rebels approaching their lines to give up. Stouter Southerners remained pinned down, hugging the ground for the little shelter it offered or huddling behind fence rails, tree stumps, and in pits they hastily scratched out of the earth with bare hands. Withdrawing in the face of such awful fire was tantamount to suicide.

Union soldiers later declared that if Hooker had taken the initiative and ordered a counterattack, the entire Confederate force would have been destroyed or captured. Hooker, however, believed he was weathering the brunt of a major assault by the entire Confederate army. Instead of sallying forth to annihilate Hood's weakened corps, Hooker ordered his men to dig in and wait for another attack—which never materialized.

During the night, surviving Confederates crawled to the sanctuary of their lines a mile south, dragging wounded comrades with them. In the dark hours the exhausted Federals were tormented by the haunting wails and moans from the dying. Unable to offer assistance until dawn, some imagined they could see the contorted faces of men pleading for their mothers or awaiting the release of death.

At dawn Union burial parties went about the grim work. They discovered Confederate bodies piled like cordwood, up to a dozen corpses huddled in ditches or crouched behind trees, many dismembered by grapeshot. Of the fifty-three hundred men who participated in the assault, eleven hundred fell. Federal casualties totaled three hundred. Hospitals in Marietta were flooded with the wounded from this single engagement, and the overflow was treated on the grounds of the courthouse, which was used as an open operating theater. Many considered it a miracle that five Southern brothers in the attack not only survived this battle but returned home safely after the war.

"Fighting Joe" Hooker, as he was known in better times, had won an impressive victory. In the year since his shattering defeat at Chancellorsville and subsequent removal from command of the Army of the Potomac, he had become skittish. Still anticipating another thrust from Hood, he sent a message to Sherman informing him of the battle and resultant Rebel losses and expressing apprehension about his right flank, adding, "Three entire corps are in front of us." Sherman, who disliked Hooker and had little confidence in him, was infuriated by the dispatch. He answered that Johnston's entire army consisted of only three corps, so he asked how they could all be massed in front of Hooker. Furthermore, Schofield was conscientiously guarding the flank in question. The inferred criticism invoked Sherman's harshest rebuke, and he severely scolded "Fighting Joe," who sulked. "Hooker was ever after incensed at Sherman" for the reprimand, Oliver O. Howard observed.

When command of an army later opened, Sherman refused to consider Hooker for the assignment, a decision that led Hooker to resign angrily from the army and seek a political career. Sherman welcomed his departure. Hooker is primarily (and wrongly) remembered for the freedom extended to female camp followers in his units, which is commonly thought to have originated the slang term for prostitutes, *hookers.*

On the Confederate side, Johnston found considerably stronger reasons for castigating Hood over his blundering in the action. Hood was censured for launching an impetuous, poorly planned, and hastily organized assault with no reconnaissance and without the knowledge or permission of his commanding officer. Hood also neglected to report the calamitous results of his ill-advised foray to Johnston. The stunning loss was senseless,

Pickets in front of Kennesaw Mountain exchange shots.

Johnston argued, a sentiment echoed by one of Hood's brigade commanders, who wrote after the battle that Hood was "totally unfit for command of a corps." Hood's contemporaries averred that he was one of the war's great divisional commanders when attacking on the orders of a superior officer, but his rash personality and poor judgment were fatal flaws, rendering him unqualified to lead a corps or army.

After the war, Johnston wrote that the fighting at Kolb's farm was ended either by "the general's [Hood's] orders or by the discretion of the troops."

It probably was the latter.

Two lessons were to be learned from Kolb's farm. The first was that troops advancing in the open against a protected enemy would be slaughtered, and the second concerned the fitness of Hood for command. Tragically, both lessons went unheeded.

Johnston's final line was anchored on Kennesaw Mountain's eighteen-hundred-foot peak. His men laboriously dragged cannon up the steep, rugged slopes by hand; from the summit those guns guarded the railroad and obstructed Sherman's route to Marietta and Atlanta.

The line began at the railroad and extended west over Kennesaw Mountain, Little Kennesaw, Pigeon Hill, a ridge that would become known as Cheatham Hill, and to the flatlands beyond. Joseph Wheeler's cavalry held the railroad; William W. Loring occupied the solid center on Kennesaw; Hardee was positioned at Cheatham Hill; and Hood anchored the left, with William Jackson's cavalry extending that flank. This six-mile-long line took advantage of the natural strength offered by the mountain, ridges, and forests, and it was fortified to the point of impregnability by the addition of extensive earthworks, artillery batteries, forward rifle pits, slashings, and chevaux-de-frise. Union veterans of Gettysburg considered it a stronger position than the one they had held at Cemetery Ridge, which was a daunting thought.

Three weeks of nearly incessant rain gave immeasurable assistance to the defenders, flooding creek beds, rendering roads impassable, and hampering Sherman's favored offensive technique, the famous flanking march. While Sherman grew increasingly frustrated by the Kennesaw Line, his officers became apprehensive for the future of the campaign. Their men and animals were sick, soggy, filthy, and generally miserable. The situation before Kennesaw had developed into a strategic stalemate that only favored Johnston; the weather compounded the problem. Sherman wanted to close

Map 15: Kennesaw Mountain Battlefield

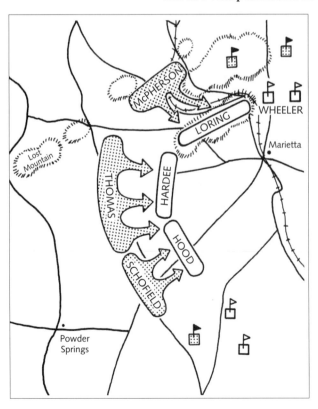

LESLIE'S ILLUSTRATED

Federal infantry and artillery try to cover their attacking comrades at Kennesaw Mountain.

with Johnston and force a decisive battle, but he admitted, "The assault would be too dear." Still, there had to be some action he could take. His memory turned to the attacks against invulnerable Lookout Mountain and Missionary Ridge seven months earlier, when his troops had unexpectedly routed the Confederates with inspired charges. Perhaps that success could be repeated.

Of the morass before Kennesaw, Sherman telegraphed Washington, "We continue to press forward on the principal of an advance against a forti- fied position. The whole country is one vast fortress, and Johnston must have fully 50 miles of connected trenches with abatis. . . . We gain ground daily fighting all the time . . . our lines are now in close contact and the fight- ing incessant with a good deal of artillery fire. As fast as we gain one posi- tion, the enemy has another all ready." Later he observed, "It was a continuous battle, lasting from June 10 to July 3," twenty-three days of con- fused combat on the Kennesaw front.

In this agitated state, Sherman began to suspect his men of having lost their desire for offensive action, a condition he blamed on trench warfare. "A fresh furrow in a ploughed field will stop the whole column, and all begin to entrench," he wrote, aiming particular venom at "Old Slow Trot"

123

Thomas. In this excited condition, Sherman considered abandoning his flanking efforts for a frontal assault on the entrenched Rebels.

"I am inclined to feint on both sides and assault the center" of the Kennesaw Line, he informed Washington. "It may cost us dearly, but in results would surpass any attempt to pass around."

Having consistently stated that he would not attack strong fortifications, Sherman justified the idea by explaining that the roads were too wet to flank. He postulated that Johnston was weary of being flanked out of successive positions and had probably strengthened the ends of his line but left the center relatively unsecured, thinking Sherman would never dare attack the forbidding trenches. By striking the weak center, Sherman believed he would split the thin gray line and destroy the two halves of the Confederate army piecemeal.

Weary of the stalemate and unable to slip around Johnston, Sherman committed his forces to one definitive battle. It would be his only rash decision of the Atlanta campaign. The Federal commander had previously stated that what occurred before Atlanta "would probably decide the fate of the Union," and he was ready to decide that fate. He also thought his soldiers were tired of the flanking tactics and desired the campaign to be determined in one final clash. The political situation in Washington also influenced Sherman's course. Lincoln desperately needed a victory, and Sherman realized he was expected to supply it.

Sherman had another reason for making the assault, a petty one that would diminish his stature as a great general. He felt he was being denied

George H. Thomas's headquarters in front of Kennesaw Mountain on July 4, 1864. Tree branches shade the tents.

a rightful share of popular attention. Grant was grabbing the headlines with his meat-grinder tactics against Lee in Virginia, and Sherman believed his successes were being unfairly overshadowed. If Sherman won a great victory, the press, which had long been hostile to him, could no longer ignore his exploits, and he would receive the publicity and adoration he rightfully deserved.

For two weeks Sherman had fought a constant and heavy skirmish action. Knowing his strength had peaked, he decided that Johnston must be finished here to put an end to the deadly chess game. "We must assail and not defend," Sherman admonished Thomas. The decision was made; the time for offensive action had arrived. The Kennesaw Line would be attacked and, hopefully, breached. The Army of Tennessee would be destroyed and Atlanta shortly captured.

In the days before the attack, Sherman commenced an artillery bombardment all along the line to soften up Confederate positions. Thomas brought 140 guns forward to pound the Rebel center, and the Confederates responded, producing a spirited artillery duel that caused little damage to either side. The Southerners soon ran low on ammunition and were ordered to conserve their fire for a full-scale assault, which Johnston could feel approaching. On the mountain, some Confederate batteries were so well targeted that during the day the positions were pounded smooth. At night the gunners would dig out their protective lunettes, and the process would begin again at dawn. The bombardment cut the forest into kindling; huge slashing splinters produced more casualties than the shelling.

Blue and gray infantry sat on their works to watch the spectacle and cheer their artillery, until an irritated enemy gunner would lob a shell at them. The men tumbled into the trenches until the shot passed, then climbed out to enjoy the show again. For three days shells screamed overhead while in the valley between the batteries the Federals continued their advance. One soldier compared the sound of constant skirmishing to a "thousand wood choppers."

Sherman was particularly irked by crowds of civilians from Atlanta who climbed Kennesaw Mountain to watch the "burrowing Yankees." After several noncombatants were killed by the shelling, Johnston forbade further casual visits. The citizens of Marietta treated the situation more seriously; their town was overrun by hundreds of wagons loaded with wounded soldiers and supplies and crowds of refugees passing south.

The Federal commander spent a week planning the assault, which would consist of two attacks, one by Thomas and the second by McPherson. Sherman's commanders were allowed to choose the men and places to attack. Thomas selected the junction of two Confederate divisions where a salient was formed and occupied by Benjamin F. Cheatham. It was enfiladed by Federal artillery that was concentrated to prepare the Rebel line for assault. McPherson chose to attack a gap between Little Kennesaw and Pigeon Hill. Schofield would not participate in the battle, but Sherman directed him to demonstrate against Hood on the day of the assault. That would prevent Hood from sending reinforcements to assist the Confederate center when the real attack opened, and it would convince Johnston his left flank was being threatened.

On June 25 Sherman issued Special Field Orders No. 25, which announced that the assault would take place at 8 A.M. on June 27. That morning broke with an ominous quiet; birds could be heard chirping in the woods. Then two hundred Federal guns opened a thunderous, hourlong bombardment of solid shot and case on the length of the Rebel position. The whole Union army advanced in a giant skirmish formation that kept the Southerners from determining the actual assaults until the last moment. Confederate guns returned fire when Federal infantry appeared, battering the troops in the valley below. Kennesaw Mountain was hammered by Yankee batteries on a ridge opposite, but this time it was gleefully answered by counterfire from the Rebels. One Southerner said, "The ground seemed to heave" under the weight of the continuous fire, while other soldiers were reminded of volcanic explosions or Niagaras of flaming fire.

Federal infantry formed a curved line two and a half miles long and probed the Southern defenses to hold the Confederates in position so they could not rush troops to the points under attack. Finding the Rebels strongly posted all along the front, they withdrew.

When the Northerners fell back at 9 A.M., Thomas charged forward with eight thousand men in five brigades to attack Cheatham Hill, three at the salient itself (soon to be called the "Dead Angle") and two a short distance farther east. The Confederates had an equal number of men defending the sector.

Thomas chose to attack with a controversial formation known as massed European infantry tactics, one of the few occasions in the Civil War where it was employed. His men advanced on a narrow front only two hundred yards wide, instead of the standard fifteen hundred yards. They were deployed in twelve closely packed ranks, a tactic designed to batter through the thin Confederate defenses, but instead they presented targets for Confederate infantry and grape-firing artillery. To make matters worse, only the front rank of Union soldiers could return the debilitating fire.

One brigade was led by Col. Daniel McCook, one of fourteen brothers and cousins famous in the Union army as the "Fighting McCooks." He recited "Horatio at the Bridge" as his men formed their columns.

The Federals scrambled from their works on a ridge opposite Cheatham Hill, and in the oppressive summer heat they bravely swept out of the woods to charge six hundred yards without cover across a wheat field. The ground was soon littered with dead and wounded as Confederate artillery tore great gaps in the ranks, which closed up and relentlessly advanced. Rebel sharpshooters took a slow, steady toll on the Yankees. At a range of one hundred yards, Confederate rifles let loose their first volley, a blast of fire and smoke that ripped the front line and stunned the Federals. Trees

Union fortifications in front of Kennesaw Mountain.

splintered from the crashing Southern fire, and one Yankee wondered if a single bird could survive a flight across the field. Men fell in appalling numbers, but those standing charged recklessly forward, taking death like "wooden men," one Confederate thought.

The Northerners rooted Confederate skirmishers out of a line of rifle pits, paused briefly at the foot of the slope to reform, then pressed up the ridge to the Confederate trenches. There they met a galling fire from infantry standing shoulder-to-shoulder, two deep, and supported by ten cannon that smashed the Union column from two sides. Rebel fire reached a deafening crescendo as a few courageous men raced to the crest of the hill and mounted the parapets, planting two flags on the enemy works. For an instant, desperate fighting enveloped the Confederate line as men in butternut savagely defended their position. They flung rocks, timbers, dirt clods, and shovels at the attackers. They bayoneted Yankees who tried to leap into the trenches. Union soldiers fell dead on top of the men who killed them, and some Rebels fell in the hand-to-hand melee.

The raging Southern fire staggered the Federal line, which reeled and started to fall back. McCook, Sherman's civilian law partner, vainly attempted to rally his men, dramatically shouting to the tormenting Confederates, "Surrender, you traitors!" He was killed only a few feet from the Southern trenches. His second and third in command were killed only seconds and minutes later. The attack sputtered, stalled, and began to recede. The Federals who had survived the ill-fated assault, however, found themselves in a dire

127

LESLIE'S ILLUSTRATED

The Fifteenth Corps formed a part of the right side of Sherman's line as the attack began on Kennesaw Mountain. The Federal commander believed that Johnston's line was thin here and susceptible to a direct assault, a tactic he had avoided thus far.

situation: The attack had obviously failed, but they could not retreat. They would have been riddled by the deadly accurate Confederate fire had they tried to retreat. Forty yards below the Rebel line on the slope of the ridge was a hollow where enemy fire could not reach, and hundreds of men sheltered there, unable to advance or retire. McCook's brigade lost 35 percent of its strength, and Union casualties at the "Dead Angle" reached 824.

Cheatham proudly reported that his men had delivered a cool, relentless fire, deliberately aiming, firing, and reloading. Some guns grew so hot they discharged when loaded. In one regiment each man claimed to have killed five Yankees. All that was required was to load and shoot; it was impossible to miss a target. Sam Watkins, a Confederate rifleman, removed ammunition pouches from fallen comrades and fired 120 rounds during the struggle. Cheatham's infantry was supported by flanking artillery that

LESLIE'S ILLUSTRATED

Also forming the right side of the line was the Seventeenth Corps. When the initial assault succeeded in capturing the first line of the Confederate works, the attackers pressed on to the second.

maintained a murderous crossfire and added to the blazing din of battle that echoed across the hills.

To the east, the other two Union brigades under Gen. Charles G. Harker were led into a more perilous situation. They lost formation climbing over their works and approached the Rebel line in uncoordinated dribbles. Confederate cannon quickly broke the back of the attack, carpeting the ground with broken men. A U.S. flag was briefly planted on the bristling Confederate works, but the Union soldiers rapidly found refuge from the crippling fire and made only occasional halfhearted forays against the enemy. Sherman's carefully orchestrated strategy had degenerated into chaos.

Shell explosions ignited the underbrush in front of the Confederate fine, putting many Federal wounded in danger of being burned alive. Rebel

Col. William H. Martin of Arkansas courageously leaped atop his trenches with a white flag and yelled to a Union officer that he was willing to observe a cease-fire so the Yankee wounded could be rescued. "Come and get your dead and wounded," he called. "We won't fire a shot until you do."

The offer was gratefully accepted, and the fighting ceased. Confederates clambered from their trenches and helped the Yankees drag their wounded off the field to safety. Federal Maj. Luther M. Sabin presented Martin with a brace of Colt revolvers in appreciation of the humane act; the soldiers reluctantly returned to their positions, and the slaughter resumed.

Harker's efforts to rally his men from horseback made him an inviting target, and a charge of canister felled the general only fifteen yards from the Rebel works. Devoted soldiers braved the storm of lead and carried Harker's body from the field. The remainder of his command was shattered by the appalling fire, and the troops promptly ended the assault by acclamation. "Our men rushed back like a herd of infuriated buffalo," said Oliver O. Howard, "running over and trampling each other under foot. I was run over and badly bruised, but glad to get off so well.

"The enemy's fire was terrific," he continued. "Our men did not stop until they gained the edge of the felled trees; a few to fall close to the enemy's parapet, but most sought shelter behind logs and rocks, in rifle holes or depressions" before they vacated the field in inglorious panic. In two hours of combat, 650 of Harker's men fell.

Some Federals later claimed they could have carried the enemy works at Cheatham Hill if they had not been forced to struggle over their own dead and wounded. That their columns had been dispersed before they struck the Confederate line also hampered the assault.

Although the slaughter was less severe at Pigeon Hill, that clash proved even less successful than the one at Cheatham Hill. Implementing a similar strategy to that of Thomas, McPherson chose to attack the gap between Little Kennesaw and Pigeon Hill because it was the junction of two Confederate divisions; there was always the hope of exploiting confusion between two commands. He selected three brigades for the attack: The first would spearhead the effort and bear the brunt of the defenders' fire so the second brigade could overrun the Confederate line, and the third would break into the Rebel rear and roll up the enemy ranks. His fifty-five hundred men would assail five thousand entrenched troops. The attack, set to begin with the general bombardment of the Kennesaw position, was synchronized with the strike against Cheatham Hill.

The Federals advanced quickly through the forested valley that separated the combatants. They sprinted between the shelter of large boulders and trees and surprised a regiment of Georgians acting as pickets. Rebels were shot and stabbed in rifle pits; in one hole two men out of eleven survived. More than one hundred skirmishers were captured before the attackers continued their rush and burst onto the center of the Confederate line undetected. Thirty feet from the trenches, McPherson's troops were blasted by murderous salvos from Confederates crouched behind earthworks, rocks, and trees. The brigades were thrown back in confusion by the massed fire; then the broken troops swung to one side and ran into an exposed valley where they were pinned down by Rebel fire from two directions and slain in awful numbers.

These men faced the same hopeless situation as their comrades at the Dead Angle. If they retreated, the Southerners would shoot them down; so hundreds hugged the ground for what poor cover was provided by natural obstacles for more than ten hours, unable to return the punishing Rebel fire. Confederates on Little Kennesaw added insult by rolling rocks on them and shouting taunts. After dark the Federals crawled back to the sanctuary of their own lines.

During the attack, other soldiers on Little Kennesaw quickly found positions from which they opened a plunging fire on the enemy attacking the base of the hill. At no point along Pigeon Hill did the Yankees near the Confederate line. They lost six hundred men in the brief assault; Southern losses were three hundred, mostly pickets captured in the rapid Union advance through the forest.

The Confederate line remained intact, but Sherman lost heavily and gained nothing. The battle wore out by 11:30 A.M., and the Federals counted losses all out of proportion to their gains or to Confederate casualties. Although brave men pressed their fight to the Confederate works, the

A hail of Rebel fire hurled back the Union advance at Kennesaw Mountain.

MOUNTAIN CAMPAIGNS IN GEORGIA

MOUNTAIN CAMPAIGNS IN GEORGIA

After pinning down the Federals and causing more than three thousand casualties, including two brigade commanders, the Confederates held their fire while the wounded were removed and the Northerners withdrew.

Northerners had failed to dent the line and died in a tempest of fire on the parapets and in the Rebel trenches.

"The sun beating down on our uncovered heads, the thermometer being 110 degrees in the shade, and a solid fine of blazing fire from the muzzles of the Yankee guns poured right into our very faces," was how a cannoneer at Cheatham Hill described the battle, "singeing our hands and clothes, the hot blood of our dead and wounded spurting on us, the blinding smoke and stifling atmosphere filling our eyes and mouths, the awful concussion causing the blood to gush out of our noses and ears, and above all, the roar of battle, made it a perfect pandemonium.

"When the Yankees fell back and the firing ceased," the Rebel continued, "I never saw so many broken down and exhausted men in my life. I was as sick as a horse, and as wet with blood and sweat as I could be, and many of our men were vomiting from excessive fatigue, overexhaustion, and sunstroke; our tongues were parched and cracked for water, and our faces blackened with powder and smoke, and our dead and the wounded were piled indiscriminately in the trenches. There was not a single man in the company who was not wounded."

Col. Robert Fulton, a Federal involved in the struggle, wrote, "The Rebels fought with a desperation worthy of a better cause. The conduct of our soldiers and officers on this occasion needs no comment; never did men show more gallantry, mounting the works, shooting the enemy, and beating them over the heads with the butts of their guns," in a futile effort.

Gen. Samuel G. French had ridden to the crest of Kennesaw Mountain on the morning of June 27 when Union artillery fire indicated an imminent battle, and he was presented with an unobstructed view of the action. "Presently, as if by magic, there sprang from the earth a host of men," he related. "In one long, wavering line of blue the infantry advanced and the battle of Kennesaw Mountain began." He was awed by the magnificent panorama of 150,000 men "arrayed in the strife of battle on the plains below." As the enemy advanced, several miles of Confederate defenses were marked by tongues of flame and blue musket smoke. Through the resultant haze French observed the struggles at Cheatham Hill and Pigeon Hill develop and dispatched reinforcements, which proved unneeded, then he watched the Union tide recede. He termed the battle "pageantry on a grand scale . . . one of the most magnificent sights ever allotted to man."

Elated by the signal victory, Johnston allowed, "The Northern troops fought very well, as usual," displaying their "characteristic fortitude" which "held them under a close and destructive fire long after reasonable hope of success was gone."

Howard observed, "We realized now, as never before, the futility of direct assault upon entrenched lines, already well prepared and well manned."

After the attacks had failed, Sherman questioned his generals about renewing the assault. Thomas replied, "We have already lost heavily today without gaining any material advantage. One or two more such assaults would use up the army."

Sherman recognized the attack had been a dismal failure, but he tried to justify the effort. "At times assaults are necessary and inevitable," he said, explaining that some end in victory, others in defeat. He was wrong to think the Kennesaw Line could be breached by storm, and later he bitterly reflected that the battle had no effect on the final outcome of the campaign. Federal losses were three thousand, including seven regimental and two brigade commanders; Confederate casualties were six hundred.

Sherman, who had shown a rare zest for offensive action at Dallas and Kennesaw Mountain, confided in a letter to his wife how the change in tactics had affected his values: "I began to regard the death and mangling of a couple of thousand men as a small affair, a kind of morning dash." But reminded of the waste, he returned to the art of maneuver.

From then Federal-occupied Pine Mountain, Federal signalmen learned the fate of their comrades at Kennesaw.

Hardee reported that a thousand dead Union soldiers lay unburied in front of his lines for two days. On June 29 a truce was declared, and Confederate and Federal soldiers cooperated in dragging decaying bodies to holes for burial. Tobacco and coffee were traded during the welcome break from combat. Some Yankees, admiring his resolute defense, requested Cheatham's autograph.

The Federals remained pinned down at Cheatham Hill, a hundred yards from the Confederate line, until the Rebels withdrew on July 3. Trenches were dug to connect the isolated men with the main Union line, but they survived for several days without food or water. Some wired mirrors to their rifles so they could aim and fire without exposing themselves. The Confederates caught on to this ruse and extended their hats on sticks over the trenches in a competition to see who could collect the most holes in their headgear and also to encourage the Yankees to waste their ammunition. The Northern soldiers recognized that the Rebels could easily overrun them, but instead the Johnnies contented themselves with pitching rocks into the hollow and calling insults to the trapped men. The Yankees were temporarily down, but their spirit was intact. They started digging a tunnel beneath the Confederate position, intending to blow it up with a large mine; but the Rebels retired before it was completed.

Sherman's desperate gamble had been a bloody failure.

A Tour of Kennesaw Mountain

This tour begins at Gilgal Church on Kennesaw-Due West Road near Marietta.

On June 10 the armies shifted to the east after Sherman flanked Johnston out of his Dallas position. While Sherman regrouped to the north and west, Johnston developed a fifteen-mile-long defensive line north of Marietta and anchored on three mountains, from west to east: Lost, Pine, and Brushy. It was known as the Brushy Mountain Line. Sherman steadily drove the Confederates out of this first line but found a shorter, stronger line behind it. This second line was anchored on Kennesaw Mountain in the center, with Brushy Mountain to the east and Cheatham Hill to the west. Rugged terrain and continuous heavy rains frustrated the Federals. The armies were stalemated for another week after Sherman's June 27 assault, but even after Sherman flanked Johnston out of the Kennesaw Mountain Line, the Confed-

To the right at Gilgal Church are reconstructed Confederate works; to the left are undisturbed earthworks.

erates paused to grapple with the Federals in two sets of fieldworks, at Smyrna and Ruff's Mill, before settling into works on the Chattahoochee River.

Most of the Gilgal Church battlefield remains unchanged from the time of the battle due to the efforts of Sydney C. Kerksis, who purchased twenty acres at the heart of the site for preservation. The Atlanta History Center operates the park, which is on the National Register of Historic Places. The site includes a 175-yard section of Union trenches, another trench of 125 yards, several shorter works leading to a creek where soldiers filled their canteens, seven rifle pits (each 50 feet long), and gravesites marked by small crosses. The remains were later moved to Marietta.

A portion of typical Civil War earthworks has been reconstructed in this small roadside park that is open to the public, the only place in Georgia where visitors can view an authentic 1860s fortification. Trenches were dug six feet deep, with the dirt piled in a protective wall facing the enemy. The inner face of the trench was reinforced with logs held in place by vertical posts driven into the ground. A head log was placed atop the trench wall for protection, and soldiers fired through the gaps between the earthen wall and head log. Logs extended from the front trench wall to the rear so that timbers dislodged by artillery fire would roll above the soldiers rather than crash down on top of them. Trees were cut down in front of the trenches to clear fields of fire and for arranging entangling abatis to slow attackers.

Portions of the Confederate line exist on both sides of the reconstructed portion, but they are rapidly succumbing to residential development. A Sons of Confederate Veterans chapter meets in the clubhouse here. Gilgal Church was several hundred yards away at the crossroads. Serving on the field here were future president Benjamin Harrison and Arthur MacArthur, father of World War II hero Douglas MacArthur. The church burned during the fighting.

When Leonidas Polk withdrew from Lost Mountain on June 9, this area became the Confederate left. On June 14–15 an eight-mile-long skirmish occurred as Sherman attacked at Gilgal, Pine Mountain, and Noonday Creek. The battle of Gilgal Church, fought on June 15, was centered here, between Federal Maj. Gen. Daniel Butterfield and Confederate Maj. Gen. Patrick Cleburne. On June 16 William J. Hardee swung his portion of the Confederate line from here back across Mud Creek.

The Federals advanced along this road from the north, passing Lost Mountain to attack Johnston's Brushy Mountain Line. George H. Thomas established his headquarters at Mars Hill Church, just south of U.S. 41-GA 3, and crossed Mascon Bridge over Allatoona Creek.

The battle of Pine Knob occurred on the same day, June 15, a mile farther east, around the intersection of Kennesaw-Due West Road and Hamilton Road. It was also a division-sized engagement aimed at the Brushy Mountain Line. In the thick woods here are well-preserved artillery emplacements and infantry trenches, including a one-thousand-yard length of works that are currently endangered by development. Their importance is that these are largely Union works—most preserved earthworks are Confederate, who had time to develop more elaborate fortifications. The three brigades of John Geary's division, caught in a Confederate crossfire, hugged the ground here and scratched out protective holes. In six hours 82 were killed, 432 wounded. Portions of the fifty-acre battlefield may be preserved.

You may want to take a side trip from Gilgal Church to visit the site where Confederate Gen. Leonidas Polk was killed while surveying Union lines with Johnston and others. In the minister's pockets were found three inspirational books inscribed for Johnston, Hood, and Hardee.

If you take this option, from the Gilgal Church parking area, turn left to continue on Kennesaw-Due West Road, turn left onto Stilesboro Road, and turn left onto Beaumont Drive to the summit.

John Bell Hood suffered severe casualties when he launched an unauthorized attack near the Kolb farm.

A short path to the right of the Georgia historical marker commemorating Polk's death leads to the twenty-foot-high marble monument placed by a Marietta Confederate veteran and his wife in 1902 at the spot where Polk was killed. The mountain also has well-preserved earthworks. This is private property, so please be considerate.

To resume the primary tour, drive back to the last intersection and turn left onto Acworth-Due West Road. At the intersection with GA 120 after 1.3 turn left onto GA 120-Dallas Highway.

At the Darby house, west of Mud Creek, Union batteries deployed and troops formed for battle amid forty-eight hours of hard rain. The road crosses Mud Creek, where the Confederates, who had swung their line after Gilgal Church, suffered terribly from Federal artillery on June 17. The Rebels occupied the ridge to the east of the creek, Yankees to the west. The Confederates withdrew from here to the Kennesaw Line.

In the 1850s brothers Wiley and Ruben Lattimore constructed houses near each other about eight miles northeast of Marietta, not far from the mill they established and operated. It was the scene of a cavalry clash on June 20, 1864, on the Marietta-Canton Road east of Kennesaw Mountain, when Confederate cavalry surprised five hundred Union horsemen under Col. Robert H. G. Minty. When the Federals withdrew at dusk they had suffered sixty-five casualties and inflicted seventy-five. A Baptist church that survived the battle, its plank sides riddled with bullet holes, was demolished in the 1960s. The Wiley Latimore house was recently destroyed for a commercial development, but there is a good chance that the Ruben Lattimore house may survive a road-widening project.

At 2.8 miles turn right on John Ward Road for .6 then turn left on Cheatham Hill Road 2 miles to the intersection with Powder Springs Road. Cross the road and immediately on your right is the Kolb farm.

Sherman probed the western end of the Confederate line for several days, and on June 22 Johnston had Hood swing his corps from the extreme eastern part of the line at Brushy Mountain behind the Army of Tennessee to extend his left here. Finding John M. Schofield's small Army of the Ohio and Joseph Hooker's corps approaching, Hood immediately attacked without reconnaissance with the divisions of Carter L. Stevenson in the center, Alexander P. Stewart to the left, and Thomas Hindman on the right. Hood advanced from the east, south of Powder Springs Road; the defending Federals were north and south of Powder Springs Road, facing east. The farmhouse was east of the Union lines. Forty artillery pieces and the fire of thousands of rifles shattered repeated determined attacks. Hood lost 1,000 men to 350 Union casualties.

This is the original 1836 home of Peter Valentine Kolb, who died in 1859. His son's widow occupied the six-hundred-acre farm (six acres remain) when Hood impetuously attacked here. The home served as Hooker's headquarters, and during the battle Union sharpshooters fired from its windows and from behind fences. Afterward, artillery and signal corps units made use of the property, also used as a hospital from June 22 to 30. Daniel Butterfield, who fought here as one of Hooker's divisional commanders, composed "Taps."

In 1964 the National Park Service restored the house, heavily damaged during the battle, to its 1864 appearance. Classified as Georgia frontier indigenous vernacular, the one-story structure originally had a dogtrot separating the two sections, each of which contained two rooms, but this was enclosed with clapboard before the Civil War. Note the four chimneys at the corners. The house is used for staff accommodations but is not currently open to the public. Visitors, however, can inspect the exterior of the home and view the family graveyard. The National Park Service had owned three corners of the intersection, and recently the fourth was purchased for preservation and saved from development. The wooded corners have trenches hastily thrown up by Union soldiers on June 22.

During the June 22 attack Schofield was ordered to demonstrate southeast of Kolb's farm. Sherman's serious assaults failed miserably, but Schofield made a lodgement in the Confederate rear, close to the Chattahoochee River, which forced Johnston to abandon the Kennesaw Line several days later.

Atop a hill a short distance to the west at the intersection of Powder Springs Road and Macland Road is the McAdoo house (also known as Melora, 1854), one of Cobb County's last surviving Greek Revival antebellum plantation homes. It is not as grand as the massive Tara of the film, but much like the one portrayed in the book version of *Gone with the Wind*. The large house has one and a half stories, the lower portion of which is stone and the upper segments built of wood. Originally the house was the centerpiece of a seventy-two-acre farm; in 1864 it was headquarters to Union Gen. Alpheus Williams, commander of one of Hooker's divisions. Earlier Williams had commanded a corps at Antietam and at Gettysburg due to casualties among high-ranking officers, and later he was given command of Hooker's corps when Hooker demanded relief.

The McAdoo house, recently saved from developers, was a Union headquarters near Marietta.

The structure, which stood between Union and Confederate lines for a time, was also a Federal hospital. Hooker probably visited from his headquarters at the Kolb farm.

In 1863 William G. McAdoo was born here. He was Woodrow Wilson's secretary of the treasury and son-in-law, ran twice for president, and was a U.S. senator from California. McAdoo's parents, fleeing Federal advances in Tennessee, purchased the house a year before Sherman arrived. During the battle it was owned by S. B. Oatman, who sold it to Col. A. S. Atkinson, son-in-law of Gov. Charles McDonald, whose Marietta home was torched by Union troops. The remains of McDonald's home are on the current property of Charlie Brown, the great-great-grandson of Georgia's wartime governor, Joseph E. Brown.

The McAdoo house would have been destroyed to allow construction of a large residential and commercial development, but it and two surrounding acres containing large oak trees were spared. The house, now occupied by offices, is on the north side of Powder Springs Road on a rise above and at the western end of a shopping center.

The Greek Revival Andrew Jackson Cheney house (2760 Bankstone Road, 1857) is found seventy-five yards off Powder Springs Road at Bankstone Road six miles southwest of Marietta. It served as headquarters for Schofield from June 22 to 30 and was visited by Sherman during inspection tours. Union Gen. Jacob Cox's division camped on the plantation before marching a mile northeast on Powder Springs Road to fight at Kolb's farm. Constructed near the intersection of the Tennessee Wagon Road and Sandtown Road, the house has two stories, the first floor of brick, the second of wood, with four rooms on each floor off a central hall. The ceilings are twelve feet high, the timbers pegged together, and on the porch are wood columns. The original cedar shake shingles are preserved under a newer roof. An exciting feature is a clearly visible five-hundred-foot-long section of the original wagon trace traveled by Civil War

Map 16: The Marietta area and Kennesaw Mountain

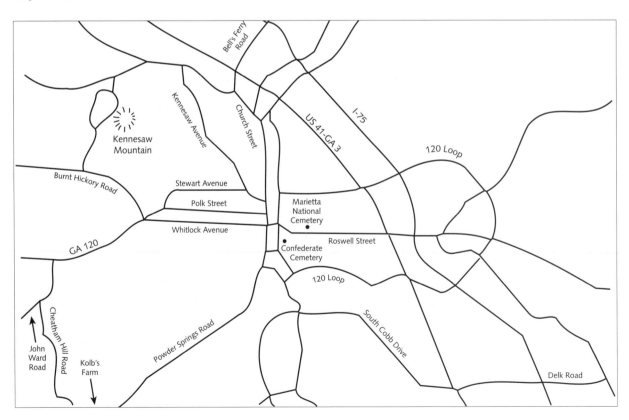

armies. Both house and road trace are scheduled to be preserved.

From the Kolb farm, retrace your route to GA 120, but along the way you may turn into the large parking area on the left side of the road where a fence, field, and woods are to the right.

On June 22 Sherman established his headquarters here to watch Thomas's five brigades form on this ridge and attack Cheatham Hill to the east.

Continue to GA 120 and turn right for .5 then turn right into the Cheatham Hill section of Kennesaw Mountain National Battlefield Park.

To the right, among the trees facing open fields over which the Federals advanced, are portions of the Confederate trenches. Cannon placed behind protective lunettes appear as they would have during the battle, firing solid balls, shell, and canister to shatter the advancing Union columns. The pink granite memorial was erected in 1964 to honor Texans who fought in the Army of Tennessee. A marker along the road indicates the site where Confederates arranged a truce to rescue Federal soldiers from fires sparked by exploding shells. Examine the markers at each of the stops on the short drive.

At .6 are a parking area and a trail leading to Cheatham Hill.

Near the edge of the parking lot is an artillery position that was instrumental in turning back eight thousand Federal soldiers from the divisions of Brig. Gens. Jefferson C. Davis and John Newton. The line was held by two of Johnston's best divisions, Patrick Cleburne's and Benjamin F. Cheatham's (Polk's former command).

As you walk the shaded quarter mile to the Dead Angle, examine the original Confederate trench line on the left. Signs mark the positions of individual units. The First and Twenty-seventh Tennessee held much of the Dead Angle. In 1864 the earthworks were deeper, and Southern soldiers crouched beneath head logs to coolly aim and fire at the Federals steadily advancing across the open field, which was much larger then.

Confederate works at the Dead Angle at Kennesaw Mountain National Battlefield Park.

On the path to the Dead Angle notice the trenches that join the main line of defense but run in the other direction. These protected soldiers at a salient when the enemy was on either side and fired artillery the length of the main works. It was also a refuge in case a portion of the work was overrun and allowed the wounded to be removed and reinforcements to rush to the front.

The Dead Angle, five miles south of Kennesaw Mountain, is the most dramatic spot on the battlefield. Here the full force of the Federal attack peaked and ebbed. A beautifully reproduced painting at a display here shows that some Union troops reached the top of the Southern trenches but were shot down. Some Confederates threw rocks at the charging Federals, bayonets inflicted wounds, and rifles were used as clubs. Near the trenches, Col. Daniel McCook, Sherman's former law partner, fell while trying to rally his men. The force of the attack was broken, and the Confederate line remained intact. Sherman lost five thousand men, Johnston only eight hundred.

Encouraged by veterans organizations, Illinois bought 60 acres of the battlefield in 1899 then donated it to the U.S. War Department in 1917, which assigned it to the National Park Service in 1933. The federal government felt it could preserve either the battlefield of Kennesaw Mountain or Peachtree Creek to commemorate the Atlanta campaign, and it chose the former. It is significant that soldiers who had fought here originated Kennesaw Mountain National Battlefield Park. The park now includes 2,884 acres, sixteen miles of hiking trails, monu-

Artillery still occupies the original Confederate positions in mass quantities atop Kennesaw Mountain.

ments, historical markers and other interpretive signs, preserved artillery emplacements, and miles of trenches.

The magnificent Illinois Monument, which stands at the crest of Cheatham Hill, was erected by the state of Illinois and dedicated on June 27, 1914, fifty years after the battle occurred, to honor the 480 men from that state who died on this slope. The marble memorial is thirty-four feet square at the base, and the shaft rises twenty-five feet. Stairs ascend the monument from the direction of the assault. Crowning the monument are two women in classical Greek garb and a seven-foot bronze soldier clutching a rifle.

At the base of the memorial is the Tunnel Monument, which seals off an excavation started by trapped soldiers who planned to burrow beneath the Confederate line and destroy it with an enormous mine like the one detonated at Petersburg, Virginia. This was made possible by the poor placement of the Confederate works, sited on the crest of the ridge, creating a dead zone where they could not see or fire upon the enemy. The military crest would have been farther down slope. The tunnel was incomplete when the Confederates withdrew. Nearby is the gravestone of an unknown soldier whose remains were discovered in 1934 by Civilian Conservation Corps (CCC) workers. It was impossible to determine for whose army he died.

A trail extends across the field, over a stream, and through the woods for six hundred yards to the spot where the Federals began their attack, an area to be examined on the way back from the Kolb farm. On the wooded slope is a monument to McCook, a two-

foot-high granite marker that commemorates the start of the assault.

Return to GA 120 and turn right. At 1.2 turn left onto Burnt Hickory Road NW. At 1.2 a parking area for Pigeon Hill is on the left.

The hill received its name from the thousands of pigeons that paused here on their migratory journeys. It was here that Sherman's secondary attack was made by three of McPherson's brigades, fifty-five hundred men, who were soundly thrown back. There were reports of Confederates on the heights rolling boulders down on the attackers, who encountered a storm of fire during their brief assault. The fields here were much more extensive then. A hiking trail from Cheatham Hill leads through the battle area to the right of well-preserved works and continues on to Little Kennesaw and Kennesaw Mountain. The short but steep trail follows the path of three Union brigades from Brig. Gen. Morgan Smith's Second Division as they attacked a Missouri brigade led by Brig. Gen. Frances Cockrell. The Fifty-seventh Ohio was only forty yards from the Confederate line when the enemy rose and unleashed devastating rifle and cannon fire. Many Union survivors took shelter among the outcrops of stone and boulders.

We will be turning right onto Old Mountain Road here, but farther north on Burnt Hickory Road is the site of the York house, Johnston's headquarters from June 10 to 19. It was destroyed by Confederate artillery fire from Kennesaw Mountain because of Union sharpshooters, and the Federals entrenched a defensive line here while confronting the mountain works. Also in the area are the Hardage house, Polk's headquarters until his death at Pine Mountain, and at the intersection of Burnt Hickory Road and Ernest Barrett Parkway, the Wallis house, headquarters of Oliver O. Howard, who founded the Freedman's Bureau following the war and for whom Howard University is named.

Turn right onto Old Mountain Road and at 1.5 turn right onto Stilesboro Road. At .5 turn into the parking area for the visitors center.

Several cannon are scattered across the grounds, which offer the best view of the imposing mountain. At the battle on June 22 Illinois troops feinted here and were engaged by Confederates from Alabama and Arkansas who were concealed in woods at the base of the mountain.

Kennesaw Mountain National Battlefield Park recently refurbished the visitors center, which doubled the size of the museum, bookstore, and library and renovated the theater. All of the exhibits are designed to illustrate both the history of the Atlanta campaign and the battle that took place at Kennesaw Mountain. Shown at regular intervals is an award-winning video that interprets the campaign and incorporates historic photographs and artwork with aerial photography, computer graphics, and reenactment footage along with period music and diary entries. Located just off I-75, Kennesaw Mountain is

A number of interpretive markers highlight the action at Kennesaw Mountain.

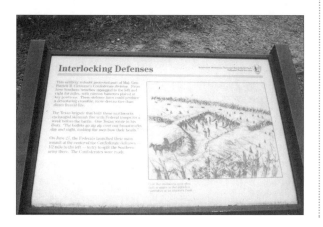

becoming one of the most popular Civil War battlefield parks in the country.

Renovations revealed a surprising fact about a flag that had been displayed at the museum for decades. The silk battle flag of the Cherokee Dragoons, hand sewn by the women of neighboring Cherokee County, has the first Confederate national flag (the Stars and Bars) on one side, but on the other side is a different design: a laurel wreath encircling the words, "Cherokee Dragoons" and a motto dating back to ancient Sparta, "Either With It Or Upon It." The dragoons trained at nearby Camp McDonald with Phillip's Legion, initially a combined unit of infantry, cavalry, and artillery. The dragoons soon joined Jeb Stuart's cavalry in Virginia, participating in more than one hundred battles and skirmishes before joining Wade Hampton as part of Joseph E. Johnston's force battling Sherman in the Carolinas. At the surrender in April 1865, only fifty of the original one-thousand-man legion remained. The flag has been restored and both sides will be displayed, but only one at a time.

Kennesaw Mountain features other flags. Governor Brown's flag was a ceremonial banner given to Georgia's chief. The flag of Company I, Seventh Georgia, a second Confederate national flag from Manassas National Battlefield, and a thirty-six-star U.S. flag are also displayed.

Museum displays include sixty-four portraits of military leaders important during the campaign (thirty-two for each army), life-sized photos of Sherman and Johnston, large sketches from Civil War artist Alfred Waud, and maps of the campaign. The park possesses two artillery tubes manufactured in Georgia and one Federal gun used in the state. A rare Georgia carbine manufactured by Crook and Brothers and the pistol of Capt. J. M. Augustine of the Fifty-fifth Illinois (killed at Pigeon Hill), are among the eleven hundred artifacts held by the park. Videos demonstrate how weapons were loaded and fired and illustrate the war's effect on the city of Marietta, inundated by refugees, wounded, and friendly and enemy armies. Other displays explain different aspects of the war, such as battle tactics, the logistics of supplying massive armies in the field, constructing miles of entrenchments, medical care of tens of thousands of wounded and ill soldiers, the presidential election of 1864 and how it was affected by the Atlanta campaign, and life on the home front.

The summit of Kennesaw Mountain offers this view of Pine Mountain.

Kennesaw Mountain National Park frequently hosts lectures and interpretive programs. Pick up a park brochure in the lobby and examine the Civil War literature available for purchase.

A steep road behind the visitors center winds to the top of Kennesaw Mountain. On weekends and during the summer a tour bus takes visitors to the summit; at other times you may drive yourself up the 1.2-mile road. On the right near the base is a monument that honors Georgia troops who served the Confederacy. There are beautiful views of the surrounding countryside as you drive up the mountain, and from the parking area near the summit is a scenic overlook of the valley below. A long flight of stairs leads to a stone observation platform with markers indicating surrounding points of interest and a memorial to the fourteen Confederate generals from Georgia who served at Kennesaw. It was dedicated in 1964, the centennial anniversary of the battle. A steep one-mile hike from the visitors center to the summit leads past rifle pits.

A trip to Kennesaw Mountain is not complete without a hike to the summit, which is steep but only one-fourth mile in length. The trail passes several recreated artillery positions in original Confederate earthworks. Some of these lunettes were leveled by Federal fire, but few casualties and little actual damage resulted from the spectacular duel. The Confederates cleared the summit for timber used in fortifications and to create fields of fire and hauled numerous cannon by hand up the precipitous slopes

of Kennesaw Mountain and Little Kennesaw. This position was held by Maj. Gen. William W. Loring's troops. The stunning view to the north allows you to imagine the panorama of war in the summer of 1864. From this peak Samuel G. French and other Confederate officers watched the awesome spectacle of one hundred thousand Union soldiers advancing in a three-mile line to probe the Southern defenses.

Kennesaw Mountain was obviously too difficult to attack directly, but on June 22 the Sixty-fourth Illinois attacked the Twenty-fifth Arkansas among the trees at the foot of the mountain. The First Alabama occupied rifle pits on the lower slopes, and Alabamians and Tennesseans defended the summit.

The summit has a number of interesting historical markers that direct visitors to observe Atlanta to the south—vulnerably close on clear days—the Allatoona Mountains to the north, and Little Kennesaw, the second peak of this double mountain to the west. We have been examining the Kennesaw Line, but Johnston's overextended first barrier, the Brushy Mountain Line, lies to the north and west and can only be appreciated from this vantage point. Lost Mountain, which you passed, is a large hump to the west; Pine Mountain, where Polk was killed, is clearly visible to the north, crowned today by a water tower and lined with homes. The site is most easily found from Gilgal Church. Brushy Mountain, a low ridge, is to the east.

Continued on page 144

Hiking the Trails of Kennesaw Mountain National Battlefield Park

A series of hiking trails, totaling sixteen miles, extend from Kolb's farm to Kennesaw Mountain and the visitors center, connecting sites of historical significance and often following trench lines. Hike the trails from either end, walk the entire trail, or visit only the sections that interest you. Since the battle at Kolb's farm occurred first and we approach the battlefield from the west, that is where we begin.

The Kolb's Farm Loop, an easy 5.6 miles (2.8 one way) may be walked from Kolb's farm to Cheatham Hill. From Kolb's farm cross Powder Springs Road and follow the trail right. It turns north through woods and fields, crossing John Ward Creek, with Confederate works to the left early and to the right near Cheatham Hill and the Dead Angle. This section of the trail ends at the Illinois Monument.

You may continue on to Kennesaw Mountain on the full trail or loop back to Kolb's farm, crossing John Ward Creek on the way. The return trail follows a low ridge through rolling hills and open fields, following the Union advance against Cheatham Hill in reverse and passing Union fortifications on the right to Cheatham Hill Road. The trail then passes Federal works to the left near the road and to the right nearer Powder Springs Road and Kolb's farm across the busy intersection.

The Cheatham Hill Loop, an easy one-mile trail, begins at the parking area at the end of the park road to Cheatham Hill and is hiked counterclockwise. At the start two guns of John W. Mebane's Tennessee Battery occupied the redoubt. The trail follows the Confederate works to the left to the Dead Angle and the Illinois

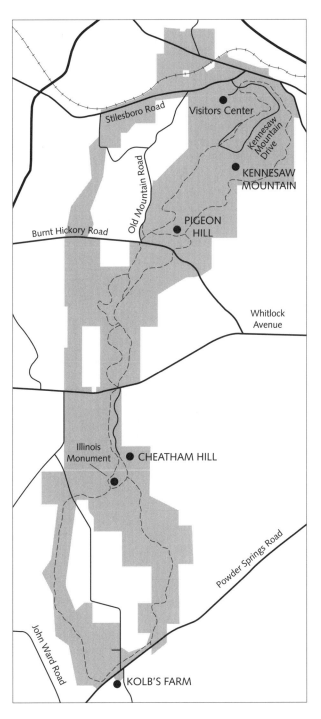

Monument then turns back to the rear of the angle and returns to the parking lot.

From the parking area at Cheatham Hill starts the Cheatham Hill Connector, an easy, level 2.6-mile one-way hike primarily through wooded areas that connect Cheatham Hill with Pigeon Hill, the next scene of significant military activity. In the .8 mile to GA 120-Dallas Road are monuments and markers, Confederate infantry trenches, and artillery positions to the left, facing open fields where Federals advanced only to be repulsed. You probably stopped to view these sites as you drove in; if you did not do so earlier, read the markers now and look around.

Across Dallas Road the trail follows Confederate works to the right among rolling hills, crosses Noses Creek on a footbridge, and passes through dense woods. Union fortifications are also encountered. The Union attacks at Pigeon Hill occurred north and south of Burnt Hickory Road. Here, south of the road near the end of the trail, attacking Union troops under Brig. Gen. Andrew A. J. Lightburn overran the Sixty-third Georgia, skirmishers whose new commander did not allow the regiment to withdraw. The Federals were soon thrown back as they approached the strong Confederate lines held by States Rights Gist. The trail ends at the parking area along Burnt Hickory Road.

The Burnt Hickory Loop is 5.7 miles and demanding, and the terrain is rugged. We would suggest making this a one-way hike. From the parking area at Burnt Hickory Road hike up the trail through Confederate earthworks to the display at Pigeon Hill. You can see Pine and Lost Mountains to the north and west. McPherson's assault here was easily repulsed. The trail continues northeast, down into a steep, rocky gorge studded with giant boulders and up wooded Little Kennesaw Mountain to additional displays, rock outcrops, an excellent view of the surrounding countryside, and extensive Confederate fortifications.

In a rifle pit at the foot of Little Kennesaw, near a series of stone lunettes, Sgt. C. E. Dale of the Ninth Texas Infantry carved "C.E. DALE IX TEX" in Roman-style lettering. He was killed on October 5 at Allatoona. Farmers found the nearly inaccessible site in 1921.

The trail switchbacks, dipping again into a steep descent and ascent through a gap separating Little Kennesaw from Kennesaw Mountain. This walk across rocky ridges leads through beautiful hardwood forests and features wonderful views southeast to Atlanta and north to ridges and mountains. It ends atop Kennesaw Mountain.

The final hiking segment is the Kennesaw Mountain Trail, 1.1 steep miles, rising one thousand feet above the visitors center at the end, or the start, of the trail. We are starting from the top. On the summit this trail begins at the signal platform, where Sherman's signalmen ordered John M. Corse to hold Allatoona because relief was en route. Confederate artillery emplacements, containing Civil War–era cannon, are passed, and there are great views of Atlanta to the south and of the mountains to the north. Next is the Georgia Overlook, a memorial to Georgia Confederate generals who fought at Kennesaw, followed by a scenic overlook, where an antebellum road was used by tourists for the views and picnics. From this point Confederates cut a road to the crest and hauled artillery up by hand. Farther down, a primary Confederate trench line is crossed. At the sign look for the original roadbed. Mountain springs, the center of a summer resort dating to the 1840s, are encountered next. Near the visitors center are rifle pits, marking the Confederate skirmish line, held by the First Alabama when Federals demonstrated here on June 27, 1864.

An alternative is to hike the modern road to or from the crest of Kennesaw Mountain, 1.2 miles and a one-thousand-foot ascent. Along that route are the Georgia Monument, two scenic overlooks, and earthworks.

Continued from page 142

On the trip down, pull into the parking area on the right and walk to the side of the road to observe the beauty of Little Kennesaw and the countryside.

You can combine an interest in history and hiking at Kennesaw Mountain. A sixteen-mile loop trail leads visitors across the park from the visitors center to Kennesaw Mountain, Little Kennesaw, Pigeon Hill, Cheatham Hill, the Kolb farm, and back across mountain peaks, pleasant meadows, wooded creek bottoms, and along eleven and a half miles of earthworks. Shorter hikes are also featured. Ask at the visitors center or refer to the Kennesaw Mountain hiking sidebar (see pages 143–44).

On Gilbert Road, a rough gravel track that is off Stilesboro Road west of the visitors center, between Stilesboro Road and Old Mountain Road, is the site of a twenty-four-gun Federal battery that pounded Confederate positions on Kennesaw Mountain.

Farther west, between Ernest W. Barrett Parkway and Stilesboro Road, in the area of Marietta Country Club, is Hardee's Salient, also known as French's Hill, an area full of Confederate street names—Ector, Cockrell, French, and the militaristic Salient and Sharpshooters. This was the pivot point when the Confederate line was swung back from Lost Mountain to Gilgal Church and then to Mud Creek. Three Union corps next attacked the salient on June 17–18, forcing Johnston to abandon the outer works and fall back to the Kennesaw Mountain Line. Earthworks, some open to the public, have been preserved within a huge development.

The Marietta Country Club, south of Stilesboro Road between Ernest W. Barrett Parkway and New Salem Road, near New Salem Church, was constructed on the site of the battle of Latimer's farm, fought June 17–18. The sixteenth and seventeenth holes were designed around earthworks, and a display case in the clubhouse contains artillery projectiles found on the grounds.

A developer has preserved two trenches, believed to have been cannon bunkers, at Stilesboro Road and Barrett Parkway in the same general area. In this instance an acre was given to the city of Marietta for the development of a public park.

The Brushy Mountain–Pine Mountain–Lost Mountain Line was the first and longest of four Confederate defensive lines constructed in Cobb County. Development has destroyed most of the line, but efforts are under way to preserve the remainder before Atlanta's inexorable growth eradicates it forever.

Brushy Mountain, along the railroad, anchored the right (northeastern) sector of the fifteen-milelong Brushy Mountain Line. It was composed of twenty-five miles of fortifications that stretched to Lost Mountain in west Cobb County, with Pine Mountain an unconnected salient. Several miles of these works remain. Brushy Mountain, which runs east to west, is low and little noticed as a natural feature. It is dwarfed by the much larger Kennesaw Mountain, which it parallels. Parts of Brushy Mountain were destroyed by construction of I-75 and I-575, which merge here, and much of the ridge was leveled for shopping centers and residential development.

Much of what remains, however, is pristine. A survey has found four separate, well-preserved sections of Confederate fortifications. One atop the ridge is two thousand feet long; another, several hundred feet below the summit, is one thousand feet in length; a third, north of the ridge, extends for twenty-five hundred feet; and the final segment, fifteen hundred feet long, is separated from the other three by the junction of I-75 and I-575 and is composed of piled rocks. Resources here were not surveyed until 1984, when important fortifications and fifteen acres of climax forest were revealed. There are plans to preserve these surviving segments of the Brushy Mountain Line and purchase easements from one to the other for a unique linear park and trail.

Adjoining NPS property is Barrett Lakes Apartments (1950 Barrett Lakes Boulevard, Kennesaw) near Town Center. Fifteen acres have been set aside as a nature preserve surrounding a seven-hundred-foot-long section of the Brushy Mountain Line. The earthworks, eight to ten feet wide and six to eight feet deep, snake along the crest of a rocky ridge. A winding, five-foot-wide interpretive trail, one-third of a mile in length, follows the trenches to the summit. At intervals the path is wider to accommodate benches and granite pillars with interpretive markers prepared by the NPS and Cobb County historians. Event panels detail the local Civil War activity of the Atlanta campaign that occurred here.

Considerable works exist on ridge lines just south of Brushy Mountain in an area known as Fort Maxson, or Hood's Fort, found on the southeastern corner of Barrett Parkway-U.S. 41. Hood's Fort is a fantastic position, with well-preserved twelve-foot-deep earth and stone trenches, an ammunition bunker, and a great view of the mountains farther north. This may have been a Confederate artillery position or a reconfigured Federal work. It was the longest held of all Confederate defenses in the area.

Hood occupied the extreme right of the Confederate line here June 14–19, and after he shifted west toward Kolb farm, dismounted cavalry assumed that responsibility. In this area on June 15 two Union brigades, equipped with seven-shot repeaters, forded Noonday Creek to drive out Confederates occupying rifle pits at the base of the ridge. The spirited attackers kept going, seizing the ridge and inflicting four hundred casualties, all but fifty of them as prisoners. The Federals were ordered to return to their lines that night.

Noted Civil War historian Phillip Secrist, head of the Georgia Civil War Commission, has one hundred yards of the Brushy Mountain Line on his current property and once owned sixty acres that held a much larger portion of the line. He sold the land with a covenant to preserve the works, which today constitute parts of people's front and back yards.

At the park entrance turn right to the traffic signal and left onto Old 41 (Kennesaw Avenue). At .3 cross the path of the contested railroad and at 1.7 is U.S. 41-GA 3. Drive straight through the intersection and at 1.8 turn right over the railroad tracks. To your left is what was once called the Big Shanty Museum, then Kennesaw Civil War Museum, but is now the Southern Museum of Civil War and Locomotive History.

Established in the 1830s as a shanty camp for railroad workers, residents changed the name of their community from Big Shanty to the more socially acceptable Kennesaw in 1870. Sherman arrived on June 9, 1864, and kept his headquarters here during operations against Kennesaw Mountain. When the fighting moved farther south, a Federal occupation force fortified the Lacy Hotel and built a stockade around it as a strongpoint on the Western and Atlantic. Hood's forces captured it in October 1864, and when Sherman marched east to Savannah in November, the Federals burned the hotel.

Big Shanty-Kennesaw is famous as the site where the Great Locomotive Chase began in 1862. Federal raider James J. Andrews and his men boarded a train pulled by the engine *General* in Marietta. When the passengers and crew disembarked for breakfast at the Lacy Hotel, Andrews and his men stole the train and started north to destroy the sixteen railroad bridges between Atlanta and Chattanooga. By cutting the railroad, they hoped to aid the Union occupation of Chattanooga, but they were thwarted in this daring attempt by the resolute pursuit of the *General*'s conductor, William A. Fuller, who chased his train on foot, with a pole car, and on three different engines, running two of them back-

A former cotton gin provided the main building of the museum formerly known as the Big Shanty Museum.

The locomotive General *was stolen by Union operatives in a daring plan to sabotage the primary railroad in Georgia.*

ward in a harrowing eight-hour journey that covered eighty-seven miles. Fuller forced Andrews to abandon the *General* near Ringgold, and all of the raiders were captured. Eight were hanged in Atlanta for sabotage, and the rest escaped or were exchanged. All but Andrews, who was a civilian, received the first Medals of Honor.

The geography of the chase sounds like a reverse of the Atlanta campaign: Marietta, Kennesaw, Acworth, Allatoona, Cass Station, Kingston, Adairsville, Resaca, Dalton, Tunnel Hill, and Ringgold. Across the tracks from the museum, in Commemorative Park, are a stone monument marking the site where the adventure began (a similar memorial north of Ringgold signifies the end of the chase) and a plaque honoring Fuller's heroic determination to recapture his engine.

Those members of Andrews's raiders who were executed following the affair are buried in the Chattanooga National Cemetery at Holtzclaw and Bailey. Their graves are clustered around a stone monument topped by a bronze replica of the *General*.

The *General* was damaged but repaired and later came under Union artillery fire on June 27, 1864, when it ran a load of ammunition to the Confederate defenders of Kennesaw Mountain. Two months later, on September 1, the *General* and another locomotive, the *Missouri,* labored south on the Macon Railroad with cargoes of munitions and quartermasters stores that John Bell Hood attempted to evacuate from Atlanta. Federal artillery at Rough and Ready (now Mountain View), where Sherman's troops had cut

the railroad, forced the engines to hastily reverse into Atlanta. At the Georgia rail yards near Oakland Cemetery, the *Missouri* was rammed into a train of ammunition cars, then the *General* and another locomotive and its cars were crashed into it, and all was set ablaze. The explosion of the five engines and eighty-six ammunition and supply cars could be heard for miles.

The *General* barely survived being scrapped following the war but was again rescued and refurbished. It was involved in two wrecks near Kingston and was featured at several reunions of Civil War veterans. Forgotten for years, the *General* was discovered on a siding in Vinings, not far from Kennesaw, restored, and featured at the 1893 Chicago World Colombian Exposition, the Atlanta Cotton States Exposition, and the 1939 World's Fair in New York before being placed on permanent display in Chattanooga. At that time the state of Georgia began a three-decade struggle for possession of the locomotive by announcing plans to display the *General* at Kennesaw Mountain or Kennesaw.

The *General* made a centennial run over the route of the chase in 1962, and over two years traveled fourteen hundred miles to appear in 120 cities. When the Louisville and Nashville Railroad, which had obtained the engine on lease from the Western and Atlantic, agreed to return the engine to Georgia in 1967, the city of Chattanooga "captured" the locomotive with a court order. After three years of litigation the *General* was returned by Federal court order to Kennesaw, appropriately one hundred yards from

Eight raiders were executed after their capture. They were reburied in Chattanooga around this monument.

where it was hijacked in 1862. The engine has been housed in this museum since 1972.

The *General,* manufactured in 1855 at Paterson, New Jersey, is a 4-4-0 steam locomotive with four driving wheels, each sixty inches in diameter. It was sold to the Western and Atlantic for eighty-five hundred dollars for the Chattanooga-to-Atlanta run and designated Engine No. 3.

The museum in which it is now displayed is a restored cotton gin donated by the city. The *General* and its tender rest on tracks with surroundings that give the illusion of a train station. There are many informative displays, including flags, weapons, dated cross-tie nails, a brick from the tunnel through Chetoogeta Ridge, a Federal ax head used to fell trees before Kennesaw Mountain, and *Gone with the Wind* mementos.

Recently, the facility began a massive $5.2 million expansion. An adjacent warehouse (1909) will house the Glover Steam Locomotive Collection. Between 1902 and 1930 the Glover Machine Works, located along the old Western and Atlantic tracks in Marietta, constructed two hundred small-gauge, short-haul steam locomotives used in timber and mining companies in twelve states and twelve foreign countries, including the construction of the Panama Canal. When the factory was destroyed in 1995, the owner donated all that remained to the Kennesaw Civil War Museum. Historians were awed by what they found: two intact locomotives, sample parts, a set of wooden templates for making engine parts, plans, drawings, complete sales records, and glass

plate negatives of every engine built. There were thirty-five filing cabinets of material. The Glover Steam Locomotive Museum will recreate the factory, featuring the two surviving engines, with a foundry and seventy-foot chimney showing how metal parts were cast and a research library.

The expanded museum will allow larger groups to view the *General* and have additional space for exhibits, a classroom, and a 113-seat theater. Films, including two Hollywood movies made about the Great Locomotive Chase—*The General,* a 1926 silent classic featuring Buster Keaton, and Disney's 1956 *The Great Locomotive Chase,* starring Fess Parker— and *Here Comes the General,* a documentary about the 1962 refurbishing of the engine, will be shown.

The Lacy Hotel and depot were at one time beside the tracks across Cherokee Street from the museum. When Union cavalry seized the town, a cannonball crashed into the second floor before bouncing down the stairs and past the family and guests at breakfast. North of the hotel and west of the railroad were the sixty acres of Camp McDonald, established by Gov. Joseph E. Brown on June 11, 1861, to train Georgia recruits. It was the largest facility in the state, training up to forty-five hundred men at a time, and one of three camps of instruction for Georgia volunteers. On July 13, 1861, a grand review of two hundred troops was held for Brown. Georgia veterans held reunions here for decades following the war. The present Kennesaw City Hall is in the middle of the campsite, which stretched from Main Street to U.S. 41.

Next door to the museum is Kennesaw Commons, a collection of restored homes where antiques and crafts are sold, and opposite it is the Kennesaw depot. Another local landmark is Wildman's Civil War Surplus, operated across the tracks from the *General* by colorful Dent Meyers. He offers a wide variety of Civil War literature for sale. Be warned: Many consider this store to be racially insensitive.

Each April Kennesaw hosts the Big Shanty Festival, celebrating the Great Locomotive Chase. It features reenactments, entertainment, arts and crafts, and good food.

A walking tour guide to Kennesaw is available locally. It highlights the site of the Lacy Hotel, the Big Shanty Restaurant (which now has a posted policy of not allowing locomotives to be parked outside unattended), and the site of Camp McDonald.

The camp was established here because of a large spring, which is preserved in a park behind the Kennesaw Municipal Building.

North of Kennesaw is the site of Moon's Station, where Andrews's raiders stopped for tools—hammers and a crowbar. Soon after the *General* departed, conductor William A. Fuller and Anthony Murphy arrived and appropriated a handcar from railroad workers to continue their pursuit. The dangerous crossroads is now closed. All that remains is a historical marker. Across Baker Road from the site was a training camp for the Georgia home guard. Thousands were trained, three hundred at a time.

North of Kennesaw is Acworth, where Sherman reconnected with the railroad after his swing west to Dallas. When the Federals started for Savannah in November 1864 much of the railroad town was torched, leaving only a dozen buildings. The city has preserved the James Lemon Antebellum Home (Lemon Street, 770-917-9153, call for limited visiting hours, 1836), used as Sherman's headquarters on June 6–9.

Retrace the route to Kennesaw Mountain and drive past the park. At .3 from the park, turn right onto Kennesaw Avenue.

On this road are several impressive and historically important antebellum homes. Oakton (581 Kennesaw Avenue, 1838) to the right, owned by Newton House, was used as headquarters by Confederate Gen. William W. Loring, and Fair Oaks (505 Kennesaw Avenue, 1862) was Johnston's headquarters during the fighting at Kennesaw Mountain. It is now open as the Marietta Educational Garden Center. At 435 Kennesaw Avenue (1849) is Tranquilla, the former home of Andrew J. Hansell, a colonel of the state militia and aide to Governor Brown. When Union officers took over, Hansell's wife refused to vacate and was allowed to remain in residence. The Archibald Howell house (303 Kennesaw Avenue, 1843) was occupied by Federal Gen. Henry M. Judah in late 1864 and early 1865. Judah received the surrender of Confederate troops at Kingston and distributed food to the civilian population in this area. The house is Greek Revival with huge columns and twenty-eight-inch-thick brick walls.

Henry G. Cole, a staunch Unionist imprisoned late in the war, built the Cole Cottage (Washington Avenue, 1861). It now houses law offices. The Bostwick-Fraser house (on Fraser Street near the Confederate Cemetery, 1844) was purchased by Anne Fraser in 1852. Although she was an Unionist, a son served the Confederacy and was killed at Gettysburg. Her daughter, Fanny, was a nurse and possibly a Confederate spy. The house and grounds were used as a Federal hospital. The impressive 1848 House (east of Powder Springs Road on Garrison Drive), a restaurant on the National Register, has the style of a Charleston plantation house and required eight years to build by John H. Glover. The center of a three-thousand-acre plantation named Brushy Park, it was owned in 1864 by William King of Roswell and was the site of a rear guard clash on July 3 as the Confederates slowly retreated to Smyrna. The house was used as a Union hospital and quarters until after the battle of Allatoona Pass in October, when it was stripped of valuables. Bullets found on the grounds are displayed, and one is embedded in an inner door.

At 2.3 turn right onto Church Street NW.

A short distance to the left, up this one-way street, is the First Presbyterian Church, built in 1852. It was used as a hospital by both armies during 1864 and was so heavily damaged by the Federals that the U.S. government paid three thousand dollars for repairs. It retains an old slave gallery as a balcony. Union forces also utilized the St. James Episcopal Church next door. It burned in 1964, but a small chapel is original and contains an organ that the Federals filled with molasses to "sweeten" the sound. In the Episcopal cemetery on Winn Street, between Polk and Whitlock, is the grave of Alfred R. Waud, a noted Civil War artist.

To the left is the interesting courthouse square. East of the square was the original Cobb County Courthouse, which Sherman fortified when he advanced on Atlanta then ordered burned when the March to the Sea began. Confederates had mustered and drilled on the square, which features a tiny replica of the *General,* on which children now play.

At .4 at the end of the square turn right onto Whitlock for .1. On the right along the tracks is Kennesaw House. Finding a parking space can be tricky, so circle the block to find one.

John H. Glover opened Kennesaw House along the railroad in 1850 as a cotton warehouse and restaurant. The brick four-story structure was purchased by Dix Fletcher and converted into the Fletcher House, a restaurant and forty-room summer resort hotel, one of the best in Georgia and frequented by those who came for the springs now behind Kennestone Hospital. The Fletchers were Northern sympathizers, and some believe Union spy James Andrews knew this and stayed here because of it.

Andrews's raiders met at the hotel the night before they stole the *General* to plan their sabotage. From August 1862 until summer 1864 Confederate casualties and refugees from fighting farther north found shelter here. Sherman briefly established his headquarters in the building while chasing Johnston on July 3 and in November. It partially burned at the start of the March to the Sea on November 11–12, 1864, losing the fourth floor and a balcony. The

The latest incarnation of the Kennesaw House contains a museum of Marietta and Cobb County history, much of it related to the Civil War.

building was reconstructed as a three-story hotel in 1867 as the Kennesaw House. Other renovations occurred in 1930 and 1979, and today the only original parts are the brick exterior, main staircase, and walnut banister. The heart pine floors were taken from old boxcars.

The Kennesaw House was most recently a restaurant, but it closed and the city of Marietta purchased the building. Since 1995 the Marietta Museum of History has been on the second floor, exploring the fascinating legacy of Cobb County and the city from prehistoric times to the present. The museum's extensive Civil War collection is housed in the same room, which contains some of the original furnishings, occupied by Andrews the night before he stole the *General.* The room, which overlooks the tracks, is also the site where the Kennesaw chapter of the United Daughters of the Confederacy was formed on July 29, 1898. There are comprehensive exhibits about the Great Locomotive Chase, the Georgia Military Institute, and the extensive combat that occurred across Cobb County. Featured are one of Sherman's twisted railroad "neckties," rifles, pistols, bayonets, and accouterments, models of the GMI campus and a 12-pounder Napoleon, locally retrieved artillery projectiles, and mannequins dressed as a Union soldier and a GMI cadet complete with short rifle.

There are many other outstanding exhibits and unique artifacts, including a mantle from a slave cabin owned by Gov. Joseph E. Brown, a large textile collection featuring dresses dating to the 1850s, a history and photographs of the hotel, and the legacy of a World War II bomber plant that evolved into Lockheed. During the war the factory employed Confederate Lt. Gen. James Longstreet's widow.

Adjacent to Kennesaw House is the Victorian Western and Atlantic passenger depot, built in 1898 on the site of the original 1840 one that Sherman burned. It currently houses the Marietta welcome center. Pick up comprehensive walking and driving tour guides to dozens of historic homes, churches, commercial structures, and cemeteries in Marietta. Acquire a handy brochure guide to the Confederate Cemetery, which is described below, prepared by the Kennesaw chapter of the UDC and the Rotary Club of Marietta. Also essential is a copy of the Cannonball Trail, prepared by the Cobb Landmarks and Historical Society, which lists seventy-one Civil War sites in the city. The welcome center offers guided walking tours, audiocassette tours for rent, and carriage rides through Marietta.

Continue on Whitlock to the traffic signal at .1 and turn left onto South Marietta Parkway SW, which becomes Powder Springs Road, for .5, and turn left onto Cemetery Street. At the end of the block after .2 turn left onto West Atlanta Street. At .1 turn left into the last cemetery entrance at a sign for the Confederate Cemetery, then turn right immediately. A Confederate monument and a cannon are on the right, a covered pavilion on the left, and the Confederate Cemetery is straight ahead.

The Marietta Confederate Cemetery was originally established on September 24, 1863, on land donated by Jane Glover, Ann Moyer, other residents, and the city of Marietta. The first burials, twenty unknown soldiers killed in a train wreck north of Marietta at Allatoona Pass in 1863, occurred on a corner of Brushy Park, which was then part of the Glover estate. During two weeks of fighting at Kennesaw Mountain five hundred casualties were buried in the hospital section. In 1866 a project was initiated to move Confederate dead from Chickamauga and battlefields of the Atlanta campaign to this Marietta location. Mary J. Green of Resaca fame and Mrs. Charles Williams of the Ladies Memorial Association directed the work, which was funded by the state of Georgia. The General Assembly granted thirty-five hundred dollars for the project, about one dollar per soldier.

The cemetery contains the graves of three thousand men, representing every state in the Confederacy, and monuments record the number sacrificed by each state. Tennessee has the most (325), and Georgia (116) ranks only fourth behind Alabama and Mississippi. Many Georgia casualties, however, would have been claimed by families and taken home for burial. The original wooden headboards deteriorated and were replaced in 1910 by marble memorials, many of them blank. Markers designate sections for the veterans from each Confederate state, plus one for Maryland and another for the men from an old soldiers home. The local UDC chapter was organized to care for the graves. The first burial was Dr. W. H. Miller on September 9, 1863, and the last, in 1989, was a soldier uncovered by construction activity. Most men who died in a local Confederate veterans

Many Southern casualties from the Atlanta campaign are interred at the Marietta Confederate Cemetery.

home were buried here, and the last survivor was a black servant, Bill Yopp, of a Confederate officer, Thomas Yopp of Dublin, who died in the home at the age of eighty-two. The former slave had raised money for the home, and other veterans gave him a medal and invited him to live there for the rest of his life.

Also interred here are Lorenzo Dow Grave, who died in 1926 at the age of 114, the oldest age any Confederate veteran reached; Russell Taylor, a GMI cadet; and John A. Blunt, a rare Confederate marine from Georgia.

Buried in the civilian portion of the cemetery is Gen. William Phillips (1824–1908). He fought in western Virginia, lost an eye, contracted typhoid, and was discharged only to find his home and factories destroyed by Sherman.

Magnificent old trees frame the grounds, and from the hillside is a beautiful view of Kennesaw Mountain to the north, symbolizing the local combat where many of these men died. The UDC dedicated a twenty-foot-tall shaft erected to the memory of the men buried here and to Cobb County's Confederate veterans on July 7, 1908. Clement A. Evans offered the principal speech, declaring this a "garden of heroes." The Georgia General Assembly adjourned early to attend. In 1911 a ten-foot-tall memorial arch was dedicated to the fallen. The gazebo, erected in 1974, is employed yearly for Confederate Memorial Day observances. The wrought-iron fence was added in the 1990s.

A bronze 6-pounder cannon, No. 27, cast in Boston by Cyrus Alger and Company, is kept on a special marble platform enclosed by a wrought-iron fence. It was used for training by the Georgia Military Institute from 1857 until 1861, when it was transferred to Savannah. The gun was abandoned when the Confederates evacuated Savannah, and Sherman sent it north as a trophy of war. It was returned in 1910 from Watervliet, New York. A Latin inscription reads, "Wisdom, the Victor over Fortune."

Recent plans call for a parking area in adjoining Brown Park, flags representing each state with burials here, and a life-sized bronze sculpture representing the three local women who helped establish and preserve the cemetery.

Just south of the cemetery and opposite it on Powder Springs Road is the 110-acre hilltop site once called College Hill, home to the Georgia Military Institute but long the property of golf clubs. The site contains the home of Arnoldus Vanderhorst Brumby, from 1851 to 1859 the superintendent of the institute, on the northwest corner of the campus. The facility had been founded in 1851 in hopes that it would become the southern West Point. GMI consisted of fourteen barracks, a classroom building, a dining hall, and a gun house, collectively valued at twelve thousand dollars.

The cadets, including Governor Brown's son Julius, helped drill Confederate recruits at Camp McDonald. When Sherman approached in 1864, 150 cadets, aged fifteen to eighteen, marched off to fight for the Confederacy. They first served at Resaca on May 14 before returning home two days later. Soon they served as a provost guard here, rounding up stragglers and dealing with refugees. Cadets guarded the Chattahoochee River railroad bridge at West Point, then occupied the River Line and Atlanta's trenches and traveled to guard the capitol in Milledgeville. They participated in the defense against Sherman's march to Savannah, fighting at the Oconee River and escaping across the Savannah River with William J. Hardee. Barred by law from fighting outside the state, the cadets marched directly up the South Carolina side of the river to Augusta and returned home ragged and emaciated. In February 1865 they were again dispatched to Milledgeville before returning to Augusta, where they helped restore order as the city was inundated by paroled Confederates from Virginia and the Carolinas. The unit was disbanded at Augusta on May 20,

1865. They surrendered their flagstaff and a large white portion of a Second National Flag, but not the corner of the flag that was the battle flag, which they had received from Mary Jones at West Point on June 21, 1864. Cadet George Coleman stuffed that portion inside his shirt and returned home. In 1932 GMI survivors presented the flag to the state; it is part of the collection in the capitol. During the war six boys died in combat, and six succumbed to disease.

Both sides used the facilities as a hospital, and George H. Thomas established his headquarters here and imprisoned Confederate captives. More than ten thousand soldiers received care, primarily in tents and beneath brush arbors. When Sherman left on the March to the Sea, he torched seventeen buildings on the campus, the courthouse, and every commercial building on the square. This site has good views of Kennesaw Mountain and other peaks.

Sherman spared Brumby's house (472 Powder Springs Road, 1854), a raised Greek Revival cottage constructed next door to the school, perhaps because the two men had been friends at West Point.

The Marietta Country Club occupied the campus for decades. When that facility moved, the land was purchased by the state and developed into the twenty-six-million-dollar Marietta Conference Center and Resort (500 Powder Springs Road), which features two hundred rooms and an eighteen-hole golf course. Brumby Hall was purchased in 1995 and restored to its 1850s appearance, and extensive gardens were planted. The structure is now a house museum used for special events at the resort.

When the school was organized, GMI received 120 short muskets and equipment, 18 short swords, and what were later presumed to be 4 brass 6-pounders with accouterments. In reality, the institute probably had 2 6-pounders and 2 12-pounders. In 1909 Gov. Joseph M. Brown, son of the wartime governor, was told that a 6-pounder, inscribed GMI, was at the Watervliet Arsenal in New York and available for $150. It was acquired by the Marietta Memorial Association and placed at the Confederate Cemetery in 1910. The piece, however, is a 6-pounder bronze field gun, not a howitzer (as had been previously thought).

In 1928 another bronze 6-pounder cadet gun, No. 2, manufactured in Boston and also inscribed GMI, was discovered in storage at Gettysburg National Battlefield Park and offered to the city of Marietta. It had been captured at Savannah and inventoried by Sherman's noted military engineer Orlando Poe. The gun was accepted in a ceremony in Pennsylvania on March 24, 1928, then mounted on a stone from Kennesaw Mountain at the Marietta Country Club. On Confederate Memorial Day, April 26, 1928, it was dedicated by Cordelia Brumby, a relative of Commandant Brumby. A crowd of thousands attended, including a few elderly cadets. The gun was displayed for sixty years. When the club moved in 1990 many expected the gun to follow, but the government had stipulated that it must be displayed on the "original soil" of the school. The state resort had an authentic wooden carriage constructed for the tube, and it is now displayed (facing north) in a hallway that connects the conference center with the resort. The Latin inscription reads, "Virtue stands because of its strength." Three mannequins are displayed near the gun: one dressed as a young cadet, another as Colonel Brumby, and a third representing Brumby's wife. Around the center and hotel are numerous prints of Civil War topics and murals of the institute circa 1851. The golf course was swept with metal detectors, and artifacts, including artillery and rifle projectiles and an 1851 GMI button, are displayed. This gun is labeled as a howitzer, but it is also a field gun.

Some controversy continues over the origin, number, type, and disposition of the GMI guns. The state and/or federal government may have given four guns to the school for artillery drill, but they were probably two 12-pounders and two 6-pounders. The lighter guns bore the state seal atop the tube and Latin inscriptions. At the institute they daily fired one round at sunset. Contrary to popular opinion, the cadets went to war as infantry and did not have artillery with them.

Two of the guns were sent to Milledgeville for the inauguration of Gov. Joseph E. Brown. At that event a cadet lost an arm while sponging one of the pieces.

Two bronze 12-pounder howitzer tubes thought to be from GMI are mounted in front of an entrance to the capitol in Atlanta. Ordered to Fort Jackson in Savannah, they were captured there in 1864 and later returned. The guns were displayed at Fort Walker near the Cyclorama in Atlanta for twenty-five years.

Return to Powder Springs Road and turn right. After .6 turn right onto Whitlock (GA 120). (Across GA 3-5-West Park Street, Whitlock becomes South Park Street and then Roswell Street NE.) Stay in the right lane until Waddel is crossed. After .3 turn left onto Haynes Street NE then almost immediately right onto Washington Street. At .2 the entrance to the Marietta National Cemetery is on the right.

The cemetery was established in 1866 on twenty-four acres donated by Henry Greene Cole, a citizen with Unionist sympathies who had once been arrested and imprisoned for his outspoken beliefs. He hoped that the Federal and Confederate dead could be buried together as a gesture of healing. When the federal government rejected his offer, he donated the land for the burial of Union soldiers. Those who fell south of Resaca and the Oostanaula River in the Atlanta campaign were buried here; the Chattanooga National Cemetery was established for all the Union men who died north of that point. After the war 10,132 men, including 3,000 unidentified casualties from the battlefields at Adairsville, Cassville, Dallas, New Hope Church, Pickett's Mill, Kennesaw Mountain, and the Atlanta battles, as well as cavalry raiders killed in Alabama, and two dozen African American troops were reinterred here. Residents constructed coffins, fences, and markers and landscaped the grounds. Because bounties of one dollar for each set of remains were offered, many poor people attempted to turn in animal bones. For many years former slaves from the Atlanta area gathered at the cemetery on Memorial Day to celebrate their emancipation.

Mountainous north Georgia was the sanctuary of draft evaders, Unionist guerrillas, and thieving raiders. The home guard and Georgia militia fought them cruelly; executions and persecutions of entire families were common. With Union Gen. George H. Thomas's permission, James G. Brown in 1864 sought to recruit a Federal unit from these hills, but he netted only three hundred.

On November 5, 1864, Col. James Findley of the First Georgia Cavalry captured twenty-one Unionists at Bucktown in Gilmer County. Four were killed in the skirmish, additional sympathizers were arrested in Dawsonville, and twelve deserters were executed on November 7 in Gainesville. In July 1887 their remains were moved to the national cemetery.

A high wall encloses the twenty-four-acre cemetery, and large oaks and magnolia trees shade the

Many Union casualties of the Atlanta campaign are buried in the Marietta National Cemetery.

graves situated on a rolling hillside. Monuments from several Northern states honor their dead, and a pavilion for ceremonies is atop the hill. As the only national cemetery in northern Georgia (another will open soon in Cherokee County), solemn services are conducted here each Memorial Day.

From this point we will proceed east to Roswell, but in the near future several significant historic sites may be opened to the public.

When Johnston withdrew from the Kennesaw Line on July 4, Sherman sent troops in rapid pursuit with McPherson racing west to reach Johnston's left flank, Schofield advancing in the center, with Thomas on the outside to the east. They were brought up short by a surprise—a double line of field works called the Smyrna–Ruff's Mill Line, backed by Johnston's entire army. Loring was on the right, Hardee in the center, and Hood to the left. Sherman struck both ends, at Smyrna and two miles to the east at Ruff's Mill, to little effect.

Little remains to commemorate the fighting at Smyrna (most landmarks were destroyed during the construction of Dobbins Air Reserve Base) or the race to the Chattahoochee River on July 4, 1864. Ruff's Mill on Concord Road between Marietta and Smyrna, however, is part of the Concord Covered Bridge Historic District, which features a scenic covered bridge at Nickajack Creek that replaced one destroyed during the war. The bridge, rebuilt in 1872, is 133 feet long, 16 feet wide, and 13 feet high. If you can get to a position to look under the span, the stone center pier dates back to the original bridge (1848).

Picturesque Nickajack Creek makes a double horseshoe loop here, forming a peninsula and a sharp drop perfect for generating waterpower. The Concord community features Ruff's Gristmill (1850s), a well-preserved brick structure behind the stone wall at the covered bridge, but it no longer contains millworks. Martin Ruff's antebellum house was an emergency hospital during the battle. The Gann house (1840s) was built by politician John Gann a quarter of a mile from the bridge. His family was forced to house, feed, and wash clothes for fifteen Union officers for a time, but their home was saved by a Masonic flag flown from an upstairs window. The house was also used as a Civil War hospital. The miller's house (1850) also survived. It and the Henry Clay Ruff house are on the southeastern side of the bridge. All are on the National Register.

Although a woolen mill, often mentioned in official records, that manufactured Confederate uniforms and a sawmill were destroyed, the gristmill was spared for its food production use. The wooden antebellum factory was rebuilt in 1869 with three stories of stone as the Concord Manufacturing Company. It burned again, was rebuilt in 1889, closed in 1912. The stone walls have recently been reinforced with steel framing. The reconstructed sawmill produced considerable timber used to rebuild the Western and Atlantic after the war. The Rock house (1900), a fieldstone summer cottage, and century-old iron railroad trestle bridge complete the historic district. This area was threatened for several decades but may become a sizable heritage park.

Sherman had hoped to attack Johnston before the Confederates crossed the Chattahoochee after abandoning the Kennesaw Mountain Line, but the Confederates frustrated him at Smyrna and Ruff's Mill then occupied an elaborate, intimidating line of fortifications. The River Line was fifteen miles northwest of Atlanta on the north bank of the Chattahoochee, protecting the Mason-Turner Ferry, which served the primary road from Atlanta to Alabama. Today the Chattahoochee, Nickajack Creek, and GA 280-Cobb Drive border it. Bankhead Highway–Veterans Parkway–U.S. 78-278–GA 8 pierces the River Line, and Oakdale Road parallels the defenses between Nickajack Creek and the Chattahoochee.

The River Line, included on the National Register, was designed and constructed by Col. Francis A.

Shoup, the thirty-year-old chief of artillery for the Army of Tennessee. It was crescent shaped, four and a half miles long, and up to one mile in depth. The position consisted of thirty-six arrowhead-shaped infantry forts called "shoupades," which were 150–200 yards apart. Each was sixteen feet high and had double pine log walls that were notched at the ends like log cabins and filled with compacted earth. The walls were twelve feet thick at the base and four feet thick at the top. These revolutionary forts, considered impervious to artillery fire, which was absorbed by the walls, were constructed on top of the ground, not dug into it. The shoupades were defended by a company of men, eighty soldiers; most of whom loaded weapons on the ground and passed them up to a firing platform, called a banquette, constructed two-thirds of the way up the wall, so the better marksmen could maintain a nearly continuous fire.

Alternating with the shoupades were two-gun redans designed to create interlocking fields of fire. The entire line was connected using deep trenches and protected by an eight-foot-high stockade with advanced rifle pits. Adding further security to the line were lunettes and redoubts containing 20-pounder Parrott rifles transported from Mobile, Alabama. The ends of the line at the river were anchored by larger artillery forts. Confederate engineers, Georgia militia, and one thousand conscripted slaves constructed the fortifications in June 1864, three weeks before they were needed.

Patrick Cleburne saw great advantages to the River Line, but John Bell Hood hated it, believing the defensive works stifled the aggression of the troops. Sherman believed they were the strongest fieldworks he had ever seen. Johnston hoped that the Federals would attack, but Sherman resorted to his best talent: flanking. The Confederates occupied the River Line for only five days, July 5–9, until McPherson swung southwest to feint a crossing on the lower Chattahoochee River, then swung behind Sherman to cross the river farther upstream at Roswell while Schofield crossed at Sope Creek. Johnston was forced to withdraw across the Chattahoochee, where he was subsequently relieved.

The revolutionary shoupades were far ahead of their time and have been compared with the Maginot line constructed by the French after World War I.

About ten shoupades remain, most on private property, but one of them and a seven-gun battery will soon be preserved in a park. The latter position, at the south end of the River Line near the mouth of Nickajack Creek where it flows into the Chattahoochee, anchored the south end of the line. The logs rotted away long ago, but the earthworks are remarkably well preserved. In 1990 Cobb County obtained 102 acres, containing fifteen hundred feet of earthworks, from a developer who received permission to level an equal length of works for construction of an industrial park. In March 2001, Cobb County deeded the works to the state. Georgia plans to clear brush, construct a parking lot, and place interpretive signage. The works may remain unimproved, but a replica of a shoupade as it would have appeared in 1864 may be constructed. Breastworks and traverse lines are still visible at the site, a high bluff on the south bank above Nickajack Creek and southwest of Smyrna. This shoupade is in an industrial area, with an airport situated directly across the river, but the site is remote and screened by heavy woods. Across the creek are the remains of a small Union artillery fort.

Another surviving shoupade in south Cobb is in an upscale gated development off Log Cabin Road near I-85 and Atlanta Road. The fort and associated earthworks were incorporated into greenspace, but they are inaccessible to nonresidents.

The Smyrna Historical and Genealogical Society (2861 Atlanta Street) is housed in a reproduction of the city's railroad depot, which was demolished in 1959. It houses historical exhibits, photographs, artifacts, and mementos. Next door is Smyrna's welcome center, housed in Aunt Fanny's Cabin, a famed former restaurant.

The Robert Mable house (1843, 5239 Floyd Road SW, Mableton, GA 30059, 770-739-0189), just north of U.S. 78–U.S. 278–Veterans Memorial Highway and just north of Maran Lane, was the centerpiece of a four-hundred-acre plantation. It was the site of a Federal camp on July 3, 1864, when several corps marched past. The structure was later used by both armies as a field hospital. The house retains its heart pine floors, hand-hewn beams, and wooden pegs. The original detached kitchen and smokehouse also survive. This is Gov. Roy Barnes's home area, and he arranged to preserve the house, including the family cemetery, as an 1840s farm and amphitheater.

When Federals approached the Israel Causey home (5909 Maxham Road, 1840), Causey loaded food and supplies on a wagon and "refugeed" to Villa Rica, leaving his wife and daughters to secure the house. Union troops occupied the house for some time, confining the women to the attic. As one soldier attempted to break into the attic, Margaret Causey whacked him in the head with a board. The soldier fell off the ladder and died of a broken neck. Two of the Causeys' sons were killed during the war and are buried in the Causey–Shady Grove Cemetery.

Vinings is named for the man who constructed the Western and Atlantic through this area. It was founded by Hardy Pace, who arrived in the 1830s, purchased ten thousand acres of land, and built an important ferry across the Chattahoochee River where Pace's Ferry Road is today as well as a gristmill, tavern, and farm. It was here at Pace's Ferry that the Confederate wagon trains, escorted by Joseph Wheeler's cavalry, barely escaped Federal pursuit after the withdrawal from Kennesaw Mountain and crossed the Chattahoochee. The pontoon bridge was cut from the north bank to swing to the Confederate shore, but instead it floated to the Union side and was seized.

Sherman established his headquarters in Pace's house and viewed Atlanta from the top of 1,170-foot-high Vinings Mountain while artillery batteries were being emplaced opposite Confederate guns across the river. The general remained for eleven days before crossing the Chattahoochee River at Power's Ferry just upriver. Oliver O. Howard then maintained his quarters here. It was from here on July 14 that Sherman issued Special Field Orders No. 35, outlining his plan to broach the Chattahoochee River. Two Federal corps crossed here on two pontoon bridges. Throughout the siege of Atlanta, munitions and supplies arrived at a railroad terminal established here, and wounded were treated and evacuated north. When Sherman abandoned the siege lines and swung southwest to sever the railroads, he heavily fortified this place. The mountain was garrisoned through the fall for use as a signal station, but the Pace house (1837) was destroyed when the Federals started for Savannah.

Pace had refugeed to Milledgeville, where he died shortly afterward. His widow retrieved his body for burial at the top of Vinings Mountain and cobbled together a new six-room home from three slave cabins. The house has been preserved and restored for use as a museum. Vinings soon became a resort spa where Gov. Joseph E. Brown built Pavilion House to encourage rail trips to the springs. The Vinings Historic Preservation Society has moved the pavilion near the Pace house.

In previous years Vinings was known for its pleasant taverns, restaurants, and shops, but developers found this refuge north of the Chattahoochee and bulldozed the rear of the mountain for office towers and hundreds of apartments, and development continues. The river, U.S. 41-GA 3, and Interstate 285 border Vinings.

Old U.S. 41 crosses the Chattahoochee at Bolton, where Johnston retreated across the river to defend Atlanta after abandoning the River Line. Artillery exchanges and cavalry clashes were frequent occurrences for weeks, and Sherman defended this same spot to protect a vital railroad bridge when he shifted most of his forces south to Jonesboro. At the Lovett School, just south of Vinings, Thomas crossed the Chattahoochee at Pace's Ferry on July 17. Other troops crossed at Power's Ferry the same day.

To continue the driving tour, from the national cemetery turn right onto Washington and right again at .4 onto the second street, which is Rock, for .1 to Roswell Street-GA 120, and turn left. After .9, at the famous Big Chicken, turn right onto U.S. 41–GA 3–Cobb Parkway. After .7 turn left onto GA 120 Loop–Marietta Parkway for 1.7 then right onto Lower Roswell Road for 2.1. Turn right onto Old Terrell Mill Road for .2 then left onto Old Paper Mill Road SE. To stop and explore the ruins, at 1 mile a parking area is off the road to the right a short distance before Paper Mill Road crosses Sope Creek. The extensive stone ruins are part of the Chattahoochee River National Recreation Area.

Follow the paths beside the creek; ruins can be found on both banks, with the most impressive remains found on the western side. This was the Marietta Paper Mill, established in 1859 and rumored to have produced paper for Confederate currency. Kenner Garrard's cavalry torched the place. On July 7, 1864, Schofield's men managed the first crossing of the Chattahoochee River here at Sope Creek, between Power's Ferry and Johnson's Ferry, and advanced

Mill ruins at Sope Creek mark the site where Union troops first forced a crossing of the Chattahoochee.

toward Buckhead, forcing Johnston's withdrawal from the River Line. Union Lt. Col. James P. Brownlow ordered his First Tennessee (U.S.) regiment to strip and cross the river with rifles, cartridge boxes, and hats. They successfully made a lodgement on the far shore and swore they would have captured many prisoners except the Confederates had the advantage of running through the bushes fully clothed.

The mill was rebuilt, burned in 1870, brought back into production, and closed permanently in 1902. A trail follows the creek for a distance, but only halfway to its confluence with the Chattahoochee River, and bends to approach the river upstream of Nickajack Creek.

An overlook deck with signage at AMIL of Sope Creek describes the Union crossing of Sope Creek in the area.

A nine-mile-long urban and historical park along the Fulton County side (the southern and Confederate bank) of the Chattahoochee from Peachtree Creek to Camp Creek is planned. On the northern bank, the Cobb County and Union side of the river, is the Chattahoochee National Recreational Area that preserves forty-eight miles of riverfront. It consists of foot trails with interpretive exhibits that explain the historic and natural features of the area. Civil War earthworks are common in the wooded areas.

Continue east on Old Paper Mill Road. At .3 on a sharp curve at Sope Creek the paper mill ruins are on the right. Continue east for 1.8. Turn left onto Johnson Ferry Road for 2.7. Turn right onto East 120-Roswell Road for 4.2. Turn left on GA 9–North Atlanta Street–GA 120-9 for .1 then turn right onto Sloan. Turn right at .1 onto Mill Street to the stop sign. Park in the large lot.

7

The Final Barrier

AFTER THE DISASTER AT Kennesaw, Sherman became convinced that further attempts to smash through the Confederate lines would be futile, wasteful exercises. He was, however, heartened by a dramatic change in the weather when the rain ceased for several days, and the countryside began to dry. With direct assault unwise and the roads finally passable, the Federal commander decided to resume his masterful flanking movements. He would cut loose from the railroad again for a swing to the west around Johnston's left and devour the remaining country before Atlanta. His troops were instructed to carry all the munitions and rations they would need for several weeks, and the advance was set in motion.

On the day of the Kennesaw assault, while George H. Thomas and James B. McPherson valiantly attacked the Confederate positions, John M. Schofield feinted around John Bell Hood, who occupied the extreme left of the Rebel front, successfully lodging his men behind Johnston by reaching the Sandtown Road and threatening the Confederate flank. Sherman called this the "only advantage of the day." Schofield, with McPherson following, would sweep around the Southern line and force Johnston to abandon Kennesaw Mountain. Thomas would play his usual role, remaining in front of the Rebels and exerting pressure on the center of their works.

On July 2 Johnston was alarmed to discover Schofield and McPherson closer to Atlanta than he was, but his resources were exhausted, and he lacked the manpower to extend his line to the west and meet Sherman's new threat. Withdrawal to a more defensible position seemed his only choice. During the night Johnston executed another of his legendary disappearances by extricating his command en masse. A weary Confederate soldier recognized Sherman's premier skill by remarking that the Union general would surely escape hell by flanking his way into heaven.

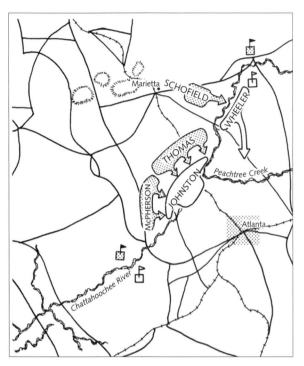

Map 17: Crossing the Chattahoochee River

Dawn on July 3 revealed no trace of the Confederate army on the mountain or in the lengthy trenches west of the citadel. Sherman watched anxiously through his glasses as Federal pickets cautiously crept up the cratered slopes to examine the powerful works atop the battered crest. The Kennesaw Line was completely vacant, and Sherman assumed his nemesis was in total retreat beyond the Chattahoochee River and would occupy the trenches that guarded the outskirts of Atlanta, "for no general, such as he," he wrote, "would invite battle with the Chattahoochee behind him." Sherman intended to pursue Johnston hotly and destroy the Confederates as they attempted to cross the river, but Johnston would baffle Sherman again, making two audacious stands before slipping over the final barrier.

The race to the Chattahoochee would be a close contest, with the winner controlling the bridges, ferries, and fords across the river. If Johnston prevailed, he would be able to defend Atlanta; if Sherman won, Atlanta and the Army of Tennessee would likely be destroyed.

Sherman and his staff quickly rode into Marietta early on the morning of July 3, but his anger was kindled by the absence of Kenner Garrard's cavalry and "Old Slow Trot" Thomas and his ponderous Army of the Cumberland. Garrard and Thomas eventually arrived, but the vanguard only covered five miles south of Marietta before it was rudely halted at Smyrna. Instead of fleeing for the protection of Atlanta, the Southern army had occupied a line of strong fieldworks constructed on a ridge behind Nickajack Creek that commanded the railroad and turned to face its pursuers. Johnston was inviting Sherman to attack, but this time the offer was declined.

At first light on July 4, Sherman rode to the front of Thomas's column, reluctant to believe that Johnston had stopped with the Chattahoochee at his back. Thomas explained that the Confederates were entrenched in force at Smyrna, but Sherman dismissed that possibility. "There is no force in your front," he admonished Thomas. "They are laughing at you."

"We will see," Thomas replied, sending forward a line of skirmishers to probe the Rebel works. Batteries of concealed guns and ranks of invisible infantry on the wooded hill hurled a murderous storm of shot at the troops, who rapidly withdrew. Sherman decided against jeopardizing his men with a frontal assault against the stout line and instructed Thomas to keep the Confederates busy while Johnston was flanked out of this position. The frustrated Sherman believed he would certainly catch the Confederates in a perilous withdrawal across the river.

Thomas opened what a Confederate called a "furious shelling" of the Rebel works, and Union troops made demonstrations against two points of Johnston's defenses. A division assaulted the left of the Confederate line, held by Hood at Ruff's Mill, and was repulsed. A second effort carried Hood's first line of works, but the Rebel front remained intact. A second Federal force had a try against Hardee's trenches at Smyrna, on the Confederate right, but found it impregnable.

Sherman wrote, "We celebrated our Fourth of July by a noisy but not desperate battle to hold the enemy there [at Smyrna] till Generals McPherson and Schofield could get well into position below him near the Chattahoochee crossings."

Events were progressing more to Sherman's taste to the west, where Schofield's and McPherson's forces faced only William Jackson's cavalry and some newly arrived Georgia militia.

In late June Georgia's intransigent Gov. Joseph E. Brown had unexpectedly dispatched three thousand Georgia militia to join Johnston's command, but with the condition that he could withdraw the men from Confederate service whenever the state required them. Most of these soldiers were poorly trained, untried young boys and old men led by Gustavus W. Smith, but Johnston nonetheless welcomed their presence. Smith resourcefully appropriated a battery of guns that were being refitted in Atlanta and reported his pitiful force for duty. Smith's cavalry deployed to patrol the Chattahoochee River crossings, and his infantry filed into place on Johnston's left flank at Kennesaw.

When Sherman initiated his flanking effort, Smith and Jackson were ordered to impede the Federal march, a task the militia performed well. They skirmished aggressively with the Federals then withdrew in good order to keep the enemy at their front. As Smith admitted, his principal response was to "get out of the way" when the two Yankee armies advanced. Faced with such overwhelming odds, the blocking force was thrown back several miles on July 3, took up a new position for the night, and on July 4 was hit hard and forced to retreat to Johnston's final line of defense on the northern bank of the Chattahoochee. There the Yankees formed a heavy skirmish line, and Smith awaited the inevitable assault by half the Federal army. Fortunately, his battery was expertly tended. The Confederates peppered the Union ranks with a deadly fire that kept the enemy at a respectful distance. In return, the Southerners received a destructive artillery fire.

Smith felt lonely when darkness fell. He was outnumbered ten to one, his flanks were dangerously exposed, and his troops had never known serious combat. Most troubling was the absence of the Confederate army. Smith dispatched a note informing Johnston that the undermanned works would be occupied by massive numbers of Union troops when they attacked at daybreak. If he did not receive a reply from Johnston by dawn, Smith intended to retreat across the Chattahoochee and save his command from certain ruin.

A Note on Casualties

When Sherman marched into Georgia, his strength was 98,800 soldiers. The number of Union troops peaked in early June at 112,819, but the siege of Atlanta took a toll. After the action at Jonesboro, Sherman counted 81,758 men in the ranks. During the campaign, estimated Federal losses totaled 4,400 killed, 23,000 wounded, and 4,500 captured or missing.

Johnston's army was comprised of 42,900 men at the beginning of the campaign and peaked at 64,600 after Polk's corps was added. Most of the Confederate casualties—3,000 killed, 19,000 wounded, and an incredible 13,000 captured, missing, or deserted—occurred after Hood took command and attacked Sherman. When Atlanta was evacuated, the thin ranks of the Army of Tennessee numbered only 35,000 soldiers.

During the night the Army of Tennessee appeared, an unruffled Johnston at its head. He commended Smith for accomplishing a difficult mission. The Georgia militia had proven themselves under fire, bravely holding off a superior force until the regulars could arrive to relieve them and resume the fight.

When Johnston abandoned Smyrna, Sherman was hard on his heels, convinced that the Confederates would hurriedly cross the river. The resourceful Johnston, however, quickly occupied the formidable works on the north side of the river, and Sherman was brought up short for a second time. Johnston had won the race by a hair, again frightening his own officers but managing to make the maneuver appear simple, to Sherman's continued mystification.

An exasperated Sherman could hardly believe the sight that greeted him. Instead of a vulnerable army feverishly attempting to span the wide river, he found Johnston's "River Line," as it became known, an extremely heavy perimeter of artillery forts and infantry trenches that Sherman called the "best line of field entrenchments I have ever seen." The bastions, log-and-earth works with walls twelve feet thick, stood at eighty-yard intervals and were linked by log stockades. Augmenting Johnston's field guns were huge siege cannon requisitioned from the defenses of Mobile, Alabama. The line was six miles long and one mile deep, occupying high ground from a ridge overlooking Nickajack Creek on the left to the Chattahoochee River on the right. The massive defenses forbade attack. The fortifications covered the railroad bridge over the river, a major wagon bridge, and three pontoon avenues that Johnston installed to ensure a safe passage if he were forced to withdraw quickly. There was adequate space for his entire army, with William W. Loring occupying the right, John Bell Hood the left, and William J. Hardee the center.

On July 5 Sherman probed the Confederate line, which he compared to a hornet's nest that released a hail of bullets and cannon fire. "I came very close to being shot myself," he remarked.

With cavalry screening the river crossings north and south of the line, Johnston waited for Sherman's reaction, which he hoped would include a debilitating assault. But Sherman, scanning the extensive works, remembered the slaughter at Kennesaw Mountain and rejected that rash action. He was astonished that Johnston had twice violated the rules of military strategy and invited combat with a wide river behind him, but such things made Johnston a worthy adversary.

On July 5 the rapidly advancing Federals chased the Confederate wagon train, which was shielded by Joseph Wheeler's cavalry, to the Chattahoochee. Under artillery fire, the wagons crossed safely at Pace's Ferry on pontoon bridges, which were cut loose to float to the southern side. One bridge swung the wrong direction in the current and was captured by jubilant Union forces, who considered it a consolation prize for having let the vital wagon train slip from their grasp yet again.

HARPER'S WEEKLY

With Kennesaw behind them and the Chattahoochee in front of them, the Federals could glimpse the city of Atlanta in the distance. It was still far from being within their grasp.

Late that day the Federals occupied Vinings on the north bank of the river. From the heights of Vinings Mountain, Sherman and Thomas first viewed the river and the prize beyond. "Atlanta is in plain view," Sherman wrote, giving the city little attention as he promptly began casting about for the most viable site to cross the barrier and flank Johnston from the River Line.

Accompanying Sherman was Maj. James Connolly, who was moved by the sight to write poetically, "Mine eyes have beheld the promised land. The 'domes and minarets and spires' of Atlanta are glittering in the sun before us, only eight miles distant." Vinings became a temporary railroad depot as Sherman built up his munitions and rations for the impending siege of Atlanta, and his wounded were carried there for evacuation north.

Sherman lost little time securing the remainder of the north bank. He sent Garrard's cavalry dashing north sixteen miles to occupy the important manufacturing center of Roswell and to probe for a crossing point. Garrard dispatched a detachment to burn the Sope Creek Paper Mills, which had manufactured newsprint, stationery, and wrapping paper since 1857.

At Roswell, Garrard drove Confederate cavalry over the Chattahoochee bridge, which was subsequently burned. Then he destroyed three factories that made cotton and wool used for Confederate uniforms. The owner of one mill raised a French flag in hopes of convincing the Federals the factory was foreign owned, but that stratagem failed. The mills were burned, and Sherman, angered by the connivance, granted advance permission to hang the next man who attempted such a charade.

The Federal troops were in high spirits. After six long weeks they had finally emerged from the wilderness of Dallas and Kennesaw. The soldiers were fighting in open country with room to maneuver, the weather was pleasant, and scouting along the banks of the Chattahoochee. They believed the end of the campaign was near.

For Sherman the first task was to cross the river in good order. He had devised a strategy for accomplishing this before leaving Chattanooga: feint south and cross north. The militia and Johnston's cavalry were responsible for holding the fords above and below the River Line, and McPherson briefly demonstrated below Atlanta to deceive Confederate scouts and initiate false reports that a Federal penetration was imminent there.

Then, on July 6, Sherman sent McPherson on a long march behind Schofield and Thomas—through the old Smyrna battlefield—to the north, where he established the extreme left of the Union line at Roswell. Schofield followed a day later, swinging around Thomas and camping at Sope Creek on July 8 to form the Federal center. Thomas had his accustomed mission: demonstrate against the River Line to keep the Confederates occupied and prevent their recognizing the dangerous operations being carried out upstream.

Future Presidents in Georgia

Among the Federal forces that invaded Georgia in 1864 was a colonel of the green Seventieth Indiana who would later make history. Benjamin Harrison, grandson of President William Henry Harrison, first led his four hundred men into combat at Resaca. They charged Hood's exposed battery with Harrison shouting, "Cheer, men, for Indiana! Forward!" The Confederate artillerists loaded canister and punished the Hoosiers, who sought safety on the ground.

When Harrison saw the Rebels' supporting infantry withdraw, he stood and led his men into the Confederate earthworks with a sword in one hand and a pistol in the other. After desperate hand-to-hand combat, the guns were captured.

At Peachtree Creek, when George H. Thomas's line was bent by a savage Confederate charge, Harrison led a spirited counterattack. His soldiers crashed into the advancing Rebels and slowly drove them back, saving the day for the Union.

Harrison left the army later that fall to occupy a seat in the U.S. House of Representatives, and in 1888 he was elected president. Although he lost the popular vote, Harrison managed to take the electoral count.

A year earlier, Brig. Gen. James Garfield had entered Georgia as chief of staff to William Rosecrans. He was forced to flee the field at Chickamauga with Rosecrans but returned to deliver instructions to Thomas, who had remained to blunt the Confederate pursuit. That act saved his reputation, and in 1880 Garfield won the presidency by a scant ten thousand votes. After four months in office, Garfield was shot by a disturbed and disappointed office-seeker. He died seven months after taking office.

In May 1865 Confederate President Jefferson Davis and Vice President Alexander Stephens were captured in Georgia and transferred to Augusta, where they boarded a ship that took them to prison in the North. As the captives were driven through Augusta, nine-year-old Woodrow Wilson, whose father was a Presbyterian minister, viewed the procession from his home. Wilson became president in 1912.

Schofield was the first to pinpoint a chink in the Chattahoochee armor, exploiting it on July 8 at the mouth of Sope Creek, five miles north of the River Line. A keen-eyed soldier found the submerged remains of an old stone fish dam, and a few men waded across, seized, and held the bank as twenty pontoon boats ferried across an additional regiment. Schofield rapidly threw a pontoon bridge, which had been hidden from Confederate view behind a ridge, across the river and passed over additional elements of his Third Division. With Jacob Cox's regiment acting as skirmishers, additional men quickly joined them to establish a bridgehead on the south bank. They raced up a high ridge three hundred yards beyond the river, routed a small camp of surprised Confederates, captured a cannon, and entrenched. Schofield rushed a second division across before Johnston was informed of the development. Without sustaining a single casualty, Sherman had breached the last barrier remaining in his path to Atlanta.

At Roswell on the following day, Garrard made up for the time he lost in Marietta by forcing a crossing at Shallowford. On July 10 Federal army engineers constructed two bridges across the river there.

Also on July 9, Union cavalry made a third crossing just south of Sope Creek. These cavalrymen dismounted, carried their guns over their heads, and waded nude—except for hats—across the river to establish another Federal position south of the Chattahoochee.

These splendid strategic maneuvers, brilliantly conceived and flawlessly executed, accomplished their purpose. Finding himself outflanked on July 8, Johnston was forced to abandon the impregnable River Line and withdraw across the Chattahoochee during the night of July 9. Once more the sound of marching feet, horse hooves, and creaking artillery crossing the wooden bridge and pontoon spans were muffled with straw and cornstalks. When all traffic had passed, the bridge was burned. The Confederates occupied the outer defenses of Atlanta, several miles north of the city on a ridge overlooking Peachtree Creek. Behind it was only the inner ring of fortifications that protected the city.

The next week saw little activity along the Chattahoochee front. Sherman marked time on the north bank and in his beachheads on the south side by resting his men, rebuilding the railroad and wagon bridges, and waiting for supplies and reinforcements to arrive at Vinings. The reconstruction of the Chattahoochee railroad bridge is still considered a significant engineering feat. In four and a half days engineers built a nine-hundred-foot-long, ninety-foot-high bridge; every stick of wood used in its construction was a tree when the construction started.

Federal and Confederate pickets watched each other warily across the river, but casualties were rare during this interlude. The men—Sherman included—bathed in the Chattahoochee, the first time many had been clean in two months. Enemies swam together, and at night Rebel and Yankee choirs and bands competed with each other and often performed together. A good deal of fraternization and trading occurred, practices that angered

To a large extent, the greatest danger to Sherman's forward progress was fraterization.

McPherson to such an extent he issued one hundred rounds to each man in the Army of the Tennessee and threatened to punish those who did not fire the ammunition. His soldiers threw the bullets into the river, and the unofficial truce between the enlisted men of both sides continued. They realized the time for killing would arrive soon enough.

Johnston was surprisingly quiet during this inactivity. He did not attempt to destroy the northern bridgeheads, nor did he attack the Federal armies as they crossed the Chattahoochee in force. Historians have questioned his acquiescence at these lost opportunities, but Johnston felt it was more important to destroy Sherman's capacity to fight in one great battle.

The lull ended when Thomas began passing his enormous army over Power's Ferry and Pace's Ferry on July 16. He and Schofield were across the following day, advancing directly on Atlanta toward Peachtree Creek. McPherson crossed the Chattahoochee at Roswell on July 17, his mission to swing east in a wide arc to occupy Decatur and destroy the Georgia Railroad that ran to Augusta, the Carolinas, and Virginia. This move would prevent Robert E. Lee from reinforcing Johnston, a lesson learned with the fearful Union defeat at Chickamauga. McPherson would pivot at Decatur and attack Atlanta from the east.

Sherman was relieved, but disturbed, that Johnston did not oppose his crossing. The Union commander correctly supposed an unpleasant surprise was being prepared for him. Johnston would certainly not allow Atlanta to be surrendered without a major effort to prevent its fall.

Johnston deployed his entire army in strong works behind Peachtree Creek and waited. Hardee held the center of the line, Hood the right, and Alexander P. Stewart, who had been appointed permanent commander of Polk's corps, secured the left. Wheeler's cavalry was sent to obstruct McPherson in Decatur while Johnston dispatched the remainder of Sherman's forces. Jackson's cavalry watched for movement south of the Chattahoochee, and the inner fortifications were occupied by the militia.

Johnston's strategy was to destroy the enemy forces as they crossed Peachtree Creek on the march to Atlanta. He would strike the seam between Schofield and Thomas, where a half-mile-wide gap beckoned, rupture the Federal line, and roll it up. At the least, he thought the attack would send Thomas and Schofield stumbling north of the Chattahoochee in disarray with serious casualties. Perhaps he could trap and destroy them against the river or send the Yankees reeling all the way back to Chattanooga; then Johnston would turn on McPherson. If the assault failed, Johnston planned to withdraw into Atlanta's defenses, which he felt could be held forever.

Johnston was ready for the showdown that had been postponed for three months. He had suffered relatively few losses, while Sherman's numerical superiority was daily reduced. The Federal commander was equally prepared for a climactic battle. Although satisfied with his territorial gains, he was impatient to close the campaign. In two and a half months Sherman had forced Johnston to abandon four strong positions and had occupied one hundred miles of valuable enemy territory, but the opposing army was intact, even stronger than it had been when the fighting began. Sherman was dependent on a single railroad to supply one hundred thousand men and twenty-five thousand animals, and some of the supplies came from faraway Louisville over five hundred miles of rickety rail that could be cut by marauding Confederate cavalry at any time.

Lincoln was also pressing Sherman. The offensive in the East had proven inconclusive as U. S. Grant and R. E. Lee fought desperate battles to a draw in Virginia's Wilderness, Spotsylvania, and Cold Harbor. Grant's casualties were mounting, and the Northern people demanded some assurance of ultimate victory. During the summer of 1864, Lincoln faced strong opposition in a grim reelection campaign, leading him for a time to believe he would be defeated in November. Lincoln needed a military victory in the field to ensure his reelection over a candidate who might make peace with the Confederacy and leave the nation permanently divided. He needed the symbol of a captured Atlanta. For both the United States and the Confederate States, the coming battles would be decisive.

A Federal supply train crosses the Chattahoochee River on a pontoon bridge.

HARPER'S WEEKLY

Johnston's trap was baited, and Thomas and Schofield were slowly advancing into it when disaster struck the Confederacy. Joseph E. Johnston was relieved of his command.

At his headquarters late on the evening of July 17, Johnston received a telegram from the War Department in Richmond. Since he had failed to stop Sherman's advance to Atlanta, and because he refused to express supreme confidence in his chances of stopping the enemy, Confederate President Jefferson Davis removed him with the terse message: "You are hereby relieved from the command of the Army and Department of Tennessee." Hood was to assume immediate control of the army. It was Davis's greatest blunder.

Johnston replied to the telegram early the following morning: orders received and complied with, command has been transferred to Hood. Johnston briefly defended his actions, adding, "Confident language by a military commander is not regarded as evidence of competence."

Davis had long been dissatisfied with the way the reticent Johnston conducted the campaign. He and his cabinet had expected Johnston to regain Tennessee, or at least whip Sherman's army, but in ten weeks' time the Federals had advanced to the outskirts of Atlanta, and Johnston would not swear he could hold the city. The rancorous Davis-Johnston feud that had ignited over rank in 1861 gained momentum over strategy and personal clashes in 1862 and 1863, and culminated in this critical year. Davis promoted Johnston's officers without consulting him, and Johnston maneuvered across northern Georgia without informing Davis of his moves or future plans. Davis only knew Johnston had relinquished a great deal of territory without fighting any major battles to hold it, and he seemed likely to surrender more.

Johnston had no friends to represent him at the Confederate court. Davis's secretary of state, Judah P. Benjamin, stated his belief that Johnston would not fight; the cabinet advised Johnston's removal. Davis also relied heavily on Braxton Bragg, the disgraced former commander of the Army of Tennessee, for military advice. Bragg harbored deep misgivings about Johnston, believing he should have taken an aggressive offensive stance to defeat Sherman before now and ridiculing his caution and defensive strategy. Davis seemed to forget that Bragg had retreated from central Kentucky to middle Tennessee and to northern Georgia—without fighting.

On July 9 Davis sent Bragg to snoop around Atlanta. Johnston resented his presence, and the reserved general refused to disclose his plans; so Bragg reported that Johnston apparently would not defend the city but would abandon Atlanta and continue to retreat. Bragg also met repeatedly with Hood, who reinforced the adviser's prejudices.

On July 17, after receiving Bragg's report, Davis telegraphed Johnston, "I wish to hear from you as to present situation and your plan of operations so specifically as to enable me to anticipate events."

Johnston replied on the same day, "As the enemy has double our numbers, we must be on the defensive. My plan of operations, therefore, depend

LIBRARY OF CONGRESS

Looking across the Chattahoochee from the Confederate line provides an insight as to how Johnston was able to maintain the position for so long. When the Southerners retreated, the bridge in the background was torched. Sherman's engineers rebuilt the bridge, but the time required allowed the Confederate commander enough time to prepare for an attack at Peachtree Creek.

upon that of the enemy. It is mainly to watch for an opportunity to fight to advantage. We are trying to put Atlanta into condition to be held for a day or two by the Georgia militia, that army movements may be freer." Davis was not satisfied with this answer, which only convinced him that Johnston would not fight for the city.

When Hood arrived to take command early on July 18, Johnston outlined his plan of attack at Peachtree Creek. In a curious turn of events, Hood and the other corps commanders urged Johnston to ignore the telegram and fight the battle, but Johnston had never disobeyed an order.

Before departing, he penned a brief farewell to his troops:

> I cannot leave this noble army without expressing my admiration of the high military qualities it has displayed. A long and arduous campaign has made conspicuous every soldierly virtue, endurance of toil, obedience to orders, brilliant courage. The enemy has never attacked but to be repulsed

167

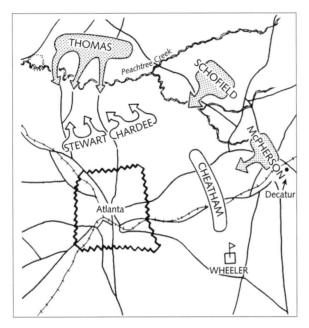

Map 18: The battle of Peachtree Creek

and severely punished. You, soldiers, have never argued but from your courage, and never counted your foe. No longer your leader, I will still watch your career, and will rejoice in your victories. To one and all I offer assurances of my friendship, and bid an affectionate farewell.

"We lifted our hats," wrote one Georgian of Johnston's farewell. "There was no cheering. We simply passed silently, with heads uncovered. Some of the officers broke ranks and grasped his hand, as the tears poured down their cheeks."

Johnston boarded a train, and by nightfall he was in Macon with his wife. His anger and disappointment must have been intensified by the knowledge that it was Hood who had written Davis and Bragg to question his strategy and lack of offensive action, and it was also Hood who had frequently thwarted his aggressive efforts. The crippled general would now determine the fate of Atlanta.

The Federal command was universally joyous over the change. "At this critical moment," Sherman wrote, "the Confederate Government rendered us most vital service. . . . The character of a leader is a large factor in the game of war and I confess I was pleased with the change."

"Much to our comfort and surprise, Johnston was removed," recorded another of Sherman's officers. The dismissal was "received by our officers with universal rejoycing," he continued. Johnston's "patient skill and watchful intelligence and courage" had stymied the Union army, he continued, and the change was seen "as equivalent to victory for us."

Sherman quickly took counsel of his officers, asking what he could expect from Hood, whom he knew by reputation to be a fighting man. McPherson and Schofield, Hood's classmates at West Point, were well acquainted with the new commander. McPherson had graduated first in the class, Schofield third, Hood forty-fourth. Hood had confessed he was "more wedded to boyish sports than academics," and the intellectual Schofield had tutored Hood in his studies. Schofield now told Sherman, "He'll hit you like hell, now, before you know it."

Sherman, pleased by the information, wondered for years why Johnston was removed. He had been baffled by Johnston's skillful defensive posture and welcomed an attack by Hood's inferior numbers. Sherman characterized Hood as "bold, even to rashness and courageous in the extreme." That attitude was shared by Confederate officers who considered him reckless and impetuous.

Davis had asked R. E. Lee's advice about replacing Johnston with Hood, who had been one of Lee's finest divisional commanders. Lee replied that the timing was bad for a change in command, and he feared it would lead to the loss of Atlanta and the army. He said Hood was a tremendous fighter but personally reckless. He recommended Hardee, who had far more experience, for the job. Lee, as usual, proved correct.

The Confederate army was heartbroken by the change in command. They held Johnston in great confidence, and their love for the general was palpable. The venerated Johnston inspired their loyalty, and they fought like demons for him because they knew he would not waste a single life in senseless combat. The soldiers were optimistic, even when the odds were overwhelmingly against them. Hardee noted Johnston was one of those rare commanders who was trusted by both his officers and enlisted men.

A Confederate captain recorded the scene after Johnston's removal was announced to the men:

> Every man looked sad and disheartened at this information, and felt that evil would result from the removal of Johnston, whom they esteem and love above any previous commander. His address touched every heart, and every man thought that his favorite General had been grievously wronged. . . . General Hood is a gallant man, but Johnston has been tried and won the confidence of the soldiery.

Another infantryman said it was "the most terrible and disastrous blow the South ever received. I saw thousands of men cry like babies—regular old fashioned boo-hoos." A sergeant wrote, "All moan the loss of our grate Leader he would have been retained in preferance to anyone else. Gen

The Fiercest Fighter in the Army ■ John B. Hood

If ever a soldier was promoted beyond his capabilities, it was John Bell Hood. What made his career an even greater tragedy is that he was one of the most ferocious fighters in the Confederate army. If Hood had remained in divisional command, he would have been regarded as an excellent subordinate officer.

Born in Kentucky in 1831, Hood graduated near the bottom of his West Point class in 1853 and was sent to the western frontier, where Indians had the first opportunity to wound the unfortunate fellow. When war broke out, Hood began his Confederate service with the retreat from Yorktown during the Peninsula campaign. He gallantly led a Texas brigade during the savage Seven Days' battles, Second Manassas, and Antietam. His conspicuous heroism brought him promotion and divisional command. He subsequently participated in the battles of Fredericksburg and Gettysburg. During the latter engagement, a severe wound cost him the use of his left arm.

Two months later Hood accompanied James Longstreet's corps to Georgia. While leading his men into the bloodbath of Chickamauga, Hood suffered a wound that forced the amputation of his right leg.

Longstreet moved on, but Hood remained in Georgia and commanded a corps under Joseph E. Johnston. During the 1864 Atlanta campaign, Hood quietly undermined Johnston's position with poison-pen letters to Richmond, which played no small role in Johnston's demotion and Hood's appointment as commander of the Army of Tennessee. Hood lost Atlanta by launching four determined, but unsupervised, strikes against Sherman's numerically superior army. Hood then abandoned Georgia to campaign in Tennessee, where he effectively destroyed his army with suicidal attacks at Franklin and Nashville.

After the war, Hood entered business in New Orleans, but ill fortune followed him. The business failed, and Hood and his wife died during a yellow fever epidemic, leaving a large number of small children to be divided among various foster homes.

The attack at Peachtree Creek failed, although for a time it threatened to succeed. Hood's troops, however, were not sufficient enough to crack George H. Thomas's line.

Hood now commands us & I hope he will be successful but the releaving of Gen Joe is dampening to his troops."

"Old Joe was our idol," added another Rebel. "Gaunt, stalwart, sunburned soldiers by the thousands would be seen falling out of line, squatting down by a tree or in a fence corner weeping like children." The diminished spirit of the army never fully recovered, although for a time they continued to fight with accustomed ferocity. Gloom permeated the Confederate ranks, leading hundreds of men to desert because they felt the cause was now lost. Personal duels were fought between Rebel pickets and Yankees who taunted Johnston's dismissal.

A cloud of fear and confusion enveloped Atlanta. The city was daily inundated with tattered refugees from the north, pathetic families clutching a few personal possessions. Trains transported more Confederate wounded, who were treated in improvised hospitals set up in schools, homes, and parks. The people of Atlanta tended the wounded and brought them all the food and bandages they could scrounge. The city was deluged by traveling morticians who opened shop in tents, and carpenters turned to making coffins. Atlanta's population doubled, reaching seventy-five thousand, and martial law was declared in an effort to curb lawlessness and apprehend deserters. The city government, newspapers, businesses, and many people were removed to Macon and other points south to escape the impending conflict. Those who remained started constructing bombproofs, dugout shelters in their basements and gardens. They remembered with dread the published accounts of Vicksburg, and they intended to be prepared for a siege.

A Tour from Roswell to Peachtree Creek

This portion of the driving tour begins at the large parking lot off Mill Street in Roswell.

At the corner of Sloan and Mill you passed The Bricks to your right, quarters erected in 1839 to house workers in the Roswell mills. They were used as a Federal hospital in 1864 and operated by the city as a library in the 1950s. The Bricks are considered one of the oldest apartments in the United States.

Below the parking lot is a cotton mill converted into a shopping complex. In Vickery Creek below are falls, a dam, and the remains of an old mill.

This is the beautiful, historic city of Roswell. It was named for Roswell King, an officer of the Bank of Darien on the coast who traveled to north Georgia in the 1830s to open a branch. Enchanted by this spot on the Chattahoochee River, he bought vast acreage and offered his friends on the Georgia–South Carolina coast ten acres each if they would settle here. Many took advantage of the offer and built fine homes that still stand. Roswell and his son Barrington established a cotton mill in the steep gorge along Vickery Creek, and other mills and factories were soon attracted to the area.

The Kings laid out the town with a square and wide streets and donated lots for the building of Presbyterian and Methodist churches, both still in existence, and a school. Roswell was a prosperous city when Kenner Garrard and James B. McPherson arrived in July 1864 to flank Johnston out of his formidable River Line, and they had orders from Sherman to burn all manufacturing facilities.

As the Federals approached, King and his family fled, reportedly with a considerable amount of gold. When Federal cavalry arrived on July 6, Theophilus Roche, a one-year employee and very temporary "owner" of the mill, raised a French flag and claimed to be a foreign neutral. When Garrard found "CSA" woven into the cloth used to make Confederate uniforms, Sherman suggested Roche be shot. Instead, Roche was merely sent north. In 1882 he sued the U.S. government for $125,000 claiming false arrest and loss of property but received no compensation.

In the Vickery Creek Gorge, King built the two-story Ivy Woolen Mill. It was joined by Roswell Mill.

Map 19: The Roswell area

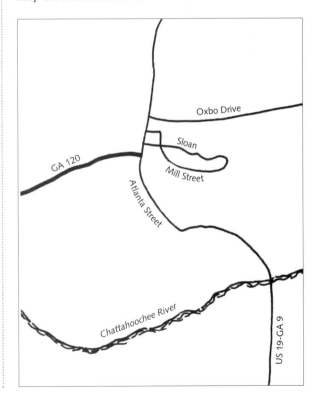

The Bricks are considered to be some of the oldest apartment buildings in the South. In 1864 they were used as hospitals.

These mill stones and gear were near the center of the fighting at Peachtree Creek.

A dam on Vickery Creek funneled water through a wooden millrace to turn a sixteen-by-twenty-foot waterwheel to provide power to six mill buildings on the hillside above the creek. The primary structure, forty feet long and fifty-three feet wide, was four stories tall. The mills produced nearly two hundred thousand yards of cloth monthly, including thirty thousand yards for Confederate uniforms.

The mills and a machine house in the gorge were destroyed during the war. Mill No. 1, originally constructed in 1854, was rebuilt but burned in 1882 and was rebuilt as the Laurel Mills. When it also burned in 1926 after a lightning strike, instead of rebuilding it, Mill No. 2 was constructed above the gorge and operated until 1975.

Long, steep stairs descend from the parking lot into Vickery Creek Gorge, where large sections of thirteen-inch-thick stone walls, machinery, the ruins of the waterwheel, and a single wooden mill building remain. The trail leads to the old thirty-foot-long dam (1835) that channeled water through a wooden millrace to turn the waterwheels. It also creates a lovely waterfall that can be heard for a considerable distance. Of the original mill complex dating to the Civil War, the only remaining structures are The Bricks, the company store (now The Public House restaurant, 605 Atlanta Street, 770-992-4646) on the highway above the existing mill-shopping complex, and the shell of the machine shop.

At the parking lot is the only remaining functional mill building in Roswell, built in 1929 and operated until 1975. Previously ravaged by vandals and vagrants, a nine-million-dollar renovation project transformed the cotton mill into an upscale retail establishment featuring shops and restaurants, and a large amphitheater has been constructed on the banks of the creek.

Sherman burned Roswell's factories and mills, but he fortunately spared the city and its fine homes. He, however, committed his most dastardly act here: the removal of the Roswell women. Noting the mill labor force was female, he directed Garrard to send them to Marietta and then north to deny their skills to the Confederacy. His orders were to "arrest all those people, male and female, connected with those factories, no matter what the clamor, and let them foot it, under guard, to Marietta, where I will send them by cars to the North. Destroy and make the same disposition of all mills. . . . The poor women will make a howl. Let them take along their children and clothing." Sherman informed Henry W. Halleck that the workers were "tainted with treason." Seven hundred women were rounded up on July 10 by Garrard and sent by wagon to join other workers from a large mill at Sweetwater Creek in Douglas County. They were given nine days' rations, and by July 15 two trainloads had been sent north to Chattanooga, Nashville, Lexington, and into Indiana.

Some were hired by families in Marietta and never left the region, but most were incarcerated in a women's prison converted from a Louisville hospital. Many worked as seamstresses and servants in place of emancipated slaves. Some women were confined for a while, others died of typhoid and measles, but others took the oath of allegiance and were released to find work. Contrary to legend, some returned to Georgia after the war. The mill workers appeared to have vanished because they were largely illiterate and wrote neither letters nor journals, and because the government did not bother to document their fate. Census records, however, prove that at least seventeen returned, and probably a number of others. One woman, Adeline Bagley Buice, and her daughter returned five years later to find her Confederate veteran husband had returned home from the war, assumed she and the girl had died, and remarried.

In Old Mill Park at Sloan and Vickery Streets is the Roswell Mill Workers Monument. The ten-foot-high granite memorial, a broken Corinthian column on a square base, represents the shattered lives of hundreds of female mill workers and their families.

Just west on Mimosa Avenue is historic Roswell Presbyterian Church (755 Mimosa Avenue, 1840), which retains the original box pews, high center pulpit, and slave balcony. In the belfry is a bronze ship's bell that was cast in Philadelphia. Following Sunday services a mini-museum is open in the rear of the church where artifacts of church history are preserved. They include the original silver communion service, which was hidden in a barrel by Fannie Whitemore until the war was over to prevent its theft by Federal troops, and a checkerboard carved on the back of a cabinet door by bored Union soldiers who removed the pews and used the church as a hospital. For whatever reason the Northerners also destroyed the hymnals.

Visiting all the historic sites in Roswell would be a profitable day's outing. A prime attraction is Bulloch Hall (180 Bulloch Street, 1840). Constructed in 1840 by one of Roswell's founders, James S. Bulloch, the two-story, heart pine structure is a true temple type Greek Revival structure with large rooms on each floor and eleven fireplaces. His daughter, Mittie, married Theodore Roosevelt here on December 22, 1853, and their son became president. In 1905 Roosevelt arrived to see his mother's home and spoke from the bandstand at the square. Bulloch's son Elliott married a fifth cousin, and they had a daughter, Eleanor, who married Franklin D. Roosevelt and became first lady. She visited during a trip to Warm Springs. The house saw service as a Federal barracks. A Civil War room features artifacts recovered from Union campsites at

Impressive Bulloch Hall was the home of James Bulloch, a founder of the town and a Confederate overseas naval agent.

Roswell in the summer of 1864. The James S. Bulloch Room contains documents and photos of these accomplished families. One case, titled "From the Civil War to the Oval Office," displays uniforms and photographs to illustrate the transformation. Bulloch himself was a noted Confederate naval agent and served in England during the war, where he was instrumental in obtaining the feared commerce raider CSS *Alabama*. Bulloch Hall can be toured and rented for special occasions.

The Archibald Smith plantation house (935 Alpharetta Street, Roswell, GA 30075, 404-993-0422; 1845) is an incredible site owned by the city and open to the public. It preserves thirteen outbuildings, including the kitchen, carriage house, barns, corncrib, and well house. Many of the furnishings are original, including an 1840s piano, crated and dispatched to Valdosta when the family refugeed in 1864. Over the mantle is a print of the noted Southern painting, *The Burial of Latane,* depicting a Confederate soldier being buried far from home. It honored the Smiths' oldest son, similarly lost in combat.

Ancient oaks frame Barrington Hall, a magnificent Greek Revival home that took five years to construct. Barrington King completed it in 1842. Great Oaks (786 Mimosa, 1841) has eighteen-inch-thick walls and was Kenner Garrard's headquarters; his troopers camped on the grounds. Mimosa Hall, built by John Dunwoody and purchased postwar by Col. Andrew J. Hansell of Marietta, is actually a reproduction; his first home burned during a housewarming party immediately after it was completed. John Minton, who fought alongside Andrew Jackson and Davy Crockett and volunteered for the Confederacy, constructed Minton House (Canton Street). He was wounded at the battle of First Manassas and returned home. Half a mile above Roswell, Naylor Hall (Canton Street, 1840) was constructed by Barrington King for his bookkeeper, H. W. Proudfoot. It was heavily damaged during the war.

Primrose Cottage (1830) was the first building erected in Roswell, a gift from King to his widowed daughter. There is also the home of Francis B. Goulding, minister, author of *Young Marooners* and *Marooners Island,* and inventor of the first sewing machine. Unfortunately he failed to obtain a patent.

The charming business district dates from 1839. The town square, where Teddy Roosevelt once spoke, was laid out in 1840 and landscaped during the Depression as a WPA project. At the end of Sloan Street is Founders Cemetery, which contains the graves of Roswell King, James Bulloch, John Dunwoody, and other founders of the city. Early settlers are also buried in the Presbyterian church cemetery (1841) and the Methodist church cemetery (1850).

The Roswell Historical Society and the city of Roswell regularly sponsor tours of the homes and the mill ruins and host re-creations of 1840s life. A walking tour featuring twenty-seven sites—mansions, cemeteries, churches, commercial buildings, and mill ruins—has been prepared by the historical society and is available from the society or visitors bureau. Walking and driving tours, both self-guided and guided, to explore the historic attractions of Roswell are available from the bureau. A seven-mile Roswell river walk is currently being developed along the Chattahoochee River.

From the mill parking area return to U.S. 19-GA 9 (Atlanta Road) via Mill Street and Sloan. Start your mileage and turn left to cross the Chattahoochee River at 1.1. While descending to the river, Allenbrook will be to the left. Allenbrook (227 Atlanta Street, 1840), a two-story saltbox built of handmade brick in 1840 to house the Laurel Mills manager (who was Roche when the Federals arrived), is the headquarters of the Roswell Historical Society and can be toured.

The river bridge is the approximate site of the original covered bridge at Shallowford. Confederates under Capt. James R. King burned it July 5, 1864, when Garrard's cavalry galloped into town, but Union engineers tore down parts of the mill buildings for the timber to quickly rebuild the bridge. In sixty hours they threw up twin spans 710 feet long, 18 feet wide, and 14 feet high. While the Federals were crossing the river, a terrible thunderstorm erupted, and lightning killed a dozen men, split ninety-foot-tall oak trees, and discharged weapons. About thirty-six thousand Federals crossed the Chattahoochee here July 13–17 and did most of the fighting at the battle of Atlanta.

As naked Union troops forded the river at Sope Creek, two cavalry regiments also crossed here. Coming under heavy rifle fire, the troopers (armed with Spencer repeaters that fired sealed metal cartridges) ducked beneath the water to eject spent cartridges, insert new ones, then popped up to aim and fire before diving again. "Look at those Yankee sons of bitches," a Confederate was heard to say. "What sort of critters be they anyway." Reportedly, two hundred Southerners allowed themselves to be captured so they could inspect the newfangled rifles.

While McPherson crossed here and advanced on Decatur to cut the Augusta railroad and descend on Atlanta from the east, Thomas crossed from Vinings at Pace's and Power's Ferries and proceeded south along Howell Mill Road and Northside Drive. Schofield crossed at Sope Creek, between Power's Ferry and Johnson's Ferry west of this point, and marched toward Buckhead.

Continue south, braving the Atlanta traffic.

Because Sherman burned all but four hundred of four thousand buildings in Atlanta, few original structures remain. Near Oglethorpe University, at the intersection of Peachtree Road and Ashford-Dunwoody Road to the east, is Southlook, the Samuel House plantation (1856), once part of a large plantation and now the clubhouse of the Peachtree Golf Club. It was used as Sherman's headquarters on July 18–19, 1864. Brookhaven, the Solomon Goodwin house (3967 Peachtree Street, 1831), was a landmark during the Atlanta campaign and bears scars from skirmishes. Although occupied and abused by the Federals, a legend contends that a loyal servant convinced soldiers not to burn the home. Meadownook

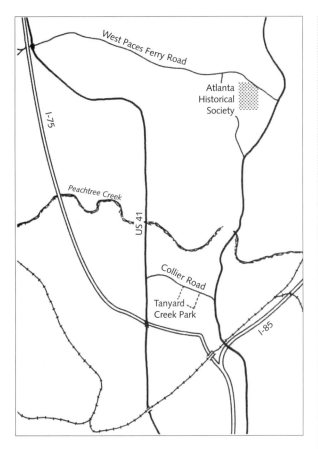

Map 20: The Peachtree Creek area

(Alston Drive at East Lake Country Club, 1832), a coastal planter style home with Greek Revival details, was home to Col. Robert Alston, who was stationed at Charleston. His wife and children stayed here during the war, and Union and Confederate generals occupied the structure. It is said that soldiers were rallied during the battle of Atlanta by slamming rifles on a rail of the staircase that is still marred. Jefferson Davis, Alexander H. Stephens, and John B. Gordon visited the house. After crossing the Chattahoochee River, Union troops camped on the grounds of Cross Roads Primitive Baptist Church (1870) at Mount Vernon Highway in Sandy Springs.

After 12.6 miles take a right on West Paces Ferry Road. At .3 turn left into the Atlanta History Center.

The Atlanta Historical Society was founded in 1926, and in 1966 it purchased the Swan house (1928) on West Paces Ferry. The Tullie Smith farmhouse (1845) was relocated here, and in 1975 McElreath Hall, housing a library and archives, opened. In 1993 a thirty-thousand-square-foot museum was dedicated. Preserved here are thirty thousand artifacts, primarily in sliding drawers kept at a constant temperature and humidity. The collection includes a walnut Queen Anne chair Jefferson Davis occupied at the last meeting of the Confederate cabinet in Washington, Georgia, a long burgundy velvet sofa Sherman used in his Atlanta headquarters, the iron safe from Atlanta's National Bank, which held the city of Atlanta's treasury ($1.64) when Sherman arrived, and a fragment of the flag of the Third Georgia, cut up rather than surrendered. There are racks of rifles, pistols, swords, and saddles, projectiles beyond number, the desk at which Margaret Mitchell pounded out *Gone with the Wind,* and the black silk bonnet of Martha Lumpkin—Marthasville, the original name of Atlanta, was named for her in 1843. The museum also holds a recently rediscovered charcoal-and-pencil mural of the battle of Atlanta by a German artist who helped create the Cyclorama. Nine feet long and nineteen inches high, it shows the Atlanta skyline in the background of its focus, the Decatur Road, where troops are depicted marching and fighting. It may have been used as a preliminary study of the existing Cyclorama from a perspective that was rejected, or for a smaller work that was never created. Another nineteen-foot-long sketch, in pen and watercolor, is believed to illustrate Stones River. The artist is Louis Kindt, who fought at Antietam at the age of sixteen and contributed to cycloramas of Gettysburg, Vicksburg, and Missionary Ridge. The artwork, executed on heavy paper with notes, was found in a box under a bed by a great-great-grandson of the artist.

The Atlanta History Center's permanent Civil War display is titled Turning Point: The American Civil War, which is comprised of ten rooms arranged in chronological order. The exhibit occupies ninety-two hundred square feet and utilizes fourteen hundred objects to explore the major themes and events of the war, including artillery and small arms, uniforms, and flags. There are large display maps to explain the sequence of events, video rooms exploring different aspects of the war, touch-screen computer learning stations to describe occurrences, dramatic dioramas, and listening stations. The personal stories of military

The Atlanta History Center uses thousands of artifacts to illustrate the lives of rank-and-file soldiers.

leaders, ordinary soldiers, government officials, and civilians are highlighted. Pivotal events of each war year are explored and linked with vital issues.

Many featured items are from the DuBose and Dickey collections. The Thomas S. Dickey Sr. Collection is the best projectile collection in the country; many of the items are one of a kind. The collector, who grew up on the southern end of Johnston's River Line, became a self-educated historian and wrote a number of books about Civil War ordnance. The Beverly M. DuBose Jr. Collection, the result of fifty years' labor, was the largest private collection of Civil War artifacts in the South.

The first display is titled 1860: Year of Crisis. It focuses on the election of 1860 with an interactive video program, photo murals, quotes, and eight maps and charts that explore four primary issues that led to the Civil War—economic differences between North and South, ideological conflicts, controversy over western expansion, and slavery. In the center of the room is a stand of flags, Confederate and Union. Featured objects include a slave badge and an abolitionist token.

The second section of Turning Point is 1861: War of Ideals, which explores the initial preparations for war, explaining how volunteers on both sides fought for their principles with the erroneous belief that war would be brief, glorious, and bloodless. Displayed are elaborate, colorful militia uniforms, ineffective body armor, portable beds, a homemade U.S. flag made by the Unionist wife of a Confederate soldier, the sword given former Georgia governor and gen-

eral Howell Cobb by the Provisional Confederate Congress in 1861, and William H. T. Walker's sword and the December 1860 letter accepting his resignation from the U.S. Army. Other artifacts include homemade trousers and socks, mass produced Union boots called Jeffersons because they had been authorized by Jefferson Davis during his tenure as secretary of war, and a wooden Confederate canteen. Along the rim of a circular room are six large photomurals of typical Americans in 1861, including soldiers, a married couple, and a slave, with quotes describing their experience.

1862: Ideals Under Fire, the third section of Turning Point, focuses on ordinary soldiers. The intense, prolonged bloodshed that produced 220,000 dead in eighteen months made hardened veterans of the joyful volunteers and sobered the nation. A video room depicts the military events of the year, supplemented by maps describing each side's strategy and what actually transpired, a feature in each succeeding room. On a platform is a recreated campsite with tent and mannequins wearing uniforms of Union and Confederate soldiers. Visitors may heft a reproduction rifle and knapsack for an idea of what soldiers carried daily. One large case has a table laid out with a Union surgeon's amputation kit, complete with fleshing knife and bone saw, and other medical material, offering a horrific glimpse of the cost of battle.

Another case illustrates how soldiers filled their many idle hours. Bibles and religious material show how some soldiers handled the stress of their duties, but other objects—liquor bottles, playing cards, and dice—demonstrate what occupied others. Mail call was important to all soldiers. One display depicts the outdated military tactics used early in the war. Combined with primitive medical technology, these tactics led to terrible battlefield losses. The army life of 180,000 black Union soldiers is explored in Now We Are Men. A large case displays rare naval uniforms, weapons, and equipment of both sides. Other extensive displays feature bedrolls, mess kits, additional everyday material, uniforms, weapons, projectiles, artillery equipment, and cavalry gear. Particularly troubling is a case of items shattered by bullets—trees, canteens, and belt buckles.

The next section of Turning Point, 1863: A War of Resources, A Test of Will, illustrates the home front and everyday civilian life and the manufacture of materials of war. The year 1863 was a time of several serious Confederate reversals and Union advances, but the South had considerable fight left. This section deals with the will of Southern civilians to support, sacrifice, and labor for the war effort.

The room starts with a video, photomurals, and maps illustrating what each side hoped to achieve and what actually occurred. The first room depicts a factory interior with simulated brick and wood beams. The space is packed with the Dickey Collection of munitions, both Confederate and Union, and details their origin and manufacture. Within this space is a diorama depicting how women hand filled and rolled rifle cartridges. Confederate and Union weapons are compared, and the large range of weapons manufactured in Georgia are displayed. Large cases show experimental and nonstandard weapons produced by the Confederacy, forced to ingenuous efforts to manufacture war materiel or import them through the blockade. Also depicted is the Union manufacturing powerhouse, including breech-loading rifles, hand grenades, and armor-piercing projectiles designed for use against ironclad warships. A large case displays every size and shape of artillery projectiles. Some of them are huge. A two-sided case explains the Union blockade and Confederate attempts to break it, featuring a flag from a British blockade-runner and imported weapons, which were more sophisticated than those the Confederacy could manufacture. Another extensive display features accouterments— canteens, belts, and cap and cartridge boxes. Interesting items are sewing kits prepared for soldiers and gifts presented to Braxton Bragg.

A period parlor has been recreated where a woman in mourning clothes weeps for the loss of her husband in battle. Displayed are a mourning veil, wooden grave marker, family Bible, and a hand-cut valentine a soldier fashioned for his wife.

1864: Year of Decision is Turning Point's finest display. That year the war entered and devastated Georgia. Battles and maneuvers brought the conflict closer to and eventually into Atlanta, where thousands of civilians refugeed, fleeing before the advancing Federals. Fighting in Virginia, Georgia, and Louisiana seemed stalemated for the Federals, presenting the very real possibility that Abraham Lincoln would lose reelection to a Peace Democrat who might negotiate a settlement with the Confederacy.

One exhibit notes the millions of women, North and South, who grieved for lost sons, brothers, husbands, and fathers.

On September 2, 1864, Sherman saved Lincoln and the Union with the capture of Atlanta.

This is the largest room in the Turning Point exhibition. It features a recreated artillery position, a 12-pounder Napoleon sheltered by gabions (earth-filled baskets), and a section of infantry works. Four artillery tubes stand in a row to demonstrate the various weapons used by both sides at Atlanta—a 12-pounder Napoleon, a Parrott rifle, an 1857 field gun, and an 1841 field gun produced at Augusta. A "Sherman necktie," a piece of railroad iron heated and wrapped around a pine tree, illustrates the final touch in the destruction of Georgia's railroads. One exhibit displays signaling equipment, both flag and telegraphic, and mapmaking. Another has an extensive time line of events in 1864, a keg torpedo like the one that sank a Union monitor, and a Coehorn mortar. Displayed are the twenty-by-ten-foot Confederate flag that flew over Atlanta when the city was surrendered, and a Union flag from the USS *Hartford,* Adm. David Farragut's flagship when he captured Mobile Bay, Alabama, another 1864 event that helped cinch Lincoln's reelection.

There is Confederate Gen. Patrick Cleburne's sword, presented just before the Atlanta campaign began, the sword carried by Confederate Gen. William H. T. Walker when he was killed at the start of the battle of Atlanta, and the sword of the officer who accepted Atlanta's surrender from its mayor. Also displayed are swords and personal items of Union Capt. Francis DeGress, whose battery was overrun at Atlanta, a Union sharpshooter's coat, artillery projectiles fired into the city, and artifacts recovered from the ashes and rubble of the city. A case contains possessions of five men who fought at Peachtree Creek and Atlanta, while another holds artillery implements. Lincoln's reelection is illustrated by a poll book used by soldiers in the election of 1864 and the colored marbles and box with which they voted. The only surviving six-mule army wagon, which carried supplies during Sherman's March to the Sea, is prominently displayed. Demonstrating the civilian plight are a box containing the clothing of a Roswell family that fled the Federals and the touching diary of Carrie Berry, a ten-year-old who survived the siege of Atlanta. Letters and diaries of soldiers and civilians relate their experiences of the battles that occurred around the city in 1864.

In one corner is a building stripped of timber for Atlanta's extensive fortifications. Inside a video explains the significance of the Atlanta campaign to the war's outcome.

1865–2000: The Search for Meaning examines the closing months of the war, Appomattox Court House, the collapse of the Confederacy, Lincoln's assassination, Reconstruction, and the war's aftermath, consequences, meaning, and relevance to the veterans, their children, and modern America. More than six hundred thousand lives were lost in the struggle that reunited the country and ended slavery. Reconstruction and the Thirteenth, Fourteenth, and Fifteenth Amendments to the Constitution set the stage for the Civil Rights movement a century later and a much stronger national government. Radical Reconstruction, the situation of African Americans, the KKK, and other topics are explored.

A circular room displays images of the ruined capital of Richmond, burned as the Confederates evacuated. Preserved here are the dress uniform coat of Confederate Gen. John B. Gordon, who surrendered Confederate forces at Appomattox Court House, an original copy of Robert E. Lee's General Orders No. 9 (his final address to the Army of Northern Virginia), Sherman's General Orders No. 65 (which ended hostilities in North Carolina, where he again confronted Joseph E. Johnston), a parole book, and loyalty oath. Other artifacts signify the end of the war: a mourning badge fashioned after Lincoln's death, dinnerware that Jefferson Davis used as he fled Richmond and entered Georgia, and the logbook of the CSS *Shenandoah,* the Confederate raider that continued to destroy Union shipping months after Lee's surrender.

Ordinary objects are often the most important artifacts, but they were generally discarded while grander artifacts survived in abundance. Particularly prized is the collection of Cpl. Charles E. Smith of the Thirty-second Ohio, who fought at Peachtree Creek and Atlanta. One side of his hand-painted canteen has an image of Fort Sumter, where the war started, and the other shows the McLean house of Appomattox Court House, where it ended. His two canvas shelter halves, which combine to form a tent and are inscribed with the names of battles in which he

Recreated Confederate earthworks, which had encircled the city, give visitors an idea of what the Federals faced.

The only army wagon that survives from Sherman's trek across Georgia is displayed at the Atlanta History Center.

participated, is one of the last surviving and can be viewed in the 1864 section. His mess kit, iron skillet, and metal dishes are also preserved.

The Atlanta History Center also displays the Medals of Honor and the sword of Capt. Albert D. Wright, a white officer who led black troops at Petersburg's savage battle of the Crater. These rare medals are marked USCT, for U.S. Colored Troops.

A corridor leads to a final exhibit, a reproduction of a soldier statue like hundreds that were dedicated at courthouse squares and cemeteries across the nation, North and South, in bronze or granite to memorialize local veterans who gave the last full measure. There is a tree trunk studded with shell fragments from the Kennesaw Mountain battlefield, felled thirty years after the war, an exhibit displaying memorabilia from veterans reunions, and the desk James Longstreet used to write his memoirs. There are also an early twentieth-century wheelchair used by a veteran, items from soldiers homes, a display of several possessions representing the military and civilian lives of the three Branch brothers of Savannah (who all fought for the South), two Confederate gravestones, and photo murals depicting the political, economic, and social influence of the war. A final video, *The Search for Meaning,* explores varied interpretations of the war.

On weekends guided tours of Turning Point are provided, and on select Sundays interpreters dress as soldiers or civilians to discuss Civil War life and demonstrate tools and equipment. Another guided tour of the gardens on the grounds describes how plants were used during the war.

Every July, on a weekend near the anniversary of the battle of Atlanta, the Atlanta History Center sponsors an encampment that illustrates everyday soldiering in both armies through troop drills, maneuvers, weapons displays, rifle and artillery firing, period music, medical practices, lectures, films, and documentaries. A twice-yearly symposium features Civil War experts discussing their research on different topics. Call for information.

The Atlanta Historical Society has created a fascinating complex and hosts a wide variety of activities and programs that can occupy a full day of exploration. On its thirty-two wooded acres are gardens, the 1840 Tullie Smith house (one of Atlanta's oldest surviving structures), and the Swan house (an Italian-style mansion of the 1920s). The eleven-million-dollar central facility hosts various exhibits.

Recently published research indicates that up to five hundred of Atlanta's eight thousand Civil War residents, composing about fifty families, were Unionists who gathered intelligence for the Federals, hid escaped prisoners of war, and smuggled food to Union prisoners. Among this group, which was composed mainly of immigrants from the North, were James L. Calhoun, former mayor and member of the Atlanta city council who surrendered the city. A number of citizens suspected of spying were arrested and released, but one was beaten to death by guards.

From the parking lot of the Atlanta History Center, turn right on West Paces Ferry to return to U.S. 19-GA 9 (which immediately becomes Peachtree Street). Start your mileage, turn right and proceed 2.5 miles to Piedmont Hospital on the right.

In front of the hospital is a large stone monument placed in 1944 by the Atlanta Historical Society. It commemorates the battle of Peachtree Creek and the Confederate and Union soldiers who fought here. South of the hospital along the sidewalk is an older WPA plaque set in stone marking the spot where Confederate troops opened the assault.

At .1 turn right onto Collier Road. At .5 to your right are the millstones and pieces of machinery from Collier's Mill, a battlefield landmark and casualty. Turn left at .1 into Tanyard Creek Park.

This preserve is Atlanta's memorial to the battle of Peachtree Creek. Created during the centennial celebration of the Civil War in 1964, nine bronze plaques were set on cement stands to describe the intense fighting that occurred in this area, but unfortunately several have been stolen. The antebellum gristmill constructed and operated by Andrew J. Collier stood 150 feet downstream on the right bank of Tanyard Creek, a tributary of Peachtree Creek that flows through this park. It was the focal point of the Confederate attack on July 20, 1864, an approach to the center of the Union line where Federals concentrated several artillery batteries that were instrumental in turning back the Confederate drive. Commanding the valiant Indiana troops here was

Col. Benjamin Harrison, a future president. On the opposite side of Tanyard Creek is the one-acre Ardmore Park on Ardmore Road, which also witnessed the Civil War combat.

In 1999 a fifteen-foot-long oak beam with metal parts—iron bars and nuts—possibly a drive shaft or paddle wheel, was found in low water at the site of the 1852 mill, destroyed the day of the battle. Portions of the mill's foundation can be seen in the creek.

After Sherman successfully crossed the Chattahoochee, Johnston withdrew south of the river and prepared to attack Thomas's Army of the Cumberland when it was partially across Peachtree Creek. When Johnston was removed from command, Hood determined to follow his former superior's battle plan. Unfortunately for the Confederate effort, the Federals had crossed Peachtree Creek and set up defensive positions on a ridge just north of here when Hood launched his ferocious assault. The Confederates attacked from the south along Collier Road, crossing through this park. Their battle line extended west to Northside Drive and east to Peachtree Road, with one division attacking from farther east across Brighton Road, and penetrating north to Peachtree Battle Avenue. The Southerners made two primary thrusts, Hardee to the east and Stewart to the west. Confederate Gen. C. H. Stevens was killed at the intersection of Twenty-eighth Street and Wycliff.

Atlanta Memorial Park, a golf-and-tennis club on Northside Drive at Woodward Way, was part of the Peachtree battlefield and has historical markers. From the hill at the entrance to the Bitsy Grant Tennis Center, the battlefield can be seen to the east, where Confederates left their works, a site marked by a stone at the intersection of Peachtree and Spring Streets. In a small park at Peachtree Battle Avenue and Peachtree Road is a memorial to Confederate soldiers dedicated by the Old Guard of Georgia. Another stone monument is at Peachtree and Palisades Road. A small stone with a plaque notes the position of Howell's Georgia Battery, where Capt. Evan Howell fired on the Federals occupying his grandfather's plantation.

From Tanyard Creek Park continue to I-75 and travel to the site of the battle of Atlanta. There are, however, several fascinating historical attractions farther down Peachtree Street, which we have just left.

Tanyard Creek Park contains several historical markers that describe the fighting at Peachtree Creek.

One of Georgia's least-known but most-spectacular Civil War attractions is to be found at Rhodes Memorial Hall (1516 Peachtree Street NW). Three beautiful Tiffany-style stained-glass windows, composed of 1,250 pieces of German glass and measuring nine to fifteen feet high and twenty-one inches wide, were made for Amos Giles Rhodes, who made a fortune through a chain of furniture stores, by the Von Gerichten Glass Company at a cost of forty thousand dollars. The windows, titled The Rise and Fall of the Confederacy, trace the history of the failed nation. The first window illustrates the formation of the new government at Montgomery, Alabama, as Jefferson Davis takes the oath of office. The second depicts the firing on Fort Sumter and the initial Southern victory at Manassas, featuring Stonewall Jackson. The third pictures the final chapter of the war at Appomattox Court House. Also shown is a proud Southerner departing his home for war then returning four years later to find his plantation in ruins. Popular legend contends that Rhodes demanded the Manassas scenes be reworked because he believed they did not depict the Federals fleeing in sufficient panic. Also represented are the Confederate Stars and Bars and the battle flag, each seal of the thirteen Confederate states, and the images of the following fifteen Southern generals, admirals, and politicians: Albert Sidney Johnston, Joseph E. Johnston, Nathan Bedford Forrest, Clement A. Evans, John B. Gordon, Joseph Wheeler, James Longstreet, P. G. T. Beauregard, M. A. Stovall, Raphael Semmes, Franklin Buchanan, Josiah Tatt-

Magnificent Rhodes Hall houses a fantastic series of stained-glass windows depicting the history of the Confederacy.

nall, Howell Cobb, Alexander H. Stephens, and Robert Toombs.

Rhodes Hall was donated to the state of Georgia in 1929 and housed the state archives until 1965, when a new facility was opened near the capitol. The windows and the intricately carved staircase of Honduran mahogany where they were displayed were removed for safekeeping then displayed at the new archives building for several decades. They were reconstructed in 1990 in their full impressive glory at the restored Rhodes Hall, which is listed on the National Register and is headquarters for the Georgia Trust for Historic Preservation. The building is interesting itself, a grand example of High Victorian that was once surrounded by 114 acres on an estate named Le Reve. Rhodes returned from a tour of Rhine River castles in Europe in the 1890s with a desire for an Americanized version of these for his home. Willis F. Denny designed the Victorian Romanesque Revival house of Stone Mountain granite. The unique four-story home, constructed 1902–4, has square towers and battlements and made extensive use of mahogany, maple, and oak, with heart pine floors. The structure has mosaics around the fireplaces and three hundred electric lights.

More than a century ago Peachtree Street was an upscale residential area. In 1899 Cornelius Sheehan constructed a brick two-story Tudor Revival residence at the corner of Peachtree and Tenth Streets. Sheehan sold the Victorian house in 1906, and in 1913 it was placed on wooden rollers and moved back forty feet to Crescent Street, where a third floor

was added beneath the original two and the structure was divided into ten apartment units called the Crescent Apartments.

Today this is the Margaret Mitchell house, on the corner of Peachtree Street and Tenth Street. In 1925 Mitchell married John Marsh and the couple moved into Apartment 1, a one-thousand-square-foot unit on the ground floor consisting of a large drawing room, a small bedroom, a tiny bathroom, and a kitchen in the rear. Mitchell was an *Atlanta Journal* society reporter from 1922 to 1926, but she was sidelined by a leg injury. While recuperating she read numerous books until her husband challenged her to write one of her own. He purchased a portable typewriter, and she wrote *Gone with the Wind* in an alcove well lighted by windows. It was a quiet, simple, happy time for Margaret (called Peggy) and John. The apartment, with dark woodwork and hardwood floors and dark faded wallpaper, was furnished with mahogany pieces from her grandparents house, Victorian furniture from her father's house, and John's simple furniture. Mitchell affectionately called the apartment The Dump. She entertained her literary friends in the cramped quarters, draping towels over her work in progress. She wrote the novel backward, from the last chapter to the first, producing up to sixty versions of a chapter, and stuffed them into manila envelopes. The novel was published to universal acclaim and a Pulitzer Prize, and the movie debuted in 1939.

The Crescent Apartments fell into disrepair and were abandoned in the 1970s. The building was nearly razed for construction of a high-rise but has managed to survive. Arsonists burned the structure on three separate occasions, twice leveling newly restored versions. Daimler-Benz spent millions resurrecting the ruins and gave ownership to the Margaret Mitchell House, Inc., a nonprofit organization that has purchased the small block surrounding the house.

The Margaret Mitchell House and Museum opened in 1997. A visitors center, originally Atlanta's first supermarket, shows a short film describing Mitchell's residence in the apartment, and a series of displays explores her life and career.

Visitors walk across the lawn to enter the front of Sheehan's Victorian residence, where stories are told of the Sheehan and Mitchell families. Tour groups are shepherded downstairs to Mitchell's apartment.

At the foot of a staircase is a recreated wooden lion's head whose nose Mitchell daily rubbed for good luck. The cramped apartment largely escaped much damage during the fires, and visitors are assured that Mitchell herself trod these actual tiles. The furniture is period (relatives own all the original pieces), and the focal point is a Remington portable typewriter, perched like the original on a small wobbly oak table in the alcove.

To the rear of the kitchen, in what was a backyard, is a museum that displays examples of Mitchell's extensive correspondence and the Civil Rights movement in Atlanta. Exit through the gift shop, filled with paper and video editions of *Gone with the Wind* and assorted memorabilia. Mitchell grew up on Peachtree and was mortally injured on the street several blocks from here.

Mitchell and Marsh moved out in 1932 and lived in several other Atlanta locations. The only other surviving residence, and their last, from 1939 to 1949, is Della Manta Apartments (1917) at Piedmont Avenue and South Prado. Designed by famed Atlanta architect Neal Reid with an American Renaissance façade, it is a few miles northeast of The Dump. At her request, Mitchell's papers were destroyed by Marsh and a secretary in the boiler room.

The new Federal Reserve Bank of Atlanta, on the corner directly north of the Margaret Mitchell house, displays Confederate currency and state bank notes in its Monetary Museum.

A short distance northeast of the Margaret Mitchell house is Piedmont Park. The Peace Statue, a deeply moving monument depicting a winged angel imploring a Confederate infantryman to lower his weapon, symbolizing reconciliation, is found at the Fourteenth Street entrance. The figures, nine feet high and eight feet wide, stand atop a nine-foot-tall granite base. The Gate City Guard gave the

Margaret Mitchell's apartment was dubbed "the Dump" by the author of Gone with the Wind.

bronze, by New York sculptor Allen G. Newman, to the city. It had been inspired by a peace mission the guard had undertaken to Union cities in 1879, and most of the cost was raised in the North. On October 10, 1911, following a massive parade, the monument was dedicated in front of fifty thousand witnesses, including four thousand Confederate veterans. Also in Piedmont Park is a large marble memorial to poet and Confederate soldier Sidney Lanier.

From the parking lot at Tanyard Creek Park, turn left onto Collier, continue west for .3 to U.S. 41 (Northside Drive), and turn left for .5. Cross the bridge over the interstate and turn right to enter I-75 South. After 5 miles leave I-75 to access I-20 East to Augusta; pay close attention to instructions at the interchange. After 4 miles take Exit 61B at Glenwood Avenue. Turn left from the ramp for .1 to the Walker Monument on the left.

8

The Siege of Atlanta

HOOD HAD BEEN GIVEN command of the Army of Tennessee to take the offensive and destroy Sherman. A subordinate noted that the new commander's eyes flashed with an indescribable light at the thought of the assignment as he set out immediately to accomplish that mission. Generally following Johnston's original plan for an assault at Peachtree Creek, Hood positioned Alexander P. Stewart and William J. Hardee (who was angry for not being chosen to succeed Johnston) to attack George H. Thomas and John M. Schofield as they crossed the stream. Benjamin F. Cheatham, who now commanded Hood's former corps, was posted to block James B. McPherson from coming to the assistance of Thomas and Schofield, who would be trapped in a pocket between Peachtree Creek and the Chattahoochee River and crushed. Then Hood would turn and dispatch McPherson.

The Confederate attack, however, appeared doomed from the start. Scheduled to begin at 1 P.M. on July 20, the action was postponed until 4 P.M. when Hood was forced to shift his line. This gave Thomas time to bring nearly his entire army across Peachtree Creek and entrench on elevated ground. Five Confederate divisions now faced seven Federal divisions—perilous odds at best.

The Confederate advance was hampered by heavy woods, thickets, and ravines. For a time an entire division was lost in the wilderness. Once organized, the lank, tattered Rebels launched a series of furious, but uncoordinated, attacks on the Federal line that accomplished several shallow penetrations; they were murderously repulsed by punishing volleys of cannon and rifle fire. The most serious Confederate thrust was parried by a counterattack led by Col. Benjamin Harrison, the future president. Some

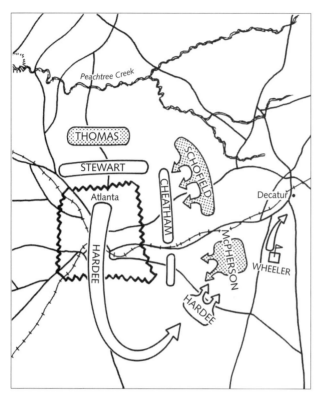

Map 21: The battle of Atlanta

Southern units took fire from several directions at once. After two hours of persistent fighting in which the Confederates gained nothing, they withdrew, having suffered 4,800 casualties while inflicting only 1,780 on the enemy.

Hood blamed the setback on Hardee for not pressing the assault with enough vigor, but Hood was responsible for much of the disaster. Absent from the scene of battle, he had chosen to direct the action from Atlanta, where he would remain throughout the fighting around the beleaguered city.

While the tempest of battle raged at Peachtree Creek, the first Federal shell dropped on Atlanta, killing a little girl. The siege had begun, a fact made clear to Atlantans by the thousands of Confederate wounded who suddenly flooded into the city, the debris of Hood's first combat.

After Hood's attack failed, he withdrew his army into Atlanta's inner defenses and contracted his lines to stave off Thomas. His new strategy involved holding the city's trenches and striking out at Sherman's armies whenever he saw an opportunity. For his part, Sherman had no intention of storming the stout fortifications that surrounded Atlanta. He intended to make a circuit of the city and destroy the four railroads that supplied Hood.

Sherman had already broken two, the Western and Atlantic and the Augusta Railroads; he expected to entice Hood out of Atlanta to protect his two remaining rail lifelines. While accomplishing this mission, Sherman welcomed fights in the open with the considerably outnumbered Confederate forces, instructing his generals to remain vigilant for Rebel sallies. The Federal commander believed this strategy would be time consuming but ultimately successful.

Hood refused to allow the bloody reversal at Peachtree Creek to deter him from continuing the offensive. He immediately turned his attention to McPherson, who was dangerously isolated to the east of Atlanta and advancing on the city from Decatur. On July 21 McPherson had told Mortimer Leggett to capture Bald Hill, a strategic post east of Atlanta. The assignment was almost suicidal, but in a brilliant strike his men swarmed over the Rebel parapets to subdue the defenders. The elevation would afterward be known as Leggett's Hill. The Federals suffered 750 casualties in what Patrick Cleburne called the most bitter fighting of his career. The loss of the important ridge placed Atlanta under Yankee artillery, and McPherson would have to be thrown back to prevent a bombardment of the city.

Without allowing his men to rest from the exertions of battle and retreat on July 20, Hood set a second full-scale attack into motion on the following day. He intended to imitate the successful tactics of the incomparable Robert E. Lee and Stonewall Jackson in Virginia by dividing his army and sending Hardee on a grand flanking march around McPherson's left, a move Jackson executed to perfection against Joseph Hooker at Chancellorsville.

Hood's plan called for Hardee to withdraw from the northeastern lines of Atlanta on the night of July 21, march through the city to the south, and be in place to attack the Federal left at dawn. When Hardee turned the flank, Cheatham was to hit McPherson's front and crush the Army of the Tennessee. Stewart and the Georgia militia would hold the city's defenses against Thomas and Schofield, preventing them from rescuing McPherson or marching into Atlanta during the battle. Joseph Wheeler was instructed to strike McPherson's rear and burn the extensive Union wagon train. Hood believed that, if properly executed, this audacious plan would send the entire Federal army reeling north of the Chattahoochee River in disorganized retreat.

Unfortunately, Atlanta was not Chancellorsville, Hood was not Lee, Hardee was not Jackson, and McPherson was not Hooker. The Confederates were exhausted from the previous battle and withdrawal, and in executing a grueling fifteen-mile march in the dark that would consume twelve hours, they would be sacrificing a second night's sleep. Then they would be expected to fight again.

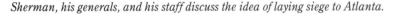

Sherman, his generals, and his staff discuss the idea of laying siege to Atlanta.

HARPER'S WEEKLY

The plan was brilliant if unrealistic. The heat was oppressive. The primitive roads were narrow, twisting, crowded, and choked with dust. Progress was slowed by heavy woods, ravines, and marshes south of Atlanta. The march was further delayed by the tardy arrival of some units, and the men suffered terribly from thirst on the long trek. Hardee's inexperienced guides retarded the advance by leading the columns into a pond, which forced a lengthy detour. The troops waited impatiently as cavalry, artillery, and ammunition wagons passed and for stragglers to rejoin the march.

The people of Atlanta realized a dramatic undertaking was afoot. All day the Confederates raised clouds of dust as troops tramped south through the city. Many feared Hood was evacuating and made preparations for occupation by Federal troops.

As the Confederates finally arrayed their battle lines, Gen. William H. T. Walker was killed by Federal pickets. It proved an ill omen.

After all the delays, the attack was launched six hours late; it initiated the fiercest combat of the Atlanta campaign. Hardee's men surged bravely forward in a furious assault on McPherson's men. A Yankee soldier said that the enemy "came tearing wildly through the woods with the yells of demons." The determined attack was marked by intensely savage fighting, but the delay had given McPherson time to extend and fortify his position, and the attack did not fall on a vulnerable flank. Hardee's initial lunge was riddled by twelve Union guns that fired one thousand rounds at the charging Rebels.

Hardee's attack degenerated into an inconclusive charge and counter-charge until Cleburne's dynamic division burst through the Federal line, capturing eight guns and seven hundred prisoners and threatening Union troops from two sides. A Yankee battery of ten guns beat back the assault, and the hole was sealed. Cleburne sacrificed 40 percent of his men in the effort, including thirty of his sixty officers.

Several hours after Hardee initiated the battle, Cheatham hit McPherson's center, ruptured the Union line, and captured ten guns, an entire regiment of Yankees, and thirteen stands of colors. As one Confederate noted, "We charged with an awful yell, but few Yankees staid to see the racket." The Confederates broke into the Union rear and routed four regiments as they steadily advanced down the line, catching the Federals from behind. McPherson's battered army received fire from two directions and jumped from one side of its works to the other to blunt successive waves of attackers. His command was severely distressed, and the entire Union line was in danger of being irretrievably shattered.

McPherson had met with his corps commanders earlier in the morning and was returning to his headquarters when the melee erupted. He quickly galloped toward a ridge where he could observe the scene and direct a defense, but he rode into an unsuspected gap in his lines just as Cleburne's men penetrated. Charging Rebels called for him to surrender; but McPherson wheeled his horse to escape, waving gallantly at the Confederate soldiers.

BATTLES AND LEADERS

Bald Hill—named such because its summit was barren of trees—was strategically situated on the eastern approach to Atlanta and formed the focal point of the battle for the city, which began on July 21. Union artillery shook up the Confederate defenders here, but it took infantry to dislodge them. McPherson anchored his line on the hill; however, Hood's attack on July 22 nearly succeeded in retaking the height.

A rattling volley knocked the Union general from his mount, and he fell dead to the ground. McPherson would never return to Baltimore to marry.

The body was recovered as the ground changed hands repeatedly, and it was brought to Sherman's headquarters and laid on a door. The Union commander wept at the sight. He ordered the corpse covered with a flag and sent the body to Marietta for transportation north. Sherman personally wrote McPherson's fiancée, who had been tormented by intemperate comments made by Secessionist family members, describing McPherson as an eclipsed "bright star" and expressing the fear that he would meet the same fate.

Sherman temporarily pushed his grief aside when he recognized the dangerous hole that Cheatham had ripped in McPherson's front. Moving quickly to seal the rupture, he ordered Schofield to redirect twenty guns on the gap. Sherman was again in his element when crisis beckoned. A staff officer noted that his "eyes flashed, he did not speak," but exhibited a "concentrated fierceness" in his face.

John "Blackjack" Logan assumed command of McPherson's army and received this order from Sherman: "Fight 'em, fight 'em, fight 'em like hell!" Logan complied, rallying his stunned men with the cry, "For McPherson and revenge!" In a fury the Army of the Tennessee relentlessly swarmed into a maelstrom of fire to restore the broken line, which is the dramatic scene of battle depicted in the famous Cyclorama.

A gale of shot from concentrated Federal artillery shredded a final Confederate charge through the hole, then Logan's men surged in counterattack to seal the gap. Men in blue and gray fought with reckless abandon in hand-to-hand fighting. Officers dueled with swords while infantrymen resorted to bayonets and swung their rifles like deadly clubs. A more bitter battle or harder fighting was not witnessed in the war. Whole battalions on each side ceased to exist, and flags and artillery pieces were repeatedly captured and lost. In one Confederate division, all the officers became casualties. A thick layer of blood covered the ground, and the groans of wounded and dying men drowned out the crashing sounds of mortal combat.

The Federals jubilantly regained their trenches and mangled three Rebel efforts to recapture them. Union batteries and seventeen thousand massed rifles formed a scathing fire that completely annihilated one assault, crumpling men like wheat before a tornado, one combatant commented.

The tide of battle had decisively turned. Wheeler had successfully driven the Yankees through Decatur, but before the wagon train could be destroyed, the cavalry was recalled to support Hardee.

After eight hours of continuous battle, darkness enveloped the field, and the fighting was halted by the exhaustion of the combatants. During the night the Rebels withdrew into the inner ring of Atlanta's defenses, leaving the Union line intact. They had suffered debilitating casualties as eight thousand men fell; the Federals lost thirty-seven hundred. It was the largest

In the fight to retake Bald Hill, a Union battery of four 20-pounder Parrotts was captured. The battery commander managed to spike the guns and evade capture. The Confederates lacked horses to remove the guns, and the battery was recaptured.

MOUNTAIN CAMPAIGNS IN GEORGIA

MOUNTAIN CAMPAIGNS IN GEORGIA

Union Gen. James B. McPherson was shot by Confederate skirmishers when he refused to surrender. He was the only Federal army commander to die in battle.

engagement of the campaign, destined to be remembered as the battle of Atlanta. The cost crippled the Confederates.

The plan had been a bold, brilliant move that could have destroyed the Army of the Tennessee, but it had failed miserably. Part of the blame could be placed on the piecemeal attacks. Four assaults were launched at four different times against unsuspected works; a single unified attack might have destroyed the opposition. Hood had also expected too much of his weary men, asking them to destroy twice their number. They tried valiantly, but they could not accomplish the impossible. Hood again placed responsibility for the failure on Hardee because of the tardy attack and poorly conducted assaults. Hood, however, had been distant from the battlefield, observing the smoke-obscured conflict from the area of Oakland Cemetery.

A truce was arranged on July 24; the wounded were collected, and the dead were buried. The number of Confederate casualties blanketing the ground was sickening. Governor Brown's brother was among the Rebel dead. The streets of Atlanta were crammed with ambulances carrying wounded to hospitals and parks in the city, where the grass was soon stained red and buckets overflowed with amputated limbs.

Curiously enough, Hood considered the battle of Atlanta a partial victory, although it had obviously not accomplished the grandiose objectives he had desired. A considerable number of Federal prisoners had been bagged; McPherson's advance had been halted, however temporarily; and

Hood strangely thought he had restored the morale of the Army of Tennessee by reintroducing them to offensive combat. The soldiers knew the truth. They had been savaged.

The siege of Atlanta now began in earnest. Sherman lobbed shells into the city, tumbling some buildings into ruins and setting others on fire. On July 28 he began a general bombardment, but he lacked the troops to establish a complete encirclement. The Union commander paid careful heed to Oliver O. Howard's warning: "Hood won't give up."

Sherman shortly decided to move west of Atlanta, intent on destroying the West Point and Macon Railroads, which shared five miles of track before branching at East Point. Political considerations led him to appoint Howard as permanent commander of the Army of the Tennessee instead of Logan, and on July 26 Howard was dispatched on a wide flanking movement around the city to cut the rails that brought supplies into Atlanta. Howard was also instructed to goad Hood into further battle, if possible.

It was possible. Learning of the threat to his lifelines, Hood sent two corps, commanded by Stewart and Stephen D. Lee, a former cavalry leader fresh from Mississippi who now commanded Hood's old unit, to intercept Howard on the western edge of the city. Expecting trouble, Howard halted the advance when scouts informed him of the approaching Confederates, and he deployed his men in a defensive position on high ground near Ezra Methodist Church. His men stripped the church to use benches and planks, supported by their knapsacks, for barricades and waited anxiously for the Southerners. The Confederates rapidly marched into view, dressed their lines of battle, and mounted several unsynchronized, piecemeal assaults beginning at 12:30 P.M. They were badly mauled as they groped forward through tangled underbrush.

The Rebels made four separate charges in three hours of terrible fighting, the last waves stumbling over dead and wounded comrades. Howard brought up his artillery to enfilade the Southern assaults, and shells rained on the attackers from two directions while bullets pelted their ranks like hail. One unit, the Twenty-fifth Alabama, lost 125 of 173 men. Confederate battle flags were shot to pieces, and Generals Stewart and Loring were wounded. Stewart, who personally led three charges, seemed for a while to be charmed, remaining unscathed for long hours while the entire Federal army appeared to blaze away at his horsed figure. Litter bearers later said it looked like hogs had been slaughtered on their stretchers.

Hardee, sent to assess the situation, reported to Hood that there was no point in continuing the attacks with such demoralized troops. They had lost five thousand men, the Federals six hundred. That night, Jacob Cox heard a Federal picket call out, "Well Johnny, how many of you are left?" A despondent Confederate replied, "Oh, about enough for another killing."

When informed of the battle, Sherman was delighted, replying that it was just what he required. "Let 'em beat their own brains out," he said somewhat excitedly.

BATTLES AND LEADERS

On July 22 the Confederates surprised McPherson's army with an early morning attack. At a critical point in the fighting, Brig. Gen. John Fuller established a new line by grabbing the colors of his former regiment and re-forming the men with his sword. As soon as the line had taken shape, they charged the Southerners and pushed them back.

The battle of Ezra Church broke the back of the Army of Tennessee. Some units had fought courageously, but others balked at advancing into the muzzles of a prepared adversary. After fighting heroically in fruitless contests at Peachtree Creek and Atlanta, many had lost heart. Desertion was soon epidemic in the Confederate ranks.

Although Hood's offenses had failed, Sherman paid homage to the Confederate soldiers. "These fellows fight like Demons and Indians combined, and it calls for all my cunning and strength" to defeat them, he remarked.

After examining the results of the Ezra Church encounter, Jefferson Davis dispatched an ironic telegram to Hood. "Stop attacking," he directed, "before you completely destroy the army." Perhaps Davis had finally realized the blunder of placing Hood in command and had come to appreciate the wisdom of Johnston's defensive strategy.

Hood was content for a month to rely on the formidable defenses of Atlanta to foil Sherman's designs. The inner ring of works, one and a half

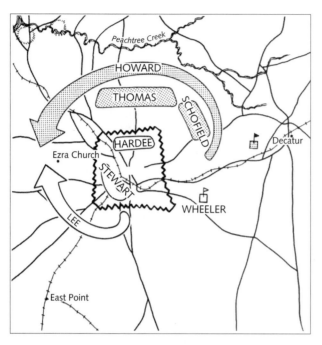

Map 22: The battle of Ezra Church

miles from the city, was ten miles in length and consisted of infantry trenches connected to batteries that provided interlocking fields of fire. The earthworks were further shielded by rows of abatis and four lines of chevaux-de-frise. Thousands of trees were felled, and neighborhoods disappeared as timber was appropriated for the extensive works, which were so vast that they "astonished" the Federals.

Sherman telegraphed Washington that the fortifications were "too strong to assault and too extensive to invest," calling Atlanta "a tough nut to crack." A frontal attack was dismissed, for "the cost would be too great and success unlikely." It also seemed improbable that Hood would sally forth again. Sherman devised a new strategy to force Hood out of Atlanta, but this plan proved to be one of Sherman's rare mistakes.

Atlanta was receiving urgently needed supplies by the two remaining railroads, one leading to West Point and Mobile, the second to Macon and Savannah. Although Sherman had always considered cavalry useless, he decided to send his horse soldiers on raids deep into Georgia to sever the railroads, make Hood evacuate Atlanta, and, as a bonus, liberate Union prisoners at Andersonville.

Sherman's "Great Raid," which kicked off on July 27, was a disaster from start to finish. Federal cavalry stumbled across western and central Georgia, managed to torch two trains, destroyed two miles of track, and laid ruin to a five-hundred-wagon procession. Then, pursued by heavily outnumbered but maniacal Confederate horsemen, each Federal cavalry detachment was annihilated. George Stoneman was defeated and captured at Sunshine Church near Macon; Edward M. McCook, a first cousin of the colonel killed at Kennesaw Mountain, saw his command shattered at Brown's Mill near Newnan; Horace Capron's brigade was scattered at King's Tanyard near Winder. The strategic gamble had completely failed by August 3, and remnants of the isolated commands trickled in for weeks, mainly on foot. More than forty-seven hundred Union cavalrymen began the raid; sixteen hundred returned. The blunder only served to resupply the depleted Confederate cavalry with captured horses and equipment.

After his cavalry failed to induce Atlanta's surrender, Sherman resumed his tedious flanking maneuvers to cut the railroads. On August 6 Schofield was sent south of the city with his army and another corps under John Palmer, but the two generals' argument over seniority wasted a day. By the time they advanced, Hardee had extended his lines to meet the threat at Utoy Creek. The Federals assaulted the Orphan Brigade, pressing through thickets and brambles to within thirty yards of the Confederate trenches. Fierce resistance caused them to falter then abandon the attack. During the night the Confederates withdrew closer to Atlanta. The following day Schofield flung his troops against the new line and suffered a more savage repulse, which led Sherman to mutter, "The enemy can build parapets faster than we can march." The Federals left eight hundred men strewn across the valley of Utoy Creek; the Confederates suffered only eighteen casualties and captured large quantities of guns and ammunition.

With this movement blocked, Sherman commenced a heavy shelling of Atlanta. He telegraphed Chattanooga for two siege guns and one thousand shells with which he planned to level every building in the city. On August 9 five thousand rounds thundered down on Atlanta, killing at least six civilians. Sherman slowly extended a viselike grip on his objective and informed Washington that he intended to "make the inside of Atlanta too hot to endure."

Conditions in the city became critical as Hood struggled to feed his thirty-seven thousand soldiers still manning the trenches and ten thousand stubborn citizens and refugees, who Sherman assumed had been evacuated. The Union commander ordered his men to fire every gun that could reach any structure in the city, whether the target was a factory, warehouse, store, church, or home. Ultimately, more than 225 cannon contributed to the "Atlanta Express."

Under a flag of truce, Hood sent a message through the lines to Sherman, criticizing his bombardment of a city filled with defenseless women and children. Sherman replied, "Even Hood must realize that war is the very science of barbarity. The city is a military target," he continued, "and will be treated as such."

August 10 was the worst day of the bombardment witnessed by Wallace P. Reed. "Ten Confederate and eleven Federal batteries took part in

At Ezra Church, Howard's Federals inflicted five times as many casualties on the Southerners as they suffered themselves.

LESLIE'S ILLUSTRATED

the engagement," he recorded. "Shot and shell rained in every direction. Great volumes of sulphurous smoke rolled over the town, trailing down to the ground; and through this stifling gloom the sun glared like a great red eye peering through a bronze-colored cloud."

One shell crashed into a house and killed a woman and her six-year-old daughter. Another woman was killed by a shell fragment while she was ironing clothes. A Confederate officer was bidding farewell to his landlady and her son when a shell burst, mortally wounding the soldier and boy. "The two victims were laid side by side on the grass under the trees," Reed wrote, "and in a few minutes both bled to death."

One young family abandoned the inner city for the security of a ridge, but they could still clearly hear "the crash when the houses were struck."

To escape the awful carnage, most families dug pits in their backyards and gardens to a depth of ten feet, then covered the holes with stout timbers and a layer of earth. Dragging tables, chairs, mattresses, and what provisions were on hand into their improvised "bombproofs," the civilians fled to their dugouts when the shelling became severe or dangerously close. Sometimes a stray shell would fall directly on the tiny entrances and entire families were instantly killed.

Federal Gen. Jacob Cox was horrified by the conditions he found in a shelter occupied by a large family: "I looked down into the pit and saw there, in the gloom made visible by a candle burning while it was broad day above, women sitting on the floor of loose boards, resting against each other, haggard and wan, trying to sleep away the days of terror, while innocent-looking children, four or five years old, clustered around the air-hole, looking up with pale faces and great staring eyes as they heard the singing of the bullets that were flying thick above their sheltering place."

The Intellectual General ■ John M. Schofield

Ohioan John M. Schofield was perhaps the least physically imposing general in the Atlanta campaign. He was short, plump, balding, and sported a long beard. Earlier he had demonstrated competence in organizing Federal forces in Missouri.

He commanded the tiny Army of the Ohio, which had earlier captured Knoxville and held it against siege by James Longstreet. After the Atlanta campaign was successfully concluded, his army was dispatched to Tennessee to deal with Hood.

When Hood skillfully slipped around the flank of Schofield's army at Spring Hill, Tennessee, that Federal force should have been destroyed. What followed, however, became one of the war's greatest controversies: Schofield's men stealthily marched past the sleeping Confederate army. Enraged the next morning to learn that the Yankees were gone, Hood pursued Schofield to Franklin and launched a foolish twilight assault against the Federals. The battle left six Rebel generals dead and crippled Hood's army. Later at Nashville, Schofield joined Thomas in pretty much destroying what was left of the Army of Tennessee.

Schofield then rejoined Sherman in the advance through North Carolina.

Schofield's talents were in the academic and administrative arenas. He was ranked seventh in the West Point Class of 1853, and for a time he tutored fellow classmate John Bell Hood. Before the war Schofield taught at West Point and, during a brief leave of absence, at Washington University in St. Louis. After the war he served as Andrew Johnson's secretary of war, as commandant of the U.S. Military Academy at West Point, and beginning in 1888, as the commanding general of the army.

By offering the starving people a generous meal, Cox coaxed twenty-one inhabitants of the bombproof into the open, the first time, he was told, they had left its protection in three weeks.

A ten-year-old girl, disappointed by the absence of a cake on her birthday, confided a sentiment to her diary that was doubtlessly shared by thousands of Atlanta citizens: "I hope by my next birthday we will have peace in our land so that I can have a nice dinner."

Civilians were visited day and night by sudden death or mutilation as shells plunged from the sky. Buildings tumbled to the ground or were gutted by flames, and always there was the sound of guns barking and explosions. People still held fast to their homes, even when faced with starvation.

A second lull descended over the battle front, coinciding with the usual southern summer doldrums. Goods were traded between the lines, and Union and Confederate songfests filled the sultry nights with music. Cotton bales soaked with turpentine provided illumination and also prevented nighttime assaults; movement during the day was discouraged by snipers.

Sherman considered the siege beneficial to the Rebels. "The enemy hold us by an inferior force," he lamented. "They besiege us." In Washington, Lincoln pondered his future life out of the presidency.

By August 25 the bombardment had apparently accomplished little, so Sherman elected to cut loose from the railroad and his supply base to try one more daring operation. Leaving Henry W. Slocum's single corps entrenched to guard the railroad bridge over the Chattahoochee River to the north, Sherman evacuated his trenches and sent the entire army, with ten days' rations, wheeling southwest of the city on a six-mile-wide front to cut those two pesky railroads that kept Hood alive. "I have Atlanta as certainly as if it were in my hand," Sherman bragged.

When the shelling abruptly ceased, Confederate pickets crept out of their holes and discovered the enemy works abandoned. For several days Hood believed Sherman had lifted the siege and had returned to Chattanooga in defeat. A victory ball was prepared, with women brought from the sanctuary of Macon to help celebrate this fortuitous event. Everyone thought Sherman was scurrying north, tail tucked between legs. Hood's failure to recognize the truth immediately was a result of Wheeler's cavalry raid north to cut the Western and Atlantic Railroad that supplied Sherman. Wheeler accomplished little damage then wandered into eastern Tennessee for a month, leaving Hood with no reconnaissance force.

Hood, however, learned the rude truth of Sherman's movement on August 30 when Howard destroyed the West Point Railroad. His soldiers did a thorough job, levering up the rails and ties, then piling the ties to form blazing bonfires, heating the rails in the center over the blaze and twisting the iron around nearby trees. Railroad cuts were filled with trees, and armed artillery shells were planted as mines to discourage repair crews.

Hood called for Hardee and sent him—accompanied by Lee's corps—to march that night to Jonesboro, fifteen miles south of Atlanta, to protect the

Sherman's engineers overlooked nothing in evaluating, adopting, and strengthening the Confederates' former entrenchments.

Macon railroad and prevent the encirclement of Atlanta. Hardee was bluntly informed that the fate of Atlanta rested in his hands. Hood believed that only half of Sherman's army was south of the city, and Hardee was expected to drive them back to the Chattahoochee. Stewart and the militia were to remain to protect Atlanta from the remainder of Sherman's troops, and Hood would stay with them again. Hood telegraphed further orders to Hardee, but the wires were soon cut by the rampaging Yankees.

Hardee's twenty-four thousand footsore men were not assembled at Jonesboro until the afternoon of August 31, which afforded Howard's seventeen thousand infantry time to entrench in a favorable position behind log-and-fence-rail barricades. When Hardee attacked at 3 P.M., the two primary assaults were again poorly coordinated. The Confederates overran the Union skirmish line, but at eighty yards they met a "terrible and destructive fire" and were solidly repulsed before the main works. Officers attempting to rally their men found the soldiers now had a horror of charging breastworks, and many refused to move forward. When a second assault was organized, it was destroyed by a six-gun battery that fired so rapidly that parts of the carriages shattered. The Rebels cowered in a ravine until a Federal counterattack routed them, Yankees calling disparaging remarks in their wake. Hardee broke off the engagement at dark, and the depleted Confederate force retired.

The dismal attack was unlike those previously executed by the Army of Tennessee. Some dispirited men, believing they were already beaten, prayed for capture, despairing of victory or even survival. Those who charged did so timidly. Hardee lost 1,700 men in the debacle; the Federals lost 180.

As Howard fended off Hardee, Schofield cut the Macon railroad at Rough and Ready just after a final train from Atlanta had passed. While the demolition was in progress, a second train approached, but the engineer spotted the troops, reversed his engine, and backed into Atlanta to inform Hood that Atlanta was now isolated. Fearing an imminent attack on the city, Hood ordered Lee's corps to return to Atlanta at 5 P.M. The men, who had marched throughout the previous night and had fought a battle during the day, now prepared for a return march into the city that night to reoccupy Atlanta's trenches. Hardee, who had withdrawn to Jonesboro, was alone, dangerously separated from the remainder of the Confederate army.

When morning dawned on September 1, Hardee commanded only one corps of five thousand men. Many of his troops had deserted or were straggling somewhere between Jonesboro and Atlanta. When Sherman realized Hardee's desperate situation, he directed all six of his corps to converge on Jonesboro in hopes of surrounding and destroying the lone Southern "army."

Map 23: The battle of Jonesboro

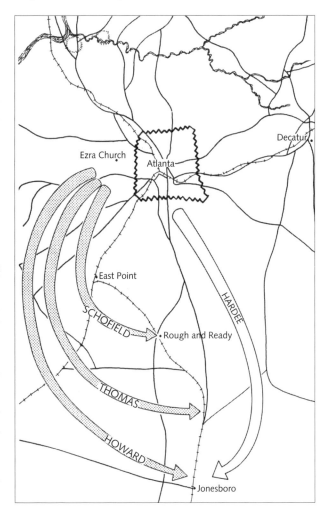

Hardee hastily improvised a line of earthworks and was subjected to an artillery bombardment that lasted all day. At 4 P.M. he was surrounded on three sides. Although one Union corps failed to arrive, Sherman felt it was too late to wait for Hardee to be corralled. He launched a vigorous assault by three divisions that struck the apex of Hardee's curved line. Excited by the knowledge that Atlanta's fall was imminent, the Yankees charged forward with abandon, ignoring holes torn in their ranks by grapeshot and leaving hundreds of their comrades writhing on the ground. They leaped the Confederate parapets and eagerly went to work with bayonets.

The Rebels, languid in attacking the previous day, resisted with a ferocity characteristic of their proud past. A battery blew gaping lanes in the surging Federal ranks, but Union counterfire splintered the carriages and forced artillery crews to abandon their pieces. The angle was smothered by vastly superior numbers, and the line was broken as savage hand-to-hand fighting erupted. Units to either side of the breach valiantly held their positions, and Hardee feverishly rushed in his puny reserves to establish a second line that miraculously firmed and fended off additional Union attacks.

Despite thirteen hundred casualties suffered in the charge, the Federals were elated, although they quivered in exhaustion. One Union officer called the attack "glorious." Sherman could easily have overwhelmed Hardee if he had bothered to make the effort, but for some unexplained reason he let the opportunity slip away.

Hardee fought off Federal advances until dark then led his decimated force six miles south along the railroad to Lovejoy Station. In addition to the eight cannon he had lost, six hundred men and a general were captured in the chaotic battle. The immortal Orphan Brigade, which had counted fifteen hundred men in Dalton, now consisted of five hundred survivors.

At Lovejoy, Hardee sent a dispatch to Hood, informing him that Jonesboro had fallen and the last railroad had been severed. Atlanta would have to be abandoned.

With a band playing "Hail, Columbia," Sherman entered Jonesboro the next day to find a grisly scene: The dead were unburied, and wounded soldiers lay abandoned in hospitals, churches, and virtually every building in town. The Federals interred two thousand bodies in mass graves.

Hood placed the blame for the defeat at Jonesboro, the loss of the railroad, and his evacuation of Atlanta on Hardee. The effort at Jonesboro must have been feeble, he said, if Hardee had only suffered seventeen hundred casualties on the first day of battle. Until he died, Hood maintained he was not to blame for the loss of Atlanta.

Following several days of elation over Sherman's reported departure, Atlanta's citizens were shocked by rumors of a great battle at Jonesboro. Crowds of stragglers and deserters flocked through the city as government stores were thrown open to the public. Hood ordered Stewart, Lee, and the

Howard's corps were kept busy with the task of destroying the railroads emanating from the Atlanta hub. Below the destruction in Jonesboro is depicted.

LIBRARY OF CONGRESS

Despite all the havoc wreaked by Sherman's armies on Georgia's railroads, the most destructive single moment had to have been the demolition of a Confederate ammunition train, necessitated by Hood's abandoning Atlanta.

militia to prepare for evacuation south to Lovejoy in the night. The despairing cries of civilians filled the darkness as the remnants of a once feared army filed silently down Peachtree Street to McDonough Road, flags furled.

With the railroads lost, Hood was unable to evacuate his trains, so he ran seven locomotives, eighty-one freight cars filled with ammunition, and thirteen siege guns to the railroad yards, evacuated every building for half a mile around, and ordered a cavalry rear guard to set torches to the rolling stock and supplies. Those present called it the most spectacular sight they ever witnessed. For five hours the ground heaved like an earthquake under the detonations, windows were shattered, and nearby buildings were pierced by shells as thousands of explosions rocked the darkness. A fireworks display like the South had never seen lit up this gloomy night. To the north, Slocum wondered if Hood was attacking Sherman. In Jonesboro, Sherman wondered whether Hood was destroying Slocum and his railroad.

In the morning Slocum's pickets found the Confederate trenches empty. Advancing farther, they met a delegation of prominent citizens led by Atlanta's mayor, who carried a white flag of truce. "Sir," he said formally to the ranking officer, "the fortunes of war has placed Atlanta in your hands. As mayor of the city I ask protection of non-combatants and private property." Late in the day Slocum's men marched into the city, bands playing as they passed bombed-out buildings to hoist the U.S. flag over city hall.

HARPER'S WEEKLY

Captured Confederates were marched north after the fighting at Jonesboro.

Sherman probed Hardee's lines at Lovejoy then marched north to occupy his prize. After 128 days of constant fighting and thirty-five thousand casualties suffered by each side, the Atlanta campaign was over.

On September 3 Sherman wired Washington, "So Atlanta is ours, and fairly won." Lincoln received the message in his study late that night and proclaimed a day of thanksgiving for the capture of Atlanta. Throughout the North one-hundred-gun salutes were fired in celebration of the stunning victory. While Atlanta held out, it remained a symbol of defeat and of Southern resistance. When the city fell, Northerners felt the war could be won. Lincoln was reelected, and the war continued to a victorious close seven months later.

A Tour of Atlanta and Jonesboro

This tour begins at the Walker Monument on the southeastern corner of Exit 61B at I-20 and Glenwood Avenue.

A cannon, its muzzle encased in concrete, marks the spot where Confederate Gen. William H. T. Walker was killed by Federal pickets at the beginning of the battle of Atlanta. Walker's death in battle surprised no one; he had been severely wounded by Indians and Mexicans and was nicknamed "Shotpouch" for rounds still embedded in his body. Walker had repeatedly resigned from the U.S. and Confederate armies over perceived slights and had engaged in a newspaper-letter war with Jefferson Davis early in the war. His body was returned to Augusta, where it rests on the grounds of Augusta College.

Drive west across I-20 on Glenwood for .8 and turn right onto Monument. Cross the first street (Metropolitan) to .3, where there is a monument similar to Walker's.

This monument marks the spot where Federal Gen. James B. McPherson unknowingly rode into advancing Confederate troops. Refusing to surrender, he spurred his horse in an attempt to escape but was shot dead from the saddle.

Turn left onto McPherson for .4, right on Moreland for .3, and left onto Memorial.

After his bloody failure at Peachtree Creek, Hood withdrew into Atlanta's inner defenses and prepared to attack McPherson, whose Army of the Tennessee was cutting Atlanta's rail link with the Carolinas and Virginia. This assault, known as the battle of Atlanta, was the largest of the campaign. The attack failed to strike the Union flank but was fierce and briefly ruptured McPherson's line. McPherson was killed, but massed Federal artillery shattered Confederate charges and sent the enemy back to their defensive trenches. Georgia Gov. Joseph E. Brown's brother was killed during the battle.

To launch his flank attack, William J. Hardee marched through the night on Peachtree Street to Five Points and down Capitol Avenue almost to the Yellow River. He was joined by Patrick Cleburne at Memorial then turned up Bouldercrest and split his forces on Flat Shoals and Fayetteville Road. Attacks were then launched all along the Federal line, which was just north of Glenwood and farther north, up Moreland, at the intersection with DeKalb, which is a focal point of the Cyclorama display. The I-20 exchange at Moreland is all that remains of Leggett's Hill, where the most desperate fighting occurred.

This monument marks the site where Union Gen. James B. McPherson was killed during the battle of Atlanta.

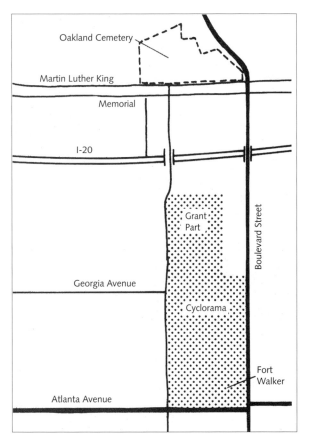

Map 24: Oakland Cemetery and Grant Park

The Confederate breakthrough occurred at More-land and the Georgia Railroad, which was the site of the DeGress battery and the Troup Hurt house and the current site of an old stone church on DeGress Avenue. A historical marker commemorates it. Sherman's headquarters at the Augustus Hurt house, where McPherson's body was carried, was on the grounds of the James Earl Carter Presidential Library just north of the battlefield. Because of Atlanta's development in this area, a true apprecia-tion of the battle of Atlanta can only be glimpsed by experiencing the Cyclorama.

At .5 on Memorial notice to the right the old depot, and at 1 mile turn right onto Oakland Avenue; at .1 turn right into Oakland Cemetery.

Established 145 years ago, Oakland Cemetery is one of Atlanta's most historic landmarks and its oldest

cemetery, now containing an estimated one hundred thousand burials. Such Georgia notables as Mar-garet Mitchell, golfing great Bobby Jones, Georgia's wartime governor Joseph E. Brown, five other gover-nors, twenty-three Atlanta mayors, and many found-ing families of the Atlanta area (including Austells, Vinings, Hapes, and Norcrosses) are buried here. Confederate Capt. Benjamin Harding Helm, Abra-ham Lincoln's brother-in-law, was buried at Oakland after suffering a mortal wound at Chickamauga. It is reported that Lincoln grieved at news of his death. In 1884 Helm was reinterred at the family plot in Eliza-bethtown, Kentucky. Confederate Vice President Alexander H. Stephens was temporarily buried at Oakland, a funeral attended by twenty thousand people in 1883, but he was reinterred at his home in Crawfordville the following year.

More than fifty thousand people wander across Oakland's eighty-eight acres each year, and historical and preservation societies conduct tours. Historic Oakland Cemetery and the city of Atlanta sponsor Sundays in the Park, a celebration of 1900-era picnic excursions and explorations of the cemetery's archi-tecture, art, and history. Information about the ceme-tery may be obtained in the visitors center in the bell tower building. An inexpensive, detailed guide to the cemetery may be purchased.

The grounds of Oakland Cemetery provide a grand view of Atlanta. A historical marker stands on the site of Mayor James E. William's home, from where Hood watched the battle of Atlanta.

Take the second left at .2 and the Confederate cemetery is on your right. At .1 turn right beside the rows of Southern graves and pass the tall Confederate monu-ment in the center of the road.

The Confederate section holds the remains of twenty-four hundred Southern soldiers. They died of wounds and disease in a complex of forty hospital buildings established at the fairground or in the intense fight-ing in the battles for Atlanta. More than sixty thou-sand soldiers were treated in the city. In 1864 the Confederate government petitioned for more burial space. Wooden headboards first marked the graves, but in 1890 those were replaced with standard government round marble headstones. Some pointed stones were added in 1951. Section C contains the graves of twenty Federals who were captured and died in local hospitals.

The sixty-five-foot-tall obelisk of Stone Mountain granite, the tallest structure in the city when it was erected on Confederate Memorial Day 1874, pays homage to the fallen Southerners. On October 15, 1870, the day of Robert E. Lee's funeral, Confederate Gen. John B. Gordon had dedicated the base. Among the libations Masons poured on it was a bottle of champagne given by a Southern lady to an officer in 1862 that was to be opened when the Confederacy won independence. A monument to the Real Daughters of the Confederacy (Real Daughters were women whose fathers served in the Confederate armed forces) is in this section. A number of civilians killed during Sherman's siege of the city are also buried at Oakland. During the Union occupation a number of graves were opened by Federal soldiers. Silver nameplates were stolen and coffins emptied and used for the burial of Northern dead.

Under a large magnolia tree to the left is the *Lion of Atlanta,* a reproduction of the famed *Lion of Lucerne.* The original honors sixteen Swiss guards who died protecting Marie Antoinette during the French Revolution. T. M. Brady carved the six-foot-high sculpture from a single fifteen-ton piece of Tate (Ga.) marble. It was dedicated on April 26, 1894, to the memory of several hundred unidentified Confederate soldiers who are buried in this plot without headstones and the thousands of others reinterred here from Atlanta's battlefields. The grieving crea-

Alfred Iverson Jr. is buried in Oakland Cemetery. He failed at Gettysburg but redeemed himself in the Atlanta campaign.

Oakland Cemetery's Lion of Atlanta *memorializes thousands of unknown casualties from the fighting around the city.*

ture, clutching a Confederate flag in one paw, is the most eloquent of hundreds of Confederate memorials found in Georgia.

Near the lion sculpture, in Block K, are buried three Confederate generals: John B. Gordon, Clement A. Evans, and Alfred Iverson Jr. Gordon (1832–1904), a delegate to both the Alabama and Georgia state secession conventions, raised the Raccoon Roughs in northern Alabama and Georgia and rose to prominence under Robert E. Lee. Fighting in every eastern battle, he was wounded five times at Antietam and nursed to health by his wife, who accompanied him throughout the war. Gordon headed the largest brigade in the Confederate army then commanded a division, led a corps, and by Appomattox had risen to command half the depleted army. Gordon, not Lee, was at the head of the Confederates who stacked their arms at one of the official ceremonies at Appomattox, then he instructed the men to return home and rebuild their lives. He was later twice governor of Georgia and served three terms in the U.S. Senate. Evans (1822–1911) was wounded five times, spent thirty years as a minister, and became a noted Confederate historian. Cavalry leader Iverson (1829–1911) served in Virginia then defeated Sherman's troopers during an Atlanta campaign raid at Sunshine Church, near his home. He had grown up in Washington, D.C., where his father served as a senator from Georgia. Their tombs are specially marked.

In family plots are the graves of Confederate generals Lucius J. Gartrell, William S. Walker, Henry K. McCay, and Isaac W. Avery and Gov. Joseph E. Brown. Gartrell (1821–91) caught Francis S. Bartow as he fell at First Manassas, where he also lost his sixteen-year-old son, Henry Clay Gartrell. Walker (1822–99) was captured in 1864 after inadvertently riding into Union lines. McCay (1820–86) was a teacher from Pennsylvania who commanded the Georgia militia at Atlanta, Griswoldville, and Doctortown. Avery (1837–97) fought at Chickamauga and was wounded at New Hope Church.

Ceremonies honoring the Southern dead have been held at Oakland since 1866 and continue today.

At .3 take a sharp right onto the rough brick pavement and a very tight right at the end of the cemetery at .1 beside the south wall. At .1 to the left is a bronze plaque.

The plaque indicates that seven of James Andrews's raiders were executed on what are now cemetery grounds. They were buried here in June 1862. Andrews was hanged from a scaffold at the corner of Juniper and Third and buried nearby. The seven were reinterred in Chattanooga National Cemetery in 1866, but Andrews's remains were not discovered and moved until a concerted effort was made in 1887. Their white marble headstones surround an impressive stone monument topped by a bronze replica of the *General,* which was dedicated in 1891 before a crowd of ten thousand. Descendants of the men in Ohio placed this marker. While being held at the Fulton County Jail, eight of the raiders escaped.

Ironically, also buried in Oakland are the three men who lost then heroically recaptured the locomotive: Conductor William A. Fuller in the northwest corner, Jeff Cain, and Anthony Murphy. The fifteen-year-old fireman of the *Texas,* Henry Haney, became

a high-ranking Atlanta fire chief. He died on November 19, 1923, outliving the last raider by one month. He is buried in Atlanta's Crestlawn Cemetery.

Beside the railroad tracks near the cemetery, at the industrial complex, was an iron rolling mill that supplied armor for Confederate ironclads. When the city was abandoned, Hood ordered the destruction of eighty-one boxcars of ammunition and seven locomotives. The explosion could be heard, felt, and seen for twenty miles. Somehow the engine *General* managed to survive the blasts. The Georgia Railroad Roundhouse, famous from post-Sherman destruction photographs, stood between the Washington Street Bridge and Piedmont Avenue.

Take the next sharp right and the first left to exit the cemetery. Oakland Avenue is one-way, so drive straight on Martin Luther King Jr. Drive and turn left onto Grant Street at .1 to Memorial. Turn left onto Memorial for .2 and right onto Cherokee for .7 to the traffic light where Georgia Avenue intersects Cherokee. Turn left into Grant Park, and the Cyclorama is directly ahead.

Cycloramas, first developed in the late 1700s, experienced a resurgence in popularity following the American Civil War and Franco-Prussian War, when victors commissioned stirring portrayals of climactic battles. The Battle of Atlanta Cyclorama has been an Atlanta landmark for decades. The canvas, which is 42 feet high, 358 feet in circumference, and weighs eighteen thousand pounds, is the largest painting in the world. Commissioned by Gen. John A. Logan to support his campaign for the vice presidency (he died before the 1888 election), it was created in 1885 and 1886 by William Wehner's American Panorama Studio of Milwaukee, which employed German artists. A dozen of them traveled to Atlanta; six drew figures of soldiers, three did nothing but landscapes, and two were responsible for producing animals. Their first work had been of Missionary Ridge, and here they had the assistance of Theodore Davis, a *Harper's Weekly* artist who had witnessed the Atlanta campaign firsthand. The artists erected a forty-foot tower at the corner of Moreland Avenue and the Georgia Railroad to examine the battlefield terrain and scrutinized the battle's history, including after-action reports and interviews with veterans of the conflict to prepare hundreds of photographs and sketches.

The forty-thousand-dollar painting, the result of two years of hard work, was first exhibited in 1887 at either Detroit or Minneapolis and toured the country until 1892. On February 22, 1892, the Atlanta Cyclorama was opened in a drum-shaped theater on Edgewood Avenue. After the theater collapsed in a freak snowstorm, the work was auctioned to Ernest Woodruff then sold to George V. Gress, who in 1898 donated it to the city of Atlanta. It was housed in the present structure in 1926, occupying an area of two thousand square feet.

The figures in the foreground, called a diorama, were added by WPA workers from 1934 to 1936. They were supervised by Joseph Llorens, Weiss Snell, and noted Atlanta artist-historian Wilbur Kurtz. The diorama blended perfectly with the painting to create a three-dimensional effect with hills, ravines, shell-blasted stumps, wagons, and 128 plaster of Paris soldiers from twenty- to fifty-inches in height, including a dead Clark Gable figure lying on the field of battle.

Unfortunately, storms damaged the roof of the building, and leaks stained the canvas and threatened to destroy the artwork. Real Georgia clay used in the diorama attracted insects and rats, and restoration attempts, including linseed oil that yellowed the work and buttermilk (which attracted more rats and required the addition of rat poison) further deteriorated it. In 1979 the Cyclorama was closed two years for a badly needed restoration. The seven hundred holes in the canvas were repaired, the terrain features and figures replaced with lightweight, durable fiberglass, and the entire building was renovated. Eight million dollars later, the Cyclorama never looked better, and it is still difficult to determine where the painting ends and the diorama begins.

At the entrance to the Cyclorama is a Civil War cannon, and in the lobby is the *Texas,* the last engine used to catch Andrews's raiders and the *General.* The *Texas* was almost scrapped in 1907, but Atlanta mayor Courtland S. Winn bought it four years later. First displayed on rails at Fort Walker, in 1936 it was restored and moved to the Cyclorama's basement. There are a gift shop and other Civil War displays, and on the second floor is a Civil War museum. It features artifacts, large photographs of the generals who participated in the Atlanta campaign, uniforms, computer touchscreens that report the action on any given day of the conflict, and an exhibit honoring the contributions of minorities to the war.

The next stop is a theater where a short film describes the events leading up to the battle of Atlanta, then visitors proceed to the Cyclorama. In earlier days, a guide illuminated points of interest with a flashlight as visitors shuffled around to examine the marvel. Today, a 182-seat theater slowly revolves as each segment of the canvas is spotlighted and a narrative, backed by music and sound effects, describes the action depicted on the canvas. After the taped tour concludes, a guide describes other interesting details in a second viewing of the work.

Nowhere can the true drama of battle be more appreciated than at the Cyclorama. The death, destruction, and heroism of soldiers fighting bravely for causes they believed in are starkly portrayed as the painting, foreground figures, music, and narrative combine to awe the viewer. The thrilling Cyclorama convinces visitors that they are on the scene of the battle of Atlanta.

Return to the traffic light at Cherokee and Georgia; turn left onto Cherokee for .4, turn left on Atlanta Avenue for .3, and turn left onto Boulevard Street. At the southeastern corner of Grant Park is the bastion named Fort Walker.

Following the 1863 debacle at Chattanooga, Atlanta began to be fortified, and those defenses soon rivaled any in the Confederacy. They consisted of infantry

Fort Walker is the only substantial Confederate fortification remaining from the battle for the city. The observation tower in this photograph has since been removed.

trenches interspersed with artillery positions like Fort Walker. The entire line was ten miles long and stood an average of one and a half miles from the center of the city. One strongpoint was at what is now the Georgian Terrace Hotel, and traces of trenches can be seen across the campus of Georgia Tech.

Fort Walker is one of the last surviving portions of the Confederate fortifications that once ringed Atlanta. It was designed by Col. Lemuel P. Grant, a pioneer citizen from Maine and railroad engineer who later donated more than 135 acres for this park. The fort is named for Gen. William H. T. Walker, who was killed at the battle of Atlanta.

The earthworks are massive. Visualize them with timber reinforcement, rows of chevaux-de-frise in front, cannon bristling over the ramparts, and lines of supporting infantry trenches extending to either side. These works made Atlanta one of the most heavily fortified cities in the world. They were so formidable that Sherman elected not to attack Atlanta. Instead, he cut the rail lines into the city and forced Hood to evacuate after the fortifications had withstood a month-long siege.

Fort Walker once contained a restored battery of cannon mounted on wooden carriages, with attendant caissons, but vandals repeatedly destroyed the woodwork. Two of the cannon are now on display inside the Cyclorama. Also missing from Fort Walker is a half-size replica of Oakland Cemetery's Lion of Lucerne, stolen long ago. The observation tower that dominated this scene for decades has been demolished. Before leaving, enjoy the beautiful view of Atlanta's skyline to the west from this vantage point.

Each July Grant Park hosts a retrospective on the battle of Atlanta, which includes a Confederate camp and other interesting events.

In 1840 Lemuel P. Grant arrived to build railroads. He made a fortune and purchased a great deal of land, six hundred acres, in southeast Atlanta, where in 1857 he constructed a huge Italianate mansion, 8,250 square feet, with twenty rooms and nine fireplaces. As a Confederate colonel, Grant designed the defenses of Atlanta, and his house was spared Sherman's torch, reportedly because of Masonic material found inside. His wife died after the war, and Grant remarried and moved in 1882. In 1902 famed golfer Bobby Jones was born here. The house changed hands seven times in a few years and became dilapi-

dated, but in 1941 Margaret Mitchell loaned newspaperman Boyd Taylor thirty-five hundred dollars to restore the mansion. Unfortunately Taylor became a hermit, living amid the ruins after repeated fires destroyed the roof and the upper floors collapsed, leaving only thick brick walls. Things have recently turned around. In 2001 the Atlanta Preservation Center purchased the Grant mansion (327 St. Paul Avenue SE) and plans to restore it as a museum and offices for their organization. It is one of only six antebellum structures left in Atlanta.

A half-mile east of Grant Park, on Confederate Avenue near Moreland Avenue, stood Georgia's Confederate Soldiers Home. Organized by the UDC in 1889, the home was a huge Victorian structure with sixty-eight bedrooms to house aging Southern veterans. The state was to operate the institution, but balked until 1901. Seventy-two aged soldiers finally took residence, but the building was soon destroyed by fire. A second home, this one built of brick, was erected in 1902. One hundred men inhabited the home in 1904; their average age was sixty. When the last died in 1948, widows of Confederate veterans found shelter there. The five women still alive in 1963 were moved from the decaying structure to quarters at Warm Springs, and the Confederate Soldiers Home was demolished. The 125-acre site is now occupied by the state area command of the Georgia National Guard.

Return to the Cyclorama's Georgia Avenue entrance and turn left onto Georgia for .8 then right onto Hank Aaron Drive-Capitol through the Turner Field area.

At .6 on the right is the Georgia Department of Archives and History, soon to be relocated to a new facility in Morrow, south of here in Clayton County. This is the repository of thousands of valuable historic documents, many dating to the Civil War.

The Georgia state capitol is on the left at .3. The roads around the capitol are one-way, so bear left beside the capitol at .1 onto Martin Luther King Jr. Boulevard (MLK hereafter). Find a place to park; your best bet is one of the nearby parking garages.

The capitol was constructed between 1884 and 1889 and cost one million dollars. The grounds of the capi-

Georgia's wartime governor, Joseph E. Brown, and his wife are memorialized in this statue on the capitol grounds.

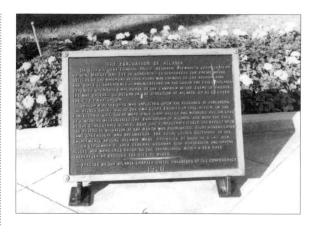

Plaques around the capitol describe the Confederate defense, defeat, and evacuation of Atlanta.

tol sport several statues and monuments of Civil War interest. A statue of Georgia's Civil War governor, Joseph E. Brown, and his seated wife is a rare husband-and-wife combination. John Brown Gordon merited an equestrian statue. He led volunteers to Virginia, where he became one of Lee's most prominent lieutenants. After the war Gordon was both governor (he was the first to occupy the new capitol), and three times elected to the U.S. Senate. Solom Borglum, brother of Gutzon, who started the Stone Mountain memorial and created Mount Rushmore, executed the statue, erected in 1907. It depicts Gordon astride Marye, a Yankee horse captured at Chancellorsville. The work stands ten feet ten inches tall. In front of the capitol are several mounted tablets that describe the battle of Atlanta, the siege of the city, and its evacuation. Two bronze 12-pounder howitzer tubes thought to be from the Georgia Military Institute in Marietta are mounted in front of one entrance to the capitol. Ordered to Fort Jackson in Savannah, they were captured there by Sherman in 1864 and later returned. The guns were displayed at Fort Walker near the Cyclorama in Atlanta for twenty-five years.

The capitol houses a large depository of Civil War flags that were carried by numerous Georgia units into battle. Unit names and battles in which they fought are often proudly stitched on the banners. Most of the flags were captured in battle or surrendered at war's end then later returned. In 1905 Gov. Joseph Terrell accepted twenty-six flags from the War Department. Many were torn or ripped in

combat by enemy fire, and bloodstains attest to the devotion of the flag-bearers. The collection now includes sixty-eight flags, fifty-two of them from the Civil War. They were once part of the old Museum of Science and Industry, displayed for decades on poles or in unprotected glass cases on basement hall walls. The flags were exposed to temperature extremes, humidity, insects, tobacco smoke, sunlight, and fluorescent lights. Those conditions and primitive past efforts at preservation (in the 1950s they were cleaned and starched) left the flags in poor shape, many nearly disintegrating.

The flags are slowly being restored as organizations like the UDC and SCV and the Georgia Civil War Commission adopt flags for expensive restorations. Restored flags are displayed, a few at a time, in a special Hall of Valor, an alcove-sized viewing room on the first floor, in climate-controlled (60 degrees) floor-to-ceiling cases that filter out UV light. The remainder are safely stored in a dark, climate-controlled room, unfurled and pressed between padded panels to await restoration. A computer touchscreen at the Hall of Valor provides a photograph and history of each flag held by the state.

The collection includes the flag of the Forty-eighth Georgia, captured at Gettysburg on July 2, 1863, after seven color-bearers fell. Gen. George A. Custer's troopers sized the flag of the Sumter Flying Artillery the day before Appomattox. The Thirty-ninth Georgia flag, representing soldiers from Dalton, was never surrendered—an officer of the unit stuffed it into his shirt and carried it to Texas.

A series of bas-relief tablets at the capitol depict many scenes of the Atlanta campaign. The two above relate to the June 27 attack at Kennesaw Mountain and the humanitarian truce that allowed the wounded to be removed and the dead buried.

One flag, the Fifty-first Georgia, captured at Fort Sanders in Knoxville, Tennessee, has a huge tear from one corner to the center and lost a stripe and three stars. Other holdings are the flags of the GMI cadets and the garrison of Fort McAllister.

Also on display inside the capitol is a marble statue of Benjamin Hill, an able supporter of Jefferson Davis in the Confederate Senate and later a U.S. senator influential in convincing President Rutherford B. Hayes to end Reconstruction. The statue was originally erected amid great ceremony at an Atlanta intersection, Hardy Ivy Park at Peachtree and West Peachtree in 1886. Newspaperman Henry Grady introduced Jefferson Davis, who was accompanied by his daughter, Winnie, the original daughter of the Confederacy. This dedication was one of Davis's last public appearances. The former president of the Confederacy was joined by former Confederate Gen. James Longstreet, who arrived from his home in Gainesville. The sight of Davis, Longstreet, and John B. Gordon together inspired the thousands of Confederate veterans present to organize a movement that launched Gordon's political career. Before that stirring moment, A. O. Bacon had been a heavy favorite in the race for governor. The statue was moved to the capitol grounds and is now in the north wing of the main floor.

In the Governor's Gallery hang large portraits of Gordon, wartime governor Joseph E. Brown, Confederate Vice President Alexander H. Stephens, U.S. Sen. and Confederate Gen. Robert Toombs, and Allen Daniel Candler, who lost an eye in the war.

In a third-floor hallway is a nearly life-sized portrait of Robert E. Lee, painted by Louis Kurz. The image, showing Lee holding his hat in one hand with the other stuck inside his jacket, once hung in the capitol in the old state library on the second floor. It was moved to the Confederate Soldiers Home and then the UDC building before becoming part of the Atlanta Historical Society's collection.

On May 29, 1893, the funeral train of Jefferson Davis entered Georgia from New Orleans at West Point, where Gov. William J. Northern and his staff boarded as an honor guard. The train reached the railroad station in Atlanta at 4:30 P.M., met by a crowd of five thousand that had been gathering for hours. Sen. John B. Gordon, former Confederate general and Georgia governor, escorted the Davis family to a location where they rested. Meanwhile, a large escort, composed of Confederate and Union veterans and led by former Confederate general and historian Clement A. Evans, followed the body, borne on an artillery caisson pulled by six iron gray horses, to the capitol. The body lay in state on a bier near the Benjamin Hill statue for three hours. An estimated forty thousand people passed to pay their respects before Davis's remains continued the journey to Richmond and burial in historic Hollywood Cemetery.

Opposite the western side of the capitol is Atlanta's city hall, site of the John Neal home where Sherman maintained his headquarters during Atlanta's occupation. From here on September 6, 1864, Sherman evicted Atlanta's remaining population, numbering 1,644, from the city, and later

John B. Gordon—Confederate general, Georgia governor, and U.S. senator—in honored with this equestrian statue.

launched the March to the Sea. From September through November 1864, tents of the Twenty-second Massachusetts Infantry, which acted as provost marshal, covered these grounds. The Confederate flag had been first raised here at Capitol Square on March 4, 1861. During the war the Fulton County Courthouse and Atlanta city hall occupied this land. They survived Sherman but were demolished for the capitol just a few years later. George H. Thomas was quartered in the Austin Leydon house, which was on Peachtree. John M. Schofield and Henry W. Slocum roomed nearby.

One of history's better ironies is that Sherman had been one of the first train passengers to reach Atlanta, then named Marthasville, when he was a young army officer in 1844. He returned after the war on January 28, 1879, as commander of America's armies, to inspect the area's military facilities, after examining his Atlanta campaign battlefields on the journey from Chattanooga. As his train approached someone shouted, "Ring the fire bells!" Sherman, however, was politely received, and he repeatedly praised the people of Atlanta for their progress since his wartime residence. He visited the site where his protégé McPherson had died, attended a military ball at McPherson Barracks, and spoke with many officials, most of whom were former Confederate leaders like former governor Joseph Brown, former Confederate general and current governor Alfred Colquitt, and Mayor James L. Calhoun, whose father had been one of Atlanta's wartime mayors. Sherman's parting advice was to stop blaming outsiders

for problems and to welcome all who wished to be a part of the city. The city has prospered since.

At the southeastern corner of city hall is a monument to Thomas Patrick O'Reilly, pastor of the Shrine of the Immaculate Conception when the Federals conquered Atlanta. He earned the respect of both Confederates and Federals by ministering to all. O'Reilly convinced Slocum to spare city hall, the courthouse, and four churches when the city was burned in November. The Shrine of the Immaculate Conception (48 Martin Luther King Jr. Drive SW, 1873) replaced the 1848 original that survived the war but was soon demolished for this structure on the same site. O'Reilly was buried in a basement crypt beneath the main altar. After an extensive fire in 1984, the church was rebuilt. The crypt was rediscovered and restored and may be visited by appointment.

Before leaving Atlanta, there are other Civil War sites and monuments that you may want to visit. Johnston's Atlanta headquarters were in the Dexter Niles house. In 1936 a WPA memorial, consisting of a stack of fifty-five cannonballs, was placed to mark the site (950 West Marietta Street NW, in front of a factory) where Johnston was relieved of command on July 17, 1864. At Marietta and Northside is the spot, indicated by a historical marker, where Atlanta mayor James Williams surrendered the city to the Twentieth Corps on September 2, 1864. A historical plaque mounted on the Wells Fargo Building (793 Marietta Street, at the corner of Northside Drive and

On the grounds of Atlanta's city hall is this phoenix tablet commemorating the unselfish service of pastor Thomas Patrick O'Reilly to both Federals and Confederates.

Marietta Street) marks the site of Fort Hood, a cornerstone of the city's northwest defenses.

Atlanta's only surviving 1855 gas lamp stands on its original position at the Five Points MARTA Station, on the corner of Peachtree and Alabama. According to tradition, the explosion of a Union shell during the siege that killed Solomon Luckie caused a hole in the base. The siege of Atlanta began with a 20-pound Parrott shell fired by John A. Logan's Twentieth Corps that killed an unidentified little girl at Ivy (now Peachtree Center Avenue) and Ellis on July 20.

Atlanta emerged as one of the South's most important cities during the Civil War. Its location deep in the Confederacy and its rail connections with most points in the struggling nation attracted numerous war industries and made the city a significant military target. On February 16, 1861, Jefferson Davis stopped at the depot at Marietta and Union on his way from Washington, D.C. (after resigning from the Senate), to Montgomery, Alabama, where he was chosen president of the Confederacy. and spoke to an enthusiastic crowd there. Davis was then entertained as the chief guest at a reception held at the Trent House, which stood at the corner of Decatur and Pryor.

When fighting erupted in Tennessee in 1862, wounded soldiers were funneled down the railroad to hospitals in Atlanta. A general hospital was built at the fair grounds, now Memorial and Flat Shoals, and a convalescent camp was situated at Marietta and Ponder. The Gate City Hotel, between Marietta and

This small mound of cannonballs marks the site of Joseph E. Johnston's headquarters in Atlanta—and the scene of his removal from command as Sherman approached the city.

Ponder, was turned into a distributing hospital. Underground Atlanta was the heart of Atlanta's business district during the war. Most of the buildings along Alabama and Pryor Streets were destroyed during the siege. A temporary Confederate hospital was set up there. The overflow was treated in the open at a park in the center of town formed by the railroad, Pryor, Decatur, and Loyd Streets, a dramatic scene depicted in *Gone with the Wind.*

On Peachtree Street not far from the capitol and Underground is Margaret Mitchell Square and a *Gone with the Wind* monument, composed of Greek Revival-like columns and a cascading fountain. The work of New York artist Kit-Yin Snyder, it was dedicated in 1986 to honor the movie's 1939 debut, which occurred at Loew's Grand Theater, long since demolished and replaced by the Georgia Pacific Center.

Officially titled *Atlanta from the Ashes* or *Rising Phoenix, The Phoenix,* an eighteen-foot-tall 1969 bronze sculpture by Italian artist Gamba Quirino was unveiled as a symbol of Atlanta's rise from the ashes of defeat during the Civil War. It was donated by the Rich Foundation on the centennial anniversary of the founding of Rich's Department Store and is now at the point of Woodruff Park at Five Points.

Over the grand staircase of the seventeen-story Candler Building (127 Peachtree Street NE, 1904) are marble portraits of Gens. John B. Gordon and Joseph Wheeler, Gov. Charles J. Jenkins, Joel Chandler Harris, Eli Whitney, and Sidney Lanier. A frieze by a European artist on the Peachtree side depicts John Ericsson, Swedish inventor of the Union ironclad *Monitor.*

After visiting the capitol, continue west on MLK past the Gordon statue. At .4 go straight on MLK; do not bear left through the tunnel. Cross a bridge, and at .3 the Georgia Dome, Philips Arena, and the CNN Center are on the right. At .6 pass through Clark Atlanta University.

A large collection of Lincoln material is housed in the Lincoln Room at Trevor Arnett Library, consisting of letters, books, pamphlets, and photographs. The material is available for scholarly research, and artifacts are displayed on special occasions.

South of Clark Atlanta University is Morehouse College (830 Westview Drive SW). Graves Hall, the

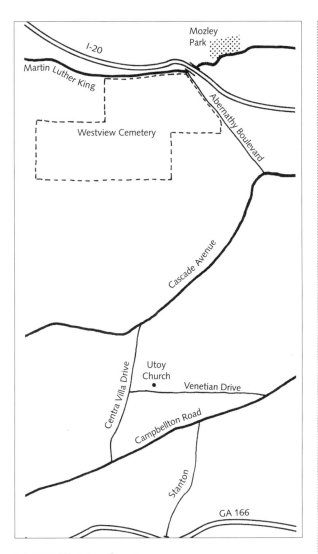

Map 25: Westview Cemetery

At 1.8 Mozley Park is on the right.

After the battle of Atlanta, Sherman shifted his pressure to the southwest in an effort to destroy the remaining railroads that connected Atlanta with Macon and West Point and to lure Hood into another costly battle. He succeeded in the latter at the battle of Ezra Church, which occurred in the area of Mozley Park. Historical markers describe the Confederate defeat and mark the site of the church. The Federals advanced from the north and formed a horseshoe-shaped defensive line. Confederate troops marched to Ezra Church along Ralph David Abernathy Boulevard, which was then known as Lickskillet Road, and attacked both sides of the Federal angle. Heavy fighting occurred at Battle Hill, northwest of Ezra Church off Waterbury Drive. The assault was a disgraceful failure and resulted in fearful Southern losses, but the railroads were temporarily saved from destruction.

Pass under I-20 and at .8 turn left into Westview Cemetery, where some of the fighting at Ezra Church occurred. (If this gate is locked, continue with the directions in the next paragraph). A fountain is directly ahead. At .1 turn right then left and circle around the Ezra Church Battle Monument, a plaque surrounded by a brick wall. Note the impressive mausoleum nearby.

Return to the cemetery entrance and turn right onto MLK. At .4 turn right onto Ralph David Abernathy

Westview Cemetery also contains this memorial to the fighting at Ezra Church, which occurred in this area west of the city.

first structure on the campus and now a dorm, occupies the highest point in Atlanta. Grading of the site for construction of the building in April 1888 uncovered the remains of a number of Confederate soldiers, who were presumably reinterred at Oakland Cemetery. Legend says they were black Confederates, but there is no supporting evidence for that claim. The four-story building was restored in 1987 and is now a dorm for 135 students.

In this area was the westernmost extension of Atlanta's fortifications. South of MLK, at Ashby and Fair, is the site of Whitehall Fort, a major position on Atlanta's defensive perimeter.

Boulevard (GA 139) and at .3 turn right into the main entrance of the cemetery. The office is on the left, and on the right is the old gatehouse.

The gatehouse retains its original bell, once tolled to announce funerals. It occupies a battlefield landmark, the Almshouse, where Civil War refugees gathered from Tennessee and north Georgia.

Drive past the office, turn left at .1 to leave the white-lined road, left at .1, left at .05, left at .3 where a sign indicates Section 70 on the corner. Straight ahead on the left is a single headstone.

This marks the grave of Lt. Edward Clingman, who died at the battle of Ezra Church. Behind the trees is a section of Confederate trench that was occupied after the battle. Federal troops later captured the position and brought up a battery of guns to shell Atlanta during the siege.

Drive straight ahead, turning right at .1 in Section 26, right again at .05 at Section 26, and return the way you came, turning right at .3 and right at .1. Turn left at .1 beside the turret-shaped water tower. At .2 on your right is a large Confederate monument.

This memorial was erected after the war by Fulton County veterans to honor their departed comrades. One hundred men are buried around the statue,

including some veterans of the Ezra Church clash. On the north side of the monument are two Confederate mortars.

When Jefferson Davis died in New Orleans in 1889, Georgia offered the Davis family a permanent grave at Westview, but Davis's widow, Varina, selected Richmond as his final resting place. Also buried here is Joel Chandler Harris, the noted author of the Uncle Remus stories, who as a boy in Putnam County witnessed Sherman's passage through central Georgia in November 1864. Some Confederate troops marched to Ezra Church on Gordon Street, which today passes Wren's Nest, Harris's home. It is open for tours.

Take the next right at .1, and at the cemetery entrance turn right onto Ralph David Abernathy Boulevard. At .8 turn right onto Cascade (GA 154) and turn left onto Centra Villa at 1.6, left at .5 onto Venetian, and at .3 turn left onto Cahaba. On this corner is Utoy Church.

The battle of Utoy Creek resulted when an impatient Sherman assaulted a Confederate position protecting the railroad. The fighting occurred west of here in what is now the Cascade Springs Nature Preserve, which is closed to the public. The Confederate line was south of Cascade (the old Sandtown road) on either side of Willis Mill Road. Utoy Church, built in 1828, is one of the oldest in Fulton County. During the Utoy Creek fighting, the church served as a Con-

This Confederate monument in Westview Cemetery honors the local veterans buried in this ground. Note the two mortars in the foreground.

The Confederates killed in the fighting at Utoy Church were interred behind the church, where a section of earthworks is also preserved.

federate hospital. Walk into the adjacent cemetery, and near the northwestern corner are the graves of the eighteen Confederates who died successfully defending the Utoy position. Several feet north is a portion of the Southern defensive line. This historic cemetery also contains the graves of four Revolutionary War soldiers, a number of Indians, and many slaves who died during a smallpox epidemic.

At the seventeenth tee on the golf course in Adams Park, just east of Centra Villa, is a historical marker that draws attention to a shallow depression that is another part of the Confederate defenses. During the final phase of the Atlanta campaign, Sherman's armies marched south through this area toward Jonesboro.

Return to Centra Villa, turn left, and at .5 is Campbellton Road. Turn left for .8 then turn right on Stanton for 1 mile. Turn left onto East Woodbury immediately after the underpass at the sign for GA 166 for .1. Bear left onto East GA 166-Lakewood Freeway.

GA 166 passes near Fort McPherson, which was established before the Civil War as a militia drilling ground. During the war Confederate recruits received their training there. Barracks and a cartridge factory were constructed here and later burned by Hood's retreating forces. Skirmishes were fought on the grounds during the battles for Atlanta. During postwar Federal occupation, the facility was named for Union Gen. James B. McPherson, killed at Atlanta. It was headquarters for the Third Militia District, whose officers included such Civil War notables as George Gordon Meade and John Pope. Within the military installation are several reminders of Confederate generals: a building named for William J. Hardee, a gate named for Alfred Iverson, and roads named for Joseph Wheeler and John Bell Hood. To the south is East Point, where the southernmost portion of Atlanta's fortifications ended.

At 2.2 follow the I-75 sign right, and at .1 follow the I-75 (to Macon) sign. Exit I-75 at 10 miles onto GA 54, which is Exit 233, the Southlake Mall, and turn right.

Historical markers describing Hardee's march to Jonesboro line the highway. Hood, thinking Sherman's movement was merely a raid, dispatched Hardee and Stephen D. Lee's corps to deal with it.

At 3.1 on Mimosa to the right is the Warren house.

The Warren house (102 West Mimosa Drive, 1859) was used during the battle of Jonesboro as a Confederate hospital. After the Fifty-second Illinois overran it on September 2, the home was used as a Union headquarters and hospital. Initials, signatures, and other graffiti left by Yankee soldiers are still visible on the interior walls.

Continue on GA 54. The Jonesboro Confederate Cemetery is on your left at .2, but you cannot turn here. Drive straight onto GA 138 to the first traffic signal at .3, turn left over the tracks, and immediately left onto McDonough Road, which parallels the railroad. At .4 turn right onto Johnson Street, and on the corner to your left is the Confederate Cemetery.

On August 19 H. Judson Kilpatrick's cavalry raid reached Jonesboro. The Federals used dismounted troopers and artillery to enter the town, where they torched large amounts of supplies and destroyed two miles of track. Entering Lovejoy the next morning, the Federals were contested by a combined force of Confederate cavalry, infantry, and militia. In a driving rain the Federals formed massed columns and charged through to McDonough. Kilpatrick returned safely to Union lines but had succeeded in disrupting the Confederate supply line for two days.

When Sherman shifted most of his forces southwest of Atlanta, he sent Oliver O. Howard west through Campbellton and Fairburn to Jonesboro, George H. Thomas in the center through Ben Hill to Red Oak, where the West Point railroad was severed, and John M. Schofield inside through Red Oak to Rough and Ready (Mountain View).

Thomas had marched through the night to Jonesboro via East Point and Rough and Ready on GA 138. William J. Hardee attacked in a futile attempt to prevent the destruction of this last rail link with Atlanta. His assault hit the Federal line just west of Jonesboro, across U.S. 41-19-GA 7 on both sides of GA 138 near the Flint River. The Confederates suffered a severe repulse. The southern part of the Federal line was along Magnolia Drive and extended to the north up Hynds Springs Road. On the second day Sherman massed most of his army and mauled Hardee, who had retreated and hastily thrown up works on the western and northern fringes of town. The heaviest fighting occurred along the railroad near this cemetery and the Warren house, which formed an angle.

During the night Hardee slipped away south to Lovejoy, while Hood destroyed supplies he could not transport and evacuated Atlanta with the remnants of the Army of Tennessee to join Hardee. Sherman entered Atlanta the following day. Confederates and Federals confronted each other at Lovejoy for several days, but no combat resulted and Sherman returned north to occupy his prize. The Atlanta campaign was over, but in November Judson Kilpatrick's horsemen drove out Joseph Wheeler's cavalry to clear the way for the Fifteenth and Seventeenth Corps at the start of Sherman's March to the Sea. The town of Jonesboro was nearly destroyed by cavalry raids and the battle, and during Sherman's occupation foragers stripped the land of provisions, leaving the citizens destitute.

The Patrick Cleburne Confederate Cemetery, named for the renowned Confederate general killed during the battle of Franklin, Tennessee, on November 30, 1864, occupies a site of heavy fighting. The Confederate dead were left on the field as the Southerners retreated; they were buried by the Federals in mass graves. Despite this circumstance, individual markers have been erected for the fallen. Blank gravestones were authorized in 1872 by the state legislature when it ordered the reinterment of eight hundred to nine hundred soldiers from the battlefield. The stones form the Confederate battle flag. In the entrance arch are embedded twelve cannonballs, and a monument in the center of the cemetery honors the men who died in the two days of fighting here.

On McDonough Street one-half mile south of the cemetery is the Pope Dixon and Son's Funeral Home (168 North McDonough Road, 1850s). A unique drive-up funeral museum behind the business displays the hearse that carried Confederate Vice President Alexander H. Stephens to his grave in 1883, from the governor's mansion in Atlanta to his home in Crawfordville. The wooden conveyance has a false bottom, and some believe that it was used to smuggle slaves to freedom. A runaway would be placed in a bottomless coffin, and when the hearse crossed into the North he would slip out and the empty coffin would be buried. Also displayed is a standard iron Civil War coffin that could be sealed and shipped considerable distances and a floral wreath from Lincoln's funeral.

At 121 South McDonough Road is the new-old courthouse (1898), where Margaret Mitchell researched *Gone with the Wind*. Near the front door is a monument honoring Confederate Chaplain Father Emiel Bliemel, killed during the battle of Jonesboro while giving last rights to Col. William Grace, a Catholic officer from Alabama. Behind that building is the old courthouse (144 North McDonough Road, 1869) on the original foundation of two earlier structures. Court was held in the Masonic hall until the courthouse was replaced. Behind it on King Street is the Gothic stone jail, and just south on the opposite side of the tracks is the stone depot (104 North Main Street). All were built in 1867 to replace the wooden structures destroyed on August 19, 1864, by Kilpatrick's raid, along with tracks and supplies stored here. The depot was moved stone by stone to its present site in 1880. The original depot had stood near the Confederate cemetery. The entire business area, which included thirteen taverns, was torched by the rampaging Federals. While the wooden interiors were lost to the fire, the brick exteriors survived the war. Two-thirds of Jonesboro, however, was destroyed.

Half the depot is occupied by the Road to Tara Museum, a much traveled establishment originally housed in the Georgian Terrace in Atlanta and then at Stone Mountain. Plans call for a battle of Jonesboro museum in the depot.

Historic Jonesboro, Inc. (P.O. Box 922, Jonesboro, GA 30237, 770-473-0197, www.gwth-jonesboro.org) maintains a museum in the Old Jail (Clayton County History Center, 125 King Street, 1869), displaying artifacts from both armies, including a Bible that stopped a Yankee bullet from piercing a Rebel heart. Historic Jonesboro sponsors an annual Civil War battle and evacuation reenactments and hosts the Tara Ball. A wonderful self-driving tour to historic sites in Jonesboro and Clayton County is available. The local tourism emphasis is the Civil War and particularly *Gone with the Wind*.

Clustered in the area are other antebellum structures, including the Stephen Carnes house (154

The Sigma Chi monument near Lovejoy commemorates the devotion of Confederate soldiers who feared that the end of the Confederacy would end their sense of fraternity.

North McDonough Street, 1850s), whose owner manufactured wagons and caskets for the Confederacy. Carnes was instrumental in reinterring the Southern dead in the Confederate cemetery. Also here are the Elliott-Morrow cottage (McDonough Street), a hospital following the battle, and the Johnson-Blalock house (155 North Street, 1840), used as a Confederate commissary where supplies were stored during 1864 and whose owner, Col. James F. Johnson, signed the Georgia secession ordinance. It was also used as a hospital. The Waldrop-Brown-Edwards home (158 South Main Street, 1860s) suffered extensive damage during the battle and was rebuilt with narrower boards. The home had been a hospital. The Burnside-Lyle house (166 South Main Street, 1870, third house on the site) was the scene of a civilian death during Kilpatrick's August raid. A cannonball fired from near the Warren house killed a man here.

Historic Jonesboro is attempting to preserve the Gayden house (158 Church Street, 1850s). Now the property of the First Baptist Church of Jonesboro, it was the home of Dr. Frances T. Gayden, a Confederate captain and surgeon and chief medical officer during the 1864 battle here. The brick structure, covered with stucco to resemble Greek revival, was a battlefield landmark mentioned by several after-action reports and marked on military maps.

East and south of Jonesboro are several interesting antebellum plantations. The Allen-Carnes plantation (1820), the oldest structure in Clayton County, and the Camp plantation (Abner Lake Jodeco Road, 1840s) sheltered Jonesboro citizens for two days, August 31 and September 1, 1864, while their homes were enveloped in carnage.

Stately Oaks, an 1839 plantation house and its original detached kitchen and other outbuildings, have been moved from their original four-hundred-acre site four miles to the north and restored (Stately Oaks Plantation Home and Historic Community, 100 Carriage Lane at Jodeco Road, P.O. Box 922, Jonesboro, GA 30237, 770-473-0197). The structure, a landmark for Sherman's armies, and the surrounding fields, which were campgrounds during the fighting around Jonesboro, hosts Historic Jonesboro's annual battle and evacuation reenactment and the Tara Ball. The house and grounds are open for tours.

The Crawford-Talmadge plantation (Lovejoy Plantation, U.S. 19 five miles south of Jonesboro, 1835) at Lovejoy is the spot where Hood gathered the tattered remnants of his shattered force after Atlanta was evacuated. Skirmishes were fought nearby, and walls of the house retain bullets.

Of all the Georgia mansions that claim to be the inspiration for the mansions Tara and Twelve Oaks described in Margaret Mitchell's classic novel, *Gone with the Wind,* Lovejoy seems to have the strongest claim. Mitchell spent many summers in this area with her grandmother and two great-aunts and heard numerous stories of the antebellum South and war from the elderly residents who had experienced the conflict. Her grandfather, Phillip Fitzgerald, owned 130 acres here, and her great-grandfather had owned 2,500 acres and thirty-five slaves. Mitchell returned to research the book in the Clayton County Courthouse records and local historical societies, and Jonesboro is featured in the book and movie. Jonesboro's association with *Gone with the Wind* is heavily promoted, and plans are regularly floated to construct a *Gone with the Wind* recreational complex in the area. Lovejoy's mistress owns the movie façade of Tara. The Fitzgerald house, previously situated several miles to the north, was moved to the Talmadge plantation.

Near Lovejoy, behind the burned ruins of the historic Crawford-Dorsey house (corner of McDonough and Freeman Roads, a half mile south of GA 3 near U.S. 19), are earthworks built for the defense of the Army of Tennessee after its retreat from Jonesboro. Cavalry skirmishes were fought here on August 20 during Kilpatrick's raid, and in November 1864, as Sherman began his March to the Sea. Permission to visit must be obtained from the Clayton Water Authority.

Just north of Lovejoy, in a landscaped park beside U.S. 41, is the Sigma Chi Monument, a one-hundred-ton cross-shaped white marble marker. After the fall of Atlanta, five Mississippi cavalrymen gathered here to discuss the potential dissolution of their common fraternity if the Confederacy was defeated. To ensure its survival, they established the Constantine Chapter. In 1939 this monument was erected to honor their devotion.

Sites Related to the Atlanta Campaign

For the most part, the path of Sherman's Atlanta campaign followed the route of the Western and Atlantic Railroad. That path became U.S. 41-GA 3, the major highway between Atlanta and Chattanooga, and today Interstate 75 follows the same route. Large portions of the armies, however, often strayed into the surrounding regions, and cavalry covered even larger areas. Because of this, several important battles and historically significant communities are bypassed in the earlier tour guides.

This section addresses that concern by including sites vital to the Atlanta campaign that are off the primary route of the armies. What follows below explores sites north and west of Atlanta then progresses to the east and south. These roads are scenic, the traffic is considerably lighter, and the cities and towns are less frenzied. Take your time and enjoy the slower pace of rural Georgia.

McPherson's Flanking Movements

At the beginning of the Atlanta campaign, in May 1864, Sherman intended to flank Johnston out of his strong Dalton position by sending James B. McPherson's Army of the Tennessee through Snake Creek Gap and south to Resaca. McPherson skirted the old Chickamauga battlefield on the present route of U.S. 27, turned east on GA 95 at Rock Springs, and moved south on GA 151 at Chestnut Flat, camping there the night of May 7. He continued east on GA 136 through Maddox Gap over Taylor's Ridge to seize Villanow and marched through beautiful Snake Creek Gap, between Mill Creek and Horn Mountains, to emerge at Resaca. When John Bell Hood withdrew to LaFayette in October 1864, closely pur-

sued by Sherman, the Confederates blocked the gap with fallen timber.

County Road 1030 runs the length of scenic West Armuchee Valley between Taylor's Ridge and Dick's Ridge to Shiloh Church, the place where Hood's leg was amputated after the battle of Chickamauga.

A famous landmark in this area is the Villanow Country Store, a red-brick three-story structure and the oldest continuously operating store in Georgia. Opened in 1840, the store has had only six owners.

The Pocket

This isolated area, which is now a national forest, contains the graves of two Confederate veterans. Samuel Pilcher served throughout the war, from 1861 until 1865, and died in 1897. The Forest Service now tends his lone grave. George W. Bailey, captured on August 13, 1864, around Atlanta and imprisoned at Fort McHenry in Baltimore, returned to raise a big family here. He died in 1907 and is buried in Fowler's Cemetery.

Floyd County Cave Spring

Ninety historic structures survive in this orderly village nestled in Vann's Valley. In October 1864 Hood met here with his superior, Gen. P. G. T. Beauregard, to discuss future operations of the Army of Tennessee. Fannin Hall, the original administration building of the Georgia School for the Deaf, was used as a hospital by both armies. The school was closed for the duration of the war but reopened in 1867. The three buildings of the school (which moved in 1973), dating to 1847, and the spring in a cave for which the community is noted are in Rolater Park. The Turner home (mid-1800s) was occupied by Federals.

Floyd Springs

A small but interesting stone monument stands in the graveyard of Floyd Springs Methodist Church. "Alexander H. Stephens Spoke Here Sept. 1860 Against Secession," it reads. Augustus Wright, a prominent local minister, judge, and U.S. congressman, invited Stephens, a University of Georgia classmate soon to become the Confederacy's only vice president, to his home in Floyd Springs, a then booming community. Stephens's reluctance to leave the Union was well known at the time.

Wright, a Confederate Congressman, was later accused of treason. After proposing that a convention of states—Union and Confederate—meet to unite the country, he lost his seat. While campaigning in Georgia, Sherman hoped to persuade the state to secede from the Confederacy. The Federal commander presented this proposal to Wright, and the Georgian traveled to Washington, D.C., where he conferred daily with Lincoln over a two-week period. Wright brought Lincoln's plan—an end to the war and gradual emancipation of slaves over a period of twenty-one years—to Jefferson Davis and Joseph E. Brown, who quickly rejected it. Wright was accused of being a spy, but few Georgians believed the charge. Back home he practiced law and raised seventeen children before his death in 1891. He is buried in Rome's Myrtle Hill Cemetery.

Farmer's Bridge

A long forgotten skirmish in the Atlanta campaign was recently commemorated. Farmer's Bridge, eight miles north of Rome, was the only span across Armuchee Creek between Summerville and Rome. On May 13 the one hundred men of Company G, Twelfth Alabama Battalion, Partisan Rangers, under Capt. William Lokey, were defending the southern bank of the creek from rifle pits and atop hills on either flank. At 8 A.M. on May 15 the brigade of Union Col. Robert H. G. Minty, composed of three regiments and two guns, arrived at Farmer's Bridge. An initial charge was repulsed, but Minty sent eight companies to cross upstream and downstream at

fords and charged the bridge again at 10 A.M. The thin Confederate line broke, and Lokey was mortally wounded. The Southerners raced seven miles to the safety of friendly infantry at Big Dry Creek. From that point the Federals commenced a retreat past Farmers Bridge to Floyd Springs.

Ten Confederates had been killed in the fighting, but their graves were lost for 130 years. Researchers found that the men had been buried in a family cemetery atop one of the hills overlooking Armuchee Creek. The existing small flat gravestones were replaced in 1998 by veterans markers, and a substantial stone monument, with plaques describing the small action and honoring the men who died in service to the South, was dedicated.

Rome

The city of Rome was an important industrial center for the Confederacy, providing desperately needed iron and munitions and serving as a convalescent center in 1863. A spur railroad line that connected with the Western and Atlantic at Kingston and three steamers on the Coosa River shipped these goods throughout the South. In addition, the fertile surrounding countryside helped feed the Confederacy. In 1863 Union Col. Abel D. Streight led two thousand horsemen on a raid to destroy Rome's industrial capacity. He was foiled by John H. Wisdom, a Confederate postal employee who rode eighty-seven miles over eleven hours from near Gadsden, Alabama, through Cave Springs and Vann's Valley to Rome on six different horses to warn of the approaching enemy. The courthouse and church bells tolled, and a train steamed to Kingston, spreading the alarm. Farmers and convalescents, old and young, barricaded the streets with cotton bales, took up planks on the covered bridges across the river and readied them for burning, and aimed two antique cannon that were feared more by its gunners than the enemy. Several hundred obsolete muskets were distributed as many civilians fled to the countryside. Confederate Gen. Nathan Bedford Forrest pursued Streight with only five hundred men and tricked the Union force into surrendering in eastern Alabama near the Georgia line. Forrest was honored in Rome on May 3, 1863. When the artillery pieces were discharged (in celebration or to disarm them), a barn was damaged

In Rome this statue honors Confederate cavalry wizard Nathan Bedford Forrest. His aggressive pursuit and capture of a large Union raiding force saved the city.

and a mule killed. Wisdom was rewarded with four hundred dollars in cash and a four-hundred-dollar silver service, and Forrest received a fine horse and one thousand dollars for the care of his wounded and sick troopers.

In May 1864 Sherman dispatched Gen. Jefferson C. Davis's division from Resaca to capture Rome. His force was preceded by Gen. Kenner Garrard's cavalry. Garrard set out on May 15, moving through Villanow to camp at Floyd Springs, then continued to Farmers Bridge on Armuchee Creek, where he skirmished with Confederate horsemen. Garrard crossed the creek at the U.S. 27 bridge, continuing to DeSoto

Hill on the east bank of the Oostanaula River near U.S. 27. Davis reached DeSoto Hill on May 17, skirmished with Confederates, and crossed the following day to capture the city. Southerners under Maj. Gen. Samuel G. French, who had arrived from Alabama, made a brief defense of Rome before withdrawing toward Kingston and Cassville to reinforce Johnston, burning the bridges and evacuating the city's hilltop forts. Rome was Sherman's headquarters in October and November 1864, and from here he sent his plans for the March to the Sea to Ulysses S. Grant for approval. Rome was garrisoned until November 10, when the Federals abandoned the city, first destroying Rome's factories, commercial establishments, several homes, and other private property. After two days of destruction Sherman wired George H. Thomas in Tennessee, "Last night we burned Rome."

Myrtle Hill Cemetery (South Broad Street and Myrtle Street) was topped by Fort Stovall during the war. Rome's Civil War attractions are concentrated in this historic cemetery. A monument to Floyd County's Confederate soldiers was erected on Confederate Memorial Day in 1887. It was first topped with an urn, and twenty years later a soldier figure was erected during a ceremony featuring fifteen hundred schoolchildren. The statue resembled a Spanish-American War Rough Rider and was eventually replaced by one more traditionally Confederate. On May 3, 1908, a statue of Nathan Bedford Forrest was dedicated. A particularly moving monument, unveiled on March 9, 1910, honors the women of the Confederacy. One side of the monument depicts a kneeling woman attending to a wounded soldier; on the opposite side a woman tells a little girl how her father died in battle. Woodrow Wilson, whose first wife is buried here, wrote the inscription. Both monuments were relocated from their original sites on Broad Street.

One plot contains the graves of 377 Confederates and 2 Federals who died in Rome hospitals and in skirmishes around the area, each marked by twenty-inch-high stones. The "Confederate Paul Revere," John Wisdom, is also buried here. A walking brochure guide of Myrtle Hill Cemetery is available from the Rome Convention and Visitors Bureau.

Myrtle Hill, where the Coosa River rises from the confluence of the Oostanaula and Etowah, both streams important to the Civil War in Georgia in

Rome's Myrtle Hill Cemetery was the site of a Confederate fort during the war. Now it is the final resting place for many who died in the area hospitals.

1864, first saw battle in September 1793 when Gen. John Sevier defeated a force of Cherokee who had attacked a settlement near Knoxville, Tennessee. In 1901 a monument was placed in the southwest corner of the cemetery by the Xavier Chapter of the Daughters of the American Revolution to honor Sevier. The cemetery is also a memorial park for World War I veterans

Outside the Rome Visitors Center (402 Civic Center Drive), which offers excellent driving and walking tours of Rome, is preserved the massive Noble Foundry lathe. The foundry produced steamship engines, locomotives (including the first manufactured in the South), and seventy cannon for the Confederacy until it was destroyed in November 1864 by Sherman's forces. The enormous machine, manufactured in 1847 in New Hampshire, survived the war to become a historical display. The lathe was too large to be transported by railroad, so it was sent by sea to Mobile, up the Alabama and Coosa Rivers to the falls, then disassembled and hauled by oxcart to the city. The Federals found it too massive and solid to be destroyed and were forced to leave it intact. Scars from sledgehammer blows are still evident. The lathe remained in use through the 1960s. Beside it is a Corliss steam engine, the type used to power the lathe and similar machinery. Noble Brothers and Dickson and Nelson also made artillery carriages and rifles. A marker at the corner of Broad Street and First Avenue notes the site of the Noble Foundry and Machine Shop, which was between the

railroad and the river. The riverbank along the Cotton Block, Broad Street between Second Avenue and First Avenue, still has holes where Noble foundry workers fired cannonballs when testing their guns.

Streight's raid frightened the residents of Rome and convinced them of the strategic importance of their city. Three thousand dollars were appropriated to construct fortifications on the many hills ringing Rome. Realizing they needed professional help, city officials soon petitioned the state for assistance. Between July 13 and October 9, 1863, Capt. James F. Laulor, a military engineer, laid out the works and impressed local slaves for labor. The only named forts were Stovall, atop Myrtle Hill, site of Rome's primary cemetery and overlooking the confluence of the Etowah and Oostanaula Rivers where the Coosa is formed; Fort Attaway, on the west bank of the Oostanaula north of downtown; and Fort Norton, atop Jackson Hill east of the Oostanaula and the only remaining fort. All were named for former residents who had been killed in the war.

Confederate Gen. Braxton Bragg ordered garrison commander Gen. Alfred Iverson to strengthen the forts with the labor of additional slaves and to emplace guns. Bragg was gone by Christmas, and Gen. William J. Hardee dispatched an engineer, Capt. John W. Green, to hurry the work. Court-martialed soldiers were sent to assist in construction. A Union spy reported that "strong fortifications are being erected." On April 24, as Sherman prepared to

The Noble Foundry lathe helped manufacture cannon for the Confederacy. It was too massive for Federal wrecking crews to destroy, but it still bears the scars from their efforts.

advance, Joseph E. Johnston ordered the Rome defenses to be completed immediately with whatever labor was necessary, soldiers and slaves.

As Federals under Jefferson C. Davis approached Rome on May 17, Forts Norton and Stovall, the works commanding all approaches to the city, fired on them. They appeared so strong, Davis recorded, "I thought [it] imprudent to storm." After the Confederates withdrew, Davis entered and described Rome as "the strongest fortified place I have seen in Dixie." Five 32-pounders, two 8-inch howitzers, and three field guns were seized.

When Hood started north toward Rome in October, the Union garrison spent three weeks reworking the fortifications to suit their defensive needs. No attack came. Hood, perhaps smarting from his losses at Allatoona Pass, chose to avoid the city.

Rome's elaborate system of earthen defenses were demolished after the war, but Fort Norton was left unmolested for 135 years. It is easily reached behind the visitors center off Turner McCall Boulevard–U.S. 27–GA 1, 20, 53. These earthworks are excellently preserved. One trench line, six feet deep and designed for artillery emplacements, curves around the southern and western crest to defend the approaches to the west across the Oostanaula. A separate system of works covers the roads from the northeast bank of the Oostanaula. This latter position fired on Davis's approaching Federals. Other gunners supported Fort Norton atop Reservoir Hill, but these works were largely destroyed by construction of the waterworks there by the WPA in 1935–36. A portion of its trenches, however, can still be seen. A 12-pounder mountain howitzer has been placed at Fort Norton, encampments are held, and there are plans for restoration.

The Rome Area History Museum (303 Broad Street) occupies two storefronts downtown. It features displays of Civil War weapons, projectiles, and documents, a topographic map of the county, a list of all casualties, and a re-creation of Ellen Axson Wilson's (Woodrow Wilson's first wife) bedroom.

The Chieftains Museum (501 Riverside Parkway Northeast, 1794), listed on the National Register, was the home of Cherokee leader Major Ridge. Preserved by the Junior Service League as a city museum, it houses exhibits of Rome's Civil War importance and also explores prehistoric Native Americans, the Cherokee, the Ridge family, and other historical, cultural, economic, and social themes of the Rome area.

Federals camped on the grounds of beautiful Oak Hill (Berry College, 1847), home of famed educator Martha Berry. Its outbuildings were destroyed during the occupation.

A monument on West 13 Street honors Texans who defended Rome and marks the site of Fort Stovall. Another memorial on West 13 Street honors the Union soldiers who captured Rome. The present Masonic Temple (336 Broad Street, the second on the same site, 1877) was built with contributions from Federals who, not knowing it was a lodge, burned the original in 1864. Jefferson C. Davis occupied the demolished Rose Hill (312 East 4 Avenue, now occupied by a pre-1911 structure), home of Maj. Charles H. Smith, the famous postwar writer known as Bill Arp. Sherman stayed in the home twice, on October 12 and between October 28 and November 2, while chasing Hood into Alabama and organizing plans for the March to the Sea respectively. The residence was burned on the latter occasion. A photograph of Sherman and his staff was taken in the front yard under what was later known as the Sherman Oak. The First Presbyterian Church (101 East Third Street, 1849) was used as a hospital and stable and for food storage. Its pews were used to bridge a river. Woodrow Wilson met his first wife here. The Methodist Church (106 East Sixth Street, 1852, now AME) was used as a Union stable. It has been stuccoed to protect the old bricks. The sanctuary of the original 1855 Baptist Church (100 East 4 Street, 1958) was used as a hospital; the basement became a stable. The church pews, used to feed the horses, were replaced in 1883.

The Floyd County Courthouse (101 West Fifth Avenue, 1892), a magnificent Romanesque structure on the National Register, was reinforced by rails torn up from Georgia's railroads by Union troops. The Federals heated the iron on pyres of railroad ties then twisted them around trees in a form known as Sherman's neckties.

West of Rome, atop Shorter Hill, at the intersection of Horseleg Creek Road and Shorter Avenue, is Thornwood, constructed in 1847 by Col. Alfred Shorter. It was occupied by an advance force of two hundred troops from Streight's command under

Capt. Milton Russell, whose duty was to secure the bridges over the Oostanaula River. They failed in their mission due to John Wisdom's warning and were captured. The mansion, however, was twice occupied by Federal soldiers, who destroyed the marble mantels and wrote names and messages in the attic in charcoal, including "You Old Reb that left your house." A column on the Greek Revival mansion is marred where a Union flag was once flown. The house is now used as an office building for Darlington Lower School.

A historical marker recently erected at the John Berryhill house marks the death site of Union Maj. Gen. Thomas E. G. Ransom. Wounded four times during the war, he commanded a corps in the Army of the Tennessee before contracting typhoid fever near Rome in October 1864, while chasing Hood into Alabama. He died here, aged twenty-nine, but was buried at Norwich University in Connecticut, where he studied and where his father was president. The school paid for the funeral.

Polk County

During Sherman's shift from Kingston to Dallas, McPherson's army swung far to the west and marched through eastern Polk County, following Euharlee Creek to Aragon, where the army camped at Peek's Spring. Other Union encampments near here included Maj. Gen. Grenville M. Dodge's corps on May 23 and Brig. Gen. Jefferson C. Davis's corps on May 24. Maj. Gen. John A. Logan's corps camped at Euharlee Creek on GA 101 on May 23. The following day the Federals turned east through Van Wert and marched to Dallas. On October 26, 1906, a Confederate monument was erected on the courthouse lawn in Cedartown. H. Judson Kilpatrick's cavalry burned the earlier courthouse and sixty-five other downtown buildings.

Haralson County

Surviving Federal cavalrymen from the Brown's Mill disaster near Newnan circled through Alabama and reached Union lines at Marietta by way of Buchanan and Draketown. The West Georgia Museum (21 West Lyon Street, Tallapoosa) has exhibits of Civil War artifacts.

Douglas County

Industry developed very early in Douglas County along the swift rapids of Sweetwater Creek, a tributary of the Chattahoochee River. By 1864 a seventeen-building mill community of one hundred employees and four hundred dependents was turning raw cotton into thread, daily generating 750 yards of cotton and wool cloth for Confederate uniforms, tents, powder bags, and blankets on six thousand spindles and ninety looms. The brick five-story mill, constructed on a stone foundation, measured 48 by 120 feet; it was the tallest structure in the Atlanta area. The waterwheel weighed fifty thousand pounds. A flour mill, a gristmill, and a shoe factory also flourished. The town had a post office, general store, and tavern. After Johnston occupied the Chattahoochee River Line, Union cavalry under Lt. Col. Silas Adams and Maj. Haviland Thompkin occupied New Manchester, finding the facilities working at full capacity. On July 9 Thompkin and eight men torched the homes in the town, a two-story warehouse, the commissary, and mill buildings. A battery of 12-pounder Napoleons was brought up to pound down the three-hundred-foot-long wooden mill dam. Two other mills on the creek, Ferguson-Merchant to the north and Alexander's to the south, were also destroyed. The damages amounted to several hundred thousand dollars.

The predominately female work force and their dependents were given as much cloth as they could carry and started a sixteen-mile march (some accounts say they were carried in wagons) to the Georgia Military Institute in Marietta. There they joined the women from Roswell and were dispatched to work in Northern mills. They arrived in Nashville on July 15, Louisville on July 20, then crossed the Ohio into Indiana. Mill superintendent Nathaniel H. Humphries was imprisoned for the remainder of the war. Controversy has raged over the treatment of the women and their ultimate fate. Most found employment in several different industries and areas. Contrary to popular myth, a number returned to Georgia, although not to New Manchester. The factories here, plagued by poor transportation, were never rebuilt. New Manchester was forgotten because of its isolation and never rebuilt.

The site is preserved in the two-thousand-acre Sweetwater Creek State Park (west of Atlanta, off the

Thornton Road exit of I-20). Archaeological excavation has revealed bolts of intact fabric and hundreds of machine parts. Large pieces of machinery were salvaged and melted down during World War II scrap-metal drives.

Sweetwater Creek has six miles of hiking trails. An easy-to-hike .6-mile section follows the old millrace along the swift, scenic creek that falls through a wooded valley to the dramatic factory ruins. This was the original road that served New Manchester. The beautiful landscape continues to a falls overlook, which provides a good view of the creek cascading over a granite cliff. This path is more strenuous. Across the creek are the remains of a gristmill and a bridge. Each September, New Manchester Days are held, including living history exercises. A historical museum/nature center is beside the trailhead.

Fulton County

Union Gen. Edward M. McCook's cavalry crossed the Chattahoochee River six miles south of Campbellton then rode through Palmetto to destroy track on the Atlanta and West Point Railroad. At Fayetteville they wrecked a Confederate wagon train, butchering horses and mules, then destroyed more track at Lovejoy before being chased through Fayetteville to Newnan.

When Sherman shifted most of his forces southwest of Atlanta to converge at Jonesboro, he sent Oliver O. Howard west through Campbellton and Fairburn. In the center was Thomas's Army of the Cumberland, which passed through Ben Hill and Red Oak, on U.S. 29 south of College Park, breaking up rails between there and Fairburn. John M. Schofield took an inside route through Red Oak to Rough and Ready.

At the northern edge of Riverdale is the log Drew Couch house, which served as headquarters for Sherman and Thomas in August 1864.

Rough and Ready Tavern, now called Mountain View (U.S. 19-41 between Hapeville and Forest Park), was visited by Union cavalry during an 1864 raid. Confederates marched through en route to the decisive conflict at Jonesboro, and Schofield's men cut the Macon Railroad there. After Atlanta's surrender, its citizens were evacuated to this point by Sherman's orders.

A monument marks the former site of the Campbell County courthouse and commemorates a series of veterans reunions.

Campbellton

In front of Campbellton Baptist Church is a UDC-WPA monument erected in 1937 to mark the site of the old Campbell County courthouse (during the Great Depression, Campbell was forced to merge with Fulton). It commemorates the devotion of Capt. T. C. Glover, a delegate to Georgia's secession convention. He raised a company and led it to Virginia, where he died at Winchester on September 9, 1864. In 1867 his wife, Elizabeth, asked survivors of Company A, Twenty-first Georgia Infantry, to hold an annual reunion here to remember their fallen comrades. They honored her request for many years, starting the long tradition of Confederate reunions. The Latham house (1829) and Masonic Lodge, both still standing, were hit by artillery fire during the siege of Atlanta.

The Methodist church cemetery has a section of Confederate soldiers who died during fighting in the area. A Union soldier is buried in the Bullard family cemetery. He was wounded in a July 4, 1864,

A memorial in Fulton County marks the site where in 1861 the first Confederate flag was unveiled in Georgia.

skirmish and died in the Bullard home. The grave was recently marked.

Campbellton is northeast of the intersection of GA 70 and GA 92.

Fairburn

In the Fairburn City Cemetery on U.S. 29 just west of town, a twenty-foot-high column, surrounded by an ornamental iron fence, was erected in honor of Confederate veterans. Col. Samuel Tate of the famous Pickens County marble quarries donated this unusual Southern memorial. At the railroad station on U.S. 29, a plaque mounted on a brick base by the United Daughters of the Confederacy (1937) marks the spot where the first Confederate flag in the state was unfurled on March 4, 1861. The design had been approved the day before in Montgomery, Alabama. The returning delegates and their wives stopped the Atlanta and West Point train in Grantville to purchase fabric. The women had crafted a flag by the time they reached Fairburn, and it flew from the train until they arrived in Atlanta. In Fairburn the Army of the Tennessee, on its way to Jonesboro, cut the West Point Railroad.

Palmetto

In July 1864 cavalry raiders burned the depot and two trains then tore up seven miles of track. Beside the old railroad station on U.S. 29, a fifteen-foot draped obelisk was erected in 1906 to mark the area where the Army of Tennessee camped on September 19, 1864, following the fall of Atlanta. Two artillery tubes are also mounted on stone. When Jefferson Davis addressed the troops on September 21, the battle-weary veterans were rude and demanded that Johnston be returned to command. Davis did not make the change, but Hardee was relieved and Hood crossed the Chattahoochee River at Pumpkintown Ferry to begin his ill-fated Tennessee campaign. Davis's ill-advised comments to newspaper correspondents here allowed Sherman to prepare for the Confederate campaign, particularly at Allatoona Pass.

Carroll County

In April 1865 part of Union Gen. James H. Wilson's cavalry passed through Carrollton. The county was raided four times by Federal foraging parties. On the courthouse square is a Confederate statue, dedicated April 26, 1910, to the county's Southern veterans.

Fayette County–Fayetteville

Union cavalry passed through the town in July 1864 and destroyed a wagon train of five hundred vehicles. They also killed thousands of horses and mules and seized four hundred prisoners. The Fife house (1855) was home to Fayetteville Academy, attended at one time by a student named Scarlett O'Hara. A Confederate monument dedicated on April 26, 1934, stands at the courthouse.

This collection of monuments in Palmetto marks the site where Jefferson Davis addressed the Army of Tennessee— and revealed Hood's plans to attack Nashville.

Peachtree City

Funds are being raised to erect a statue of Confederate Maj. Gen. William J. Hardee in Peachtree City. Hardee fought throughout the Civil War in the western theater and commanded a corps in the Army of Tennessee during the Atlanta campaign. When John Bell Hood struck north in the fall of 1864, Hardee was left with little resources to contest Sherman's March to Savannah. Trapped in Savannah with nine thousand assorted troops cobbled together from various sources, Hardee ingeniously constructed a scratch pontoon bridge and stealthily escaped to South Carolina as Sherman closed in on the city.

Coweta County—Newnan

During his siege of Atlanta, Sherman sent Gen. Edward M. McCook's cavalry to destroy the Macon Railroad. Turned away from Griffin by the timely arrival of Joseph Wheeler's horsemen, McCook intended to move through Newnan, at that time crowded with refugees from the fighting to the north, cross the Chattahoochee, and return to Union lines. Wheeler, however, put McCook's rear guard to flight at Line Creek, and the Federals entered Newnan on July 30, 1864, to find an unexpected contingent of Confederate troops bolstered by convalescents and boys. A volley caused the Federals to bolt, and McCook attempted to make a stand at nearby Brown's Mill. The Confederates, outnumbered three

This monument marks the battle of Brown's Mill, where one of Sherman's cavalry raids came to grief during the Atlanta campaign.

The Newnan Confederate Cemetery offers ample proof that the city hosted many hospitals during the war.

to one, captured one thousand men, twelve hundred horses, and two guns and released five hundred Confederate prisoners.

A small stone slab honoring Wheeler's victory at Brown's Mill was placed at the intersection of Millard Farmer Road and Old Corinth Road, three miles southwest of Newnan. In July annual reenactments are often held. Recent funding has saved two important Newnan-area Civil War landmarks. One hundred twenty acres of the Brown's Mill battlefield, off Rickety Back Road, is to be converted into a historic site with hiking and biking trails and historical markers. In Newnan, the old railroad depot, where the opening shots were fired, has been donated to the historical society and will be restored.

During 1864 every train coming into the hospital center of Newnan was packed with wounded men. More than ten thousand soldiers were cared for in seven field hospitals, including the Baptist and Presbyterian churches (the Methodist church was the only church used for religious services), homes, and other buildings. Dr. Samuel H. Stout, medical director of the Department of Tennessee, supervised the hospitals. Under the trees around the courthouse, men rested under twelve-by-one-hundred-foot sheds. Of 268 Confederate soldiers buried at Oak Hill Cemetery (Bullsboro and Jefferson Streets), only 2 are unknown. In 1951 the federal government erected marble headstones over the graves. A stone monument honoring the dead is in the cemetery.

A twenty-two-foot-high Confederate monument dedicated in 1885 stands on the courthouse square.

The memorial weighs thirty-two thousand pounds and cost two thousand dollars. Also on the grounds is a large memorial to William Thomas Overby, who was born in Coweta County (his birthplace is indicated by a historical marker east of Newnan on GA 34). Captured in 1864 with five other men while serving behind enemy lines in Virginia with John S. Mosby's partisan rangers, all were hanged as guerrillas. Mosby retaliated in kind, and his men were afterward treated properly as prisoners of war. The former courthouse was struck by several Union cannonballs during the skirmish.

The twenty-four-year-old Overby, often called the Nathan Hale of the Confederacy, was hanged September 23, 1864, near Front Royal, Virginia, in the Shenandoah Valley. Offered his life in exchange for revealing Mosby's location, Overby refused. He was buried in the nearby family cemetery of another Confederate executed on the same day. The Coweta County chapter, Sons of Confederate Veterans spent

With this marker, Newnan honors native son William T. Overby, one of Mosby's rangers, who was executed in 1864 in Virginia. His remains were returned home 130 years later.

years negotiating with the property owner and Virginia and Georgia state courts before obtaining permission to bring Overby home. In 1996 a group of Georgians traveled to Virginia and disinterred a few bones from his grave. In Newnan the remains were placed in a reproduction period wooden coffin covered by a Confederate flag, with a portrait of Overby on top. The remains lay in state December 28, 1996, in the Coweta County courthouse, surrounded by Confederate banners and attended by an armed honor guard of reenactors wearing black armbands and representing each branch of the military. On December 29 the coffin was borne to Oak Hill Cemetery on a horse-drawn caisson to join 268 brothers in arms. Three hundred reenactors and three hundred spectators attended the ceremony, where former governor Lester Maddox spoke.

The city of Newnan has restored the Male Academy Museum (30 Temple Avenue), which is operated by the Newnan-Coweta Historical Society. It houses a large collection of Civil War artifacts—weapons, equipment, and a battle flag from Company I, Thirty-seventh Georgia—and occasionally features special Confederate exhibits.

Three red-brick buildings on College Street, including College Temple (73 College), then a school for girls, were used as hospitals. Wheeler's headquarters was temporarily established at Buena Vista (87 LaGrange Street). The Virginia house (corner of East Washington and Jefferson, 1865) was a hotel that once had a second-story balcony from which Jefferson Davis spoke.

Liberty Hill

West of GA 29, between Franklin and LaGrange, is Liberty Hill, where a public well in the tiny community survives. It was used in 1864 when Federal cavalry, fleeing the disaster at Brown's Mill, stopped for water.

Glenn

Buried in the Mount Zion Methodist Church cemetery in Glenn (on GA 109 near the Alabama Line) is Pleasance D. Wilson, a soldier in the Army of Northern Virginia and the blacksmith who shod Robert E. Lee's famed horse Traveller. Two miles west of Glenn, just off GA 109 near the intersection of CR

These slabs bear a poem describing the plight of a Federal cavalry raider who died in western Georgia during the Atlanta campaign.

218 and CR 211, is the Adamson Cemetery where an unidentified Federal soldier who died on the trek from Brown's Mill is buried. A poem relating his saga was carved on concrete slabs by N. B. Adamson in 1928.

DeKalb County–Decatur

There are many significant sites east of Atlanta, particularly in Decatur. Fighting during the battle of Atlanta swirled through the town, but it escaped destruction then and later, when Union soldiers rampaged at the start of the March to the Sea.

When the battle of Atlanta began, Union troops circled east of the city to cut the Augusta Railroad. As Confederate commander John Bell Hood attacked James B. McPherson's Army of the Tennessee, Joseph Wheeler's cavalry attacked McPherson's wagon train in Decatur and drove back wagons, troops, and two batteries. Initially successful, the assault was halted when Hood's action failed. An engraved stone on the campus of Agnes Scott College indicates the main scene of the battle, and a second stone at the old courthouse records further

fighting that day. A draped granite obelisk on the grounds honors DeKalb's Confederate veterans. The original monument fell and broke while being erected in 1907.

On the first day of the March to the Sea, Henry W. Slocum's left wing, with Sherman present, marched out of Atlanta on the Decatur Road and passed through town, destroying considerable property.

Ironically, DeKalb County voted against secession on January 2, 1861. The old courthouse (101 Court Square) now houses the DeKalb Historical Society, which has assembled an impressive exhibit titled Johnny Reb and Billy Yank: The Life of the Common Soldier. A prized artifact is the wedding dress of Elizabeth Gresham, who in July 1847 married Joseph E. Brown, Georgia's wartime governor. The society has also restored several important Civil War–era houses (720 Trinity Place). The Swanton house (1825), which was used as headquarters by several Federal generals, including Brig. Gen. Thomas W. Swooney, has bullets from the battle still embedded in the walls. A local tale claims that a Union soldier was held captive under the eaves of an upstairs closet after the battle of Atlanta. The Mary Gay house was the home of a heroine who refused to evacuate her home when Union troops occupied the town. Gay later picked up bullets and shells to exchange for food. After the war she wrote a book describing her trials, *Life in Dixie During the War,* which *Gone with the Wind* author Margaret Mitchell used for reference.

The old DeKalb County courthouse in Decatur houses a notable Civil War museum and features a Confederate monument on the grounds.

Women gathered daily at Mason's Corner, at the intersection of Clairmont Avenue and Ponce de Leon Avenue, to sew uniforms for a regiment of local men, the DeKalb Light Infantry. On Sycamore Street is High house, where Sherman is thought to have watered his horse at an ivy-covered well.

In the city cemetery, on Commerce Drive near Barry Street, is a six-foot cruciform tablet erected in 1984 to honor Decatur's Confederate dead. The intrepid Mary Gay is buried here. Nearby is an Italian marble obelisk that was slipped through the blockade to mark the grave of Charles Murphy, who died before he could serve as a delegate to Georgia's secession convention. He had expressed the hope that he would not live to see Georgia leave the Union, and he did not.

North of Decatur is Tucker, which preserves the Browning Courthouse, also known as Tucker Militia District 572 Courthouse. The one-room white clapboard structure (1860) was a landmark during the battle of Atlanta. It is thought to have been appropriated as Sherman's headquarters or by other Union officers during the raid to destroy facilities in Stone Mountain on July 18, 1864. Used by a justice of the peace until January 1977, it was threatened by road construction until relocated and placed on a foundation of stones from an old mill.

The DeKalb Convention and Visitor's Bureau and the DeKalb Historical Society have prepared an excellent driving tour to towns, churches, homes, and other points of interest in the county.

Sherman was up to 2 A.M. on July 20 giving orders before the battle of Atlanta at Houston Chapel, since destroyed, in DeKalb County.

Stone Mountain Village

The historic village of Stone Mountain is filled with shops and restaurants. The Stone Mountain Cemetery, near the intersection of Silver Hill Drive and Memorial Drive, has a Confederate section in which 150 soldiers are buried. They died of wounds or disease during the war, and several were killed defending Stone Mountain against a Union cavalry raid in July 1864, when the railroad was demolished and the town of New Gibraltar (as Stone Mountain was then called) was burned. After the war fifty veterans were buried here over the next sixty years, the last was

Pvt. Melton A. Herndon, who died in 1933. On the corner of Ridge Avenue and West Mountain Street is the Stillwell House, a prewar tourist inn and later Confederate hospital.

The fantastic Confederate memorial carved into Stone Mountain is examined in *To the Sea,* the companion volume to this book.

Belmont

Federal cavalry under Kenner Garrard retreated from Flat Rock (Flat Shoals) and were bottled up by Wheeler along U.S. 278 east of I-285.

Barrow County – Winder

The final undoing of Sherman's cavalry during the Atlanta campaign occurred on August 3, 1864, five miles northwest of Winder at King's Tanyard. Two brigades that escaped from Sunshine Church in Jones County intended to resupply in Athens, but they turned west when they were repulsed there. One brigade reached Federal lines, but that of Col. Horace Capron was surprised by Confederate cavalry at Winder (Jug Tavern), resulting in the capture of 430 Federals. Only Capron and 6 men reached Sherman—on foot.

At Triangle Park in Winder's Rosehill Cemetery is a small granite monument honoring the unknown Confederate dead. One Southerner killed at Jug Tavern (Winder) was reburied here in 1907. Research identified the soldier in 1971 as Martin Van Buren Parkhurst of Kentucky.

Walton County – Social Circle

Because of important railroad facilities, Federal cavalry visited Social Circle in July 1864 to destroy the line and interrupt Hood's communications with Augusta. The destruction was repeated on a much larger scale on November 17 during Sherman's March to the Sea.

Covington

On July 22, 1864, Federal Gen. Kenner Garrard led a cavalry raid that destroyed a newly constructed hospital center of thirty buildings, four wagon bridges, two railroad bridges over the Yellow and Alcovy Rivers, and six miles of track between the Alcovy and Lithonia. This action disrupted transportation between Atlanta and Augusta and guaranteed that Hood would not be reinforced from Virginia or the Carolinas. Garrard burned the depot, two thousand bales of cotton, large amounts of government supplies and trains, and captured two hundred prisoners. On July 27 George Stoneman camped nearby on his way to destruction at Sunshine Church. Sherman and the Left Wing camped in the area on November 17–18 and crossed the rivers on pontoon bridges.

More than twenty thousand sick or wounded soldiers from the Atlanta area were treated in Covington's hospitals under the supervision of Samuel Stout, medical director for the Army of Tennessee. Many who died were reinterred near their homes after the war, but the graves of sixty-seven known and eight unknown men remain in Southview Cemetery at the end of Davis Street.

Morgan County–Madison

The students at two female colleges cared for Confederate casualties in hospitals and made clothing and blankets for them from carpets. This city was visited in July 1864 by Col. Silas Adams's retreating Federal cavalry, which burned Confederate stores.

Hickory Hill Farm (6080 Bethany Road, 1830) in nearby Buckhead was a Union hospital following an area skirmish in July 1864. (For a comprehensive description of Madison's extensive Civil War history and attractions see *To the Sea,* the companion volume to this book.)

Jones County–Sunshine Church

On July 31, 1864, Col. Silas Adams led his retreating brigade through Eatonton to Sunshine Church (known now as Round Oak), where it was destroyed by Confederate Gen. Alfred Iverson. Captured officers went to Macon, enlisted men to Andersonville, and their horses were given to the Orphan Brigade (the First Kentucky [C.S.]). During Sherman's March to the Sea in November, out of revenge, Federals burned the church, where many of their comrades had received treatment after the battle. The replacement church (on GA 11 between Monticello

Union raiders visited historic Clinton during the summer and fall of 1864.

and Gray, 1880) is north of the battle site. B. F. Morris, a Federal cavalryman wounded in the battle who was cared for by a local family for two months, returned in 1890 to preach here. Jesse Hunt, whose wife, Mary, had cared for prisoners while he and seven brothers were serving the South, was invited to a veterans reunion dinner in Ohio. In front of Sen. John Sherman, the general's brother, Jesse examined the silverware and commented, "I was just seeing if this was my wife's silver the Yankees carried off." Their daughter married Union soldier John T. Creigh, who moved south at the urging of W. F. Gladden, a Sunshine Church veteran who had purchased property nearby and helped carry Mary to her grave.

Clinton

In July 1864 two thousand Union cavalry entered the town and destroyed half a million dollars' worth of property in the area before pushing on toward Macon. They returned, pursued by Confederates, and skirmished in the streets and burned the jail.

The Iverson-Edge house (1821) was home to Alfred Iverson, who defeated Edward M. McCook at Sunshine Church, literally defending his home. His father had been an U.S. senator.

Griswold

Samuel Griswold bought four thousand acres here after the railroad was built between Savannah and Macon and constructed an enormous factory that produced nine hundred gins a year and other facilities that produced bricks, soap, and candles. He also built a twenty-four-room, three-story mansion and sixty cottages for his workers. In 1862 the gin factory was converted to manufacture Colt navy pistols. A Union cavalry raid destroyed most of these structures in July 1864, and repeated visits by blue troopers in November during Sherman's March to the Sea completed the destruction.

Wilkinson County—Gordon

In July 1864 George Stoneman's cavalry entered Gordon to destroy the depot, 11 locomotives, and 140 cars loaded with supplies for Hood's army. They torched other railroad facilities at McIntyre and Toomsboro. When Sherman's army arrived in November, other structures were burned, and Gordon was virtually leveled.

Bibb County—Macon

Because the city was a railroad hub, Macon served as an important arsenal, armory, and logistical center for the Confederacy, with quartermasters distributing supplies, ordnance, and munitions via rail across the struggling nation. Artillery, small arms, and ammunition were also manufactured. When fighting began around Atlanta in 1864, Macon became headquarters for Georgia's military hospitals and a refugee center. Dr. James M. Green supervised eleven hospitals,

Macon's City Hall served as Georgia's last capitol of the war when, in November 1864, the legislature and governor fled Milledgeville to escape Sherman's March to the Sea.

After the war the Southern dead from a dozen hospitals around Macon were reinterred at Rose Hill Cemetery.

aided by many women from the city. When Milledgeville was captured in November, the state government was relocated to Macon, where the last session of Georgia's Confederate legislature met in 1865. Camp Wright, named for Gen. Marcus J. Wright, known after the war for collecting Confederate military records, was established nearby in early 1864.

Union cavalry twice menaced Macon. On July 30, 1864, Gen. George Stoneman's cavalry unlimbered some guns across the Ocmulgee River at the Dunlap Farm but found Macon protected by fifteen hundred militia with Joseph E. Johnston (recently relieved of command in Atlanta), Howell Cobb, and Gov. Joseph E. Brown present. The Federals abandoned the attempt. In November of the same year Kilpatrick's cavalry feinted on Macon while Sherman passed to the east on the march to Savannah.

Several blocks north of Rose Hill is Riverside Cemetery (Riverside Drive), which has a remarkably preserved artillery battery, part of the line that twice repulsed Union attackers. Within the earthwork is the grave of famed boxer "Young" Stripling.

On the grounds of Ocmulgee National Monument (1207 Emery Highway) is a large artillery position blocking a major road on what was the Dunlap Farm, the property of Samuel E. Dunlap. During the July raid against Macon, the Federals tore down stables and built temporary breastworks with the timbers, but the militia held them off. In November 1864 nine guns, primarily 12-pounder Napoleons, fired at Union skirmishers during the battle of Walnut Creek. Follow the Dunlap Trail to the works.

Some of the Confederates who were killed in the area or died in Macon's hospitals are buried in Riverside Cemetery.

Artillery deployed in Riverside Cemetery helped to turn back Federal cavalry raids in July 1864.

The two brief attacks against Macon produced only one tiny act of destruction. During the July raid a single cannonball hit the sidewalk in front of Judge Asa Holt's home, pierced a column, and bounced into the parlor. The Cannonball House and Confederate Museum (856 Mulberry Street), an elegant 1853 Greek Revival structure, has been restored to its Civil War condition by the Sidney Lanier Chapter of the UDC, which purchased the house in 1963. The chairs in the dining room have been upholstered with needlepoint copies of Southern state seals used during the war. Behind the house, in the old servants quarters, is a Confederate museum where the prized artifact is Mrs. Robert E. Lee's rolling pin.

The old Railroad District—south of the restored train depot on the railroad and bordered by Seventh, Pine, and Hawthorne Streets and a swamp, now occupied by railroad yards—was the site of Camp Oglethorpe (1844), a drill-parade ground for area militia and a fairground before the war and later used as a prison for Federals. The first eight hundred internees arrived from Tennessee after the battle of Shiloh in April 1862, and more were sent from Libby Prison when the Union Peninsula campaign threatened Richmond. The three-acre facility was phased out by October then reinstated in the spring of 1864 to accommodate the masses of prisoners captured during the Atlanta campaign, the fighting in Virginia, and Nathan Bedford Forrest's operations in northern Mississippi. It came to be used as a prison for Union officers; Andersonville held only enlisted personnel. At Oglethorpe, up to fourteen hundred men

were confined at one time, enclosed by a twelve-foot-high board fence and guarded by four 12-pounder guns and sentries spaced every ten yards.

When Federal cavalry threatened to liberate the prison in July 1864, six hundred men were sent to Savannah and six hundred more to Charleston. Union Gen. George Stoneman missed one of the trains by only fifteen minutes at Gordon. Stoneman, taken prisoner at Round Oak, was briefly held here. Two other Federal generals were also incarcerated here: Truman Seymour and Alexander Shaler. Ironically, Shaler once commanded the infamous Federal prison camp at Johnson's Island, Ohio. Hearing of Sherman's successes in the Atlanta campaign, the captives staged an enthusiastic celebration on July 4, 1864, featuring small U.S. flags, patriotic speeches,

The Confederate Women's Monument in downtown Macon pays homage to the devotion of Southern women.

The most prominent of Macon's Confederate monuments features one of the tallest soldier statues ever created.

and singing. Nervous Confederates added two cannon to discourage a spontaneous breakout. Although escapes were rare, these prisoners made

grand plans. One tunnel discovered by Confederate authorities was 180 feet long. It was designed for a mass escape that planned to seize the arsenal, capture locomotives, then launch a rescue of the prisoners at Andersonville. Worship services were held regularly, as were classes in French, German, logic, and other subjects, and the officers purchased the library of a local citizen for five hundred dollars. Many of the officers had money and could afford to purchase good food. Some Southerners were briefly imprisoned here after James H. Wilson seized the city. The prison dead were reburied at Andersonville.

Many additional Civil War attractions may be found in *To the Sea,* the companion to this book.

A cannonball crashed through the front door of the since-named Cannonball House, which is now home to a Civil War museum.

CONCLUSION

The Importance of the Atlanta Campaign

THIS MORNING, AS FOR some days past, it seems exceedingly probable that this administration will not be reelected."

That was how Abraham Lincoln evaluated his future on August 28, 1864. After reflecting on the year's war news, the president expected the Democrats to win the White House in three months and, as one of the first acts of the new administration, to sign a peace treaty with the Confederate States of America.

The year had begun on a hopeful note when Ulysses S. Grant, newly appointed general in chief of the armies of the United States, devised a three-part offensive that would strike Rebel forces across the country. In the South he would send Sherman to strike a death blow against Atlanta. Sherman rapidly reached the outskirts of the city with minimal losses, but as the war dragged on and each hot summer day passed, citizens of the North became discouraged at the fruitless siege.

In the far western theater of operations, Grant sent Nathaniel Banks to invade the Red River region of Louisiana with a substantial force. After allowing the Federals to penetrate the region deeply, the Confederates savagely turned on Banks. In May, Union forces stumbled back to safety, having lost eight thousand men, nine ships, and fifty-one cannon. Northerners had been thoroughly disgusted at the debacle.

The hopes of most Northerners for a quick end to the war were pinned on Grant's actions as he led the massive Army of the Potomac into Virginia's wilderness in May. Robert E. Lee gave Grant a typical welcome, lashing out against a vastly superior force and inflicting seventeen thousand Union casualties.

Earlier Federal generals would have taken this as an invitation to retreat, but Grant bore in relentlessly. He shifted east to Spotsylvania and

233

launched one of the war's largest assaults. He nearly succeeded in splitting Lee's army in half, but the attack failed and cost him eighteen thousand additional troops.

Undaunted, the tenacious Union commander again shifted east, this time to Cold Harbor. Lee had anticipated the move and had established a labyrinth of concealed works. There Grant believed the works were vulnerable to attack, but his infantrymen obviously disagreed, sewing their names on their clothing on July 2 so their bodies could be identified and sent home for burial following the upcoming battle. The attack on June 3, one day later, lasted ten minutes and cost eight thousand men.

Grant managed to elude Lee and appeared at Petersburg, south of Richmond, but he had wasted his advantage, and the Confederates blocked him again. The war in Virginia settled into a brutal, ten-month-long siege that was a forerunner to the trench warfare of World War I.

Newspapers in the North labeled Grant the "Butcher," and people clamored for Lincoln to remove him. The president, however, stood firm, realizing that Grant had inflicted crippling losses on Lee. The public could only see three seemingly bungled campaigns—a disgusting continuation to three years of bungled war—and growing lists of men killed, mangled, and missing.

War weariness had settled over the North, seriously weakening the public's resolve to continue the seemingly endless struggle. The human loss—sons, fathers, husbands, and brothers—was a horrible burden to bear. To that were laid crushing taxes to pay for the continuation of the war and the abandonment of long cherished freedoms in an attempt to crush criticism of the war's conduct. In 1863 there had been massive riots in Northern cities to protest a draft, nasty disturbances that saw blacks hung from lampposts and soldiers firing on civilians in the streets. Most people believed the war, with its attendant evils on the battlefield and at home, would continue for several years.

Citizens wondered aloud if the war's goals justified the price that was being paid. Preserving the Union and ending slavery were sound moral causes, but the individual Northerner would not suffer materially if the Confederacy was allowed its independence. It would be much easier to set the South free and end the suffering.

The impending election could stop the long struggle. The Democratic Party offered George B. McClellan as the only man who could save the country. McClellan was still a war hero in the eyes of many Americans, despite a crushing defeat by Lee at the Seven Days' battles and the stigma of having allowed Lee to escape following Antietam. The Democrats protested that the Federal government had vastly increased its powers, and they accused Lincoln of usurping the rights of states. They claimed that Lincoln wanted to be a dictator and that the long, costly war was a failure. At the ballot box people would have a chance to change what they believed had gone wrong with America.

While the Democratic Party was resurgent, the Republicans were deeply divided. Lincoln's renomination had been bitterly opposed, and throughout the summer the Republicans had attempted to replace him with another candidate.

Then Atlanta fell. "Atlanta is ours, and fairly won." That simple telegraphic message struck the North like a thunderbolt. Victory! The war could be—indeed was even now being—won. The Union could be preserved. With that now established as a certainty, a negotiated settlement seemed cowardly, and the Democratic claim was made a lie. One of the South's great armies had been soundly whipped, and her second most important city conquered.

Five days after Lincoln's spirits had struck their lowest point, his leadership was vindicated. Exactly two months later, Americans voted. Lincoln won 55 percent of the popular vote, gaining 212 electoral votes to McClellan's 21. The public had regained its commitment to continue the war, retaining the man who would prosecute it to a victorious conclusion.

The presidential election of 1864 had been of paramount importance to Southerners, who realized the significance of a potential McClellan victory. After three years of war, the Confederacy had been seriously weakened, but it remained a dangerous adversary. The South, however, had suffered far greater casualties, relative to its population, than had its Northern enemy. Even the most optimistic did not believe the Confederacy could survive four more years of war against so determined a foe as Lincoln.

Atlanta's loss proved to be a deathblow to the Confederacy. Lee, hopelessly entangled at Petersburg, could never hope to regain the offensive. Southern fortunes could only be redeemed in Georgia, and that hope had been crushed.

By late 1864 Atlanta had come to symbolize Southern resistance. With its loss and Lincoln's reelection, Confederate morale plummeted. As Northern hopes soared, Southerners lost heart, and their armies suffered an epidemic of desertions.

Political consequences aside, the military effects of the Atlanta campaign dealt a crushing blow to Rebel fortunes. Sherman had inflicted thirty-five thousand irreplaceable casualties on the Army of Tennessee. That once great army would fight valiantly until the end of the Civil War, but its thin, ragged ranks would never again pose a serious threat to Union forces.

The loss of Atlanta's manufacturing facilities was immediately felt throughout the Confederacy. The South had always suffered shortages of cannon, rifles, munitions, uniforms, boots, and dozens of other vital items. Now those things were virtually unobtainable.

The destruction of Atlanta's railroad connections spelled doom for Lee in Virginia. On those rails had been channeled the agricultural bounty of Mississippi, Alabama, and Georgia through the Carolinas to feed the Army of Northern Virginia. Now Lee's men would starve at Petersburg until the war ended.

The Deaths of Two Noble Warriors

An accidental postwar meeting aboard a cruise ship sparked a long friendship between William T. Sherman and Joseph E. Johnston. The former adversaries visited each other and corresponded. At Ulysses S. Grant's funeral in 1885, they stood shoulder-to-shoulder.

Sherman had just turned seventy-one when he died of asthma on February 14, 1891. The North was plunged into mourning as New York City prepared for the funeral, which was attended by more than thirty thousand soldiers. President Benjamin Harrison, a veteran of the Atlanta campaign, was present, as were two former presidents and many government officials.

Also in attendance was a former Confederate adversary who was capable of forgiving wartime unpleasantness. Johnston served as an honorary pallbearer. When Sherman's coffin was placed on a caisson, Johnston stood beside it, bareheaded in a freezing rain.

"General," someone pleaded with him, "please put on your hat. You'll get sick."

"If I were in there," Johnston replied solemnly, "and he were standing here, he would not be wearing his hat."

Johnston fell ill and died a month later at the age of eighty-four.

Strategically, the Confederate flank had been breached. Union armies could drive easily to the Gulf Coast and capture Mobile or, more important, sally to the Atlantic Ocean via Savannah or Charleston and reinforce Grant in the trenches at Petersburg.

Atlanta was not only fairly won, but the war as well.

APPENDIXES

BIBLIOGRAPHY

INDEX

APPENDIX A

Confederate Valor at the Battle of Ringgold Gap

O N NOVEMBER 24, 1863, Joseph Hooker forced Confederate troops from a strong position atop Lookout Mountain, Tennessee, in a glorified skirmish that has been romanticized as the "Battle Above the Clouds" because of the heavy fog that had settled over the mountain. On November 26, Hooker, George H. Thomas, and Sherman stormed Missionary Ridge and routed the remainder of the Confederate army that was besieging Chattanooga, sending it reeling back into Georgia through Ringgold Gap and on to Dalton.

Irish-born Patrick Cleburne, who had risen from private to general, provided the only measure of Confederate heroism at Missionary Ridge. Sherman's troops advanced to within fifty yards of his line, but Cleburne's hard-pressed warriors forced them back then counterattacked and threw the Federals off the ridge. While the rest of the Confederate army fled in disorder, Cleburne's four-thousand-man division executed an orderly withdrawal from the mountain while protecting the rear of the retreating Confederate army. That night Cleburne received orders to make a stand in the steep gorge of Ringgold Gap.

Braxton Bragg, the commander of the Army of Tennessee, feared that the Federals would organize an immediate pursuit that would destroy his disorganized force. He was particularly concerned about his long and painfully slow train of supply and hospital wagons that stretched for miles along the poor, deeply rutted roads leading to Dalton. Their capture would cripple the army's ability to defend the route to Atlanta, and Cleburne was ordered to check the Federal pursuit until the wagons were safely behind Rocky Face Ridge above Dalton.

Cleburne had only thirty minutes to deploy his men in the gap and on both sides of the ridge. It was 8 A.M. when Federal skirmishers drove back the Confederate cavalry and Hooker formed his battle lines in front of Cleburne. The Confederate wagon train was still in sight, rocking desperately down the tracks leading south; only Cleburne could stave off total disaster for the demoralized Confederates.

The Federal soldiers advanced confidently, but a well-served Rebel artillery battery delivered a punishing fire that broke one Federal flank, the soldiers diving for cover behind the railroad bed. Hooker's artillery responded, and shells fell in the town, endangering civilians and tearing large chunks of stone from the railroad depot.

A Federal advance up one slope was checked by crackling volleys of Confederate rifle fire. Southern soldiers heaved boulders down the mountain at the enemy and hurled smaller rocks at the Federals, taking many of their stunned targets captive. When the Confederates swept down the slope in pursuit, they routed the Federals and captured sixty prisoners.

After the battle had raged for two and a half hours, the determined Union troops reeled back in confusion with heavy losses. Hooker wisely elected to await reinforcements before renewing the assault. Cleburne's stubborn defense had halted the Federal momentum.

As soon as Cleburne received word that the wagons were safe behind the hastily constructed defenses at Dalton, his men withdrew proudly. His casualties were twenty killed, while Federal losses were estimated at several hundred. For this action Cleburne was thanked by a resolution passed by the Confederate Congress, and he was afterward known as the "Stonewall of the West."

APPENDIX B

"Hold the Fort, for I Am Coming"

The Battle of Allatoona

O NE OF THE FIERCEST battles of the Civil War occurred at Allatoona, but not as part of the Atlanta campaign. The battle of Allatoona occurred five months later, in October 1864. John Bell Hood had succeeded to the command of the Army of Tennessee and had dashed his army against Sherman's forces four times, virtually destroying his own command. In September he withdrew from Atlanta, which surrendered and was occupied by the Federals.

Camped at Lovejoy, Georgia, with a disgruntled army that wanted Joseph E. Johnston returned to command, Hood decided to drive north and destroy the railroad, Sherman's line of supply and communication. He further intended to invade Tennessee, capture Nashville, regain the state for the Confederacy, and draw Sherman out of Atlanta in pursuit.

Unfortunately for the Confederate cause, after reviewing Hood's near mutinous troops, President Jefferson Davis delivered a speech to the men detailing Hood's plans; the Confederate press dutifully published the information. Sherman always maintained that his best source of intelligence came from reading Southern newspapers; so, forewarned, he alerted and reinforced his garrisons along the railroad to Chattanooga and dispatched George H. Thomas and his massive army to Tennessee. Two other divisions strengthened Chattanooga, and another was sent to Rome, Georgia.

Federal cavalry had occupied Allatoona late in May while Confederate and Union forces were fighting around Dallas. Sherman was so impressed by the natural strength of the position that he ordered the Confederate fortifications expanded and garrisoned the post with one thousand men. He then established his main supply depot here for the remainder of the Atlanta campaign. By the fall of 1864 the town consisted of eight stores,

In May, at the beginning of the campaign, Sherman had bypassed the village of Allatoona, aware of the strength of the position. Hood, however, attacked the Union garrison here in October 1864, hoping to draw Sherman out of Atlanta. This image by George Barnard shows one of the barely visible forts situated on the heights to the left.

eight homes, a railroad depot, and several new, large warehouses that contained a million rations of hardtack and nine thousand head of cattle.

There were two main forts at Allatoona, one on either side of the railroad cut. The strongest of the two redoubts, shaped like a star, was on the western side. Both forts were strongly protected by log stockades, abatis, and three rows of outer trenches. Additionally, the Federals cleared a field of fire that stretched for hundreds of yards, and artillery emplaced in the redoubts covered all approaches. Deadly repeating rifles were carried by many of the Federal soldiers, and these provided a formidable defense. The men had personally bought these guns, which held fifteen shots, for fifty-one dollars each. It turned out to be a wise investment. Confederate soldiers, who would gain a great respect for the weapons, said that they could be loaded on Sunday and fired the rest of the week!

On September 29 Hood left camp at Lovejoy and moved north to Dallas; Sherman left Henry W. Slocum to guard Atlanta and started north after the

Confederates. Hood sent a force to capture a four-hundred-man garrison at Acworth. Another three-thousand-man division under Samuel G. French was dispatched to capture Allatoona, fill the railroad cut with rock, earth, and logs, and destroy a railroad bridge over Allatoona Creek.

Unknown to French, the garrison at Allatoona had been doubled in strength by the arrival of 1,050 men under John M. Corse. At first Corse had traveled to Rome, but finding no danger from Rebels there, he had returned south to Allatoona just hours before the battle began.

French left Big Shanty and arrived at Allatoona at 1 A.M. on October 5. Placing twelve guns on a hill twelve hundred yards south of the pass, he positioned his men to surround the star fort from three sides and waited for dawn to launch the assault.

At 7 A.M. French sent a message to the Federal commander informing him that his works were surrounded and demanding the immediate surrender of the garrison to avoid the "needless effusion of blood." French guaranteed that the prisoners would be treated humanely and allowed five minutes for a reply.

Corse rejected the ultimatum, stating, "We are prepared for the 'needless effusion of blood' whenever it is agreeable with you." Confederate gunners immediately opened a deadly fire on the enemy works.

By 9 A.M. all the Confederate troops had been deployed across the rough terrain. Their artillery continued to pound the star fort until the infantry closed on the works; Federal cannon returned the fire briskly.

With a bloodcurdling scream, the Confederates leaped from the forest surrounding the fort and charged forward. Corse later wrote, "A solid mass of gray advanced from the woods and started up the hill, with artillery support from the rear." As the Federal officer ordered his men to fire on the Rebel infantry, he quietly prayed, "Oh, that Sherman might come."

The initial Confederate charge routed the Federals from their first line of outer works, but an intense fire from the second line stopped the Rebels cold. The Confederates regrouped then charged recklessly, carrying the second line and continuing the mad dash to fall on the third line, which the Union troops defended desperately. During the ensuing hand-to-hand fighting, rifles were used as clubs, bayonets flashed, and rocks were hurled when no other weapons were at hand. Some of the defenders were captured; others escaped by scrambling for the cover of the fort.

The Confederates had suffered heavy casualties, but they dressed their lines and charged the last line of defense. The desperate Federals fired their repeating rifles so quickly that the guns grew too hot to hold; half the soldiers fired while the other half crouched below the parapets and waited for their rifles to cool. Inside the fort, the ferocity of the Confederate assault and the pounding from their artillery took a heavy toll on the Union soldiers. The dead were propped up against the earthworks to give the false impression that the fort was strongly defended; corpses were hit repeatedly. The gun crews were so decimated that the wounded were propped up beside the weapons to pull the lanyards and send charges of grapeshot screaming point blank into the charging Confederate lines.

The Federal artillery and repeating rifles staggered the advancing gray lines. The Rebels wavered then reeled back to the third line of trenches. Confederate officers rallied their men then led them into the storm of hot metal to close on the fort from all directions. They were yards from the final ramparts when they received an incredible order: disengage and withdraw. The dazed, exhausted attackers staggered back into the woods.

French had received a message from Hood advising him that a large force of Federal reinforcements was advancing over the railroad from Kennesaw. French feared that if he did not withdraw then, he would be cut off from Hood and captured. He later reported that the order he gave to withdraw gravely depressed him. After such heroic sacrifice from his men, he had been forced to call off the attack just minutes before the fort would have been overrun or forced to surrender. To the soldiers inside the fort, it appeared that they had been saved by divine intervention.

The battle of Allatoona was a relatively minor affair, but no battle in the Civil War was more fiercely fought or brought forth more valor by troops of both sides. The carnage was terrible. The Confederates suffered 798 casualties, the Federals 706, or 30 percent of all the men engaged. French lost 70 officers killed or wounded, proving again that in the Civil War officers led their men into battle at the fore.

Hood's maneuver had forced Sherman to leave the comfort of his headquarters in Atlanta temporarily and to take to the field again. The Union commander had just reached his observation post on the crest of Kennesaw Mountain, where months before his men had met disaster, as the battle at Allatoona began. He watched anxiously through his glasses as clouds of smoke marked the scene of the desperate struggle. Starting a column of troops marching north to relieve Corse, Sherman knew they would not arrive in time to affect the fighting. As they marched, they fired buildings to mark their progress by pillars of fire and smoke for Sherman. They would not arrive at Allatoona until early on the following day.

Sherman recorded: "I followed Hood, reaching Kennesaw Mountain in time to see in the distance the attack on Allatoona, which was handsomely repulsed by Corse." The Federal commander later called it "one of the fiercest and more gallant battles of the war."

Hoping to encourage Corse to defend his position and not surrender, the Union commander ordered that this message to Allatoona from Kennesaw Mountain be sent throughout the fighting: "Sherman says hold fast; we are coming." Thinking that relief was imminent, Corse held out heroically, but he paid a bloody price.

Early in the battle Corse was severely wounded when a minié ball tore away half his face. During the battle he drifted in and out of consciousness, but his subordinates ably carried on the defense. On the following day, he displayed a mixture of bravado and anxiety in a message he signaled to

BATTLES AND LEADERS

Samuel G. French's division attacked from the west and north and came very close to seizing the pass. Corse's Federals managed to rally and hold. News of approaching Union reinforcements inclined French to withdraw.

Kennesaw Mountain: "I am short a cheek bone and an ear, but am able to lick all hell yet! My losses are quite heavy. Where is Sherman?"

When Sherman saw Corse after the battle, he remarked: "Corse, they came damn near missing you, didn't they?" Corse was a West Point dropout, but that day he proved himself to be a better man that many who graduated at the top of their class.

On his way to join Hood at New Hope Church, French stopped and bombarded a Federal blockhouse on Allatoona Creek into submission, capturing 250 prisoners. Sherman chased Hood to Rome, Resaca, Dalton, and Tunnel Hill. Hood attacked Sherman's railroad garrisons, capturing several and being driven away from others, but he never stopped to engage Sherman in a pitched battle. Sherman allowed Hood to move into northern Alabama unmolested, happy to have him far from the action. He returned to Atlanta to plan his devastating March to the Sea, which would be unopposed. Hood, meanwhile, marched on into Alabama and ultimately Tennessee, failing in his efforts to cut off Sherman's supply route. In Tennessee he would destroy the Army of Tennessee as an effective fighting force by dashing his men in a desperate, but futile, assault at Franklin then waiting for his army to be shattered at Nashville by Thomas.

Accounts of the battle of Allatoona were given extensive play in Northern newspapers. The evangelist Phillip Paul Bliss was so inspired that he wrote the moving hymn, "Hold the Fort," which he introduced at a revival meeting in Chicago. It can still be found in some hymnals.

Ho! my comrades! See the signal, Waving in the sky!
Reinforcements now appearing, Victory is nigh.
"Hold the fort, for I am coming," Jesus signals still;
Wave the answer back to heaven, "By His grace we will."

See the mighty host advancing, Satan leading on;
Mighty men around us falling, Courage almost gone!
See the glorious banner waving! Hear the trumpet blow!
In our Leader's name we triumph, Over every foe.
Fierce and long the battle rages, But our help is near;
Onward comes our great Commander, Cheer, my comrades, cheer!

APPENDIX C

Driving Snake Creek Gap

FOLLOWING THE ROUTE THAT James B. McPherson used to sneak around Rocky Face Ridge and threaten Resaca makes a scenic Saturday outing. Begin at the Chickamauga National Battlefield Park, where you may want to spend most of the day exploring the museum and numerous monuments and enjoying a driving tour of the park that marks the largest battle in the western theater of the Civil War.

Exit the battlefield on U.S. 27-GA 1 south. Turn left onto GA 95 and left again on GA 90-151. This intersection was called Chestnut Flat, where McPherson camped for the night of May 7. Continue south to the intersection with GA 136 (Lookout Mountain Scenic Highway) and turn left. Maddox Gap, then called Ship's Gap, winds gently across Taylor's Ridge and enters the beautiful West Armuchee Valley. McPherson seized this strategic gap with no opposition.

At the bottom of the ridge, you might want to take S1030-706 south to Shiloh Church, where John Bell Hood recovered from the loss of a leg after the battle of Chickamauga. This side trip dramatically demonstrates the beauty of Georgia's valley and ridge district. Taylor's Ridge rises to the right; Johns Mountain is to the left.

Return to 136 and continue east to Villanow, which McPherson seized on May 8. The name of the settlement was taken from a Jane Porter novel, *Thaddeus of Warsaw.* If you have the time, just east of Villanow is a sign directing you south on S822-714 six miles to Keown Falls Scenic Area and the Pocket. Keown, on the eastern slope of Johns Mountain, is one of the few waterfalls in this part of Georgia. Picnicking and hiking are the attractions at Keown Falls, and just south of it is a pleasant wooded area with a spring and stream where camping is permitted at the Pocket.

McPherson continued directly from Villanow to seize Snake Creek Gap by surprise on May 8 and threaten Johnston's flank at Dalton. GA 136 shears sharply south in the pass between Mill Creek Mountain to the north and Horn Mountain to the south. The scenic pass is very narrow and several miles long, and the ridges rise spectacularly on both sides of the road. Emerging from the pass you can continue east on 136 to I-75 and the features described at Resaca, or continue south on 136-Connector into Calhoun.

APPENDIX D

Chronology

1863

December 27. Joseph E. Johnston arrives in Dalton to command the Confederate Army of Tennessee.

1864

February 22–27. George H. Thomas's Federal Army of the Cumberland unsuccessfully probes Dalton's defenses to determine Confederate strength then withdraws.

March 18. In Nashville, Ulysses S. Grant receives command of all Union armies; he places William T. Sherman in charge of the western armies.

April 9. Grant issues orders that, when he attacks Lee in Virginia, Sherman is to move into Georgia and destroy the Army of Tennessee.

May 1–7. Moving south from Chattanooga and Red Clay, Tennessee, the Army of the Cumberland and the Army of the Ohio advance through Ringgold, Catoosa Springs, Varnell, and Tunnel Hill to face Confederate defenses at Rocky Face Ridge near Dalton.

May 8–12. Federals launch diversionary attacks against Buzzard Roost Gap, Dug Gap, and the Crow Creek Valley.

May 9. James B. McPherson's Federal Army of the Tennessee sneaks through Snake Creek Gap but pulls back when faced with Confederate resistance at Resaca, wasting a golden opportunity to destroy Johnston.

May 11–13. Sherman advances to Resaca through Snake Creek Gap, and Johnston withdraws from Dalton to oppose him.

May 13–15. Sherman's assaults against the Confederate line at Resaca are repulsed, but he successfully places a force behind Johnston.

May 16–18. Confederates retreat through Calhoun and Adairsville, fighting delaying actions against Union pursuit. Federals capture industrial center of Rome.

May 19. Johnston draws the Army of the Ohio into an ambush at Cassville, but John Bell Hood fails to attack. After establishing a second position, Johnston's generals counsel retreat and the Confederates withdraw across the Etowah River to Allatoona.

May 23–25. Sherman sweeps southwest to Dallas, while Johnston hurries to intercept him.

May 25. Joseph Hooker's Federals launch determined attacks against Hood's corps but are decimated by concentrated Confederate fire at New Hope Church.

May 27. Sherman, believing he is turning the Confederate flank, is repulsed with loss at Pickett's Mill. Johnston directs Hood to attack Sherman's flank, but Hood reports unfavorable conditions for the assault.

May 28. Johnston, hoping to catch McPherson withdrawing, attacks a strongly held Union position at Dallas and is thrown back.

June 1–6. After constant skirmishing near Dallas, Sherman shifts to the railroad at Big Shanty, and Johnston moves to fortify three high points north of Marietta.

June 14. Confederate Gen. Leonidas Polk is killed on Pine Mountain. Southern forces retreat that night to prevent their encirclement.

June 15–20. Confederates forced to retreat from Lost Mountain. A running battle ensues with encounters at Gilgal Church and Mud Creek.

June 22. Hood leads an unauthorized and unprepared strike against Federals at Kolb's farm and loses heavily.

June 27. Weary of the stalemate before Marietta, Sherman attacks Kennesaw Mountain at two points and is soundly defeated, losing two thousand men to four hundred Confederate casualties.

July 2. Finding that Sherman has slipped McPherson and John M. Schofield between his forces and the Chattahoochee River, Johnston abandons Kennesaw Mountain.

July 3–4. Johnston slows Sherman at a line of fortifications established at Smyrna.

July 5. Flanked out of Smyrna, Johnston withdraws to a strong position on the north bank of the Chattahoochee.

July 9. Federal troops effect two crossings of Johnston's River Line, forcing the Confederates to withdraw south of the river.

July 13. Braxton Bragg arrives in Atlanta to assess the Confederate situation. His report to President Jefferson Davis is critical of Johnston's performance.

July 17. Sherman crosses the Chattahoochee with all three armies; two march directly on Atlanta, while McPherson swings east to Decatur. Jefferson Davis relieves Johnston from command of the Army of Tennessee, replacing him with Hood.

July 20. As Thomas crosses Peachtree Creek, Hood launches a furious attack that is repulsed with a loss of five thousand men.

July 21. McPherson moves toward Atlanta from Decatur, capturing positions that threaten the city with bombardment.

July 22. Confederate Gen. William J. Hardee's corps execute a daring night march to reach McPherson's flank but find it was extended during the night. In the campaign's fiercest fighting, McPherson is killed and the Union line is temporarily pierced, but Confederate forces are decisively beaten and suffer considerable casualties.

July 22–August 27. Atlanta is besieged and subjected to intense bombardment.

July 28. Sherman sends the Army of the Tennessee west around Atlanta, and Hood dispatches Alexander P. Stewart and Stephen D. Lee to stop the movement. Lee fails, and Confederate losses are heavy in a battle at Ezra Church.

July 27–August 4. Sherman's grand cavalry strike south of Atlanta is defeated at Brown's Mill, Sunshine Church, and Jug Tavern.

August 6. Sherman's attempt to break a vital railroad by attacking near Utoy Church is thwarted.

August 25–30. Most of Sherman's forces circle south to destroy the two remaining railroads that supply Atlanta. Hood believes Sherman has retreated.

August 30–31. Discovering his rail lines severed, Hood realizes his precarious position and sends Hardee south to dislodge Sherman. Attacking at Jonesboro, Hardee is repulsed.

September 1. Sherman gathers most of his army at Jonesboro and almost destroys Hardee, who escapes south to Lovejoy. That night Hood destroys his army's supplies and evacuates Atlanta.

September 2. Federal troops occupy Atlanta.

September 3. Sherman telegraphs Washington, D.C., "So Atlanta is ours, and fairly won."

APPENDIX E

Resources

The Atlanta campaign tour can be completed in as little as two days, or it can be stretched out to a full-length vacation. If your time is limited, the tour can be done in portions. This book has been designed to accommodate either approach. Visits to the sites can be enhanced by contacting any of the following sources for information on what to see and do along the way.

I advise adventurous travelers to secure county maps from the state, currently available for $1.50 each from the Department of Transportation, 2 Capitol Square, Atlanta, GA 30334. The counties covered in the tour are Catoosa, Whitfield, Gordon, Bartow, Paulding, Cobb, Fulton, and Clayton. A good map of Atlanta is also essential. These maps will enable you to keep up with the tour on maps and will be invaluable if you decide to stray off the tour route.

GEORGIA

The Georgia Department of Industry, Trade, & Tourism, P.O. Box 1776, Atlanta, GA 30301. (404) 656-3590; (800) VISIT-GA. www.georgia.org

Georgia State Parks & Historic Sites, 205 Butler Street, Suite 1354, Floyd Tower East, Atlanta, GA 30334. (404) 656-3530; (800) 864-7275. www.gastateparks.org

Georgia Battlefields Association, 2331 Fireside Court, Jonesboro, GA 30236-2671. www.georgiabattlefields.org

CATOOSA COUNTY

Catoosa County Area Chamber of Commerce, 7734 Nashville Street, P.O. Box 52, Ringgold, GA 30736. (706) 965-5201; fax (706) 965-5219; www.catoosa.com

www.gatewaytogeorgia.com/ringgold.html.

Georgia Visitor Information Center, Ringgold, I-75 South, GA/TN line. (706) 937-4211.

Catoosa County Historical Society, 1611 Deitz Road, P.O. Box 113, Ringgold, GA 30736-5441.

Old Stone Church Museum, Box 113, Ringgold, GA 30736. (706) 935-5232.

WHITFIELD COUNTY

Tunnel Hill Historical Foundation, P.O. Box 114, Tunnel Hill, GA 30755. (706) 673-5152.

Battle of Tunnel Hill Reenactment, (800) 331-3258.

Dalton Convention & Visitors Bureau, 2211 Dug Gap Battle Road (30720), P.O. Box 2046, Dalton, GA 30722. (706) 272-7676; fax (706) 278-5811; (800) 331-3258. Daltoncvb@alltel.net

Crown Gardens and Archives, Whitfield-Murray Historical Society, 715 Chattanooga Avenue, Dalton, GA 30720. (706) 278-0217.

Blunt House, 506 South Thorton Avenue, Dalton, GA 30720. (706) 278-0217. By appointment Whitfield-Murray Historical Society (706) 278-0217.

The John Hamilton House, 701 Chattanooga Avenue, Dalton, GA 30720. By appointment Whitfield-Murray Historical Society. (706) 278-0217.

Dalton Depot Restaurant & Trackside Café, 110 Depot Street, Dalton, GA 30720. (706) 226-3160.

Prater's Mill Foundation, 848 Shugart Road, Dalton, GA 30720; P.O. Drawer H, Varnell, GA 30756. (706) 275-6455. Pratersmill@dalton.net www.pratersmill.org

GORDON COUNTY

Calhoun-Gordon County Convention & Visitors Bureau and Welcome Center (also Blue and Gray Trail), 300 South Wall Street, Calhoun, GA 30701. (706) 625-3200. www.gordonchamber.org

Friends of Resaca Battlefield, Inc., P.O. Box 1098, Resaca, GA 30735. (706) 602-2224.

For news of the annual Resaca reenactment: P.O. Box 919, Resaca, GA 30735-0919. www.battleofresaca-gdra.org

New Echota State Historic Site, 1211 Chatsworth Highway NE, Calhoun, GA 30701. (706) 624-1321.

Oakleigh, 335 South Wall Street, Calhoun, GA 30701. (706) 629-1515. www.oakleigh.com

MURRAY COUNTY

Chatsworth-Murray County Chamber of Commerce and Welcome Center, 126 North Third Avenue, Chatsworth, GA 30705. (706) 695-6060.

Chief Vann House State Historic Site, 82 Georgia Highway 225 North, Chatsworth, GA 30705. (706) 695-2598; fax (706) 517-4255. VannHouse@alltel.net

BARTOW COUNTY

Cartersville–Bartow County Convention & Visitors Bureau and Welcome Center, 101 North Erwin Street, P.O. Box 200397, Cartersville, GA 30120. (770) 387-1357; fax (706) 386-1220; (800) 733-2280. www.notatlanta.org
Also ask for Chieftains Trail brochure.

Adairsville Great Locomotive Chase Festival, (770) 773-3451.

Adairsville Visitor Information, 116 Public Square, Adairsville, GA 30103. (770) 387-1357; (800) 733-2280. www.notatlanta.org

Barnsley Gardens Resorts, 597 Barnsley Gardens Road, Adairsville, GA 30103. (770) 773-7480. www.barnsleyinn.com

Kingston Confederate Memorial Museum, 13 East Main Street, Kingston, GA 30145. (770) 387-1357.

The History Center, 13 Wall Street, P.O. Box 1239, Cartersville, GA 30120. (770) 382-3818.

Etowah Valley Historical Society, P.O. Box 1886, Cartersville, GA 30120. (770) 606-8862. www.evhsonline.org; evhs@evhsonlint.org

Roselawn, 224 West Cherokee Avenue, Cartersville, GA 30120. (770) 387-5162. www.roselawnmuseum.com

Lake Allatoona Recreational Facilities and Visitors Center, P.O. Box 487, Cartersville, GA 30120. (770) 382-4700.

Etowah Indian Mounds State Historic Site, 813 Indian Mounds Road SE, Cartersville, GA 30120. (770) 387-3747.

Euharlee Covered Bridge and Museum, 1116 Covered Bridge Road, Cartersville, GA 30120. (770) 607-2017.

Weinman Mineral Museum, 51 Mineral Museum Drive, Cartersville, GA 30184. (770) 386-0576. www.chara.gsu.edu/-weinman

Red Top Mountain State Park, 653 Red Top Mountain Road SE, Cartersville, GA 30121. (770) 975-4226.

POLK COUNTY

Cedartown Welcome Center, 518 Main Street, Cedartown, GA 30125. (770) 749-1652.

Polk County Chamber of Commerce, 604 Goodyear Street, Rockmart, GA 30153. (770) 684-8760.

Polk County Historical Society Museum & Gardens, 205 North College Street, P.O. Box 203, Cedartown, GA 30125. (770) 748-0073. polkhist.home.mindspring.com

PAULDING COUNTY

Paulding County Chamber of Commerce, 455 Jimmy Campbell Parkway, Dallas, GA 30157. (770) 445-6016. www.pauldingcountygeorgia.com

The Paulding County Museum, 295 North Johnston Street, Dallas, GA 30157. (770) 505-3485.

Pickett's Mill Battlefield State Historic Site, 4432 Mount Tabor Road, Dallas, GA 30157. (770) 443-7850; fax 443-7851. picketts@innerx.net

The Friends of Civil War Paulding County, Inc., P.O. Box 861, Hiram, GA 30141. www.thehellhole.org

Paulding County Historical Society, P.O. Box 333, Dallas, GA 30132. (770) 948-5915.

COBB COUNTY

Acworth Visitor Information Center, 4367 Senator Russell Square, Acworth, GA 30101. (770) 974-7626.

Southern Museum of Civil War and Locomotive History (the old Kennesaw Civil War Museum), 2829 Cherokee Street, Kennesaw, GA 30144. (770) 427-2117; (800) 742-6897. www.thegeneral.org

Kolb Farm Coalition, 1165 Ward Creek Road, Marietta, GA 30064. bhovey@mindspring.com

Kennesaw Mountain National Battlefield Park, 905 Kennesaw Mountain Drive, Kennesaw, GA 30152. (770) 427-4686; fax (770) 528-8399. http:www.nps.gov/keno

Marietta Museum of History, 1 Depot Street, Suite 200, Marietta, GA 30060. (770) 528-0431; fax (770) 528-0450. dcox@city.marietta.ga.us; www.mariettasquare.com/history

Marietta Welcome Center & Visitors Bureau, No. 4 Depot Street, Marietta, GA 30060. (770) 429-1115; (800) 835-0445; fax (770) 428-3443. www.mariettasquare.com

Marietta Conference Center and Resort and Brumby Hall and Gardens, 500 Powder Springs Road, P.O. Box 4041, Marietta, GA 30061. (770) 422-6030.

Marietta National Cemetery, Cole Street and Washington Avenue, Marietta, GA 30060. (770) 429-1115.

Cobb County Convention & Visitors Bureau, One Galleria Parkway, Atlanta, GA 30339. (678) 303-2625; (800) 451-3480.

Kennesaw Historical Society, Inc., 2829 Cherokee Street, Kennesaw, GA 30144. (770) 975-0877.

Cobb County Historic Preservation Commission, 191 Lawrence Street, Marietta, GA 30060. (770) 528-2010; fax (770) 528-2161. www.cobbcounty.org/community/hst_pres/ hp_map.htm

City of Smyrna, 2800 King Street, Smyrna, GA 30080. (770) 434-6600. www.ci.smyrna.ga.us

Smyrna Historical and Genealogical Society and Museum, 2861 Atlanta Street, Smyrna, GA 30082.

The Great Locomotive Chase Web site: www.andrewsraid.com

ATLANTA-FULTON COUNTY

Chattahoochee River National Recreation Area, 1978 Island Ford Parkway, Atlanta, GA 30350-3400. (770) 399-8070; fax (770) 392-7042. http://www.nps.gov/chat

Historic Roswell Convention & Visitors Bureau (also Roswell Historical Society and Historic Roswell Tours), 617 Atlanta Street, Roswell, GA 30075. (770) 640-3253; 640-3252; (800) 776-7935. www.cvb.roswell.ga.us; info@cvb.roswell.ga.us

Bulloch Hall, 180 Bulloch Avenue, Roswell, GA 30075. (770) 992-1731; fax (770) 587-1840.

Naylor Hall, 1121 Canton Street, Roswell, GA 30075. (770) 642-9409; fax (770) 642-9994. www.naylorhall.com

The Public House, 605 Atlanta Street, Roswell, GA 30073. (770) 992-4646; fax (770) 992-8320.

Atlanta Convention & Visitors Bureau, 233 Peachtree Street NE, Suite 100, Atlanta, GA 30303. (404) 521-6600; (800) 285-2682. www.atlanta.com

Atlanta History Center, 130 West Paces Ferry Road NW, Atlanta, GA 30305-1366. (404) 814-4000; fax (404) 814-4186. www.atlantahistory.com

Historic Oakland Cemetery, 248 Oakland Avenue SE, Atlanta, GA 30312. (404) 658-6019. www.oaklandcemetery.com

Atlanta Cyclorama, 800 Cherokee Avenue SE, Atlanta, GA 30315. (404) 624-1071; 658-7625; fax (404) 658-7045. www.bcaatlanta.org

Rhodes Hall-The Georgia Trust for Historic Preservation, 1516 Peachtree Street NW, Atlanta, GA 30309-2916. (404) 885-7800; fax (404) 875-2205. www.georgiatrust.org

Georgia Department of Archives & History, 330 Capitol Avenue SE, Atlanta, GA 30334. (404) 651-6469. www.sos.state.ga.us/archives

Federal Reserve Bank of Atlanta Visitors Center and Monetary Museum, 1000 Peachtree Street NE, Atlanta, GA 30309-4470. (404) 498-8764. www.frbatlanta.org

Margaret Mitchell House & Museum, 990 Peachtree Street, Atlanta, GA 30309. (404) 249-7015; fax (404) 249-7188. www.gwtw.com

Georgia State Capitol, 206 Washington Street, Capitol Square, Atlanta, GA 30334. (404) 656-2844. www.sos.state.ga.us

Georgia Capitol Museum, 431 State Capitol, Atlanta, GA 30334. (404) 656-2846. www.sos.state.ga.us

Shrine of the Immaculate Conception, 48 Martin Luther King Jr. Drive, Atlanta, GA 30334. (404) 521-1866.

DEKALB COUNTY

Atlanta's DeKalb Convention & Visitors Bureau, 750 Commerce Drive, Suite 200, Decatur, GA 30030. (404) 378-2525; (800) 999-6055. www.atlantasdekalb.org

Old Courthouse on the Square, 101 East Court Square, Decatur, GA 30030. (404) 373-1088. www.dekalbhistory.org

Historic Complex of DeKalb Historical Society, 720 West Trinity Place, Decatur, GA 30030. (404) 373-1088. www.dekalbhistory.org

Georgia's Stone Mountain Park, Highway 78, Stone Mountain, GA 30086. (770) 498-5690. www.stonemountainpark.com

Stone Mountain Welcome Center, 891 Main Street, Stone Mountain, GA 30083. (770) 879-4971.

CLAYTON COUNTY

Clayton County Convention & Visitors Bureau & Welcome Center, 104 North Main Street, Jonesboro, GA 30236. (770) 478-4800; (800) 662-7829. www.gwtw.cc

Warren House, 102 West Mimosa Drive, Jonesboro, GA 30236. (770) 477-8864.

Jonesboro Depot Welcome Center, 104 North Main Street, Jonesboro, GA 30236. (770) 478-4800 (same number for Jonesboro battle reenactment); (800) 662-7829.

Road to Tara Museum, Jonesboro Depot, 104 North Main Street, Jonesboro, GA 30236. (770) 478-4800. www.ccps.ga.net

Antique Funeral Museum, Pope Dickson & Son Funeral Home, 168 McDonough Street, Jonesboro, GA 30236. (770) 478-7211. www.popedixon.com

Stately Oaks Plantation, 100 Carriage Lane, P.O. Box 922, Jonesboro, GA 30237. (770) 473-0197; fax (770) 473-9855. www.gwtw-jonesboro.org

FLOYD COUNTY

Greater Rome Convention & Visitors Bureau and Welcome Center, 402 Civic Center Drive, Rome, GA 30161. (706) 295-5576; (800) 444-1834.

Rome Area History Museum, 305 Broad Street, Rome, GA 30161. (706) 235-8051. www.romegeorgia.com; rahm.roman.net

Chieftains Museum, 501 Riverside Parkway, Rome, GA 30162-0373. (706) 291-9494; fax (706) 291-2410. www.chieftainsmuseum.org/

Historic High Country Travel Association, 527 Broad Street, Rome, GA 30161. (706) 802-5680.

Northwest Georgia Historical and Genealogical Society, P.O. Box 5063, Rome, GA 30162-5063.

DOUGLAS COUNTY

Douglasville Welcome Center, 6694 East Broad Street, Douglasville, GA 31034. (770) 947-5920.

Sweetwater Creek State Conservation Park, Mount Vernon Road, P.O. Box 816, Lithia Springs, GA 30122. (770) 732-5871.

Friends of Sweetwater Creek State Park, P.O. Box 816, Lithia Springs, GA 30122. www.friendsofsweetwatercreek.org

COWETA COUNTY

Coweta County Convention & Visitors Bureau Welcome Center, 100 Walt Sanders Memorial Drive, Newnan, GA 30265. (770) 254-2629; (800) 826-9382. www.coweta.ga.us

Male Academy Museum, 30 Temple Drive, Newnan, GA 30263. (770) 251-0207.

HEARD COUNTY

Heard County Chamber of Commerce, 121 South Court Square, Franklin, GA 30217. (706) 675-0560.

Heard County Historical Center and Museum, 151 Shady Street, Franklin, GA 30217. (706) 675-6507.

HARALSON COUNTY

Haralson County Chamber of Commerce, 70 Hub Drive, Waco, GA 30182. (770) 537-5594.

West Georgia Museum of Tallapoosa, 185 Main Street, Tallapoosa, GA 30176. (770) 574-3125.

Haralson County Historical Society, Old Haralson County Courthouse, P.O. Box 585, Buchanan, GA 30113.

MACON-BIBB COUNTY

Downtown Welcome Center, 200 Cherry Street (31201), Terminal Station, P.O. Box 6354, Macon, GA 31208-6345. (800) 768-3401. (912) 743-3401. www.maconga.org

Cannonball House, 856 Mulberry Street, Macon, GA 31201. (912) 745-5982.

Hay House, 934 Georgia Avenue, Macon, GA 31201. (478) 742-8155; fax (478) 745-4277. hayhouse@bellsouth.net

Rose Hill Cemetery, 1091 Riverside Drive, Macon, GA 31208. (912) 751-9119.

Ocmulgee National Monument, 1207 Emery Highway, Macon, GA 31217. (912) 752-8257.

Woodruff House, 988 Bond Street, Macon, GA. (912) 752-2715.

Middle Georgia Historical Society, Inc., Sidney Lanier Cottage, 935 High Street, Macon, GA 31201. (912) 743-3851.

BIBLIOGRAPHY

Bailey, Ronald H. *Battles for Atlanta.* Alexandria, Virginia: Time-Life Books, 1985.

Bailey, Sue C., and William H. Bailey. *Cycling Through Georgia: Tracing Sherman's March from Chickamauga to Savannah.* Atlanta: Susan Hunter, 1989.

Barnard, George N. *Photographic Views of Sherman's Campaign.* New York: Dover Publications, 1977.

Blue & Gray Magazine's History and Tour Guide of the Atlanta Campaign. Columbus, Ohio: Blue & Gray Enterprises, 1996.

Boyd, Kenneth W. *The Historical Markers of North Georgia.* Atlanta: Cherokee Publishing Co., 1993.

Brown, Fred, and Sherri M. L. Smith. *The Riverkeeper's Guide to the Chattahoochee.* Atlanta: CI Publishing, 1994.

Brown, Joseph M. *The Mountain Campaigns in Georgia.* Buffalo, N.Y.: Matthews, Northrup, and Co., 1890.

Bryan, T. Conn. *Confederate Georgia.* Athens: University of Georgia Press, 1953.

Bull, Rice C. *Soldiering.* San Rafael, Calif.: Presidio Press, 1977.

Carter, Samuel, III. *The Siege of Atlanta.* New York: Ballantine Books, 1973.

Castel, Albert. *Decision in the West: The Atlanta Campaign of 1864.* Lawrence: University Press of Kansas, 1992.

Catton, Bruce. *Never Call Retreat.* Garden City: Doubleday and Co., 1965.

Connelly, Thomas L. *Autumn of Glory: The Army of Tennessee.* Baton Rouge: Louisiana State University Press, 1971.

Cox, Jacob D. *Atlanta.* New York: Charles Scribner's Sons, 1882.

Crossroads of Conflict: A Guide for Touring Civil War Sites in Georgia. Atlanta: Historic Preservation Division of the Georgia Department of Natural Resources, 1990s.

Cumming, Kate. *The Journal of a Confederate Nurse.* Savannah: Beehive Press, 1975.

Davis, Stephen. "Atlanta Campaign, Actions from July 10 to September 2, 1864." *Blue & Gray Magazine,* August 1989.

Davis, William C. *The Orphan Brigade.* Baton Rouge: Louisiana State University Press, 1980.

Evans, Clement A., ed. *Confederate Military History.* Vols. 6 and 12. Atlanta: Confederate Publishing Co., 1899.

Evans, David. *Sherman's Horsemen: Union Cavalry Operations in the Atlanta Campaign.* Bloomington: Indiana University Press, 1996.

Foote, Shelby. *The Civil War, A Narrative: Red River to Appomattox.* New York: Random House, 1974.

Gay, Mary. *Life in Dixie During the War.* Atlanta: Darby Publishing Co., 1979.

Georgia: A Guide to Its Towns and Countryside. Athens: University of Georgia Press, 1940.

Hitt, Michael. *Charged with Treason.* Atlanta: Library Research Associates, 1992.

Hoehling, A. A. *Last Train from Atlanta.* New York: Thomas Yoseloff, 1956.

Hood, John B. *Advance and Retreat.* Bloomington: Indiana University Press, 1952.

Horn, Stanley F. *The Army of Tennessee.* Norman: University of Oklahoma Press, 1952.

Howard, Blair. *Battlefields of the Civil War: A Guide for Travelers.* Edison, N.J.: Hunter, 1994.

Johnston, Joseph E. *Narrative of Military Operations.* Bloomington: Indiana University Press, 1959.

Kelly, Dennis. "Mountains to Pass, a River to Cross: The Battle of Kennesaw Mountain and Related Action from June 10 to July 9, 1864." *Blue & Gray Magazine,* June 1989.

Kennett, Lee. *Marching Through Georgia: The Story of Soldiers & Civilians During Sherman's Campaign.* New York: HarperCollins, 1996.

Kerksis, Sydney C., comp. *The Atlanta Papers.* Dayton, Ohio: Morningside Press, 1980.

Kerlin, Robert H. *Confederate Generals of Georgia and Their Burial Places.* Fayetteville, Ga.: Americana Historical Books, 1994.

Kurtz, Wilbur B. *Atlanta and the Old South.* Atlanta: American Lithograph Co., 1969.

Lenz, Richard J. *The Civil War in Georgia: An Illustrated Traveler's Guide.* Watkinsville, Ga.: Infinity Press, 1995.

Logue, Victoria, and Frank Logue. *Touring the Backroads of North and South Georgia.* Winston-Salem: John F. Blair, 1997.

McCarley, J. Britt. "Atlanta Is Ours, and Fairly Won." *Atlanta Historical Journal,* Fall 1984.

McDonough, James Lee, and James Pickett Jones. *War So Terrible: Sherman and Atlanta.* New York: Norton, 1987.

McInvale, Morton R. *The Battle of Pickett's Mill.* Atlanta: Georgia Department of Natural Resources, 1977.

Miers, Earl S. *The General Who Marched to Hell: William Tecumseh Sherman and His March to Fame and Infamy.* New York: Dorset Press, 1990.

Nichols, George W. *The Story of the Great March.* New York: Harper and Brothers, 1865.

Nisbet, James C. *Four Years on the Firing Line.* Edited by Irwin W. Bell. Jackson, Tenn.: McCowat-Mercer Press, 1963.

Richardson, Eldon B. *Kolb's Farm: Rehearsal for Atlanta's Doom.* Privately published, 1979.

Roth, Darlene R. *Architecture, Archaeology, and Landscapes: Resources for Historic Preservation in Unincorporated Cobb County, Georgia.* Marietta: Cobb County Historic Preservation Commission, 1988.

Rowell, John W. *Yankee Artillerymen.* Knoxville: University of Tennessee Press, 1975.

Scaife, William R. *Campaign for Atlanta.* Atlanta: Privately published, 1985.

———. *The March to the Sea.* Atlanta: Scaife, 1993.

———. "Sherman's March to the Sea: Events from September 3 to December 21, 1864." *Blue & Gray Magazine,* December 1989.

Scruggs, Carroll P. *Georgia Historical Markers.* Helen, Ga.: Bay Tree Grove, 1976.

Sherman, William T. *Memoirs of General William T. Sherman.* New York: DaCapo Press, 1984.

Symonds, Craig L. *A Battlefield Atlas of the Civil War.* Baltimore: Nautical and Aviation Publishing Co. of America, 1983.

Upson, Theodore F. *With Sherman to the Sea.* Baton Rouge: Louisiana State University Press, 1943.

War of the Rebellion Official Records. Series 1, Vol. 38. Washington, D.C.: Government Printing Office, 1891.

Watkins, Sam R. *Co. Aytch.* New York: Collier Books, 1962.

Yates, Bowling C. *Historical Guide for Kennesaw Mountain National Battlefield Park and Marietta, Georgia.* Marietta: Privately published, 1976.

INDEX